Privatising Border Control

Privatising Border Control

Law at the Limits of the Sovereign State

Edited by
MARY BOSWORTH AND
LUCIA ZEDNER

OXFORD
UNIVERSITY PRESS

OXFORD
UNIVERSITY PRESS

Great Clarendon Street, Oxford, OX2 6DP,
United Kingdom

Oxford University Press is a department of the University of Oxford.
It furthers the University's objective of excellence in research, scholarship,
and education by publishing worldwide. Oxford is a registered trade mark of
Oxford University Press in the UK and in certain other countries

First Edition published in 2022
Impression: 1

Published in the United States of America by Oxford University Press
198 Madison Avenue, New York, NY 10016, United States of America

British Library Cataloguing in Publication Data
Data available

Library of Congress Control Number: 2022937832

ISBN 978–0–19–285716–3

DOI: 10.1093/oso/9780192857163.001.0001

Printed and bound in the UK by
TJ Books Limited

Transferred to digital printing 2023

Acknowledgements

We would like to thank all the contributors for their excellent work, and for sticking with this project during a pandemic. Thanks to Elspeth Windsor for help with copyediting, Victoria Taylor for help with the Index, and to Samuel Singler for managing all the technology at the hybrid workshop held in Oxford in June 2021. We are grateful to All Souls College, University of Oxford for co-funding and hosting the workshop, and to all its staff, especially Marie Giraud and Cristina Fernandez-Crespo, for supporting it. Mary would like to acknowledge the British Academy, who contributed towards the cost of the event as part of her grant IC4/10000160 'Privatising Border Control and Sovereign Power'. Thanks also to Fiona Briden at Oxford University Press and to K (Viji) Vijayalakshmi at Newgen KnowledgeWorks for their hard work in seeing this book through to publication.

Contents

List of Contributors

Editors

Mary Bosworth is Professor of Criminology at the University of Oxford, where she is a Fellow of St Cross College. Concurrently, Mary is Professor of Criminology at Monash University, Australia. In Oxford, Mary founded and is the director of Border Criminologies, an interdisciplinary research group focusing on the intersections between criminal justice and border control. Her research focuses on immigration, detention, and deportation. She is particularly interested in how border control practices uphold and generate notions of race, gender, and citizenship, and how those who are confined and who work in detention and deportation negotiate their daily lives.

Lucia Zedner is a Senior Research Fellow at All Souls College, Professor in the Faculty of Law, and a member of the Centre for Criminology at the University of Oxford, and she is concurrently Conjoint Professor in the Law Faculty, University of New South Wales. She was elected a Fellow of The British Academy in 2012 and Overseas Fellow of the Australian Academy of Law in 2015. Her current research explores what grounds the authority of the state to exercise coercive power over citizens and non-citizens within, at, and beyond its borders, and examines how citizenship is conditional on compliance. Earlier works include *Security* (Routledge 2009), *Preventive Justice* (OUP 2014, ppbk 2015) with Andrew Ashworth, and *Changing Contours of Criminal Justice* (OUP 2016), co-edited with Mary Bosworth and Carolyn Hoyle.

Contributors

Ana Aliverti is a Reader in Law at the School of Law, University of Warwick. She holds a DPhil in Law (Oxford 2012), an MSc in Criminology and Criminal Justice (Distinction, Oxford 2008), an MA in Sociology of Law (IISL 2005), and a BA in Law (Honours, Buenos Aires 2002). Her research explores questions of national identity and belonging in criminal justice, and of law, sovereignty, and globalisation. She is the author of *Crimes of Mobility* (Routledge 2013) and *Policing the Borders Within* (OUP 2021). Ana is also co-director of the Criminal Justice Centre at Warwick, and she serves on the editorial boards of *Theoretical Criminology*, *Punishment & Society*, *Revista Española de Investigación Criminológica*, and the *Howard Journal of Crime and Justice*.

Didier Bigo is Professor of International Political Sociology at Sciences Po Paris CERI, France and a part-time professor at King's College London, Department of War Studies. He recently co-directed, on the topic of migration and security, Yannis A Stivachtis, Didier Bigo, Thomas Diez, Evangelos Fanoulis, and Ben Rosamond (eds), *The Routledge Handbook of Critical European Studies* (Routledge 2021).

Jennifer Chacón is Professor of Law, Stanford Law School. Her research focuses on the fields of immigration law, constitutional law, and criminal law and procedure. It has been funded by grants from the National Science Foundation and the Russell Sage Foundation. She is a co-author of the casebook *Immigration Law and Social Justice* (Aspen Press), now in its second edition (2021), and of numerous articles, essays, and book chapters on citizenship, immigration, border control, and human trafficking.

Federica Infantino is a Marie Sklodowska-Curie Fellow at the Migration Policy Centre, European University Institute, and Lecturer at the Université Libre de Bruxelles. Her research focuses on the actors and organisations that put migration and border control into action. She is particularly interested in the diffusion of practices and the involvement of private companies. Building on ethnographic methodologies and comparative perspectives, her research has analysed the day-to-day implementation of policy instruments of migration and border control, the Schengen visa policy, and immigration detention and removal. On those topics, she has published several articles and book chapters. She is also the author of the books *Outsourcing Border Control* (Palgrave Macmillan 2016) and *Schengen Visa Implementation and Transnational Policymaking* (Palgrave Macmillan 2019).

Valsamis Mitsilegas is Professor of European and Global Law and Dean of the School of Law and Social Justice at the University of Liverpool. His research interests and expertise lie in the fields of European criminal law; migration, asylum, and borders; security and human rights, including the impact of mass surveillance on privacy; and legal responses to transnational crime, including organised crime and money laundering. He is the author of seven books, including *The Criminalisation of Migration in Europe* (Springer 2015) and *Policing Humanitarianism* (with Carrera, Allsopp, and Vosyliute, Hart 2019).

Ian Peacock is a PhD candidate in the sociology department at the University of California, Los Angeles. Ian's research concerns international migration, immigration policy and enforcement, organisations, and research methods.

Peter Ramsay is Professor in Law at the London School of Economics and Political Science. His work is focused on understanding the criminal law as a foundational element of sovereign democratic states. His book *The Insecurity State* explores the relationship between the expanding scope of the UK's criminal law and the contemporaneous decay of its national sovereignty.

Emily Ryo is Professor of Law and Sociology at the University of Southern California Gould School of Law. Her current research focuses on immigration, criminal justice, legal attitudes and legal non-compliance, and procedural justice. She approaches these issues through innovative interdisciplinary lenses, using diverse quantitative and qualitative methods. As an empirical legal scholar, she has published widely in leading sociology and law journals. She served as an American Bar Foundation/JPB Foundation Access to Justice Faculty Scholar in 2020–2021.

Samuel Singler is a Departmental Lecturer at the Centre for Criminology, University of Oxford. Samuel's research examines novel border security technology, with a focus on the role of the International Organisation of Migration (IOM) in Nigeria.

Malcolm Thorburn is Professor of Law at the University of Toronto Faculty of Law where he holds the Research Chair in the Legal, Ethical and Cultural Implications of Technological Innovation. His writing focuses on theoretical and comparative issues in criminal justice and public law including criminal law and procedure, sentencing, policing, constitutional rights, and proportionality reasoning.

Hallam Tuck is a doctoral student in the Centre for Criminology, University of Oxford, researching the intersections of privatisation, borders, and punishment within Criminal Alien Requirement prisons in the United States of America.

Ashwini Vasanthakumar is Associate Professor and Queen's National Scholar in Legal and Political Philosophy at Queen's Law School, Canada and a researcher at the Institute for Futures Studies in Stockholm, Sweden. Her current research examines political authority and membership in the context of migration, focusing in particular on the relationship between migrants and the political communities they have left.

Anthea Vogl is a Senior Lecturer in Law at the University of Technology Sydney, Australia. Her research addresses refugee and migration law and racialised practices of border control, focusing on the use of administrative powers to regulate refugees and non-citizens. She lectures in Administrative Law and Legal Theory, and co-runs a Refugee Law Clinical course. In 2018 she was a Visiting Fellow at the Humbolt University Berlin Institute for Integration and Migration Research (BIM), and in 2019 she was awarded a Social Impact Practice Grant for clinical work with refugee legal organisations in Australia. Her monograph *Judging Refugees: Oral Testimony in Refugee Status Determination* is under contract with Cambridge University Press.

Border Control, Privatisation, and the State

An Introduction

Lucia Zedner and Mary Bosworth

I Introduction

This collection of essays explores the growing use of the private sector and private actors in border control and its implications for our understanding of state sovereignty and citizenship. In so doing, the book makes a sustained empirical and conceptual contribution to the interdisciplinary body of scholarship on border control, with a particular focus on legal and criminological accounts. It also contributes a new dimension to academic enquiry into the privatisation of policing and punishment. These domains, once regarded as central to the state's police power and its monopoly on violence,[1] are increasingly outsourced to private providers. While several important works explore the privatisation of policing, penalties, and imprisonment,[2] as yet few scholars have turned their attention to the privatisation of border controls,[3] even though these operate at the very limits of the sovereign state and are fundamental to its jurisdiction and, not least, its authority to decide who is a citizen.

Both before the disruption of the COVID-19 pandemic (on which more below), and in novel ways since, states everywhere, but particularly in the Global North, have increasingly turned to criminal law and the criminal justice system to manage migration. Many breaches of immigration law have been criminalised, and foreign nationals are now routinely identified in court and in prison as possible subjects for deportation. Police at the border and within the territory refer foreign suspects to immigration authorities for expulsion.[4] Within the immigration system itself, institutions and practices have sprung up that adopt criminal justice logics and methods: most obviously detention in immigration removal centres,[5] but also reporting centres, and

[1] Thomas Hobbes, *Leviathan* (OUP 2008) 1651, ch XXX, 'Of the Office of the Sovereign Representative'; John Locke, *Two Treatises of Government* (CUP 1988) 1690, ch IX, 'Of the Ends of Political Society and Government'.

[2] Tom Daems and Tom Vander Beken (eds) *Privatising Punishment in Europe?* (Routledge 2018); Malcolm Feeley, 'The Unconvincing Case against Private Prisons' (2014) 89(4) Indiana Law Journal 1401; Alon Harel, 'Why only the State may Inflict Criminal Sanctions: The Case against Privately Inflicted Sanctions' (2008) 14(2) Legal Theory 113.

[3] Although, see Monish Bhatia and Victoria Canning, 'Misery as Business: How Immigration Detention Became a Cash-cow in Britain's Borders' in Kevin Albertson, Mary Corcoran and Jake Phillips (eds), *Marketisation and Privatisation in Criminal Justice* (Policy Press 2020); Devyani Prabhat (ed), *Privatisation of Migration Control: Power without Accountability?* (Emerald Books 2021).

[4] Ana Aliverti, *Policing the Borders within* (OUP 2021).

[5] Mary Bosworth, *Inside Immigration Detention* (OUP 2014); and Infantino, in this volume

Lucia Zedner and Mary Bosworth, *Border Control, Privatisation, and the State* In: *Privatising Border Control.*
Edited by: Mary Bosworth and Lucia Zedner, Oxford University Press.
DOI: 10.1093/oso/9780192857163.003.0001

deportation itself in its reliance on security escorts, cellular vehicles, and mechanisms of control and restraint.[6]

While the state asserts its sovereignty to sort the 'deserving' and the 'undeserving' to determine who may stay and who must leave, it has increasingly outsourced the implementation of these decisions by privatising the practice of border control. In Britain, Australia, the US, and Canada, the immigration systems rely heavily on private corporations, the voluntary sector, and private actors to police immigration, both at the territorial border and within it. In these countries, it is largely private security firms that build and staff immigration detention centres. These same firms arrange and enforce the deportation and removal of foreign nationals. In some ports (for example, at the London St Pancras Eurostar terminal), private security staff check the passports of those leaving the country.[7] Across the Channel, private security employees patrol the freight lanes at Calais, looking for asylum seekers and irregular migrants in lorries.[8] Further afield still, private companies run visa processing services at overseas points of departure in so-called sending countries, for example Morocco and Algeria.[9] Even EU member states like France and Italy, which have largely retained state oversight over border control within their territories, depend on private sector and voluntary sector organisations, whether in the day-to-day operation of aspects of their detention centres[10] or in access to the data surveillance programmes funded by the EU and built by private security firms.[11] In Europe, as in the US,[12] the border is secured via assistance from 'big tech' companies, which build data surveillance programs and share (at least some of) the details they gather with the state.[13]

Although the state is never wholly absent, as immigration officers check passports on entry, and determine whether individuals are to be detained, deported, or removed, many of these decisions made by state officials depend on the work of private security agents to identify potential suspects, either through algorithms or by finding them on lorries. Private companies, sometimes operating in partnership with voluntary sector organisations, monitor foreign nationals in the community, hold them in detention centres, or escort them on to planes for deportation. Such developments are amplified and legitimated by familiar racialised assumptions about who is an unauthorised traveller and whose immigration status is irregular. As well as conventional privatisation

[6] Bosworth and Singler, in this volume.

[7] At the time of writing, this service is provided by Mitie Care and Custody, a company that also holds contracts for managing immigration removal centres in the UK, and the escorting contract for moving immigration detainees within the UK, and escorting them on deportation flights.

[8] Mary Bosworth, 'Immigration Detention and Juxtaposed Border Controls on the French North Coast' (2020) European Journal of Criminology <https://doi.org/10.1177/1477370820902971> accessed 16 December 2021

[9] Frederica Infantino, *Outsourcing Border Control: Politics and Practice of Contracted Visa Policy in Morocco* (Palgrave 2016).

[10] On Italy and the role of NGOs in immigration detention centres, see Guissepe Campesi, 'Hindering the Deportation Machine: An Ethnography of Power and Resistance in Immigration Detention' (2015) 17(4) Punishment & Society 427; for a discussion of the work of the legal charity CIMADE in French detention centres, see Nicolas Fischer, 'The Detention of Foreigners in France: Between Discretionary Control and the Rule of Law' (2013) 10(6) European Journal of Criminology 692.

[11] Bigo, in this volume.

[12] Chacón, in this volume.

[13] See also Sanja Milivojevic, *Crime and Punishment in the Future Internet: Digital Frontier Technologies and Criminology in the Twenty-first Century* (Routledge 2021).

through contracting out to private firms, in many countries the state also extends legal responsibilities to enforce border control to a much wider population of private citizens who are required to verify the status of migrants and report those who do not have the required paperwork, and to check and report on visa holders.[14]

As these immigration control practices, and the logic they espouse, have become unfixed from the border to permeate everyday life,[15] they have reshaped social relations and, arguably, the nature of citizenship itself. Thus, for example, concerns over border control draw into question the rights and presence of black and minority ethnic citizens, who may have to prove their legal status in a variety of interactions with state and private sector agents.[16] At the same time, whole new criminal justice institutions—such as the all-foreign national 'criminal alien requirement' (CAR) prisons in the US federal system—which are almost entirely filled with ethnic minority prisoners, have been established to facilitate deportation.[17]

Third-sector organisations, which have traditionally conceived of their role in humanitarian terms, have not been unaffected by these developments. On the one hand, the criminalisation of aid to migrants has forced some to change their activities to avoid prosecution,[18] while on the other hand, generous funding has attracted other groups, including—in the UK—homeless and rough sleeper charities,[19] to work alongside the state in managing asylum seekers and irregular migrants.[20]

Finally, in its restrictive response to the COVID-19 crisis, Australia demonstrated the potential risks of a staunch commitment to border control for the rights and protections of all citizens. Not only did Australia pursue a vigorous system of quarantine hotels, in some cases run by the same private sector agents who otherwise operated immigration detention facilities, but in reducing the number of daily flights and the permitted reasons for departure or return, the Australian government departed radically from the legal and ethical obligations towards citizens that were formalised with the creation of passports.[21]

In drawing attention to the contracting-out of state migration control, this collection seeks to refocus debates around matters of sovereignty and state power to acknowledge the very significant role now played by private actors. At the border, the state exercises its ultimate right to determine membership, whether voluntarily or by force. The exercise of these powers is inseparable from the state's right and duty to determine who may enjoy hospitality as a guest, who is allowed to enter, who may remain, and who may enjoy the protections and liberties of citizenship. The justification and moral authority for exercising these coercive powers is commonly held, even in the highest courts, to depend on their administration being entrusted to organs of the state.[22] It might be considered paradoxical, therefore, that governments around the

[14] Ana Aliverti, 'Enlisting the Public in the Policing of Immigration' (2015) 55(2) British Journal of Criminology 215; Zedner, in this volume.

[15] Aliverti, *Policing the Borders within* (n 4).

[16] Aliverti, *Policing the Borders within* (n 4) 106.

[17] Chacón and Tuck, in this volume; Mary Bosworth, Alpa Parmar and Yolanda Vázquez (eds), *Race, Migration and Criminal Justice: Enforcing the Boundaries of Belonging* (OUP 2018).

[18] Mitsilegas, in this volume.

[19] Zedner, in this volume.

[20] Vogl, in this volume.

[21] John Torpey, *The Invention of the Passport: Surveillance, Citizenship and the State* (CUP 2018).

[22] Thorburn and Ramsay, in this volume.

world so readily delegate their authority to police the borders of their territorial jurisdiction to commercial security firms, non-governmental organisations (NGOs), and private actors.[23]

On one view, the privatisation of border control adds new actors and further layers of control that amplify and extend state power far beyond the physical precincts of the border and thus may be considered to enhance or even extend state sovereignty.[24] On another view, some forms of outsourcing—for example the delegation of immigration monitoring and reporting responsibilities to NGOs, professionals, and private citizens—undermine state control by delegating decision-making to non-state, charitable, and humanitarian organisations, and even to private citizens. These forms of outsourcing allow decisions about undocumented migrants to be made by individuals who lack training, are not public officials, and may not consider themselves to be acting in a public capacity, and who consequently may have little regard for values like justice, fairness, and non-discrimination.

The costs of such arrangements in moral and ethical terms are manifold. In more straightforwardly financial terms, these costs are also evident, most obviously in the price tag attached to the contracts for providing border control services; often these are for sums that, as Chacón makes clear for the US,[25] can reach dizzying heights. From a different perspective, abundant evidence of the negative impact of these practices on individuals and communities speaks to another kind of tariff. In the slipshod provision of COVID-19 quarantine facilities for travellers to Australia during the pandemic, for example, where private contractors failed to supply personal protective equipment, provided inadequate training to security guards, breached hygiene protocols, and permitted those quarantined to leave the building, an additional toll emerged in the form of a further wave of cases and renewed lockdown in Australia's second-largest city, Melbourne, which ultimately endured one of the longest periods of lockdown in the world.[26] Finally, questions might be raised about the rationale and enduring support for the deportation infrastructure in the UK, when 75 per cent of deportations fail.[27] In all cases, the private sector appears not only to bear the risk for the state, but also to generate new points of vulnerability and new risks, not least to health and personal safety.

The contributions to this volume offer a variety of views on the implications of these privatised arrangements for our understandings of state sovereignty. While Peter Ramsay suggests that privatisation demonstrates the decay of sovereignty, Mary Bosworth and Samuel Singler perceive it as a new hybrid form of governance that calls into question old binaries about the public and private sectors.[28] For Emily Ryo and Ian Peacock, such matters may offer grounds for challenging practice, even though, as

23 Vasanthakumar, in this volume.

24 Mitsilegas, in this volume.

25 Chacón, in this volume.

26 See Renju Jose, 'Melbourne Readies to Exit World's Longest COVID-19 Lockdown' (*Reuters*, 21 October 2021) <https://www.reuters.com/world/asia-pacific/melbourne-readies-exit-worlds-longest-covid-19-lockdowns-2021-10-20/> accessed 16 December 2021. In the UK, when similar policies were adopted, the cost took a different form still, with female travellers complaining of unwanted and sinister sexual attention from the private border guards employed in privately run quarantine hotels.

27 Bosworth and Singler, in this volume.

28 Ramsay, and Bosworth and Singler, both in this volume.

Jennifer Chacón reminds us, many of the examples cited follow entrenched patterns inherent to 'racial capitalism', which have proven impervious to change.[29]

II Structure and Themes of the Book

The book is structured in four sections, the first of which examines 'The Limits of State Sovereignty'. Jennifer Chacón starts this section with a detailed analysis of the irredeemably racialised quality of privatised border controls, private detention, and deportation. She argues that privatisation works exactly as intended to evade transparency and accountability 'by design' in furtherance of the aims of racialised surveillance capitalism. It is not so much, therefore, that state authority is undermined by privatisation, but rather that weakened state oversight and poor accountability provisions are designed into contracts for services precisely so that the state can escape liability. Qualified immunity for private companies and non-disclosure agreements (NDAs) further undermine transparency, as they allow companies to assert commercial secrecy and their employees to claim immunity from disclosure to escape public accountability. In turn, Chacón suggests that the US Federal Government resists freedom of information requests on security grounds, further limiting transparency, and allowing the state to create a racially differentiated system of border controls, permeable for some but not others.

Turning to the EU, Valsamis Mitsilegas examines the increasingly restrictive state responses to civil society and humanitarian organisations, which seek to rescue migrant boats in the Mediterranean and Aegean Seas. Notwithstanding the protections of international human rights law and maritime law, such organisations have come under increasing pressure from EU member states, which have criminalised their activities and charged them with facilitating human trafficking and colluding with smugglers. Mitsilegas argues that states thus attempt to assert their sovereignty over border control by deliberately fostering a 'hostile environment' for civil society actors seeking only to uphold the rule of law and to defend the rights of migrants. In response, as Mitsilegas shows, NGOs and civil society actors 'turn the tables' on the state by actively contesting state overreach of its sovereign power.

Whereas it may be tempting to view such a muscular defence of the border as an outward-facing confirmation of the strength of the sovereign state to command control over its territory, assert national autonomy, and demand the respect of other powers, in his contribution to this section, Peter Ramsay suggests otherwise. In his view, the energetic defence of national borders, harsh immigration policies, and the identification of outsiders as threats may be less a display—still less evidence—of state power than a symptom of its decay. As rapid globalisation weakens the nation state, states respond defensively, resort to criminalisation of immigration breaches, and invoke emergency powers as if the life of the nation were under threat.[30] In Ramsay's view, resort to the criminalisation of immigration offences, or 'crimmigration', should

[29] Ryo and Peacock, and Chacón, both in this volume.

[30] Ramsay, in this volume. See also Lucia Zedner, 'The Hostile Border: Crimmigration, Counter-terrorism or Crossing the Line on Rights?' (2019) 22(3) New Criminal Law Review 318.

be understood less as an assertion of state power, but rather as an admission of weakness, or perhaps better as a means of masking the waning of its sovereignty by laying the blame for failures of the state on impoverished foreigners.

Essays in the second section turn to 'Legitimacy and the Rule of the Law at the Border'. Adherents of classical liberal theory see the state as fulfilling an essential and irreducible role in its exercise of the police power or 'nightwatchman'[31] role within and at the border. Some, like Dorfman and Harel, regard it is as axiomatic that only the state has standing to exercise coercive control over its citizens and that such powers cannot, therefore, be contracted out.[32] Others reject the primacy of the state–citizen relation, and its attendant rights and obligations, to adopt a cosmopolitan world view that declines to distinguish between citizens and non-citizens,[33] refuses to regard fundamental rights as tied to citizenship,[34] and gives no special priority to the state.[35] On this view, the state has no special standing or relationship upon which basis to claim primacy over coercive powers.

In his chapter, Malcolm Thorburn argues that the state has standing because only it can act in the name of the polity. For Thorburn, private actors lack standing to carry out border controls and cannot assume state powers to coerce, not least because they lack the necessary ethos of public office. For him, the key question is whether 'privatising border control is *intrinsically* illegitimate'.[36] Thorburn defends a 'statist' argument and notes that, although the positions taken by 'statists' vary, they share the view that only the state may exercise coercive power over its citizens and that, therefore, only the state may police and punish. Even in respect of non-citizens, the state itself encapsulates what migrants seek. They journey not merely in search of food, shelter, and blankets, but in the hope of full membership of a political community, enjoyment of the protections enjoyed by citizens, and, ultimately, full rights of democratic participation. On this view, argues Thorburn, to give up on the state is also to give up on all it offers, not least democratic governance and the rule of law.

Some scholars of privatisation have questioned these assumptions. Both critics and advocates of privatisation have called into question the so-called state monopoly thesis.[37] They challenge the legitimacy of the state monopoly over the police power on several grounds. Some argue that what matters is less the legitimacy or standing of the actor, whether state or private, than the justness of the practices by which coercive power is exercised. In her contribution to this volume, Ashwini Vasanthakumar contends that the legitimacy of a given policy or practice is not sufficient to determine

[31] Malcolm Thorburn, 'Reinventing the Night-watchman State?' (2010) 60(2) University of Toronto Law Journal 425.

[32] Avihay Dorfman and Alon Harel, 'Against Privatisation as Such' (2015) 36(3) Oxford Journal of Legal Studies 1.

[33] Klaus Günther, 'World Citizens between Freedom and Security' in David Dyzenhaus (ed), *Civil Rights and Security* (Routledge 2009).

[34] David Cole, 'Against Citizenship as a Predicate for Human Rights' (2007) 75 Fordham Law Review 2541.

[35] Pauline Kleingeld and Eric Brown, 'Cosmopolitanism' (2002) *The Stanford Encyclopedia of Philosophy* <https://plato.stanford.edu/entries/cosmopolitanism/#PoliCosm> accessed 8 December 2021.

[36] Thorburn, in this volume.

[37] Clifford Shearing, 'Reflections on the Refusal to Acknowledge Private Government' in Jennifer Wood and Benoit Dupont (eds), *Democracy, Society and the Governance of Security* (CUP 2006) 11–32; Feeley 'The Unconvincing Case against Private Prisons' (n 2).

the legitimacy of the state, which should rather rely on intrinsic arguments. While Vasanthakumar concedes that the state has standing to police its citizens, she questions the legitimacy of its authority over non-citizens, who are not parties to the social contract, and over whom, at the border, the state is 'deficient as a public agent' and has, therefore, only limited powers to admit, exclude, or deport.[38] On these grounds, she suggests that non-state actors mitigate this deficit and even enhance the legitimacy of border controls.

In the face of the many 'successes' of privatised border control, other scholars draw attention to the flaws and defects that prompt growing resistance to privatisation. In their chapter, Emily Ryo and Ian Peacock observe that the involvement of private security in the provision of immigration detention in the US has not only facilitated massive investment in, and expansion of, the immigration detention estate, but has also attracted potent resistance. A growing disinvestment campaign by US banks since 2019, and increasing political and legal challenges in the US and elsewhere, have drawn public attention to the immorality of contracting-out and, not least, of 'profiting from human misery'.[39] Opponents of privatised detention have revealed the prevalence of inhumane conditions, neglect, abuse, and even deaths in private facilities, and the need for greater transparency and accountability, and for fresh public debate about the legitimacy of privatised controls. Ryo and Peacock thus analyse 'anti-privatisation frames' to explore their limits and their implications for conceptualising, illuminating, and advancing debates.

Privatisation of policing and punishment are often seen to undermine state power by transferring day-to-day decision-making from public officials to private firms and private actors in ways that reduce transparency and accountability, and limit avenues of redress for misuse of that power.[40] For many state-centric thinkers, the privatisation of core state functions is prima facie illegitimate.[41] Yet, others see privatisation as a positive development that allows for entrepreneurship, innovation, economy, and efficiency in the delivery of punishment.[42] Applied to border controls, privatisation provokes even more debate about how it should be understood, not least because privatisation here embraces a wider array of practices and a larger cast of actors.

In the third section, on 'Outsourcing or Undermining State Authority', contributors draw on a range of empirical work to study such matters. Hallam Tuck begins with a detailed account of a novel, but familiar, form of punishment: the US Federal 'Criminal Alien Requirement' (CAR) prisons. These all-foreign national establishments are designed to facilitate deportation following criminal conviction. As the sole privatised institutions within the federal system, CAR prisons make concrete the ties between racial capitalism and border control, set out earlier by Chacón, and also demonstrate how such matters reshape fundamental ideas of justice. Those serving time in CAR prisons not only receive differential and lesser treatment while incarcerated

[38] Vasanthakumar, in this volume.
[39] ibid.
[40] Daems and Vander Beken (n 2).
[41] Harel (n 2).
[42] Malcolm M Feeley, 'Privatizing Criminal Justice: An Historical Analysis of Entrepreneurship and Innovation' in Tom Daems and Tom Vander Beken (eds), *Privatising Punishment in Europe?* (Routledge 2018) 18–44; Feeley, 'The Unconvincing Case against Private Prisons' (n 2).

than US citizens but face an additional penalty—deportation—for their actions. In his analysis of the historical policy roots of these institutions, Tuck demonstrates how successive US governments deployed racialised fears over 'criminal aliens' to lobby for the privatisation of state functions.

A determination to normalise and depoliticise practices of border control and deportation may also explain government contracting-out of immigration detention, internal transfers, and overseas escorting to achieve removal and deportation. As Federica Infantino, Mary Bosworth, and Samuel Singler argue in their chapters in this section, these practices are better understood not at the macro level of privatisation writ large, but at the micro level of quotidian immigration control practices, which are revealed only through empirical study. In her contribution, Infantino focuses on the perspectives and experiences of border control actors on the ground to gain a fuller understanding of how power is exercised on the micro level, to consider how privatised detention officers make sense of their roles, their primary obligation to meet key performance indicators (KPIs), and assess the impact of the drivers of economy and efficiency on their day-to-day decision-making. The imperatives of 'new public management' (NPM) combine to make outcomes, as measured, for example, by successful deportations, the primary metric of success, irrespective of how or by what means they are achieved. By thus governing at a distance, the state seeks to deflect, and largely succeeds in deflecting, responsibility for the exercise of coercive force over would-be migrants. It thereby distances itself from responsibility for the risks and resulting harms of forcible deportation.

This distancing tactic is also advanced by ensuring the low visibility of privatised border control practices. As Bosworth and Singler make clear, private companies commonly charter flights that depart at midnight to withdraw deportee resistance from the public eye and to reduce public scrutiny of deportation practices generally. If and when things do go wrong, the state is then able to invoke termination of contract as a swift means to deflect responsibility for violence against deportees that results in injury or even death. Privatisation of deportation also conceals the racialised assumptions and practices of private security guards, which result in darker-skinned deportees more often being subject to physical restraints than lighter-skinned fellow travellers in a super-fine grading of deportees by skin colour and race. These micro-level empirical enquires shine a bright light on inequities and abuses that the state would prefer to obscure. Bosworth and Singler's observations reveal that privatisation may, above all, be a means by which the state outsources the exercise of coercion entailed in border control and, by so doing, obscures its racism and sheer brutality.

While criminologists invoke the image of the 'shadow carceral state'[43] to describe penal practices lying beyond conventional state punishment, the contributions to this volume reveal that the outsourcing of border control extends far beyond the state to activities over which the state has little or no aegis, and that operate, not under the state's auspices, but far apart from it. In the final section, 'Practices of Privatisation at the Border', contributors examine how outsourcing entails a much larger population— consisting of workers for NGOs and charities, professionals, and even private

[43] Katherine Beckett and Naomi Murakawa, 'Mapping the Shadow Carceral State: Toward an Institutionally Capacious Approach to Punishment' (2012) 16(2) Theoretical Criminology 221.

individuals— who are encouraged, inveigled, or legally obliged to carry out immigration status checks, to verify immigrants' right to rent, to work, to obtain healthcare or attend classes, and to report those of 'irregular' status to the authorities.[44]

In addition to corporate activities, those of immigration lawyers, of migrant charities and lobby groups, and other NGOs also play an important part in the management of migrant populations, but they may operate at odds with, or even in direct opposition to, the state. In so far as non-governmental and humanitarian groups intervene to enable migrants to continue their journeys safely across land and sea, and seek to facilitate border crossings, their activities may pose a threat to state control of the borders of its sovereign territory territories, or even be recast as criminal collusion with people smugglers and human traffickers.[45] While commercial security companies dominate the field of privatised border control and detention, non-governmental organisations (NGOs) also play an increasingly important role as they are inveigled into active partnership with state immigration control policies in a radical shift from care to compliance, with requirements to police and report undocumented migrants.

As Anthea Vogl makes clear in her contribution in this section, many NGOs have been captured as agents of state policing, deterrence, and complicity in deportation, even when seeking to fulfil their avowed humanitarian roles in providing support to newly arrived migrants. In Australia, for example, humanitarian NGOs contracted by the state are subject to mandatory reporting requirements, and voluntarily dominate in making reports to the so-called 'Dobbing-in Service', even though reporting may result in individuals being denied the very services that the NGO purports to provide. Such reporting serves not only to police migrants within the community, but to render their lives so difficult as to encourage 'self-deportation' or voluntary return. The policy of engaging NGOs and private citizens to report on irregular migrants is part of a larger practice of seeking to create conditions so inhospitable that they induce voluntary departure. In the UK, for example, the explicit introduction of the 'Hostile Environment' policy had such an aim: it actively encouraged, and even obliged, citizens, professionals, and charity workers to collaborate in the creation of a dense network of checks and controls explicitly designed to discourage and deter undocumented immigration.[46]

The social contract of classical liberal political theory posits a settlement by which citizens subject themselves to the authority of the sovereign state in return for its promise of protection. The social contract is thus simultaneously a source of state power to command and to exercise sovereign power over citizens. It follows that the imposition on private actors of obligations to police immigration constitutes a significant outsourcing of the state duty to protect because it makes citizens, not the state, responsible for tackling the threat ostensibly posed by illegal or undocumented migrants. In her chapter, Lucia Zedner suggests that the imposition of positive

[44] Zedner, in this volume.

[45] The UK government has declared itself committed to take tougher action against anyone facilitating a migrant's illegal entry, whether for profit or on humanitarian grounds: HM Government, *New Plan for Immigration Policy Statement* (HMSO 2021) 37 <https://assets.publishing.service.gov.uk/government/uploads/system/uploads/attachment_data/file/972517/CCS207_CCS0820091708-001_Sovereign_Borders_Web_Accessible.pdf> accessed 8 December 2021.

[46] Zedner, in this volume.

obligations on citizens to check migration status and to report 'illegals'[47] is problematic because it partially inverts the social contract by making citizens stand in for the state and even assume responsibility for policing, ostensibly for their own protection. That said, the fact that those citizens who fail to fulfil these positive obligations are liable to criminal fines and may be subject to prosecution and imprisonment for their non-payment, makes clear that they remain subject to state coercion and punishment for non-compliance. While the imposition of positive obligations upon citizens may not constitute privatisation in the conventional sense, the fact that, in the UK at least, citizens engaged in checking migrant status have been held by the Court of Appeal to act in a private capacity[48] implies that citizens police migrants not as agents of the state but as private actors.[49] Zedner concludes that by assigning border-policing duties to private citizens, the state cedes sovereign power and undermines its own legitimacy.

In respect of the corporate provision of border security services, an intriguing suggestion by Didier Bigo in his chapter is that the combined impact of globalisation and the digitisation of immigration controls, which operate well beyond state borders, is to create new forms of 'corporate sovereignty', not least that exercised by global tech companies. On this view, to focus our attention on the physical border is to ignore the fact that migration controls also operate elsewhere, above and beyond the border. To overlook the significance of these technological advances, argues Bigo, is to miss the relationship between corporate power, the less visible operation of technological border controls, and the transnational logics of the digitalised border.[50] According to Bigo, to focus on questions of state sovereignty is to miss the fact that sovereignty has largely been decoupled from the state as the border is no longer under state control. Rather, it has been dissolved, fragmented, and redistributed among multiple private actors, a guild of data managers, and IT system engineers, whose new data highways have transformed the very meaning of border control.

III Conclusion

As the contributors to this volume make clear, the privatisation of border controls takes many forms and encompasses widely varying practices, ranging from the contracting-out to private security firms of border control functions formerly undertaken by state officials; to the assumption of monitoring and other interventions by NGOs, and even private citizens, to entirely new technologies of control. The tasks and roles privatised range from the provision of services like cleaning, catering, and transport, to control functions such as detaining, guarding, and escorting by private security companies. Monitoring immigration status and reporting irregularities are duties outsourced to charities, NGOs, professionals (including doctors, professors, and teachers), as well as to private citizens like landlords. In addition, new tools of digital security and data highways operate above and beyond the border, well away from public view.

47 Catherine Dauvergne, *Making People Illegal* (CUP 2008).
48 *SSHD v Joint Council for The Welfare of Immigrants* [2020] EWCA Civ 542 [80].
49 Zedner, in this volume.
50 Zedner, in this volume.

In all these examples, we see how the nature and implications of border control arrangements have implications for understanding state power and control more broadly. Nonetheless, it is open to question whether these diverse practices share sufficient commonality to be considered under the single term 'privatisation', or whether contracting-out to private firms should be distinguished from the reassignment of responsibilities for border control to NGOs and individual citizens. Is the state still exercising sovereign control at the border? Or is the border now better understood as a complex web of entities—state, commercial, charitable, civilian, and individual—that operate not only at the physical margins of state territory, but also at distant points of departure, along commercial travel and migrant routes, along digital borders and data highways, and even embedded in daily life throughout civil society?

These are not merely definitional questions. Whether private actors remain largely under the direction and command of state officials, operate subject to the strictures of contract terms, or act independently to exercise their discretion has significant implications for the rule of law and the legitimacy and fairness of border control practices. So too, the nature, scale, and technological and legal form of the transfer directly affect how far the involvement of non-state actors in practices of border control constitutes the subcontracting, extension, delegation, or outsourcing of state power.

The chapters in this volume make a significant contribution to identifying, clarifying, and classifying the varied practices of non-state border control, though there remains scope for yet more extensive, systematic, and more granular accounts of the operation of privatised border controls to determine which forms of outsourcing enhance, which weaken, and which—by non-compliance, opposition, or subversion—directly challenge state sovereignty. No less important are questions about the changing shape of the state and changes in the modes and in the legal channels by which the state exercises its police power. These changes include resort to criminalisation of immigration law, or 'crimmigration', but also extensive recourse to non-criminal measures for regulatory and even penal purposes, veiled by the label of administrative law.

As the Afterword by Aliverti's generously observes, the contributions to this volume engage in 'robust intellectual enquiry' to subject the complexities of border control to 'scrupulous examination from a range of disciplinary standpoints, methodological approaches and jurisdictions'.[51] She rightly identifies three critical concepts—privatisation, border controls, and state sovereignty—that structure the volume, and give coherence to, and provide continuity throughout, chapters that range widely across jurisdictions, and across the gamut of border control practices. As editors, we began with the puzzle of why the state, at the very borders of its sovereign jurisdiction, would so readily cede its powers to private companies, organisations, and actors, and with what consequences for the legitimacy of its authority to govern. Aliverti reflects that 'it may seem paradoxical that a volume on the privatisation of border controls tells us so much about the state and its place in broader structures of contemporary governance'.[52] But this was the very intuition we invited our contributors to explore and to test. As the richness of their contributions reveals, there is much to be said

[51] Aliverti, in this volume.
[52] ibid.

about what privatising border control reveals about the limits of the sovereign state. While a final account of the implications of the privatisation of border control for our understanding of state power and sovereignty remains contested, these topics invite continuing scrutiny, both for their own sake, and for their effects on state authority, on membership of the polity, and for the legitimacy of the diverse laws, procedures, and practices by which borders are governed today.

References

Aliverti A, 'Enlisting the Public in the Policing of Immigration' (2015) 55(2) British Journal of Criminology 215

Aliverti A, *Policing the Borders within* (OUP 2021)

Beckett K and Murakawa N, 'Mapping the Shadow Carceral State: Toward an Institutionally Capacious Approach to Punishment' (2012) 16(2) Theoretical Criminology 221

Bhatia M and Canning V, 'Misery as Business: How Immigration Detention Became a Cash-cow in Britain's Borders' in Albertson K, Corcoran M, and Phillips J (eds), *Marketisation and Privatisation in Criminal Justice* (Policy Press 2020)

Bosworth M 'Immigration Detention and Juxtaposed Border Controls on the French North Coast' (2020) European Journal of Criminology

— — *Inside Immigration Detention* (OUP 2014)

— —, Parmar A, and Vázquez Y (eds), *Race, Migration and Criminal Justice: Enforcing the Boundaries of Belonging* (OUP 2018)

Campesi G, 'Hindering the Deportation Machine: An Ethnography of Power and Resistance in Immigration Detention' (2015) 17(4) Punishment & Society 427

Cole D, 'Against Citizenship as a Predicate for Human Rights' (2007) 75 Fordham Law Review 2541

Daems T and Vander Beken T (eds), *Privatising Punishment in Europe?* (Routledge 2018)

Dauvergne C, *Making People Illegal* (CUP 2008)

Dorfman A and Harel A, 'Against Privatisation as Such' (2015) 36(3) Oxford Journal of Legal Studies 1

Feeley M, 'The Unconvincing Case against Private Prisons' (2014) 89(4) Indiana Law Journal 1401

Feeley M, 'Privatizing Criminal Justice: An Historical Analysis of Entrepreneurship and Innovation' in Daems T and Vander Beken T (eds), *Privatising Punishment in Europe?* (Routledge 2018)

Fischer N, 'The Detention of Foreigners in France: Between Discretionary Control and the Rule of Law' (2013) 10(6) European Journal of Criminology 692

Günther K, 'World Citizens between Freedom and Security' in Dyzenhaus D (ed), *Civil Rights and Security* (Routledge 2009)

Harel A, 'Why only the State may Inflict Criminal Sanctions: The Case against Privately Inflicted Sanctions' (2008) 14(2) Legal Theory 113

HM Government, *New Plan for Immigration Policy Statement* (HMSO 2021) <https://assets.publishing.service.gov.uk/government/uploads/system/uploads/attachment_data/file/972517/CCS207_CCS0820091708-001_Sovereign_Borders_Web_Accessible.pdf>

Hobbes T, *Leviathan* (OUP 2008)

Infantino F, *Outsourcing Border Control: Politics and Practice of Contracted Visa Policy in Morocco* (Palgrave 2016)

Kleingeld P and Brown E, 'Cosmopolitanism' (2002) *The Stanford Encyclopedia of Philosophy* <https://plato.stanford.edu/entries/cosmopolitanism/#PoliCosm>
Locke J, *Two Treatises of Government* (CUP 1988)
Milivojevic S, *Crime and Punishment in the Future Internet: Digital Frontier Technologies and Criminology in the Twenty-first Century* (Routledge 2021)
Prabhat D (ed), *Privatisation of Migration Control: Power without Accountability?* (Emerald Books 2021)
Shearing C, 'Reflections on the refusal to acknowledge private government' in Wood J and Dupont B (eds), *Democracy, Society and the Governance of Security* (CUP 2006)
Thorburn M, 'Reinventing the Night-watchman State?' (2010) 60(2) University of Toronto Law Journal 425
Torpey J, *The Invention of the Passport: Surveillance, Citizenship and the State* (CUP 2018)
Zedner L, 'The Hostile Border: Crimmigration, Counter-terrorism or Crossing the Line on Rights?' (2019) 22(3) New Criminal Law Review 318

Cases

SSHD v Joint Council for The Welfare of Immigrants [2020] EWCA Civ 542

PART I
THE LIMITS OF STATE SOVEREIGNTY

1

Same As It Ever Was? Race, Capital, and Privatised Immigration Enforcement

Jennifer Chacón

I Introduction

Privatisation exists in the context of capitalist systems and is structured by capitalist logics. Privatisation refers to the government's use of 'private entities to implement government programs or to provide services to others on the government's behalf'.[1] Public officials 'shift public functions into private hands', on the theory that market-style competition can increase the efficiency and cost-effectiveness of these services.[2] While privatisation has additional aims and effects,[3] its leading justification—market efficiency[4]—turns on the promise of private financial gain to individuals and entities who perform services on behalf of the government. These gains are distinct from performing salaried work on behalf of the government. A government worker is remunerated for her labour and ingenuity. But privatised governmental services carry with them the additional promise of profit for private individuals who can perform governmental services for less than the labour and material costs of those services as performed by government workers. In this way, privatised governmental services generally require the extraction of profit from somewhere other than the labour and ingenuity of the person with whom the government contracts.[5]

[1] Gillian E Metzger, 'Privatization as Delegation' (2003) 103 Columbia Law Review 1367, 1370. See also Steven Rathgeb Smith, 'Review: The Privatization Decision: Public Ends, Private Means by John D Donahue. New York, Basic Books, 1989' (1991) 106(1) Political Science Quarterly 1379 (Privatization … describe[s] a variety of strategies that entail the delegation of public responsibility to the private sector).

[2] See, eg Martha Minow, 'Public and Private Partnerships: Accounting for the New Religion' (2003) 116 Harvard Law Review 1229, 1230 ('a useful definition [of privatization] encompasses the range of efforts by governments to move public functions into private hands and to use market-style competition'). See also Jody Freeman, 'Extending Public Law Norms through Privatization' (2003) 116 Harvard Law Review 1285, 1287.

[3] See, eg Jon D Michaels, 'Privatization's Pretensions' (2010) 77 University of Chicago Law Review 717, 718–19 ('[P]olicymakers turn to privatization for more than the customary, and ostensibly exclusive, objective of providing the public with the same goods and services more efficiently than the government bureaucracy can. They use government contracting in a way that substantively alters (or temporally ossifies) the very policies they are supposed to be neutrally administering.').

[4] See, eg Freeman (n 2), 12 ('[I]t is fair to say that pragmatic arguments [for privatization] typically draw on economic conceptions of the advantages of private over public service provision.); see also John D Donahue, *The Privatization Decision: Public Ends, Private Means* (Basic Books 1989), 57 (identifying 'superior efficiency' as the promise that drives general interest in privatization); David A Super, 'Privatization, Policy Paralysis, and the Poor' (2008) 96 California Law Review 393, 400 ('economic efficiency' is privatization's 'measure of success').

[5] Contracting also raises oversight challenges that are distinct from, and more intractable than, the problem of government employee oversight. See Thomas J Laubacher, 'Simplifying Inherently

Jennifer Chacón, *Same As It Ever Was? Race, Capital, and Privatised Immigration Enforcement* In: *Privatising Border Control*. Edited by: Mary Bosworth and Lucia Zedner, Oxford University Press.
DOI: 10.1093/oso/9780192857163.003.0002

In the sphere of private immigration enforcement in the US, privatisation operates as a mechanism of racialised capitalist extraction. The structure of the global economy, constructed over the long historical arc of colonialism, in conjunction with the particular operation of US immigration law, ensures that capitalist accumulation relating to immigration enforcement has a racial dimension. The people who are surveilled, tracked, and caged are overwhelmingly from the Global South—racialised as Black and Latinx in the US.[6] The people who profit most are overwhelmingly US citizens racialised as white. Private companies profit from the detention of hundreds of thousands of people, who are held for varied and indeterminate lengths of time in private immigration detention centres as they await status determinations.[7] Private companies profit from the intrusive ankle monitor surveillance of non-detained immigrants in removal proceedings.[8] Private social media companies and data aggregators profit from the sale to the government of information gathered from their users and other sources in service of the project Anil Kalhan calls 'immigration surveillance'.[9]

A burgeoning literature critically analyses privatised immigration enforcement, particularly immigration detention, in the US. These critiques point out various problems that privatisation creates in the immigration enforcement sphere: downward pressures on expenditures on food, infrastructure, and services in detention facilities, which generate degraded conditions of confinement; opaque chains of responsibility that frustrate immigrants' access to counsel in detention facilities and undermine accountability for injuries and other harms suffered; and distortions of the mechanisms of democratic governance.[10] Other literature evaluates the growth of immigration surveillance, though this literature has generally been less concerned with privatisation, and more concerned with state power.[11] This chapter fuses those critiques of privatisation and state power, and situates them in a broader historical framework,

Governmental Functions: Creating a Principled Approach from its Ad Hoc Beginnings' (2017) 46 Public Contract Law Journal 791, 818 (citing Kimberly N Brown, '"We the People," Constitutional Accountability, and Outsourcing Government' (2013) 88 Indiana Law Journal 1347, 1352 ('Even if the capacity for more oversight was built into the acquisition system, the threat of not renewing a contract or more judicial scrutiny will not create the same level of day-to-day accountability that government employees face.')).

[6] Though this term has its critics, I use it in this chapter to describe individuals previously described as Latino/Latina both because it signals greater inclusion of indigenous identities and also because it is more inclusive of those who identify as queer or nonbinary. See Concepción de León, Another Hot Take on the Term 'Latinx', *New York Times* (New York, 21 November 2018), available at <https://www.nytimes.com/2018/11/21/style/latinx-queer-gender-nonconforming.html> last accessed 1 September 2022.

[7] John Burnett, 'As Asylum Seekers Swap Prison Beds for Ankle Bracelets, Same Firm Profits' (*National Public Radio*, 13 November 2015); César Cuautémoc García Hernández, *Migrating to Prison: America's Obsession with Locking Up Immigrants* (New Press 2019).

[8] Burnett (n 7).

[9] See, eg the discussion accompanying nn 35–46. Kalhan defines immigration surveillance as 'technologies [that] have transformed a regime of immigration control, operating primarily upon noncitizens at the territorial border, into part of a more expansive regime of migration and mobility surveillance, operating without geographic bounds upon citizens and noncitizens alike': Anil Kalhan, 'Immigration Surveillance' (2014) 74 Maryland Law Review 1, 2.

[10] See, eg César Cuauhtémoc García Hernández, 'Naturalizing Immigration Imprisonment' (2015) 103 California Law Review 1449; Mariela Olivarez, 'Intersectionality at the Intersection of Profiteering & Immigration Detention' (2016) 94 Nebraska Law Review 963.

[11] See, eg Kalhan (n 9); Eunice Lee, 'The End of Entry Fiction' (2021) 99 North Carolina Law Review 565, 614–24 (describing recent expansions in immigration surveillance).

arguing that the expansion of private immigration enforcement and public–private surveillance partnerships in the criminalised and securitised space of immigration is not, at its core, a new phenomenon. Placing current trends in the broader sweep of history reveals how contemporary privatisation schemes in the US continue the 400-year march of racial capitalism, in which private property owners have *always* appropriated purportedly public governance mechanisms to extract profit from certain racialised populations. Reframed this way, it is possible to view the harms and systemic distortions generated by privatisation not as accidental glitches, but as predictable features of the US political economy.

The chapter proceeds in four sections. Section II provides a descriptive account of privatised immigration enforcement practices in the US, with a particular focus on immigration surveillance. Section III presents critiques of the resulting hybrid public–private immigration enforcement system, with attention to the distinct contexts of immigration detention and immigration surveillance. Section IV identifies the ways that this hybrid enforcement system frustrates two purported normative goals of good democratic governance: transparency and accountability. Finally, and intentionally provocatively, section V argues that the features mapped in the earlier parts of the chapter are not at all new. The apparent pathologies of privatisation might more properly be understood and assessed as the latest iteration of a deeply entrenched, extractive system of racial capitalism.

II Privatised Immigration Enforcement in the US

Over the last fifty years, governments in the US have turned increasingly to private companies and contractors to perform services once performed by government employees.[12] Municipal governments led the way about five decades ago, using private contractors to provide services like electric power, collecting garbage, putting out fires, and even running jails. Those moves were held up by free market advocates as an example for the Federal Government,[13] which happily followed suit. Though the groundwork was laid by movement activists in the era of the Republican President Ronald Reagan, and championed by him,[14] the Democratic President Bill Clinton made bipartisan the embrace of privatisation, and private contracts have become a growing feature of Federal Government administration in the decades since. This is true even in governmental spheres like policing and the fighting of wars: functions that are typically seen as quintessentially governmental given the government's purported monopoly on the legitimate use of force and violence.[15]

[12] Jody Freeman and Martha Minow, 'Introduction: Reframing the Outsourcing Debates' in Jody Freeman and Martha Minow (eds), *Government by Contract: Outsourcing and American Democracy* (Harvard University Press 2009) 1, 7–8; Jon D Michaels, 'Beyond Accountability: The Constitutional, Democratic, and Strategic Problems with Privatizing War' (2004) 82 Washington University Law Quarterly 1001, 1013–20 (describing these trends, particularly in military contracting).

[13] See, eg Philip E Fixler and Robert W Poole Jr, 'The Privatization Revolution: What Washington can Learn from State and Local Government' (1986) 37 Politics Review 68 (touting the benefits of federal prison privatization, citing the example of state and local efforts in this regard).

[14] Smith (n 1) 175.

[15] See, generally, Michaels, 'Beyond Accountability' (n 12).

The agency charged with federal immigration enforcement, the Department of Homeland Security (DHS), has been a significant consumer of private contractor services since its creation in late 2002. In March 2020, the US Government Accountability Office (GAO) published a report documenting their analysis of the DHS's service contracts.[16] Of the four agencies within DHS that the GAO chose to study, three were DHS's immigration agencies: Immigration and Customs Enforcement (ICE), Customs and Border Protection (CBP), and US Citizenship and Immigration Services (USCIS).[17] The GAO report notes that 'DHS obligated about $70.7 billion, or 76 per cent, of its $93.7 billion in total contract obligations on services from fiscal years 2013 through fiscal year 2018'.[18] The single largest category to which this funding is applied is guard services.[19] The second-largest share of DHS contractor spending is on information technology and communication services (13 per cent of the 2018 DHS budget), followed by information technology hardware and software services (approximately 4 per cent of the DHS budget).[20] More than half of DHS's spending on outside contractors went to jobs that the GAO characterised as 'services in need of heightened management attention', and the percentage of funds going to those jobs increased substantially under President Trump.[21] This included almost $2.5 billion in DHS contracts.[22] The 2020 GAO report found that DHS lacked a consistent plan for federal oversight of these contracts, and that 75 per cent of the contracts they reviewed identified no specific oversight activities designed to ensure that contractors are not performing 'inherently governmental functions' such as policymaking.[23]

Immigration enforcement constitutes a significant portion of DHS's insufficiently supervised expenditures. Since it began operation in March 2003, DHS has spent $333 billion on immigration enforcement.[24] In 2021, the combined budget for Customs and Border Protection (CBP) and Immigration and Customs Enforcement (ICE) was $26 billion.[25]

What has been 'privatised' in the sphere of immigration enforcement? DHS spent over $2.7 billion in 2020 on immigration detention,[26] and about three-quarters of US immigration detention is privatised.[27] This explains why the single largest category

[16] United States Government Accountability Office (GAO), *DHS Service Contracts: Increased Oversight Needed to Reduce the Risks Associated with Contractors Performing Certain Functions* (May 2020).

[17] ibid 2. The only other agency studied was the Office of Procurement Operations (ibid).

[18] ibid 17. That number hovered between $14 billion and $15 billion in the Obama era, but quickly climbed under President Trump, to $18.9 billion in 2018, the last year recorded in the study (ibid). The report notes that '[t]his increase in service contract obligations was largely driven by increases in Federal Emergency Management Agency and CBP service contract obligations, which grew by $2.2 billion and $927 million respectively' (ibid 18).

[19] ibid 19. This made up about 14% of DHS spending in 2018 (ibid).

[20] ibid 20.

[21] ibid 21.

[22] ibid 22.

[23] ibid 1. For a discussion of the broader question of what constitutes an 'inherently governmental function', see Laubacher (n 5) 799.

[24] American Immigration Council (AIC), *The Cost of Immigration Enforcement and Border Security* (20 January 2021), available at <https://www.americanimmigrationcouncil.org/sites/default/files/research/the_cost_of_immigration_enforcement_and_border_security.pdf> last accessed 1 September 2022..

[25] ibid.

[26] Department of Homeland Security (DHS), *Budget-in-Brief: Fiscal Year 2020* (2019), 3.

[27] Livia Luan, *Profiting from Enforcement: The Role of Private Prisons in US Immigration Detention* (Washington DC, 2 May 2018).

of contracting expenditure for DHS is on private guard services.[28] In 2020, the US also spent $5 billion on border wall construction along the US–Mexico border,[29] and again, a significant portion of that funding went to private contractors.[30]

Another important site of privatisation is enforcement-related surveillance and data aggregation. In recent years, the US government has entered into large contracts with private companies that have developed technology to aggregate public data (including law enforcement data, like arrest records) and privately collected data (such as mobile phone data). For example, the private company Palantir has $1.5 billion in contracts with the US government and has been contracting with DHS since at least 2011:[31] 'Palantir's software synthesizes the data that an organization collects ... [b]uilding virtual pipelines [to] ... merge all the information into a single platform'.[32] In 2020, DHS had $94 million in contracts with Palantir.[33]

Palantir technology has played an important role in ICE investigative practices in recent years. Palantir's ICM technology provides ICE with the tool to merge data about an individual's addresses, family members, employment, educational records, telephone records, and immigration histories. It also includes data from a tip line where members of the public can report people to immigration enforcement,[34] and it aggregates information from social media.[35] Through its FALCON mobile app, Palantir provides ICE agents with access to this information in the ICM database, as well as geospatial data.[36] DHS agents used FALCON in a 2017 worksite enforcement operation in New York City,[37] and FALCON is commonly used in workplace enforcement raids, which rose 640 per cent from 2017 to 2018 under President Trump.[38] During the Trump administration, the ICM database was used for a workplace raid in New York City in 2018 and in a large-scale Tennessee meatpacking raid in April 2018.[39] ICE also used ICM to arrest children at the border in 2017, before the height of the family separation crisis.[40]

Palantir is not the only company assisting DHS with surveillance and dataveillance. In recent years, immigration enforcement agents have increasingly monitored social media accounts as part of their enforcement work. Private companies have played an

[28] GAO (n 16).

[29] DHS (n 26).

[30] Sandra Sanchez, 'Terminating Border-wall Contracts Would Cost "Billions," Says CBP Head, but US has Options' (*Border Report*, 15 December 2020).

[31] Mijente, The National Immigration Project of the National Lawyers Guild, & Immigrant Defense Project, *The War against Immigrants: Trump's Tech Tools Powered by Palantir* (Mijente, August 2019) 8, 12.

[32] Michael Steinberger, 'Does Palantir See too Much?' *New York Times Magazine* (New York, 21 October 2020)

[33] Mijente and others, *The War against Immigrants* (n 31) 12, and 13–15, for a full list of federal contracts.

[34] Spencer Woodman, 'Transition Adviser Peter Thiel Could Directly Profit from Mass Deportations' (*Intercept*, 12 December 2016). Anthea Vogl notes a parallel development in Australia, in this volume, in her analysis of the 'National Allegation Assessment Team Dob-In Line' in Australia.

[35] Lee (n 11) 624.

[36] George Joseph, 'Data Company Directly Powers Immigration Raids in Workplaces' (*WNYC*, 16 July 2019).

[37] ibid.

[38] Mijente and others, *The War against Immigrants* (n 31) 4.

[39] ibid 10.

[40] Mijente, 'Palantir Played Key Role in Arresting Families for Deportation, Document Shows' (Mijente, 2 May 2019).

essential role in aggregating and providing that data, which is largely contained on private social media platforms. For example, in 2016, DHS paid the data analytics firm Giant Oak $1.4 million to provide them with the capability of searching the web (including the dark web) and social media to compile comprehensive dossiers of individuals targeted for investigation.[41] In 2017, the Trump administration spent almost $3 million more on contracts with Giant Oak.[42] Other companies provide the government with similar services. Thomson Reuters' CLEAR technology 'is powered by personal information: data from credit agencies, cellphone registries, social-media posts, property records, utility accounts, fishing licenses, internet chat rooms and bankruptcy filings, all fused and vetted by algorithm to form an ever-evolving, 360-degree view of U.S. residents' lives'. ICE also contracted with Thomson Reuters for continuous monitoring and alerts on 500,000 identities every month.[43]

Data compiled by other private companies supplement DHS's ability to track the movements of those under surveillance. Vigilant Solutions, a California company recently acquired by Motorola, has contracted with ICE since 2017, when ICE gained access to their database: the world's largest privately run database of licence plate scans. Vigilant Solutions has captured more than 5 billion images of licence plates, continuously and automatically at the rate of thousands per minute. Now ICE agents 'can see precisely when and where vehicles of interest have been spotted during the previous five years, and they can upload 2,500-plate "hot lists" that trigger immediate iPhone alerts whenever a target is scanned by a camera in the network'.[44]

DHS contracts with private companies extend to the most intimate details of private lives, including an individual's genetic makeup. In May 2019, the US government contracted with ANDE, a Massachusetts-based Rapid DNA testing company, to conduct a Rapid DNA test on migrants at the southern border of the US to screen for what Trump administration officials pejoratively and unjustifiably called 'fake families'.[45] And in mid-June 2019, ICE entered into a $5.2 million contract with June Bode Cellmark Forensics, Inc, to conduct Rapid DNA testing on the border to detect what the agency problematically labelled 'fraudulent families'.[46] Notwithstanding the obvious privacy concerns raised by this governmental collection of DNA, failure to submit to the testing was weighed by the DHS as a negative factor in its assessment of the legitimacy of the claims of incoming migrants to a parent–child relationship.[47] This DNA collection was done despite the fact that Congress has never authorised

[41] McKenzie Funk, 'How ICE Picks its Targets in the Surveillance Age' *New York Times Magazine* (New York, 2 October 2019).

[42] Thomas Brewster, 'Trump's Immigration Cops just Spent $3 Million on these Ex-DARPA Social Media Data Miners' (*Forbes*, 27 September 2017).

[43] Funk (n 41); see also Lee (n 11) 624–25 (discussing DHS's $2.4 million contract with Pen-Link for software to collect and analyse social media data).

[44] Funk (n 41).

[45] Priscilla Alvarez and Geneva Sands, 'Exclusive: DHS to Start DNA Testing to Establish Family Relationships on the Border' (*CNN*, 1 May 2019).

[46] Immigration and Customs Enforcement, 'ICE Awards New Contract for Rapid DNA Testing at Southwest Border, Expands Pilot Program' (*US Immigration and Customs Enforcement* 2019).

[47] Saira Hussain, 'ICE's Rapid DNA Testing on Migrants at the Border is yet another Iteration of Family Separation' (*Electronic Frontier Foundation*, 2 August 2019).

ICE to conduct DNA testing, and, in fact, failed to pass legislation that would have done so.[48]

Finally, companies have profited from the use of electronic monitors in immigration enforcement efforts.[49] Ankle monitors are used as alternatives to detention for immigrants in removal proceedings (though often these function more as a form of net-widening than simple substitution).[50] Since 2004, ICE has delegated its authority for the administration of these monitors to a private company, BI. BI manages the agency's Intensive Supervision Appearance Program (ISAP), which includes the issuance of ankle monitors for individuals released from civil immigration detention.[51] Notably, BI is a subsidiary of GEO Group, the largest provider of private immigration detention services in the US, so the same company profits from immigration detention and from the ankle monitors that ICE requires some immigrants to wear when they are released from civil immigration detention.[52] Ankle monitors are sometimes also imposed upon immigrants as a condition for release from *criminal* custody, and they can also be a contractually required guarantee for the private lenders that post required cash bonds for release from immigration detention.[53] Ankle monitors issued for these purposes are often provided by a different private company (Libre by Nexus is the primary provider).[54] Indeed, because of the use of monitors as a bond guarantor, some people have to wear (and pay for) two different ankle monitors from two different companies at the same time. The prices immigrants pay for their own monitoring through these devices are quite high.[55]

In short, a great deal of immigration enforcement beyond detention and border infrastructure has been privatised. Many of these privatised enforcement systems involve the surveillance of immigrants: their physical persons and vehicles, their use of social media, and other electronic data relating to nearly every aspect of their lives.

III The Effects of Privatisation

Many of the criticisms of privatisation in the sphere of immigration enforcement focus on immigration detention. Criticisms of private detention can be sorted into three broad categories: (1) conditions arguments—that private facilities provide worse conditions for detainees than public facilities; (2) moral arguments—that it is morally objectionable for private companies to profit from the liberty deprivations of others;

[48] ibid.

[49] For a full discussion of the use of ankle monitors in the immigration enforcement context, see Julie Pittman, 'Released into Shackles: The Rise of Immigrant E-Carceration' (2020) 108 California Law Review 587, 593.

[50] ibid.

[51] ibid.

[52] Angelika Albaladejo, 'How a Private Prison Company Profits from Biden's Broken Immigration Pledge' (*Newsweek*, 29 September 2021) ('GEO group is "making money at both ends of the system," said Julie Mao, an immigration attorney and deputy director of Just Futures Law. "Once [immigrants are] released from detention, they're putting on the ankle shackles or requiring people to do the SmartLINK app." ').

[53] Pittman (n 49) 590.

[54] Gus Bova, 'Bound to Pay' (*Texas Observer*, 26 September 2017).

[55] ibid.

and (3) political arguments—that the growing privatisation of detention interferes with the democratic process.[56] Some of these critiques have parallels in the privatised world of surveillance, though, as this section makes clear, the parallels are not neat, and the privatisation of surveillance also raises unique concerns.

The clearest point of convergence of the critiques of privatisation of detention and of surveillance are in the third category: the distorting effects that privatisation can have on democratic governance.[57] Concerns about the deleterious effect of privatisation on the democratic process are not new.[58] In the realm of detention, critics have argued that private companies are able to override popular preferences when they lobby as special interest groups that are well placed to 'exploit the path dependency and the classic bureaucratic expansionism of federal government actors',[59] pushing for expansion of services and programmes that might otherwise be unlikely public priorities. At the same time, privatisation renders the entire system more opaque, building roadblocks for people who seek accountability for abuse and neglect in detention.[60]

When it comes to data surveillance, the same concerns exist. First, individuals who stand to profit from the sale of their surveillance technologies to the government have a strong motive to push for expansive uses of those technologies, whereas the public may be less motivated to track and push back on these expansions in surveillance. While the threat of excessive surveillance—unlike the more targeted threat of immigration detention—does generate substantial public opposition at times, the opacity of these programmes shields them from widespread public opposition. Privatised immigration surveillance thus poses challenges for democratic accountability and transparency. As in the detention industry, contracting with private actors becomes a way to obscure unpopular or legally problematic work.

In recent years, employees of industries responsible for private surveillance, including very high-ranking corporate executives, have rotated in and out of government office.[61] While they are in government, they may have incentives to push for more expansive reliance on the technologies that their companies provide, and to encourage government investment in the industries that generate revenue for them. As surveillance functions are privatised, private actors gain access to public databases, which can be monetised as part of the aggregation services that they sell to private parties. Private companies also participate in enforcement programmes that expand the reach and depth of their aggregation capabilities.

[56] Jennifer M Chacón, 'Privatized Immigration Enforcement' (2017) 52 Harvard Civil Rights–Civil Liberties Law Review 1, 20–21.

[57] For a discussion of these distortions, see Ramsay, in this volume.

[58] See, eg Paul R Verkuil, *Outsourcing Sovereignty: Why Privatization of Government Functions Threatens Democracy and what we can do about it* (CUP 2007) 23–24.

[59] Chacón (n 56) 38 (citing César Cuauhtémoc García Hernández, 'Naturalizing Immigration Imprisonment' (2015) *103 California Law Review* 1449, 1498).

[60] Chacón (n 56) 38–39; see also Marie Gottschalk, *Caught: The Prison State and the Lockdown of American Politics* (Princeton University Press, 2015) 72 ('observing that [p]rivate prisons and correctional services are subject to even less accountability and scrutiny than public ones').

[61] See, eg Eliana Johnson, 'Donald Trump's "Shadow President' in Silicon Valley' (*Politico*, 26 February 2017) (reporting that the founder and high-ranking staff at Palantir took high-ranking jobs within the Trump administration).

In contrast to the political critiques, the conditions critiques of private detention facilities have no ready parallels in the surveillance world. In the detention context, 'conditions' critiques can be divided into two distinct arguments. The first concerns living conditions, including medical care, food (quality and quantity), the cleanliness of the facility, educational resources for children in detention, etc. Conditions in both public and private facilities are often poor,[62] but there is at least some evidence that conditions can be worse in private facilities.[63] The second argument is a due process argument; namely, that detainees in private facilities have a harder time exercising their rights than those in public facilities. Here again, there is some indirect supporting evidence, most notably that detainees in private facilities are less likely to win their appeals.[64]

For those surveilled, it seems unlikely that conditions would improve if public employees rather than private contractors were charged with data surveillance and aggregation. On the other hand, it is quite possible that the employees of private companies engaged in data surveillance are worse off than public employees who are, or otherwise might be, tasked with similar work. There is an extensive literature charting the decline of working conditions that has accompanied the hollowing out of public sector employment, including in the prison industry.[65] The public sector reduces its own labour costs by outsourcing governance tasks to more precarious, private workforces with fewer benefits and less job security. In the surveillance realm, as in immigration detention, the shift to private contractors may worsen conditions for workers.[66]

The moral arguments against private prisons and detention facilities—undergirded by the notion that the state alone should run institutions designed to interfere with liberty interests—also lack neat analogues in the world of surveillance.[67] Indeed, concerns about surveillance historically have tended to focus on the risk of government overreach rather than on arguments for public monopoly or greater concentration of such resources in the hands of the state. But recent critiques of surveillance capitalism point to the harms of concentrating personal information in the hands of a few powerful tech companies: a trend that is exacerbated by government reliance on these same companies to amass and package personal data for enforcement purposes.[68]

62 Chacón (n 56) 22–24.

63 See, eg American Sociological Association, 'Private Detention of Immigrants Deters Family Visits, Study Finds' (*Science Daily*, 23 August 2016), <https://perma.cc/S8MF-DN88> accessed 17 November 2021 (finding that family visits were less frequent in private facilities than in public ones).

64 See, eg Center for American Progress, *How For-profit Companies Are Driving Immigration Detention Policies* (18 December 2015) 8, <https://perma.cc/V5PR-KDAS> accessed 17 November 2021.

65 See, eg Robert Jay Dilger and others, 'Privatization of Municipal Services in America's Largest Population Cities' (1997) 57 Public Administrative Review 21, 24 (noting reduced wages and benefits as a cost of privatisation); Richard Michael Fischl, '"Running Government like a Business": Wisconsin and the Assault on Workplace Democracy' (21 June 2011) Yale Law Journal Online 47, <https://www.yalelawjournal.org/forum/running-the-government-like-a-business-wisconsin-and-the-assault-on-workplace-democracy> accessed 1 September 2022. (noting greater job security for public employees than private employees).

66 Such arguments have been made in the context of private prisons, for example: Geoffrey Schotter, *Prisons for Profit: A Look at Prison Privatization* (ACLU of Ohio, 2011) 13–14 (citing various studies).

67 For explorations of the philosophical critiques of privatised enforcement and detention, see Ashwini and Malcolm, in this volume.

68 See Shoshana Zuboff, *The Age of Surveillance Capitalism: The Fight for a Human Future at the New Frontier of Power* (Public Affairs 2019) 386–88.

Indeed, as discussed in the final section of this chapter, the state's commodification of border control has been an important driver of the rise of surveillance capitalism.[69]

IV The Legal Black Holes of Privatisation

The transfer of responsibilities from public agencies to private companies generates significant legal obstacles to two important goals of good democratic governance: governmental accountability and transparency. Under US law, governmental actors have unique legal constraints, as well as unique shields from legal liability. The restrictions of the US Constitution—prohibiting, for example, the abrogation of free speech or free exercise of religion,[70] unreasonable searches and seizures,[71] cruel and unusual punishment,[72] and denials of equal protection of the law[73]—apply to the government (Federal, State, and local), but not to private individuals. Laws regulating private conduct, on the other hand, generally do not flow directly from the Constitution. The Constitution does govern the conduct of private companies engaged in 'state action',[74] but courts construe 'state action' quite narrowly.[75] Most of the work of private companies collecting data on users, for example, falls outside this domain.

At the same time, government actors can avail themselves of certain legal immunities that are not applicable to private actors. The Federal government has the power to pre-empt state law, to dictate the limits of regulation of its conduct, and to specify whether, where, and when it can be sued.[76] In theory, these protections should not apply to private companies. As a practical matter, however, private contractors benefit from these sovereign shields. Private companies—including private immigration detention providers—are sometimes able to claim the mantle of governmental immunity for their conduct when they are sued.[77] Legal scholars Elengold and Glater have documented how 'contractors have relied on their relationship with the [US] federal government to escape accountability without precisely defining or distinguishing the sovereign-shield doctrines, using prevailing doctrinal confusion to push the boundaries of the doctrines'.[78]

Unlike governmental actors, private companies can also fall back on defences that are available to them in their private capacities. These companies can justify, on 'trade

[69] Kalhan (n 9) 77–80 (discussing how the US government has used appeals to border control and national security to overcome common objections to mass surveillance, without ensuring appropriate limits on the collection and use of the data).

[70] US Constitution, amend I.

[71] ibid amend IV.

[72] ibid amend VIII.

[73] ibid amend XIV; *Bolling v Sharpe*, 347 US 497 (1954) (holding that the requirements of equal protection applied as against the federal government through the 5th Amendment Due Process Clause).

[74] *Terry v Adams*, 345 US 461 (1953); *Shelley v Kraemer*, 334 US 1 (1948), *Burton v Wilmington Parking Authority*, 365 US 715 (1961).

[75] See, eg *Jackson v Metropolitan Edison*, 419 US 345 (1974) (heavily regulated private utility company granted monopoly by the state not a state actor).

[76] Kate Sablosky Elengold and Jonathan D Glater, 'The Sovereign Shield' (2021) 73 Stanford Law Review 969, 971.

[77] ibid 975.

[78] ibid 973.

secrets' grounds, their refusal to provide information about their services in response to Freedom of Information Act (FOIA) requests.[79] Information that the government would be required to provide, private companies can shield.[80] The public–private partnership thus allows 'the federal executive branch and its corporate servants to evade accountability to individual consumers, states, and even other federal overseers in ways that neither could in isolation'.[81]

David Sklansky theorised that one problem emerging at the intersection of criminal law and civil immigration law is the rise of 'ad hoc instrumentalism', which he defines as 'a rising tendency to treat legal rules and legal procedures as interchangeable tools, to be brought to bear pragmatically and instrumentally on an ad hoc basis'.[82] The permeability of the civil/criminal boundary thus allows those acting on behalf of the government to evade accountability when they fail to protect guaranteed rights of immigrants, and to obscure the source of these rights violations. Like the civil/criminal boundary, the public/private boundary is another place where the intersection of legal regimes can allow for these kinds of 'instrumental' uses of law in ways that are similarly detrimental to the rights of migrants. Private companies can often claim the sovereign shield when sued, while evading the constitutional limits that apply to the sovereign. At the same time, the government can contract away obligations in ways that shield its own activities under the mantle of trade secrets and other laws protecting private actors or simply disclaim any relevant action at all.[83]

V Privatisation as Racial Capitalism

Over time, courts and legislatures might be expected to begin doing a better job of regulating the novel configurations and technologies that facilitate privatised immigration enforcement. Indeed, there are legislative proposals designed to address some of the specific problems that have emerged out of new privatisation trends and technologies. Some US states have debated, and enacted, laws to prohibit private immigration detention facilities in their jurisdictions.[84] Some have introduced or passed

[79] The Freedom of Information Act, 5 USC § 552 (FOIA), enacted during the Johnson administration, is the principal legal tool through which third parties can seek records in the possession of a government agency.

[80] See, eg *Food Marketing Institute v Argus Leader Media*, 139 S Ct 2356 (2019) (protecting private contractor from disclosure of 'sensitive information' based solely on the government's assurance that the data would remain confidential).

[81] Elengold and Glater (n 76) 974.

[82] David Alan Sklansky, 'Crime, Immigration, and Ad Hoc Instrumentalism' (2012) 15 New Criminal Law Review 157, 157.

[83] See, eg *United States v Reddick*, 900 F.3d 636 (5th Cir 2018) (finding no government search where government officials were the first humans to view, without a warrant, files that were flagged by a private company's electronic screening system, and forwarded directly to local law enforcement); *United States v Miller*, 982 F.3d 412, 427 (6th Cir 2020) (same). But see *United States v Wilson*, No 18-50440, 2021 WL 4270847 (9th Cir Sept 21, 2021) (finding that the government's warrantless search of defendant's email attachments premised on a tip generated by an artificial intelligence scan of the data by a private tech company violated the Fourth Amendment).

[84] Suzanne Monyak, 'State Bills Banning Private Immigration Detention Gain Traction' (*MSN*, 25 May 2021).

legislation to limit or prohibit the uses of camera surveillance of drivers' licences.[85] Lawmakers have also made efforts to regulate the ways that government agencies[86] and social media companies collect, use, and share private data.[87]

On the other hand, regulation of data privacy in the US is far less robust than in Europe.[88] The US Supreme Court is also likely to impede future regulation in this field, given its increasingly expansive view of the First Amendment's protections for wealthy individuals[89] and corporations.[90] This suggests that the problem is not just an inability to develop the legal tools to regulate novel technologies, but a systemic tolerance for the kinds of surveillance and control that have been unleashed.

Technologies—whether in the form of passports or drones, driver's licence databases, or apps that aggregate personal data—are merely tools used in service of broader projects. Shoshana Zuboff cautions against focusing on technological tools at the expense of focusing on the systemic logic 'that imbues technology and commands it into action'.[91] Zuboff identifies that logic as 'surveillance capitalism', which she defines as 'a new economic order that claims human experience as free raw material for hidden commercial practices of extraction, prediction, and sales'.[92]

Current developments in privatised immigration enforcement could be understood as manifestations of surveillance capitalism. Companies sell to the government, and profit from, the technological capability to surveil, collect data upon, and predict the behaviour of huge numbers of people. Both public and private actors seek to justify these efforts in surveillance, prediction, and manipulation as essential to 'border security', even as private companies reap significant profits from their efforts, through the direct sale of their services, and through their further accumulation of monetisable personal data, obtained through their work with the government. The companies managing the technology can also use this information to manipulate the behaviour of their customers and users.

At the same time, to think about the current harms of privatisation in this sphere as the manifestation of some new form of extractive 'surveillance capitalism' risks missing what is old about it. In a slightly different context, Gerald Lopez cautioned:

[85] Mike Dennison, 'House Endorses Bill Banning Use of License Plate Scanning in Montana' *Montana Standard* (Butte, 9 March 2015); Mike Maharrey, 'California Senate Committee Passes Bill to Limit ALPR Data Retention, Help Block National License Plate Tracking Program' (*The Tenth Amendment Center Blog*, 25 March 2021); Mike Maharrey, 'Massachusetts Committee Holds Hearing on Bills to Limit ALPR Data, Help Block National License Plate Program' (*The Tenth Amendment Center Blog*, 25 June 2021); Garrett Brnger, 'Data Trackers: License Plate Scanning Technology Raises Privacy Questions' (*WILL & Illinois Public Media*, 25 April 2015).

[86] See, eg The Driver's Privacy Protection Act of 1994 (DPPA or Act) 18 USC § 2721–25 (regulating the disclosure of personal information contained in the records of state motor vehicle departments (DMVs)).

[87] The Children's Online Privacy Protection Act (COPPA); The Communications Decency Act.

[88] The US lacks an analogue to the EU General Data Protection Regulation.

[89] See, eg *Americans for Prosperity Foundation v Bonta*, 141 S Ct 2373 (2021) (interpreting the First Amendment to prohibit a California law requiring that charities and non-profit organisations operating in California provide California's Attorney General's Office with the names and addresses of their largest donors).

[90] For a critique of the doctrinal evolution of the First Amendment into a shield for corporations, see Erwin Chemerinsky, 'Not a Free Speech Court' (2011) 53 Arizona Law Review 723.

[91] Zuboff (n 68) 15.

[92] ibid v.

> Monstrous and destructive as criminal justice is in 2019, especially as enhanced by technological innovations, monstrous and destructive as it will likely remain barring a radical transformation, the criminal justice system has long been monstrous and destructive. I do not buy that what we experience today is novel or only of recent vintage. I do not because I personally know it is not. Most of what these networks of systems, institutions, and individuals do in 2019 is not different at all from what they did in dealing with those of us who lived in East LA in the 1950s (and in earlier decades still). Indeed, what feels eerie for someone like me, and perhaps for others who lived within targeted communities during earlier eras, is how the present is utterly reminiscent of the past.[93]

Lopez reminds us that racialised repression is not new, and that symbiotic ties between enforcement agencies, and between those agencies and private entities in the protection of the interests of property owners, are not new. Nor is the commodification of the control of racialised populations. Much is familiar in the repressions of our age: the ever-recurring strands of authoritarianism, taking aim at racialised targets.

Though perhaps novel in their particular technological forms, the racial logics of the extractive immigration enforcement system of the United States—which relies on racialised bodies 'out of place' as its *raison d'être*—functions exactly as capitalism always has.[94] Cedric Robinson long ago rejected the idea that racialisation and racial oppression are merely coincidental with capitalism; in his view, modern iterations of capitalism evolved out of racialism in Europe, where racialism is understood as the creation of racial distinctions that legitimise hierarchical relationships as natural.[95] Robinson maintained that the conjunction of racism and capitalism—'racial capitalism'—drove and thrived upon racialised slavery, dispossession, and genocide. Robinson's critical description of capitalism identifies the ongoing reinscription of racial difference in furtherance of accumulative practices, such as those at the heart of the contemporary border security industrial complex.

What would it mean to think about these new public–private enforcement strategies not as wholly new, but as a feature of a continuous landscape of racial capitalism: a landscape in which surveillance capitalism has long had a presence? Shifts in US immigration law over time have been driven by the needs of capital for labour, and racial categories and hierarchies have been both the product of, and the means of achieving,

[93] Gerald P López, 'Growing Up in Authoritarian 1950s East LA' (2019) 66 UCLA Law Review 1532, 1536–37.

[94] See, eg Nicholas Mirzoeff, 'Artificial Vision, White Space and Racial Surveillance Capitalism' (2020) 36 AI & Society 1295 (tracing racial surveillance capital over the *longue durée* of settler colonialism).

[95] See Cedric Robinson, *Black Marxism: The Making of the Black Radical Tradition* (3rd edn, UNC Press 2020). As Robin DG Kelley explains, in Robinson's view, 'Capitalism and racism ... did not break from the old order but rather evolved from it to produce a modern world system of "racial capitalism" dependent on slavery, violence, imperialism, and genocide. Capitalism was "racial" not because of some conspiracy to divide workers or justify slavery and dispossession, but because racialism had already permeated Western feudal society. The first European proletarians were *racial* subjects ... and they were victims of dispossession (enclosure), colonialism, and slavery *within Europe*. Indeed, Robinson suggested that racialization within Europe was very much a *colonial* process involving invasion, settlement, expropriation, and racial hierarchy.' Robin DG Kelley, 'What did Cedric Robinson Mean by Racial Capitalism?' (*Boston Review*, 12 January 2017). For additional discussions and applications of this notion of racial capitalism, see also Ruth Wilson Gilmore, *Golden Gulag: Prisons, Surplus, Crisis, and Opposition in Globalizing California* (University of California Press 2007); Jodi Melamed, 'Racial Capitalism' (2015) 1 Critical Ethnic Studies 76.

these ends. In the early days of the Republic, US states exercised migration control at and within their borders, focusing their powers to deny entry and expel on free Black residents, Black people who had escaped enslavement, poor people, the disabled, and others who were deemed likely to impose burdens on the public purse.[96] The external national border was relatively permeable; internal borders were more likely to be policed. And that policing was deliberately structured to foster white racial dominance, Black enslavement, and the expropriation of the land of Indigenous peoples.[97]

In the mid nineteenth century, this approach to border and population control shifted. The US Federal government increasingly asserted its authority over immigration control.[98] The notion that the central government should control the flow of migration was emerging not only in the US, but throughout the world. With the formal legal abolition of slavery—the system that previously formed the most significant means of the control of labour mobility[99]—colonial powers like the UK increasingly drew on racialised notions of nationality to control the movement of 'free labour'.[100] As Radhika Mongia and others have argued, the emergent racialised migration management schemes are the genealogical heart of modern Western state formation.[101]

Management of these increasingly regulated 'racial borders', to use Tendayi Achiume's formulation,[102] was performed by national bureaucracies, and it was achieved through the collaboration of public and private entities. As Aristide Zolberg has pointed out, for example, in the mid nineteenth century, before the existence of systematic federal laws of immigrant exclusion, the regulation of migration to the US was achieved indirectly, through the regulation of common carriers—namely, the shipping industry.[103] Nor did these public–private collaborations end with the bureaucratisation and expansion of federal power in the twentieth century. Private entities continued to play an integral role in shaping US border enforcement strategies, while race continued to offer the conceptual justification for these enforcement strategies.[104]

[96] Gerald Neuman, 'The Lost Century of Immigration Law' (1993) 93 Columbia Law Review 1833.

[97] Jennifer M Chacón, 'Immigration and Race' in Devon Carbado, Emily Houh, and Khiara M Bridges (eds), *The Oxford Handbook of Race and Law in the United States* (OUP 2022); Anna O Law, 'The Myth of "Open Borders"' *The Washington Post* (Washington DC, 21 September 2021).

[98] See, eg *The Passenger Cases*, 48 US 283 (1849); *Chy Lung v Freeman*, 92 US 275 (1875); and *Henderson v Mayor of City of New York*, 92 US 259 (1875); *Chae Chan Ping v United States*, 130 US 581 (1889), also known as the Chinese Exclusion Case (declaring Congress's plenary power over the exclusion of immigrants); *Fong Yue Ting v United States*, 149 US 698 (1893) (declaring Congress's plenary power to authorise the deportation of non-citizens, pursuant to Congress's authorised procedures).

[99] And, indeed, the only form of migration control actually mentioned in the US Constitution. See US Const, Art 1, cl 9.

[100] Radhika Mongia, *Indian Migration and Empire: A Colonial Genealogy of the Modern State* (Duke University Press, 2018).

[101] ibid; see also E Tendayi Achiume, 'Racial Borders' (forthcoming 2022) Georgetown Law Journal; Lucie Cheng and Edna Bonacich (eds), *Labor Immigration under Capitalism: Asian Workers in the United States before World War II* (University of California Press, 1984) (examining Chinese migration to the US as a product of labour demands in the US and the growing surplus of labourers in China as a result of the economic stagnation generated by colonial practices).

[102] Achiume (n 101).

[103] Aristide Zolberg, *A Nation by Design: Immigration Policy in the Fashioning of America* (Harvard University Press, 2008).

[104] See, eg Kelly Lyttle Hernández, *City of Inmates: Conquest, Rebellion, and the Rise of Human Caging in Los Angeles, 1771–1965* (University of North Carolina Press, 2017) (reviewing the central importance of racial animus toward Mexicans as the justification for the criminal prohibitions on illegal entry and re-entry,

How, then, might we understand current privatisation trends against this backdrop of a long-lived public–private partnership in racialised migration management? For almost two centuries now—since the formal abolition of slavery—borders have been constructed and enforced to remain permeable to some bodies, but impassible to others. Technologies, from passports to biometric scanners, have been created and deployed to effectuate differentiated mobility—not neutral or universal mobility—both within empires and ultimately between and among nation states.[105] Mobility has been parcelled out in racialised fashion to answer the needs of capital and to justify—or distract from—policy choices that allocate resources to the wealthy and powerful.

Ultimately, then, modern borders themselves can be understood as the longstanding products of public–private partnerships, with the Westphalian nation state as an outgrowth of an emergent colonial world order designed around racialised capitalist extraction. It is hardly surprising that the policing of sovereign borders has allowed and continues to allow for capitalist extraction from racialised, subjugated populations. In the US today, surplus value is extracted from workers in situations of precarity generated by their immigration status.[106] Such extraction occurs as the state pivots away from public sector workers with their relatively robust pension and benefits plans, to subcontractors without comparable benefits, in staffing detention centres. A largely non-white workforce, often including the detainees themselves,[107] disproportionately staffs the lowest paid positions in these privatised enforcement sectors,[108] while a largely white, wealthy workforce parachutes in and out of high-ranking governmental work, steering lucrative contracts in the direction of their industry, so that they and their disproportionately white and wealthy shareholders can profit from these contracts in the private sector.[109] Everything old is new again.

and the role that labour demands of private employers played in ensuring that criminalisation, rather than quotas, would govern Mexican migration).

[105] Mongia (n 100).

[106] Nicholas De Genova, 'The Deportation Regime: Sovereignty, Space, and the Freedom of Movement' in Nicholas De Genova and Nathalie Peutz (eds), *The Deportation Regime* (Duke University Press 2010) 38–39.

[107] See, eg Zusha Elinson, 'Detention Operators Face Suits over $1-a-Day Work Programs for Migrants' *Wall Street Journal* (New York, 21 July 2018); Tracy Jan, 'These GOP Lawmakers say it's Okay for Imprisoned Immigrants to work for a $1 a day' *Washington Post* (Washington DC, 16 March 2018); Yana Kunichoff, '"Voluntary" Work Program in Private Detention Centers Pays Detained Immigrants $1 a Day' (*Prison Legal News*, 15 August 2012).

[108] See, eg Brett C Burkhardt, 'Who is in Private Prisons? Demographic Profiles of Prisoners and Workers in American Private Prisons' (2017) 51 International Journal of Law, Crime and Justice 24 (using Bureau of Justice Statistics data to demonstrate that private federal prisons 'employ officers that are disproportionately female and black or Hispanic').

[109] For a discussion of the revolving door of tech industry executives and the Federal Government, see, eg Carlotta Alfonsi, 'Taming Tech Giants Requires Fixing the Revolving Door' (*Kennedy School Review*, 18 February 2020); Olivia Solon and Sabrina Siddiqui, 'Forget Wall Street—Silicon Valley is the New Political Power in Washington' *The Guardian* (London, 3 September 2017); For a discussion of the demographics of shareholders see, eg Lydia Saad and Jeffrey M Jones, 'What Percentage of Americans Owns Stock?' (*Gallup News*, 13 August 2021).

References

Achiume ET, 'Racial Borders' (forthcoming 2022) Georgetown Law Journal

Albaladejo A, 'How a Private Prison Company Profits from Biden's Broken Immigration Pledge' (*Newsweek*, 29 September 2021)

Alfonsi C, 'Taming Tech Giants Requires Fixing the Revolving Door', (*Kennedy School* 18 February 2020)

Alvarez P and Sands G, 'Exclusive: DHS to Start DNA Testing to Establish Family Relationships on the Border' (*CNN*, 1 May 2019)

American Immigration Council (AIC), *The Cost of Immigration Enforcement and Border Security* (20 January 2021), <https://www.americanimmigrationcouncil.org/research/the-cost-of-immigration-enforcement-and-border-security>

American Sociological Association, 'Private Detention of Immigrants Deters Family Visits, Study Finds' (*Science Daily*, 23 August 2016), available at <https://perma.cc/S8MF-DN88>

Bova G, 'Bound to Pay' (*Texas Observer*, 26 September 2017)

Brewster T, 'Trump's Immigration Cops just Spent $3 Million on these Ex-DARPA Social Media Data Miners' (*Forbes*, 27 September 2017)

Brnger G, 'Data Trackers: License Plate Scanning Technology Raises Privacy Questions' (*WILL & Illinois Public Media*, 25 April 2015)

Brown KN, '"We the People," Constitutional Accountability, and Outsourcing Government' (2013) 88 Indiana Law Journal 1347

Burkhardt BC, 'Who is in Private Prisons? Demographic Profiles of Prisoners and Workers in American Private Prisons' (2017) 51 International Journal of Law, Crime and Justice 24

Burnett J, 'As Asylum Seekers Swap Prison Beds for Ankle Bracelets, Same Firm Profits' (*National Public Radio*, 13 November 2015)

Center for American Progress, *How For-profit Companies are Driving Immigration Detention Policies* (18 December 2015), available at <https://perma.cc/V5PR-KDAS>

Chacón JM, 'Privatized Immigration Enforcement' (2017) 52 Harvard Civil Rights–Civil Liberties Law Review 1

Chacón JM, 'Immigration and Race' in Carbado D, Houh E, and Bridges KM (eds), *The Oxford Handbook of Race and Law in the United States* (OUP 2022)

Chemerinsky E, 'Not a Free Speech Court' (2011) 53 Arizona Law Review 723

Cheng L and Bonacich E (eds), *Labor Immigration under Capitalism: Asian Workers in the United States before World War II* (University of California Press, 1984)

Dennison M, 'House Endorses Bill Banning Use of License Plate Scanning in Montana' *Montana Standard* (Butte, 9 March 2015) Dennison M, 'House Endorses Bill Banning Use of License Plate Scanning in Montana' *Montana Standard* (Butte, 9 March 2015)

Department of Homeland Security (DHS), *Budget-in-Brief: Fiscal Year 2020* (2019)

Dilger RJ and others, 'Privatization of Municipal Services in America's Largest Population Cities' (1997) 57 Public Administrative Review 21

Donahue JD, *The Privatization Decision: Public Ends, Private Means* (Basic Books 1989)

Elengold KS and Glater JD, 'The Sovereign Shield' (2021) 73 Stanford Law Review 969

Elinson Z, 'Detention Operators Face Suits over $1-a-Day Work Programs for Migrants' *Wall Street Journal* (New York, 21 July 2018)

Fischl RM, '"Running Government like a Business": Wisconsin and the Assault on Workplace Democracy' (2011) 47 Yale Law Journal Online, available at <https://www.yalelawjournal.org/forum/running-the-government-like-a-business-wisconsin-and-the-assault-on-workplace-democracy

Fixler PE, and Poole RW Jr, 'The Privatization Revolution: What Washington can Learn from State and Local Government' (1986) 37 Politics Review 68

Freeman J, 'Extending Public Law Norms through Privatization' (2003) 116 Harvard Law Review 1285.

— — and Minow M, 'Introduction: Reframing the Outsourcing Debates' in Freeman J and Minow M (eds), *Government by Contract: Outsourcing and American Democracy* (Harvard University Press 2009)

Funk M, 'How ICE Picks its Targets in the Surveillance Age' *New York Times Magazine* (New York, 2 October 2019)

Gilmore RW, *Golden Gulag: Prisons, Surplus, Crisis, and Opposition in Globalizing California* (University of California Press 2007)

Gottschalk M, *Caught: The Prison State and the Lockdown of American Politics* (Princeton University Press 2015)

Hernández CCG, *Migrating to Prison: America's Obsession with Locking Up Immigrants* (New Press 2019)

— —, 'Naturalizing Immigration Imprisonment' (2015) 103 California Law Review 1449

Hernández KL, *City of Inmates: Conquest, Rebellion, and the Rise of Human Caging in Los Angeles, 1771–1965* (University of North Carolina Press, 2017)

Hussain S, 'ICE's Rapid DNA Testing on Migrants at the Border is yet another Iteration of Family Separation' (*Electronic Frontier Foundation,* 2 August 2019)

Immigration and Customs Enforcement, 'ICE Awards New Contract for Rapid DNA Testing at Southwest Border, Expands Pilot Program' (US Immigration and Customs Enforcement 2019)

Jan T, 'These GOP Lawmakers Say it's Okay for Imprisoned Immigrants to Work for a $1 a Day' *Washington Post* (Washington DC, 16 March 2018)

Johnson E, 'Donald Trump's "Shadow President" in Silicon Valley' (*Politico*, 26 February 2017)

Joseph G, 'Data Company Directly Powers Immigration Raids in Workplaces' (*WNYC*, 16 July 2019)

Kalhan A, 'Immigration Surveillance' (2014) 74 Maryland Law Review 1

Kelley RDG, 'What did Cedric Robinson Mean by Racial Capitalism?' (*Boston Review*, 12 January 2017)

Kunichoff Y, '"Voluntary" Work Program in Private Detention Centers Pays Detained Immigrants $1 a Day' (*Prison Legal News*, 15 August 2012)

Laubacher TJ, 'Simplifying Inherently Governmental Functions: Creating a Principled Approach from its Ad Hoc Beginnings' (2017) 46 Public Contract Law Journal 791

Law AO, 'The Myth of "Open Borders"' *Washington Post* (Washington DC, 21 September 2021)

Lee E, 'The End of Entry Fiction' (2021) 99 North Carolina Law Review 565

López GP, 'Growing Up in Authoritarian 1950s East LA' (2019) 66 UCLA Law Review 1532

Luan L, *Profiting from Enforcement: The Role of Private Prisons in US Immigration Detention* (Washington DC, 2 May 2018).

Maharrey M, 'California Senate Committee Passes Bill to Limit ALPR Data Retention, Help Block National License Plate Tracking Program' (*The Tenth Amendment Center Blog*, 25 March 2021)

— — , 'Massachusetts Committee Holds Hearing on Bills to Limit ALPR Data, Help Block National License Plate Program' (*The Tenth Amendment Center Blog*, 25 June 2021)

Melamed J, 'Racial Capitalism' (2015) 1 Critical Ethnic Studies 76

Metzger GE, 'Privatization as Delegation' (2003) 103 Columbia Law Review 1367

Michaels JD, 'Beyond Accountability: The Constitutional, Democratic, and Strategic Problems with Privatizing War' (2004) 82 Washington University Law Quarterly 1001

— —, 'Privatization's Pretensions' (2010) 77 University of Chicago Law Review 717

Mijente, 'Palantir Played Key Role in Arresting Families for Deportation, Document Shows' (*Mijente*, 2 May 2019)
Mijente, The National Immigration Project of the National Lawyers Guild, & Immigrant Defense Project, *The War against Immigrants: Trump's Tech Tools Powered by Palantir* (*Mijente*, August 2019)
Minow M, 'Public and Private Partnerships: Accounting for the New Religion' (2003) 116 Harvard Law Review 1229.
Mirzoeff N, 'Artificial Vision, White Space and Racial Surveillance Capitalism' (2020) 36 AI & Society 1295
Mongia R, *Indian Migration and Empire: A Colonial Genealogy of the Modern State* (Duke University Press, 2018)
Monyak S, 'State Bills Banning Private Immigration Detention Gain Traction' (*MSN*, 25 May 2021)
Neuman G, 'The Lost Century of Immigration Law' (1993) 93 Columbia Law Review 1833.
Olivarez M, 'Intersectionality at the Intersection of Profiteering & Immigration Detention' (2016) 94 Nebraska Law Review 963
Pittman J, 'Released into Shackles: The Rise of Immigrant E-Carceration' (2020) 108 California Law Review 587
Robinson C, *Black Marxism: The Making of the Black Radical Tradition* (3rd edn, UNC Press 2020)
Saad L and Jones JM, 'What Percentage of Americans Owns Stock?' (*Gallup News*, 13 August 2021)
Sanchez S, 'Terminating Border-wall Contracts would Cost "Billions," Says CBP Head, but US has Options' (*Border Report*, 15 December 2020)
Schotter, G, *Prisons for Profit: A Look at Prison Privatization* (ACLU of Ohio, 2011) 13–14 (citing various studies)
Sklansky DA, 'Crime, Immigration, and Ad Hoc Instrumentalism' (2012) 15 New Criminal Law Review 157
Smith SR, 'Review: The Privatization Decision: Public Ends, Private Means by John D. Donahue. New York, Basic Books, 1989' (1991) 106(1) Political Science Quarterly 1379
Solon O and Siddiqui S, 'Forget Wall Street—Silicon Valley is the New Political Power in Washington' *The Guardian* (London, 3 September 2017)
Steinberger M, 'Does Palantir See too Much?' *New York Times Magazine* (New York, 21 October 2020)
United States Government Accountability Office (GAO), *DHS Service Contracts: Increased Oversight Needed to Reduce the Risks Associated with Contractors Performing Certain Functions* (May 2020)
Verkuil PR, *Outsourcing Sovereignty: Why Privatization of Government Functions Threatens Democracy and what we can do about it* (CUP 2007)
Woodman S, 'Transition Adviser Peter Thiel could Directly Profit from Mass Deportations' (*Intercept*, 12 December 2016)
Zolberg A, *A Nation by Design: Immigration Policy in the Fashioning of America* (Harvard University Press, 2008)
Zuboff S, *The Age of Surveillance Capitalism: The Fight for a Human Future at the New Frontier of Power* (Public Affairs 2019)

Cases

Americans for Prosperity Foundation v Bonta, 141 S Ct 2373 (2021)

Bolling v Sharpe, 347 US 497 (1954)
Burton v Wilmington Parking Authority, 365 US 715 (1961)
Chae Chan Ping v United States, 130 US 581 (1889)
Chy Lung v Freeman, 92 US 275 (1875)
Fong Yue Ting v United States, 149 US 698 (1893)
Food Marketing Institute v Argus Leader Media, 139 S Ct 2356 (2019)
Henderson v Mayor of City of New York, 92 US 259 (1875)
Jackson v Metropolitan Edison, 419 US 345 (1974)
Shelley v Kraemer, 334 US 1 (1948)
Terry v Adams, 345 US 461 (1953)
The Passenger Cases, 48 US 283 (1849)
United States v Miller, 982 F.3d 412, 427 (6th Cir 2020)
United States v Reddick, 900 F.3d 636 (5th Cir 2018).
United States v Wilson, No 18-50440, 2021 WL 4270847.

Legislation

The Children's Online Privacy Protection Act (COPPA)
The Communications Decency Act, Pub L No 104-104, 110 Stat 133, codified as amended in scattered sections of 47 USC
The Driver's Privacy Protection Act of 1994 (DPPA or Act), 18 USC § 2721–25
The Freedom of Information Act, 5 USC § 552.

2

Contested Sovereignty in Preventive Border Control

Civil Society, the 'Hostile Environment', and the Rule of Law

*Valsamis Mitsilegas**

I Introduction

The chapter explores the evolving relationship between private actors and state sovereignty in the field of border control, by examining legislative developments from the perspective of a preventive, securitised paradigm of immigration control. The analysis will focus primarily on Europe, and on measures taken by European states and the European Union (EU), to demonstrate how both border controls and state sovereignty have been transformed in this process. While traditional analysis of the privatisation of border control has focused on instances where the private sector is being co-opted by the state to exercise border controls, with private actors in effect strengthening state sovereignty, the present contribution addresses a relatively under-researched aspect of the relationship between private actors and the state in border control, in instances where privatisation is viewed not as a boost, but rather as a threat to state sovereignty. The framing of private actors as a threat to the state is linked to the growing intervention of private actors—and, in particular, civil society and non-governmental organisations (NGOs)—in order to address the fundamental rights, rule of law, and humanitarian shortcomings preventive border control entails. Private actors intervene to secure the rights of migrants and to remedy the consequences of state action or inaction in the field and are thus seen to contest state overreach in the exercise of border control. The chapter will focus on attempts by states, and by the EU, to create a 'hostile environment'[1] for civil society in the field of border control. In creating such a hostile environment, states aim to assert their sovereignty, disregarding their fundamental rights and rule-of-law obligations in order to uphold the preventive paradigm of border control. The chapter will examine the evolution of the hostile environment by critically evaluating the emergence of a multilayered system of control of private

* This paper was presented at the Workshop on Privatising Border Control: Law at the Limits of the Sovereign State, held at All Souls College on 28/29 June 2021. I would like to thank the workshop participants for their feedback, and Mary Bosworth and Lucia Zedner for their comments on an earlier draft. The usual disclaimer applies.

[1] On the emergence of the hostile environment discourse in the UK, see Zedner, in this volume. For further analysis of hostile environment policies, see Sheona York 'The "Hostile Environment"—How Home Office Immigration Policies and Practices Create and Perpetuate Illegality' (2018) 32(4) Journal of Immigration, Asylum and Nationality Law 363.

Valsamis Mitsilegas, *Contested Sovereignty in Preventive Border Control* In: *Privatising Border Control.*
Edited by: Mary Bosworth and Lucia Zedner, Oxford University Press. © Valsamis Mitsilegas 2022.
DOI: 10.1093/oso/9780192857163.003.0003

actor activities by the state, ranging from the criminalisation of activities by a variety of actors to the introduction of 'duties of obedience' imposed on the private sector. The chapter examines the impact of the criminalisation of private actors on the rule of law, in particular the expansion of unaccountable state power and arbitrariness and the lack of legal certainty coupled with the limitation, or at times impossibility, of legal or judicial protection of those targeted.[2]

II Rethinking Privatisation in the Emerging Paradigm of Preventive Border Control: From the Commercial Sector to Civil Society

The creation of a hostile environment targeting migrants first, and by association civil society, must be viewed within the context of the emergence of a preventive paradigm of border control, whereby prevention, securitisation, and privatisation are linked. Preventive border control is framed here as another example of preventive (in) justice. The term 'preventive justice', developed by Ashworth and Zedner, has been used regarding domestic criminal law as extending its scope to gradually remove the link between criminalisation and prosecution on the one hand and the commission of concrete offences on the other, focusing on the prevention of future harms.[3] Here, preventive justice is understood more broadly as the exercise of state power in order to prevent future acts considered to constitute security threats.[4] Preventive justice is thus forward- rather than backward looking: it aims at preventing potential threats rather than punishing past acts, and introduces a system of justice based on the creation of suspect or undesirable individuals on the basis of risk assessment.[5] In the field of preventive border control, the preventive justice paradigm is fleshed out in a number of paradigmatic changes, all expressions of a profound change in the law of the border itself.[6] As Bigo has noted, the notion of the border is very often considered a materialised line between two spaces.[7] This static conception of the border has been central to the emergence of traditional systems of border control. Under these systems, entry

[2] These aspects of the rule of law are all elements of what I have characterised elsewhere as the rule of law *ex post*, which includes principles that are applicable after the enactment of legislation (including legal certainty, prohibition of arbitrariness, effective judicial protection, and the protection of human rights): Valsamis Mitsilegas, 'Rule of Law: Theorising EU Internal Security Cooperation from a Legal Perspective' in Raphael Bossong and Mark Rhinard (eds), *Theorising Internal Security Cooperation in the European Union* (OUP 2016) 109–28. They encompass formal/procedural and substantive dimensions of the rule of law (see Paul Craig, 'Formal and Substantive Conceptions of the Rule of Law: An Analytical Framework' [1997] Public Law 467; Tom Bingham, *The Rule of Law* (Allen Lane 2010).

[3] Andrew Ashworth and Lucia Zedner, *Preventive Justice* (OUP 2014).

[4] Valsamis Mitsilegas, 'The Security Union as a Paradigm of Preventive Justice: Challenges for Citizenship, Fundamental Rights and the Rule of Law' in Valsamis Mitsilegas and Sergio Carrera (eds), *Constitutionalising the Security Union. Effectiveness, Rule of Law and Rights in Countering Terrorism and Crime* (CEPS 2017) 2–18.

[5] Valsamis Mitsilegas, *EU Criminal Law After Lisbon* (Hart 2016) ch 9.

[6] Valsamis Mitsilegas, 'The Law of the Border and the Borders of Law—Rethinking Border Control from the Perspective of the Individual' in Leanne Weber (ed), *Rethinking Border Control for a Globalizing World—A Preferred Future* (Routledge 2015) 15–31.

[7] Didier Bigo, 'Frontier Controls in the European Union: Who is in Control?' in Didier Bigo and Elspeth Guild (eds), *Controlling Frontiers: Free Movement into and within Europe* (Ashgate 2005) 52.

controls occurred in a specific place (the external border of the state) by checking the identification of the traveller, thus leading to 'the invention of the passport'.[8] The control of the border in these territorial terms constitutes a prime projection of state sovereignty, by granting the state the power to decide who may enter its territory, and who may not.[9] However, this static conception of border control has been challenged in recent years. Globalisation and Europeanisation have led to a profound transformation of border controls, focusing increasingly upon the prevention and deflection of migration flows via the proliferation of externalised immigration controls[10] with border controls extended in time and space.[11] The emergence of this preventive, externalised paradigm of border control is inextricably linked with the securitisation of migration and the development of what Bigo has called an (in)security continuum transferring the security considerations of crime control to the field of migration.[12] The (in)security continuum is reflected in the terminology of 'border security' in the field of border control[13] and in the growing criminalisation of migration, not only of migrants but also of those who assist them.[14]

The role of private actors in the emergence of preventive border control has been significant. Thus far, the analysis has focused on privatisation as a delegation of border control functions by the state to the private sector, particularly to commercial entities[15] through the imposition of carriers' liability[16] and, more recently, through the

[8] John Torpey, *The Invention of the Passport: Surveillance, Citizenship and the State* (CUP 2000).

[9] Malcolm Anderson, *Frontiers: Territory and State Formation in the Modern World* (Polity 1996).

[10] Valsamis Mitsilegas, 'Immigration Control in an Era of Globalisation: Deflecting Foreigners, Weakening Citizens, Strengthening the State' (2012) 19 Indiana Journal of Global Legal Studies 3; Bernand Ryan and Valsamis Mitsilegas (eds), *Extraterritorial Immigration Control: Legal Challenges* (Brill 2010); Valsamis Mitsilegas, 'Extraterritorial Immigration Control in the 21st Century: The Individual and the State Transformed' in Bernand Ryan and Valsamis Mitsilegas (eds), *Extraterritorial Immigration Control: Legal Challenges* (Brill 2010) 39–66.

[11] Mitsilegas, 'The Law of the Border' (n 6).

[12] Didier Bigo, *Polices en Réseaux. L'Expérience Européenne* (Presses Sciences Po 1996).

[13] For reflections on 'border security', see, inter alia, Katja Franko Aas and Mary Bosworth (eds), *The Borders of Punishment: Migration, Citizenship, and Social Exclusion* (OUP 2013); Elspeth Guild, *Security and Migration in the 21st Century* (Polity 2009); Valsamis Mitsilegas 'Border Security in the European Union. Towards Centralised Controls and Maximum Surveillance' in Elspeth Guild, Helen Toner, and Anneliese Baldaccini (eds), *Whose Freedom, Security and Justice? EU Immigration and Asylum Law and Policy* (Hart 2007) 359–94; Valsamis Mitsilegas, 'Human Rights, Terrorism and the Quest for "Border Security"' in Marco Pedrazzi and others (eds), *Individual Guarantees in the European Judicial Area in Criminal Matters* (Bruylant 2011) 85–112.

[14] Valsamis Mitsilegas, *The Criminalisation of Migration in Europe: Challenges for Human Rights and the Rule of Law* (Springer 2015).

[15] Galya Lahav, 'Immigration and the State: The Devolution and Privatisation of Immigration Control' (1998) 24(4) Journal of Ethnic and Migration Studies 675; Virginie Guiraudon, 'De-nationalizing Control: Analysing State Responses to Constraints on Migration Control' in Virginie Guiraudon and Christian Joppke (eds), *Controlling a New Migration World* (Routledge 2001) 31.

[16] Elspeth Guild, 'Moving the Borders of Europe' (The inaugural lecture delivered during the official ceremony on the occasion of the assumption of the professorship of the CPO Wisselleerstoel at the University of Nijmegen, the Stichting Steunfonds Juridisch (Post) Doctoraal Onderwijs on 30 May 2001, ch 6); Sophie Scholten, *The Privatisation of Immigration Control through Carrier Sanctions* (Brill 2015); Theodore Baird, 'Carrier Sanctions in Europe: A Comparison of Trends in 10 Countries' (2017) 19 European Journal of Migration and Law 307; Erika Feller, 'Carrier Sanctions and International Law' (1989) 1 International Journal of Refugee Law 48; Frances Nicholson, 'Implementation of the Immigration (Carriers' Liability) Act 1987: Privatising Immigration Functions at the Expense of International Obligations?' (1997) 46 International and Comparative Law Quarterly 633; Tilman Rodenhauser, 'Another Brick in the

imposition on carriers of duties to collect and transfer to state authorities passenger data under Advanced Passenger Information (API) and Passenger Name Record (PNR) schemes.[17] Privatisation here is inextricably linked to the externalisation of immigration control[18] and has served not to weaken, but rather to strengthen, state sovereignty by proliferating levels of border control, with the private sector complementing, rather than replacing, the state.[19] In addition to the co-option of the private sector through delegation of border control tasks imposed by law, another dimension of co-option involves the development of contractual relationships between states and the private sector in key aspects of border control, including detention, removal, and surveillance. In both cases, the state's co-option strategy involves either the commercial sector or other entities involved for profit. In the case of delegation by law, the implementation of duties by private entities involves considerable compliance costs, with carriers complying under threat of state sanctions;[20] in the case of the development of public–private contractual relationships, the involvement of the private sector is motivated by profit-making.[21] In both cases, the coercive power of the state is amplified.

This chapter aims to move the debate forward by focusing on a different dimension of the relationship between the state and the private sector in the field of preventive border control, examining instances where the involvement of private actors is perceived not as a boost, but rather as a threat to state sovereignty. The framing of activities of private actors as a threat to state sovereignty has emerged following the growing intervention in recent years of non-profit, non-governmental organisations—but also, increasingly, individual citizens—to undertake search and rescue of migrants and secure their access to EU territory, to address inaction by states, and to fill the protection gap by complying with moral and legal obligations under international refugee, humanitarian, and human rights law, and the law of the sea. Privatisation of border control here takes the form of the proactive intervention by civil society, which operates in place of, rather than in addition to, the state, and whose objectives are seen to be at odds with state sovereignty. The clash between states and civil society has intensified with regard to saving lives at sea in what has increasingly been characterised as the shifting humanitarian border or borderland.[22] On the one hand, NGOs intervene to

Wall: Carrier Sanctions and the Privatization of Immigration Control' (2014) 26 International Journal of Refugee Law 223.

[17] Valsamis Mitsilegas, 'Contrôle des étrangers, des passagers, des citoyens: Surveillance et anti-terrorisme' (2005) 58 Cultures et Conflits 155–82; Mitsilegas, 'Border Security' (n 13); Elif Mendos Kuskonmaz, *Privacy and Border Controls in the Fight Against Terrorism* (Brill 2020).

[18] Mitsilegas, 'Extraterritorial Immigration Control in the 21st Century' (n 10).

[19] Mitsilegas, 'Immigration Control in an Era of Globalisation' (n 10); Thomas Gammeltoft-Hansen, 'The Rise of the Private Border Guard. Accountability and Responsibility in the Migration Control Industry' in Thomas Gammeltoft-Hansen and Ninna Nyberg Soerensen (eds), *The Migration Industry and the Commercialization of International Migration* (Routledge 2013) 128, 129.

[20] Scholten (n 16).

[21] See Infantino; Bosworth and Singler; Ryo and Peacock; and Bigo, all in this volume.

[22] Franko Aas and Grundhus talk about the 'humanitarian borderland' as alluding to an uncertain, intermediate space or region which is neither lawless nor marked by a well-functioning rule of law–with policing framed and legitimised through the language of humanitarianism and human rights, but operating in inhumane conditions in multi-jurisdictional spaces with unclear lines of responsibility: Katja Franko Aas and Helene OI Grundhus, 'Policing Humanitarian Borderlands: Frontex, Human Rights and the Precariousness of Life' (2015) 55 British Journal of Criminology 1. On the intersection between the humanitarian and the

address state inaction and ensure the safety and rights of migrants. On the other hand, states use the rhetoric of saving lives at sea to legitimise the interception of migrants at sea.[23] Franko has noted that this clash reflects a growing disagreement about how to deal with border deaths—with criminalisation and inaction on the one hand and unconditional priority given to search and rescue on the other—in which NGOs base their action on staking claims on the moral authority of their intervention.[24]

In addition to their moral responsibilities, NGOs, instead of the state, increasingly act to uphold legal responsibilities which states deliberately attempt to evade through preventive border control. State inaction in this context is inextricably linked with the exercise of sovereignty as an uncritical state-sponsored prevention agenda in migration management, aiming to prevent access of migrants to their external border and their territory. In this preventive paradigm, states act in contravention of European human rights norms that apply to everyone—citizens and migrants alike—by securitising migrants and those who help them, and by attempting to keep migrants beyond legal protection in the first place. By assisting migrants and attempting to uphold rights and the rule of law, civil society is seen to pose a threat to unfiltered state sovereignty and power over border control. In addressing this perceived threat, states have enacted a number of policies aiming to create a hostile environment against migrants, extending to private actors and, in particular, civil society, which is seen as assisting them. The creation of such a hostile environment generates rule-of-law challenges at two levels: at the level of depriving migrants of access to territory and to law, with the protections that the latter entails;[25] and at the level of enhancing state arbitrariness leading to abuses of law not only against migrants but also against those who help them.

III Laying the Foundations of the Hostile Environment: Criminalising Humanitarianism

A key strand of the preventive border control paradigm has been the criminalisation of migration. The introduction of criminal offences targeting the conduct of migrants—criminalising breaches of administrative regulations regarding entry and stay—is a prime example of this trend,[26] with the state proceeding to 'make people illegal'.[27]

penal after entry, at the stage of return, see Mary Bosworth, 'Penal Humanitarianism? Sovereign Power in an Era of Mass Migration' (2017) 20 New Criminal Law Review 39.

[23] Violeta Moreno-Lax, 'The EU Humanitarian Border and the Securitization of Human Rights: The "Rescue-Through-Interdiction/Rescue-Without-Protection" Paradigm' (2018) 56 Journal of Common Market Studies 119.

[24] Katja Franko, 'The two-sided Spectacle at the Border: Frontex, NGOs and the Theatres of Sovereignty' (2021) 25 Theoretical Criminology 379.

[25] Valsamis Mitsilegas, 'Extraterritorial Immigration Control, Preventive Justice and the Rule of Law in Turbulent Times' in Juan Santos Vara, Sergio Carrera, and Tineke Strik (eds), *Constitutionalising the External Dimension of EU Migration Policies in Times of Crisis: Legality, Rule of Law and Fundamental Rights Reconsidered* (Edward Elgar 2019) 290–308.

[26] Ana Aliverti, *Crimes of Mobility* (Routledge 2015); Mitsilegas, 'The Criminalisation of Migration in Europe' (n 14).

[27] Catherine Dauvergne, *Making People Illegal* (CUP 2011).

This criminalisation of migrants has been accompanied by the criminalisation of civil society—in another guise of the (in)security continuum, whereby the illegality of migrants is extended to those who help them. The construction of a hostile environment against civil society via criminalisation occurs in two main ways: through the enactment of broadly defined offences criminalising assistance to migrants, including humanitarian assistance; and through prosecutorial uses and abuses of these provisions and of other—unrelated—criminal and administrative law provisions aiming to neutralise civil society. The criminalisation of human smuggling—or in EU law terms the facilitation of unauthorised entry—is emblematic of the enactment of broad criminal offences targeting help for migrants. Criminal law here has developed under shaky normative foundations (with the harm addressed by criminalisation ranging from unclear to purely symbolic). It is oriented towards the prevention of future acts by the perpetrators, but also by others (the migrants involved) and is drafted in all-encompassing terms.[28]

Compared with international law, the definition of smuggling at EU level is particularly broad,[29] and has allowed the overuse of criminal law at national level. The EU framework directive defines the 'facilitation of unauthorised entry, transit and residence',[30] accompanied, in the light of the first pillar competence limits regarding criminalisation at the time,[31] by a third pillar framework decision confirming that conduct defined as facilitation in the directive is a criminal offence.[32] Both instruments of what is rather 'old' law by EU standards predate by far the entry into force of the Lisbon Treaty and they have been negotiated and adopted with minimal scrutiny and debate.[33] The EU Facilitation Directive goes further than the UN Palermo Convention Smuggling Protocol[34] in that it dispenses with the condition of obtaining a financial or other material benefit for the smuggling offence to be established.[35] The directive calls upon member states to adopt criminal sanctions for 'any person who intentionally assists a person who is not a national of a Member State to enter, or transit across, the territory of a Member State in breach of the laws of the State concerned on the entry or transit of aliens'.[36] Instigation, complicity, and attempt are also criminalised.[37] The Facilitation Framework Decision contains a general obligation for member states to criminalise such conduct,[38] includes a general provision on

[28] Valsamis Mitsilegas, 'The Normative Foundations of the Criminalisation of Human Smuggling: Exploring the Fault Lines between European and International Law' (2019) 10 New Journal of European Criminal Law 68.

[29] For a comparison, see ibid.

[30] Council Directive 2002/90/EC of 28 November 2002 defining the facilitation of unauthorised entry, transit and residence [2002] OJ L328/4 ('Facilitation Directive').

[31] For an overview, see Valsamis Mitsilegas, *EU Criminal Law* (Hart 2009), ch 2.

[32] Council Framework Decision 2002/946/JHA of 28 November 2002 on the strengthening of the penal framework to prevent the facilitation of unauthorised entry, transit and residence [2002] OJ L328/1 ('Facilitation Framework Decision').

[33] For background, see Valsamis Mitsilegas, Jörg Monar, and Wyn Rees, *The European Union and Internal Security* (Palgrave/Macmillan 2003) 106–08.

[34] See Mitsilegas, 'Normative Foundations of the Criminalisation of Human Smuggling' (n 28).

[35] Art 1(1)(a) of the Facilitation Directive.

[36] ibid.

[37] ibid art 2.

[38] See arts 1(1), (3), and (6) of the Facilitation Framework Decision.

sanctions,[39] which may be accompanied by confiscation,[40] and imposes high levels of sanctions in certain aggravating circumstances.[41]

Notwithstanding the lack of specificity as regards the level of criminal sanctions to be imposed by member states, it is clear that the scope of criminalisation at EU level is very broad, as it can cover any form of assistance to enter or transit the territory of an EU member state in breach of what is essentially administrative law (such as travelling without travel documents). The EU approach aims to prevent entry into EU territory, and targets not only the smugglers, but also the smuggled. The negative impact that the EU approach towards criminalisation has had on third-country nationals wishing to apply for asylum is evident. In a departure from international law, where human smuggling is criminalised in the context of the pursuit of financial gain, EU law emphasises preventive border control and the punitive targeting of migrants and those who help them as its main aims.[42]

The Facilitation Directive attempts to address the issue of overcriminalisation by granting member states the discretion not to impose sanctions for human smuggling and instead to apply their national law and practice to humanitarian assistance cases.[43] However, this provision is discretionary, and its value in redressing the balance set by the broad definition and criminalisation of human smuggling under EU law is questionable. According to a recent Commission report, only seven member states specifically include, in domestic law, an exemption from punishment for facilitation of humanitarian assistance.[44] By using the threat of criminal sanctions, the EU measures on human smuggling aim to deter individuals and organisations from coming into contact and assisting any third-country national wishing to enter an EU member state. An issue paper by the Council of Europe Commissioner for Human Rights notes, 'the message which is sent is that contact with foreigners can be risky as it may result in criminal charges'.[45] This message is reinforced by the very broad criminalisation of human smuggling in the national law of member states, for example the criminalisation of any contact with irregular migrants not only at the point of entry but within the territory of the state,[46] and, as expressly called for by the Facilitation Directive, the criminalisation of attempts to smuggle. As Spena has noted, commenting on Italian law, the fact that this law does not require that the conduct be successful, with smuggling crimes deemed to be committed independently of the attainment of the result, creates a condition teleologically linked to illegal entry.[47] The preventive continuum

[39] Infringements are punishable by effective, proportionate, and dissuasive penalties which entail extradition: ibid art 1(1).

[40] ibid art 1(2).

[41] ibid art 1(3).

[42] Mitsilegas, 'Normative Foundations of the Criminalisation of Human Smuggling' (n 28).

[43] Art 1(2) of the Facilitation Directive.

[44] European Commission, 'Staff Working Document—REFIT Evaluation of the EU Legal Framework against Facilitation of Unauthorised Entry, Transit and Residence' SWD (2017) 117 final, 14.

[45] Council of Europe Commissioner for Human Rights, *Criminalisation of Migration in Europe: Human Rights Implications* (Issue Paper prepared by Elspeth Guild, 2009) available at <https://rm.coe.int/16806da917> accessed 18 November 2021.

[46] See the ruling of *Areios Pagos* (the Greek Supreme Court AP 1344/2016).

[47] Alessandor Spena, 'Migrant Smuggling: A Normative and Phenomenological View from Italy' in Vincenzo Militello and Alessandro Spena, *Between Criminalization and Protection: The Italian Way of Dealing with Migrant Smuggling and Trafficking within the European and International Context* (Brill Perspectives in Transnational Crime 2019) 26.

between the criminalisation of facilitation of irregular entry and the criminalisation of entry per se is evident.

The targeting of civil society through the overcriminalisation of human smuggling is here to stay in EU law. The Commission's evaluation of the EU anti-smuggling framework states, generally, that there is limited evidence that social workers, family members, or citizens acting out of compassion have been prosecuted for human smuggling.[48] In its latest intervention on the EU Pact on Migration and Asylum, the Commission declined to introduce new legislation in the field, merely producing non-legally binding guidance on the implementation of the EU framework.[49] This approach is not adequate to address the multiple attempts across the EU to criminalise—if not demonise—the humanitarian work of civil society and to create a 'hostile environment' against humanitarian action.[50] The use of the broad anti-smuggling criminal law framework plays a key part in this process, with a wide range of actors ranging from individuals to NGOs being targeted.[51] Developments in recent years related to the criminalisation of civil society for providing search and rescue at sea and humanitarian assistance to migrants, including on the high seas and in the territory of third countries, constitute a key example of preventive criminalisation. States have targeted NGOs via a combination of the overcriminalisation and sustained stigmatisation of civil society organisations.

The use of criminal law to generate a hostile environment for NGOs' involvement in search and rescue operations is evident in a number of NGO prosecutions in Italy, with well-reported cases including those against Iuventa/Jugend Rettet, Proactiva Open Arms, and Sea Watch 3. The case of *Iuventa/Jugend Rettet* involved the seizure of the vessel for the crime of facilitating illegal entry (alleged handovers of migrants to NGOs). *Proactiva Open Arms* also involved seizure for facilitation of illegal entry where the crew chose to disregard the code of conduct set out by the Italian authorities to control the operations of NGOs on the high seas[52] and rescue migrants before Libyans arrived in the Libyan search and rescue (SAR) area. *Seawatch 3* involved the arrest of Captain Carola Rackete for the offence of resisting a public officer and resisting a warship, and for colliding with an Italian patrol boat while docking in port. The case involved the rescue of migrants on board an unsafe vessel in the Libyan SAR area. An entry ban on Seawatch 3 vis-à-vis Italian waters was imposed but the order of the Guardia di Finanza was disregarded.[53]

These cases are part of a general trend of criminal law being used in targeting and attempting to neutralise humanitarianism and search and rescue at sea in the name of

[48] European Commission, 'REFIT Evaluation' (n 44) 21.

[49] Communication from the Commission, Commission Guidance on the implementation of EU rules on definition and prevention of the facilitation of unauthorised entry, transit and residence 2020/C 323/01, [2020] OJ C 323/1.

[50] For a detailed analysis of targeting NGOs on the ground, see Sergio Carrera and others, *Policing Humanitarianism: EU Policies Against Human Smuggling and their Impact on Civil Society* (Hart 2019).

[51] Council of Europe Commissioner for Human Rights, *Lives Saved. Rights Protected. Bridging the Protection Gap between Refugees and Migrants in the Mediterranean* (Council of Europe 2019).

[52] See s V.

[53] Stefano Zirulia, 'Is that a Smuggler? The Blurring Line between Facilitating Illegal Immigration and Providing Humanitarian Assistance at the European Borders' in Gian Luigi Gatta, Valsamis Mitsilegas, and Stefano Zirulia (eds), *Controlling Immigration through Criminal Law* (Hart 2021) 235–66.

state sovereignty in border control with civil society organisations treated essentially as smugglers.[54] Not only is the criminal law of human smuggling, broadly drafted, used to prosecute humanitarian NGOs, but prosecutors also use other avenues of criminal law including anti-mafia legislation and increasingly offences unrelated to migration such as failure to comply with administrative law on environmental protection, health and safety on board and failure to comply with state orders under the Navigation Code.[55] This multiple targeting of NGOs aims at neutralising them; suspending or stopping their work via the use of seizure and confiscation of vessels,[56] entry bans, and increasingly exit bans from the territorial waters.[57] In addition to the serious challenges this aggressive stance poses for the respect of international and EU human rights, refugee law, and humanitarian obligations, the overuse and abuse of criminal law—increasingly linked not to immigration but to administrative violations[58]—also poses significant rule-of-law/legal certainty challenges. Individuals and organisations are targeted on the basis of a variety of laws, including legislation which is too broad, and whose aims are unclear, and in a system where prosecutions are coupled with the imposition of criminal and administrative measures whose aim is in essence to halt the humanitarian action of civil society. These concerns persist in view of the use of criminal law on human smuggling and related offences; to evoking offences of life endangerment;[59] and to targeting individual citizens undertaking humanitarian assistance,[60] as well as migrants themselves.[61]

In the absence of the political will for law reform to restrict the scope of criminal law related to human smuggling and in the face of multiple attacks on NGOs by prosecutorial and other state authorities, the courts may seek to limit overcriminalisation, protect human rights, and uphold the rule of law. Some steps in this direction have been taken in Italy, where courts appear gradually to be upholding limits to criminalisation of NGOs and preventive sanctions such as entry bans on grounds of necessity and in respect of rescue at sea and refugee law obligations.[62] A key example has been the ruling of the Italian Corte di Cassazione in the well-publicised prosecution of

[54] For further examples, see the Report of the Expert Council on NGO Law, *Using Criminal Law to Restrict the Work of NGOs Supporting Refugees and Other Migrants in Council of Europe Member States*, Thematic Study prepared by Dr Carla Ferstman, Expert Council on NGO Law CONF/EXP (2019), December 2019 ('Ferstman Report') <https://rm.coe.int/expert-council-conf-exp-2019-1-criminal-law-ngo-restrictions-migration/1680996969> accessed 18 November 2021.

[55] Marta Minetti, 'The Facilitators Package, Penal Populism and the Rule of Law: Lessons from Italy' (2020) 11 New Journal of European Criminal Law 335.

[56] For further details, see the Report of the EU Fundamental Rights Agency (FRA), 'December 2020 update—NGO ships involved in search and rescue in the Mediterranean and legal proceedings against them' <https://fra.europa.eu/en/publication/2020/december-2020-update-ngo-ships-involved-search-and-rescue-mediterranean-and-legal> accessed 12 August 2021.

[57] ibid.

[58] See ibid. The FRA noted an increasingly common use of measures of an administrative, rather than criminal, nature, based on the laws of navigation and safety at sea, and a decrease of measures against individuals.

[59] <https://www.infomigrants.net/en/post/30947/afghan-migrant-charged-with-endangering-his-sons-life-in-greece-speaks-out> accessed 12 August 2021.

[60] See the examples in the Ferstman Report (n 54) 85–86.

[61] <https://www.ecre.org/greece-survivor-sentenced-to-146-years-imprisonment-amid-deaths-in-camps-and-at-borders/>. See also <https://www.law.ox.ac.uk/research-subject-groups/centre-criminology/centreborder-criminologies/blog/2021/06/criminalising> accessed 12 August 2021.

[62] Zirulia, 'Is that a Smuggler?' (n 53).

Carola Rackete.[63] The prosecution did not involve human smuggling but prosecution on the grounds of resisting public officials and resistance and violence against warships. In a significant ruling in favour of humanitarianism, the *Cassazione* rejected the appeal to uphold the charges by giving precedence to the duty of rescue as enshrined in international law and to obligations under international refugee law, and rejecting the argument that a ship constitutes a safe place for the purposes of rescue at sea. The court accepted that bringing migrants recovered during rescue activities in international waters, also in the face of an express ban on entry into territorial waters and/or in the absence of authorisation to dock, constitutes fulfilment of the duty of rescue at sea.[64] The *Cassazione* ruling can be read as enshrining a 'right of resistance' against state action that is in breach of hierarchically higher legal principles.[65] The ruling is a welcome development, which sends a clear signal to the executive and to the prosecutors that the end does not justify the means in the name of border control and that well-established principles of international law, including international humanitarian law, law of the sea, and refugee law, must be observed in the management of migration flows at sea. By recourse to international law, the *Cassazione* built a line of defence for humanitarian action against a sustained attack on civil society by state institutions.

A parallel development limiting the application of criminal law on smuggling to individuals/citizens providing humanitarian assistance has occurred in France, in a case concerning the prosecution of two individuals for facilitation offences relating to migrants crossing the land border between Italy and France in Val Roya. This litigation led to the examination of the extent of the humanitarian exception to the criminalisation of human smuggling by the French Conseil Constitutionnel in the '*Fraternité*' ruling.[66] The ruling is significant in that the Conseil Constitutionnel used the constitutional principle of *fraternité* as the basis of the freedom to provide humanitarian assistance, without consideration of the lawfulness of the assisted person's stay in the national territory.[67] However, the Conseil Constitutionnel went on to balance (or, in its words, to reconcile) the principle of *fraternité* with the safeguarding of public order, within whose framework the fight against irregular migration falls.[68] The Conseil Constitutionnel accepted the limitation of criminalisation in cases of facilitating irregular movement on humanitarian grounds, without this limitation being extended to cases of irregular entry.[69] The court's ruling leaves the preventive aim of the criminalisation of the facilitation of irregular entry intact. Yet, the ruling is of significance in engaging a fundamental—albeit ambivalent—constitutional principle in French law with the need to take into account humanitarian conduct in the context of immigration control. The ruling can be seen as developing (admittedly in the limited sphere of humanitarian conduct after entry) what has accurately been described as a 'humanistic, universal, and liberal ideal', applicable to citizens and foreigners alike,

[63] Cass. pen., s III, 16 January 2020 (dep 20 February 2020), n 6626, Pres. Lapalorcia, Est. Gai, ric. Rackete.

[64] Stefano Zirulia, 'La Cassazione sul caso Sea Watch: le motivazioni sul l'illegitimita dell arresto di Carola Rackete' Sistema Penale (20 February 2020).

[65] ibid point 7.

[66] Decision no 2018-717/718 QPC.

[67] ibid para 8.

[68] ibid paras 9–10.

[69] ibid para 12.

closer to the principle of human dignity than to an idea of national kinship.[70] The principle of human dignity may form a key foundation to rethink the uncritical overcriminalisation of human smuggling as promoted by EU and national law and to decriminalise acts of citizenship towards those in need. Evoking the principle of *fraternité* in the context of humanitarian assistance may contribute more broadly towards developing constitutional protective principles in respect of humanitarian actors and those receiving humanitarian assistance.

IV Destabilising the Rule of Law: Criminalising Legal Advice

Another step in the creation of a hostile environment with the aim of quashing resistance to states' preventive border control policies has been action by states targeting not only humanitarian actors, but also the legal profession who defend civil society actors from prosecution and uphold migrants' rights. Recent years have witnessed the growing targeting and stigmatisation of the legal profession in its immigration work, with state policies ranging from vilification to outright criminalisation. In the UK, only recently the Home Secretary used loaded language with regard to the legal profession, transferring the illegitimacy of human trafficking to immigration lawyering and framing legal representation as unwanted 'activism'.[71] Lawyers are thus being reconceived from defenders of the rule of law to 'bad faith' citizens, who are in the same category as traffickers and illegal migrants. In Italy, according to reports, human rights lawyers were secretly recorded by prosecutors.[72] And in Hungary, as will be seen below, providing legal assistance to migrants has been criminalised. These developments can be seen as gravely challenging the rule of law in liberal democracies. State discourse and legislation criminalising the legal profession for exercising its roles in upholding the law and holding the state to account for its violations, are worrying steps in a process whereby immigration controls erode the rule of law.

The question of whether criminalising legal advice is compatible with EU law is currently before the Court of Justice of the European Union (CJEU), with the Opinion of Advocate General Rantos delivered, and the ruling of the CJEU pending at the time of writing.[73] The case concerns the introduction in Hungary of the criminal offence of organising activity designed to enable asylum proceedings to be brought by persons who do not meet the criteria for the granting of international protection established by national law.[74] The Hungarian Constitutional Court attempted to limit the impact

[70] Editorial (2019) (15) EuConst 183–93, 189.

[71] According to the UK Home Secretary Priti Patel, '[t]hose defending the broken system—the traffickers, the do-gooders, the leftie lawyers, the Labour Party—they are defending the indefensible'. She said, '[o]ur broken system is enabling this international criminal trade. It is disregarding the most vulnerable, elbowing women and children in need to the side.' <https://www.theguardian.com/politics/2020/oct/25/lawyers-ask-johnson-and-patel-to-apologise-for-endangering-colleagues> accessed 12 August 2021.

[72] <https://www.theguardian.com/world/2021/apr/09/italian-prosecutors-secretly-recorded-human-rights-lawyers#:~:text=Prosecutors%20in%20Italy%20have%20secretly,were%20complicit%20in%20people%20smuggling> accessed 12 August 2021.

[73] Opinion of AG Rantos, Case C–821/19 *European Commission v Hungary* ECLI:EU:C:2021:143

[74] ibid para 27.

of such criminalisation by stating that the provision does not penalise negligent conduct, but exclusively acts which are committed deliberately, on the basis of a 'clear intention' to commit the offence. The Constitutional Court added that the provision did not cover altruistic behaviour which satisfies the obligation to assist those who are deprived and in need, but it is for the courts adjudicating on the substance, in their judicial practice, to determine the circumstances in which an organising activity may be treated as humanitarian aid.[75] The Advocate General found these arguments unconvincing. He first pointed out the element of uncertainty inherent in legal representation in the asylum procedure:

> in principle, any organisation or person wishing to provide assistance necessarily acts with the intention of enabling the person being assisted to initiate asylum proceedings and may, at the very least, have doubts as to whether or not that person meets the requirements to be eligible for international protection. Doubts as to the veracity of applicants' claims are inherent in the asylum procedure, which is conducted precisely with the aim of establishing whether the conditions for the granting of international protection are satisfied. It is for the competent national authorities, and not legal advisers or organisations or persons offering assistance to applicants for international protection, to assess whether the reasons given in the application justify international protection being granted in accordance with the conditions imposed by the national legislation.[76]

The Advocate General noted the enactment of restrictive asylum legislation in Hungary and pointed out that in view of these developments any person or organisation providing assistance to applicants for international protection will be well aware of the fact that, in those circumstances, those applications are very likely to fail and that person or organisation therefore risks criminal prosecution.[77] Criminalising assistance provided to applicants for international protection could have a particularly significant deterrent effect on all persons or organisations who knowingly try to promote a change in legislation or a more flexible interpretation of national law, or even claim that the relevant national law is incompatible with EU law. Moreover, 'developing' the national legislation or making it easier for applicants to access the asylum procedure or humanitarian aid, even if it is very doubtful or, as in the present case, very unlikely that the applicants satisfy all of the conditions laid down by national law for obtaining international protection, generally forms part of the legitimate objectives of an organisation which assists applicants for international protection.[78] Penalising only activities carried out in an organised manner is not sufficient to eliminate the restrictive nature of the offence, as the organisations which provide assistance to applicants for international protection and which are the main addressees of that provision carry out, by definition, an 'organised activity' and national law is capable of hindering the activities of almost all persons or organisations providing assistance to applicants for

[75] ibid para 33
[76] ibid para 34.
[77] ibid para 35.
[78] ibid para 36.

international protection.[79] According to the Advocate General, criminal prosecution of persons or organisations that facilitate the initiation of asylum proceedings is not a legitimate penalty under EU law, but that finding in no way prejudices the possibility of introducing criminal penalties where the activities are not limited to assisting applicants for international protection in making their application and initiating asylum proceedings, but are genuine attempts to facilitate illegal immigration.[80] The Advocate General has thus recommended that the CJEU finds that national law criminalising the provision of legal advice is incompatible with EU law, and has attempted to distinguish the provision of legal advice from the facilitation of unauthorised entry.

V Demanding Obedience: From the Hostile to the Compliant Environment?

Lucia Zedner tracks the shift in the rhetoric of the UK government from a focus on the hostile environment to an emphasis on a compliant environment whereby private actors are required to assume immigration control-related duties in-country.[81] In the case of preventive border control in Europe, the move towards establishing a compliant environment is additional to efforts to criminalise civil society and consists of the adoption of a broader series of measures aiming to ensure obedience, or at least to prevent what is perceived as disobedience,[82] of private actors towards the state. Disobedience, expressed through decisions private actors take in the course of humanitarian action (in particular regarding saving lives) that are at odds with states' emphasis on preventive border control, is perceived as a direct threat to state sovereignty. This threat perception is linked with the adoption of a discourse treating private actors, and in particular NGOs, as colluding with smugglers and traffickers, which has the effect of stigmatising and delegitimising humanitarian action.[83] The state considers that these private actors must be 'reined in' as they are perceived to operate too independently and contrary to state interests.[84] New measures demand obedience of private actors with state guidelines and policies in respect of immigration control and sea patrols. The creation of a hostile environment via the threat of prosecution and the imposition of criminal sanctions is gradually being complemented by attempts to establish a compliant environment through the imposition of obligations on private actors to comply with a series of legal and regulatory requirements

[79] ibid para 39.

[80] ibid para 37.

[81] Zedner, in this volume.

[82] Mann has called private rescue operations in the Mediterranean a form of transnational maritime civil disobedience: Itamar Mann, 'The Right to Perform Rescue at Sea: Jurisprudence and Drowning' (2020) 11 German Law Journal 598.

[83] On the process of delegitimisation of NGOs, see Eugenio Cusumano and Matteo Villa, 'From "Angels" to "Vice Smugglers": The Criminalization of Sea Rescue NGOs in Italy' (2021) 27 European Journal on Criminal Policy and Research 23.

[84] 'According to Greek Government sources, "not all NGOs are the same"—the quote goes on to distinguish between NGOs who are registered with the state and others who pose a threat to national security' <https://www.lifo.gr/now/greece/ti-symbainei-me-tis-mko-poy-katigoroyntai-gia-kataskopeia> accessed 12 August 2021.

and state instructions. It also has the potential to transform citizenship and trust, and the relationship between the individual and the state, by creating a climate of mistrust towards citizens and civil society and a 'chilling effect' on independent citizen action.

A key example of the shift towards obedience has been the introduction by the Italian authorities of a code of conduct which was presented to humanitarian organisations for signature in August 2017. The code of conduct was mandated by the European Commission as part of a package of measures to address the perceived migration 'crisis' in Italy at the time.[85] It reflects dissatisfaction with humanitarian efforts on search and rescue at sea and was an attempt to control humanitarian operations. The code of conduct stated, inter alia, that NGOs should not enter Libyan territorial waters unless in exceptional circumstances and under previous authorisation; that NGO vessels' shipmasters should notify their involvement in SAR operations to their flag state; that NGOs are expected to constantly inform the Italian Maritime Rescue Coordination Centre (MRCC) and execute its instructions; and that NGOs are to loyally cooperate with the public security authorities in relation to their intended place of disembarkation, transmitting all relevant information in advance. Moreover, NGOs are expected to declare all their sources of financing to both the flag state and the Italian government.[86] The code of conduct is a clear effort to subsume civil society efforts within the objectives and limits of state intervention, and a number of its provisions may lead to breaches of international and EU law. Non-compliance with its provisions has been used in order to introduce criminal prosecutions,[87] although the ruling of the *Cassazione* limits somewhat its adverse effects.[88]

The approach taken by the Italian authorities, of seeking obedience under a code of conduct which NGOs must sign, is reflective of a general trend aiming to control and monitor the activities of civil society. In Greece, in addition to measures subsuming humanitarian aid under state instruction,[89] emphasis has been placed on the establishment of a government-approved register of NGOs,[90] linked with a political

[85] Action plan on measures to support Italy, reduce pressure along the Central Mediterranean route and increase solidarity, Better coordination of Search and Rescue activities (SAR) in the Central Mediterranean, Brussels, 4.7.2017 SEC(2017) 339 called on Italy to draft, in consultation with the Commission, and on the basis of a dialogue with the NGOs, a Code of Conduct for NGOs involved in SAR activities.

[86] Eugenio Cusumano, 'Straightjacketing Migrant Rescuers? The Code of Conduct on Maritime NGOs' (2019) 24 Mediterranean Politics 105.

[87] See s II above.

[88] The Code of Conduct has not been repealed, at the time of writing. The new Italian administration is at pains to indicate a more protective change of direction <https://www.interno.gov.it/it/stampa-e-comunicazione/interventi-e-interviste/lamorgese-ue-fermi-sbarchi-dalla-libia-nuovo-patto-sui-migranti> accessed 12 August 2021. The most recent Italian legislation (the Lamorghese decree – Law Decree 21 October 2020, n 130, converted into Law 18 December 2020, n 173), however, maintains an entry ban whose violation is accompanied by criminal sanctions; but it also introduced a 'search and rescue clause', following the ruling in *Cassazione*. I am grateful to Stefano Zirulia for these points.

[89] According to Greek legislation, sanctions are not imposed for SAR and transport of those in need of international protection 'as long as police and coast guard authorities are informed'. See Nikolaos Chatzinikolaou, 'Crimmigration in Greece: A Story of Exceptional Derogations from the Rule of Law within a Permanent Situation of Emergency' in Gian Luigi Gatta, Valsamis Mitsilegas, and Stefano Zirulia (eds), *Controlling Immigration through Criminal Law* (Hart 2021) 189–90.

[90] See Meena Masood, Greece's Silence: Analysing the Greek Response to the Global Compact for Safe, Orderly and Regular Migration (GCM) (*RLI blog on Refugee Law and Forced Migration*, 5 July 2021) <https://rli.blogs.sas.ac.uk/2021/07/05/greeces-silence-analysing-the-greek-response-to-the-global-compact-for-safe-orderly-and-regular-migration-gcm> See also <https://www.kathimerini.gr/society/561103948/oi-draseis-toy-ypoyrgeioy-metanasteysis-gia-ton-elegcho-ton-mko/> and <https://www.statewatch.

discourse portraying activists as being linked with irregular flows and smuggling,[91] but also with money laundering[92] and espionage,[93] treating civil society organisations as a threat to national security.

Efforts to ensure the obedience and control of civil society in this manner clearly reflect the exercise of state sovereignty, but may have serious adverse consequences, not only for the rights and lives of migrants and asylum seekers, but also for the place of civil society in a democratic society and for the exercise of freedom of association. The implications of attempting to control the work of civil society were highlighted by the CJEU in a ruling concerning Hungary's 'Transparency Law', which required NGOs to declare their financing from abroad.[94] The preamble to the 'Transparency Law' stated that 'support from unknown foreign sources [to civil society organisations] is liable to be used by foreign public interest groups to promote—through the social influence of those organisations—their own interests rather than community objectives in the social and political life of Hungary' and that that support 'may jeopardise the political and economic interests of the country and the ability of legal institutions to operate free from interference'.[95] The demonisation of civil society by the state and its framing as an 'enemy to the state' and to state sovereignty is clear.

The Court of Justice found that the Hungarian law was in breach of the EU Charter of Fundamental Rights, and in particular of the rights of privacy and data protection, and importantly, of the right to freedom of association. The CJEU emphasised, by reference also to the case law of the European Court of Human Rights, that 'the right to freedom of association constitutes one of the essential bases of a democratic and pluralist society, inasmuch as it allows citizens to act collectively in fields of mutual interest and in doing so to contribute to the proper functioning of public life'.[96] The right includes the possibility for that association to act in the meantime, which means, inter alia, that an association must be able to pursue its activities and operate without unjustified interference by the state.[97] The Court of Justice stressed the 'chilling effect' that the Hungarian law would have on the activities of civil society. It noted that the obligations of declaration and publicity imposed by those provisions are such as to limit the capacity of the associations and foundations at issue to receive financial support sent from other member states or third countries, having regard to the dissuasive effect of such obligations and the penalties attached to any failure to comply with them.[98] The Court added that the systematic obligations imposed on the associations

org/news/2021/march/greece-crackdown-on-civil-society-groups-working-with-refugees/> accessed 12 August 2021.

[91] See the words of the Greek immigration minister Mitarakis, who blamed Turkey and NGOs for arrivals in Lesvos: <https://www.iefimerida.gr/politiki/mitarakis-toyrkia-mko-somalon-lesbo> accessed 12 August 2021.

[92] <https://www.hrw.org/news/2018/11/05/greece-rescuers-sea-face-baseless-accusations> accessed 12 August 2021.

[93] <https://www.lifo.gr/articles/greece_articles/298457/ti-symvainei-me-tis-mko-poy-katigoroyntai-gia-kataskopeia> accessed 12 August 2021.

[94] Case C–78/18, *Commission v Hungary*, ECLI:EU:C:2020:476.

[95] ibid para 3.

[96] ibid para 112.

[97] ibid para 113.

[98] ibid para 116.

and foundations falling within the scope of the Transparency Law to register and present themselves under the designation 'organisation in receipt of support from abroad' are liable to have a deterrent effect on the participation of donors resident in other member states or in third countries in the financing of civil society organisations falling within the scope of the Transparency Law and thus to hinder the activities of those organisations and the achievement of the aims which they pursue.[99] These obligations are, the Court added, of such a nature as to create a generalised climate of mistrust vis-à-vis the associations and foundations at issue, in Hungary, and to stigmatise them.[100] In this manner, the Court of Justice's ruling reflects the profound adverse effects of stifling the activities of civil society organisations for citizenship and the rule of law in a democratic society. Independent civil society actors are framed as enemies of state sovereignty, not to be trusted by the public.

Notwithstanding these effects of demanding obedience and controlling civil society on fundamental rights and the rule of law, the recent proposals on the EU Pact on Immigration and Asylum appear to normalise and Europeanise state control over the private sector. The Commission has recommended cooperation between Member States in relation to operations carried out by privately owned or operated vessels for the purpose of search and rescue activities and has called on flag and coastal member states to exchange information, on a regular and timely basis, on the vessels involved in rescue operations and the entities that operate or own them.[101] The Commission Recommendation clearly stigmatises the private sector through its claims of linkages between private sector activities and criminality: it is expressly stated that it is 'essential to avoid a situation in which migrant smuggling or human trafficking networks, including criminal organisations trafficking people or engaging in forms of exploitation assimilated to slavery, take advantage of the rescue operations conducted by private vessels in the Mediterranean'.[102] Intervention vis-à-vis private search and rescue is further justified on the grounds that SAR has become the 'predominant activity' of certain NGOs.[103] It is implicit that this form of intervention is undesirable and must be controlled under the pretext of criminality and health and safety arguments which require registration and monitoring.[104] The impact of private action on state migration management (and thus state sovereignty) is expressly mentioned,[105] implying that private sector humanitarian interventions pose an undue burden on states of disembarkation.

The combination of this growing control of the private sector and the reluctance to decriminalise elements of the currently broad and abuse-prone offences of human smuggling at EU level demonstrate an attempt to neutralise or dismantle private sector—and in particular civil society—efforts to ensure that human rights are

[99] ibid para 118.
[100] ibid.
[101] Commission Recommendation (EU) 2020/1365 of 23 September 2020 on cooperation among Member States concerning operations carried out by vessels owned or operated by private entities for the purpose of search and rescue activities [2020] OJ L 317/23.
[102] ibid Preamble recital 9.
[103] ibid recital 8.
[104] ibid recital 12.
[105] ibid recital 13.

respected and lives are saved in the face of increasingly restrictive preventive border policies by European states. Limits to the capacity of civil society may leave more and more migrants unprotected, leaving commercial vessels as the only non-state actors able to assist. The latter are increasingly being placed under pressure to comply with state instructions on managing migration flows and on SARs, including transferring and disembarking migrants in the territory of third countries such as Libya, effectively requiring commercial vessels to contribute to pushbacks.[106] Commercial vessels are thus increasingly being placed under a conflict of interest between obeying state instructions and being in breach of international, European, and national law.[107] The extent to which commercial carriers will cooperate with state authorities in breach of their international law obligations or decide to clash with the state following the example of civil society actors remains to be seen.

VI Conclusion: Sovereignty versus Rights? Civil Society Organisations as Rule-of-Law Defenders

This chapter has attempted to map the evolution of the relationship between private actors and state sovereignty in the field of border control when the activities of private actors are seen as a threat to state sovereignty. States have increasingly exercised sovereign power while disregarding their human rights, humanitarian, and rule-of-law obligations. The securitisation and criminalisation of migration has led to a preventive approach aiming to place migrants outside the law, in contravention of the foundational European human rights paradigms set out in the European Convention on Human Rights and in the EU Charter of Fundamental Rights, where rights are enjoyed by all, not only by citizens. In this process, the illegality of the migrants, in the eyes of the state, is increasingly reassigned to those who assist them. Preventive measures have resulted in expansion of the remit and use of criminal law against private actors (ranging from NGOs to lawyers to individual citizens) acting with humanitarian motives to uphold human rights and the rule of law; an overuse and abuse of criminal law provisions by prosecutors; and a shift from immigration-related criminal law to increased recourse to measures of administrative compliance and control with the aim of neutralising or dismantling civil society organisations.

All these efforts aim at reinforcing a preventive paradigm of border control by stopping people reaching the sovereign territory of European states and the legal safeguards they offer. In addition to their adverse impact on human rights, SAR obligations, and refugee law, practices targeting civil society have profound rule-of-law implications in multiplying instances of state arbitrariness and unaccountable executive action while providing limited, if any, avenues for remedies for affected individuals. Unlike the system of privatisation of border control through delegation

[106] Anuscheh Farahat and Nora Markard, *Places of Safety in the Mediterranean*, Report for the Heinrich Böll Stiftung (2020) 36 et seq.

[107] See allegations and current litigation on 'privatised pushbacks' resulting from state instructions to private commercial vessels: <https://www.theguardian.com/global-development/2020/may/19/exclusive-12-die-as-malta-uses-private-ships-to-push-migrants-back-to-libya>; <https://www.glanlaw.org/nivincase> accessed 12 August 2021.

and co-option, where the majority of private actors are for-profit entities required to comply with state-imposed duties or to undertake border control-type tasks for profit, the main private actors targeted under the hostile environment are civil society organisations and private citizens. Such organisations and citizens have not hesitated to undertake action against the wishes of the state in order to address state illegality and to ensure compliance with human rights and humanitarian norms. Civil society actors have not hesitated to clash directly with the state preventive agenda on border control, engaging in action outside and on the border and in state territory, and in extensive litigation to defend themselves from state enforcement action and in strategic litigation. In this manner, civil society actors have emerged as key defenders of the rule of law. In addition to their search and rescue operations, NGOs have increasingly initiated strategic litigation to document and affirm breaches of human rights by states,[108] and they have set up systems to systematically monitor state preventive border control practices in order to flag up human rights abuses.[109] Civil society and in particular non-governmental organisations have thus been 'turning the tables' on the state[110] to emerge as key proactive actors in the field of border control: contesting state sovereignty and challenging the paradigm of preventive border control and the human rights and rule of law deficit it entails.

References

Aas KF and Bosworth M, *The Borders of Punishment: Migration, Citizenship, and Social Exclusion* (OUP 2013)

Aliverti A, *Crimes of Mobility* (Routledge 2015)

Anderson M, *Frontiers: Territory and State Formation in the Modern World* (Polity 1996)

Ashworth A and Zedner L, *Preventive Justice* (OUP 2014)

Baird T, 'Carrier Sanctions in Europe: A Comparison of Trends in 10 Countries' (2017) 19 European Journal of Migration and Law 307

Bigo D, *Polices en Réseaux. L'Expérience Européenne* (Presses Sciences Po 1996)

— —, 'Frontier Controls in the European Union: Who is in Control?' in Bigo D and Guild E (eds), Controlling Frontiers: Free Movement into and within Europe (Ashgate 2005)

Bingham T, *The Rule of Law* (Allen Lane 2010)

Bosworth M, 'Penal Humanitarianism? Sovereign Power in an Era of Mass Migration' (2017) 20 New Criminal Law Review 39

Carrera S, Mitsilegas V, Allsopp J, and Vosyliute L, *Policing Humanitarianism: EU Policies Against Human Smuggling and their Impact on Civil Society* (Hart 2019)

[108] Itamar Mann and Julia Mourão Permoser, *Visibility and Crime at Sea* (*VerfBlog*, 9 July 2021) <https://verfassungsblog.de/visibility-and-crime-at-sea/> accessed 12 August 2021.

[109] Angela Smith, 'Battles over Migrant Rescue Take to the Skies with Civilian Counter-surveillance' (2021) (*Centre for Criminology: Border Criminologies Blog*, 24 June 2021) <https://www.law.ox.ac.uk/research-subject-groups/centre-criminology/centreborder-criminologies/blog/2021/06/battles-over> accessed 12 August 2021; see also <https://www.theguardian.com/global-development/2021/jul/02/libyan-coastguards-fired-on-and-tried-to-ram-migrant-boat-ngo> accessed 12 August 2021.

[110] Maximilian Steinbeis, 'Normal Times' (2021) (*VerfBlog*, 9 July 2021) <https://verfassungsblog.de/normal-times/> accessed 12 August 2021.

Chatzinikolaou N, 'Crimmigration in Greece: A Story of Exceptional Derogations from the Rule of Law within a Permanent Situation of Emergency' in Gatta GL, Mitsilegas V, and Zirulia S (eds), *Controlling Immigration Through Criminal Law* (Hart 2021)

Council of Europe Commissioner for Human Rights, *Criminalisation of Migration in Europe: Human Rights Implications* (Issue Paper prepared by Elspeth Guild, 2009) <https://rm.coe.int/16806da917>

— —, *Lives Saved. Rights Protected. Bridging the Protection Gap between Refugees and Migrants in the Mediterranean* (Council of Europe 2019)

Craig P, 'Formal and Substantive Conceptions of the Rule of Law: An Analytical Framework' [1997] Public Law 467

Cusumano E, 'Straightjacketing Migrant Rescuers? The Code of Conduct on Maritime NGOs' (2019) 24 Mediterranean Politics 105

— — E and Villa M, 'From "Angels" to "Vice Smugglers": The Criminalization of Sea Rescue NGOs in Italy' (2021) 27 European Journal on Criminal Policy and Research 23

Dauvergne C, *Making People Illegal* (CUP 2011)

EU Fundamental Rights Agency (FRA), 'December 2020 update—NGO ships involved in search and rescue in the Mediterranean and legal proceedings against them'
<https://fra.europa.eu/en/publication/2020/december-2020-update-ngo-ships-involved-search-and-rescue-mediterranean-and-legal>

European Commission, 'Staff Working Document—REFIT Evaluation of the EU Legal Framework against Facilitation of Unauthorised Entry, Transit and Residence' SWD (2017) 117 final

Farahat A and Markard N, *Places of Safety in the Mediterranean*, Report for the Heinrich Bóll Stiftung (2020)

Feller E, 'Carrier Sanctions and International Law' (1989) 1 International Journal of Refugee Law 48.

Fertsman C, *Using Criminal Law to Restrict the Work of NGOs Supporting Refugees and Other Migrants in Council of Europe Member States*, Thematic Study prepared by Dr Carla Ferstman, Expert Council on NGO Law CONF/EXP', December 2019 <https://rm.coe.int/expert-council-conf-exp-2019-1-criminal-law-ngo-restrictions-migration/1680996969>

Franko K, 'The Two-sided Spectacle at the Border: Frontex, NGOs and the Theatres of Sovereignty' (2021) 25 Theoretical Criminology 379

Franko Aas K and Grundhus HOI, 'Policing Humanitarian Borderlands: Frontex, Human Rights and the Precariousness of Life' (2015) 55 British Journal of Criminology 1

Gammeltoft-Hansen T, 'The Rise of the Private Border Guard. Accountability and Responsibility in the Migration Control Industry' in Gammeltoft-Hansen T and Nyberg Soerensen N (eds), *The Migration Industry and the Commercialization of International Migration* (Routledge 2013)

Guild E, *Security and Migration in the 21st Century* (Polity 2009)

Guiraudon V, 'De-nationalizing Control: Analysing State Responses to Constraints on Migration Control' in Guiraudon V and Joppke C (eds), *Controlling a New Migration World* (Routledge 2001)

Kuskonmaz E Mendos, *Privacy and Border Controls in the Fight Against Terrorism* (Brill 2020)

Lahav G, 'Immigration and the State: The Devolution and Privatisation of Immigration Control' (1998) 24(4) Journal of Ethnic and Migration Studies 675

Mann I, 'The Right to Perform Rescue at Sea: Jurisprudence and Drowning' (2020) 11 German Law Journal 598

Mann I and Permoser JM, 'Visibility and Crime at Sea' (*VerfBlog*, 9 July 2021) <https://verfassungsblog.de/visibility-and-crime-at-sea/>

Masood M, 'Greece's Silence: Analysing the Greek Response to the Global Compact for Safe, Orderly and Regular Migration (GCM) (*RLI Blog on Refugee Law and Forced Migration*, 5 July 2021) <https://rli.blogs.sas.ac.uk/2021/07/05/greeces-silence-analysing-the-greek-response-to-the-global-compact-for-safe-orderly-and-regular-migration-gcm>

Minetti M, 'The Facilitators Package, Penal Populism and the Rule of Law: Lessons from Italy' (2020) 11 New Journal of European Criminal Law 335

Mitsilegas V, 'Contrôle des étrangers, des passagers, des citoyens: Surveillance et anti-terrorisme' (2005) 58 Cultures et Conflits 155

— —, 'Border Security in the European Union. Towards Centralised Controls and Maximum Surveillance' in Guild E, Toner H, and Baldaccini A (eds), *Whose Freedom, Security and Justice? EU Immigration and Asylum Law and Policy* (Hart 2007)

— —, *EU Criminal Law* (Hart 2009)

— —, 'Extraterritorial Immigration Control in the 21st Century: The Individual and the State Transformed' in Ryan B and Mitsilegas V (eds), *Extraterritorial Immigration Control: Legal Challenges* (Brill 2010)

— —, 'Human Rights, Terrorism and the Quest for "Border Security"' in Pedrazzi M and others (eds), *Individual Guarantees in the European Judicial Area in Criminal Matters* (Bruylant 2011)

— —, 'Immigration Control in an Era of Globalisation: Deflecting Foreigners, Weakening Citizens, Strengthening the State' (2012) 19 Indiana Journal of Global Legal Studies 3

— —, *The Criminalisation of Migration in Europe: Challenges for Human Rights and the Rule of Law* (Springer 2015)

— —, 'The Law of the Border and the Borders of Law—Rethinking Border Control from the Perspective of the Individual' in Weber L (ed), *Rethinking Border Control for a Globalizing World—A Preferred Future* (Routledge 2015)

— —, *EU Criminal Law After Lisbon* (Hart 2016)

— —, 'Rule of Law: Theorising EU Internal Security Cooperation from a Legal Perspective' in Bossong R and Rhinard M (eds), *Theorising Internal Security Cooperation in the European Union* (OUP 2016)

— —, 'The Security Union as a Paradigm of Preventive Justice: Challenges for Citizenship, Fundamental Rights and the Rule of Law' in Mitsilegas V and Carrera S (eds), *Constitutionalising the Security Union: Effectiveness, Rule of Law and Rights in Countering Terrorism and Crime* (CEPS 2017)

— —, 'Extraterritorial Immigration Control, Preventive Justice and the Rule of Law in Turbulent Times' in Vara JS, Carrera S, and Strik T (eds), *Constitutionalising the External Dimension of EU Migration Policies in Times of Crisis: Legality, Rule of Law and Fundamental Rights Reconsidered* (Edward Elgar 2019)

— —, 'The Normative Foundations of the Criminalisation of Human Smuggling: Exploring the Fault Lines between European and International Law' (2019) 10 New Journal of European Criminal Law 68

— —, Monar J, and Rees W, *The European Union and Internal Security* (Palgrave/Macmillan 2003)

Moreno-Lax V, 'The EU Humanitarian Border and the Securitization of Human Rights: The "Rescue-Through-Interdiction/Rescue-Without-Protection" Paradigm' (2018) 56 Journal of Common Market Studies 119

Nicholson F, 'Implementation of the Immigration (Carriers' Liability) Act 1987: Privatising Immigration Functions at the Expense of International Obligations?' (1997) 46 International and Comparative Law Quarterly 633

Rodenhauser T, 'Another Brick in the Wall: Carrier Sanctions and the Privatization of Immigration Control' (2014) 26 International Journal of Refugee Law 223

Ryan B and Mitsilegas V (eds), *Extraterritorial Immigration Control: Legal Challenges* (Brill 2010)

Scholten S, *The Privatisation of Immigration Control through Carrier Sanctions* (Brill 2015)Smith A, 'Battles over Migrant Rescue Take to the Skies with Civilian Counter-surveillance' (*Centre for Criminology: Border Criminologies Blog*, 24 June 2021) <https://www.law.ox.ac.uk/research-subject-groups/centre-criminology/centreborder-criminologies/blog/2021/06/battles-over>

Spena A, 'Migrant Smuggling: A Normative and Phenomenological View from Italy' in Militello V and Spena A, *Between Criminalization and Protection: The Italian Way of Dealing with Migrant Smuggling and Trafficking within the European and International Context* (Brill Perspectives in Transnational Crime 2019)

Steinbeis M, 'Normal Times' (*VerfBlog*, 9 July 2021) <https://verfassungsblog.de/normal-times/>

Torpey J, *The Invention of the Passport: Surveillance, Citizenship and the State* (CUP 2000)

York S, 'The "Hostile Environment"—How Home Office Immigration Policies and Practices Create and Perpetuate Illegality' (2018) 32(4) Journal of Immigration, Asylum and Nationality Law 363

Zirulia S, 'Is that a Smuggler? The Blurring Line between Facilitating Illegal Immigration and Providing Humanitarian Assistance at the European Borders' in Gatta GL, Mitsilegas V, and Zirulia S (eds), *Controlling Immigration Through Criminal Law* (Hart 2021)

— —, 'La Cassazione sul caso Sea Watch: Le motivazioni sul l'illegitimita dell arresto di Carola Rackete' Sistema Penale (20 February 2020)

Legislation

Commission Recommendation (EU) 2020/1365 of 23 September 2020 on cooperation among Member States concerning operations carried out by vessels owned or operated by private entities for the purpose of search and rescue activities [2020] OJ L 317/23

Council Directive 2002/90/EC of 28 November 2002 defining the facilitation of unauthorised entry, transit and residence [2002] OJ L328/4

Council Framework Decision 2002/946/JHA of 28 November 2002 on the strengthening of the penal framework to prevent the facilitation of unauthorised entry, transit and residence [2002] OJ L328/1

Cases

Areios Pagos (the Greek Supreme Court AP 1344/2016)

Case C–78/18, *Commission v Hungary*, ECLI:EU:C:2020:476

Decision no 2018-717/718 QPC

Cass. pen., s III, 16 January 2020 (dep 20 February 2020), n 6626, Pres. Lapalorcia, Est. Gai, ric. Rackete

3

The Borders of Sovereignty

Peter Ramsay

I Introduction

There is an intimate connection between immigration control and the sovereignty of the state. As Katja Franko puts it, '[t]he prerogative to decide the right of entry into the country is one of the essential traits of any sovereign state.'[1] However, perceptive commentators have pointed out that the punitiveness associated with immigration control in recent decades appears to be a response to the increasing difficulty that states experience in controlling the flow of migrants, and to indicate 'the limits of the sovereign state'.[2] Citing David Garland, Mary Bosworth suggests that '[i]n such a world harsh policies about foreigners may ... "pose as a symbol of strength but ... should be interpreted as a symbol of weak authority and inadequate controls"'.[3] For Alessandro Spena, the criminalisation of violations of immigration rules is a sign of the state's 'waning authority'.[4]

To understand the contemporary practices of border control, it is essential to understand that they are the effect of waning sovereignty. However, there is also a tendency to assume that the source of this weakening sovereign power is *exogenous* to nation states themselves; to be found in the process of globalisation that has caused increased migrant flows. Bosworth cites Zygmunt Bauman's argument that nation states have been 'stripped of a large part of their sovereign prerogatives and capacities by globalization forces which they are impotent to resist, let alone to control'.[5] For Spena, 'globalization has ... made states far less autonomous than they have traditionally claimed to be, hence impinging not only on their external sovereignty, but also on their internal sovereignty, which largely depends on the former'.[6] Franko draws on Saskia Sassen to argue that 'the globalizing condition' has destabilised 'the central categories and building blocks of the national penal domain'.[7]

[1] Katja Franko Aas, 'The Ordered and the Bordered Society: Migration Control, Citizenship, and the Northern Penal State' in Katja Franko Aas and Mary Bosworth (eds), *The Borders of Punishment* (OUP 2013) 29. See also Juliet Stumpf, 'The Crimmigration Crisis: Immigrants, Crime, and Sovereign Power' (2006) 56 American University Law Review 367, 410; Nicholas De Genova and Nathalie Peutz, *The Deportation Regime: Sovereignty, Space, and the Freedom of Movement* (Duke University Press 2010) 2.

[2] Mary Bosworth, 'Border Control and the Limits of the Sovereign State' (2008) 17 Social & Legal Studies 199.

[3] ibid 210.

[4] Alessandro Spena, 'The Double-deviant Identity of the Mass-foreigner and the Lack of Authority of the Crimmigrationist State' (2019) 22(3) New Criminal Law Review 301, 310.

[5] Bosworth (n 2).

[6] Spena, 'The Double-deviant Identity of the Mass-foreigner' (n 4) 310.

[7] Franko Aas (n 1) 20.

Peter Ramsay, *The Borders of Sovereignty* In: *Privatising Border Control.* Edited by: Mary Bosworth and Lucia Zedner, Oxford University Press. © Peter Ramsay 2022. DOI: 10.1093/oso/9780192857163.003.0004

Here I will question that assumption and suggest that both the privatisation of border control and the criminalisation of violations of immigration rules are evidence that the decay of national sovereignty has causes that are primarily *endogenous* to the nation states that have engaged in them. I first review the existing normative debate over the privatisation of border control to show how it demonstrates the domestic sources of the decline of sovereign authority, before explaining why 'crimmigration' offences also reveal an endogenous waning of sovereignty. After that I suggest that the primary reason for this endogenous decline is to be found in the political decay of the nation state itself. Throughout I draw on the UK as an example, but I would be surprised if the argument had no wider relevance.[8]

II Sovereignty and the Privatisation of Border Control

There is a debate over the legitimacy of the privatisation of core state functions between two schools of thought. Malcolm Thorburn refers to the two schools respectively as 'statists', for whom the state has a privileged status in the execution of certain coercive public functions, and 'moral individualists', for whom the exercise of such coercion is subject to the same moral considerations whoever carries them out.[9] This normative philosophical debate about the legitimacy of privatisation is not my direct concern here,[10] but reviewing the debate does provide a very clear answer to the question of political sociology that is my concern: what is the historical relationship between privatisation and state sovereignty? Whether or not privatisation of border control is regarded as justifiable, it is antithetical to state sovereignty.

On the statist side of the debate, Thorburn points out that the state is made up of 'interconnected public offices', and that these public offices 'exist only in order to solve the fundamental problem of the state of nature' by serving 'public purposes'—that is, those purposes in which diverse private interests may find some common interest—as opposed to private interests, which are in competition with each other.[11] As a result, Thorburn argues:

> the reason why we are so concerned that offices should serve public purposes rather than private ones ... is that the only justification for one person to hold coercive power over another in a liberal legal order is to secure the civil condition ... To act for private reasons is to do precisely what public offices are designed to preclude.[12]

For this reason, the individuals appointed to hold public offices cannot be appointed by private actors, according to their own rules, but only by public procedures; and as

[8] Its precise application might, nevertheless, be quite different in a state such as Italy where, as Zelia Gallo has argued, the state's internal sovereignty was always more 'contested' and uncertain. See Zelia A Gallo, 'Punishment, Authority and Political Economy: Italian Challenges to Western Punitiveness' (2015) 17(5) Punishment & Society 598, 609–12.

[9] See Thorburn, in this volume.

[10] For what it is worth, my own sympathies in this debate are with the 'statists'.

[11] Thorburn, in this volume.

[12] ibid.

officials these persons are protected from the influence of private interests by various specific privileges and prohibitions. In other words, private border agents are simply not public officials. When the state delegates any of its activities to private agents, they become private activities, albeit private activities licensed by the state.

The private character of this privatised coercion is reflected in the lack of political integration into the hierarchy of public offices which constitutes the state. For Dorfman and Harel, when the state's activity is contracted out to private agencies, it becomes activity that is done *for* the state rather than *by* the state.[13] Critically, even though the privatised practice of such an activity may be regulated by contract and by public law, it is not subject to the 'direct influence' of higher political representatives that characterises the activities of the public bureaucracy. The contracted private actors do not have to defer to the guidance of their political masters in their deliberations over how they deploy their discretionary powers. Rather their relation to the ends and means of public officials is governed by contract, and they must use their own reason in fulfilling their obligations.

The mediation of a contract with a private employer standing between the state's political representatives—government ministers—and their agents converts the agents' acts into private acts. This conversion of a public activity into a private one has profound implications for the state's sovereignty when it is introduced into the execution of those coercive activities which provide the state's *raison d'être* as the public entity with a claim to represent the unity of all subjects. To understand these implications, it is necessary to keep in mind two distinctions and relationships that are fundamental to the state, but which are often obscured. The first is the distinction and relationship between legal supremacy on the one hand and political authority on the other. The second is between public office and the individuals who occupy the office. Let us consider each in turn.

Dorfman and Harel rely on a conventional concept of state sovereignty: that of 'a supreme authority within a territory'.[14] But the word 'sovereignty' can be confusing since it denotes both a *legal* supremacy within a territory and the factual *political* basis of that legal supremacy.[15] The supremacy of a state's law within a territory is only as good as the practical political authority that the state commands. The state's authority rests on its claim to be the political association of all its citizens—a unity of all of them—that is represented by the state's sovereign institutions, and which individual citizens are therefore obliged to obey. In this sense, a state enjoys sovereignty only if its laws are sufficiently obeyed within its territory. The degree of obedience that is sufficient will be context-specific, but it will have to be enough for the state to be treated as an autonomous agent, not least by other states. It is this *internal*, domestic aspect of sovereignty as a relation of representation, authority, and accountability between the public offices of government and citizens that can easily be overlooked when the focus is on non-citizens crossing borders, where the *external* aspect of sovereignty is more prominent.

[13] See, generally, Avihay Dorfman and Alon Harel, 'The Case Against Privatization' (2013) 41 Philosophy & Public Affairs 67.

[14] ibid 97.

[15] See Martin Loughlin, 'Why Sovereignty?' in Richard Rawlings, Peter Leyland, and Alison Young (eds), *Sovereignty and the Law* (OUP 2013) 35.

The second relationship is that between the public offices that comprise the sovereign state and the individuals who occupy the offices and who decide on and execute its policies as public officials. It does not follow merely from their occupation of those offices that those individuals understand, or necessarily respect, the requirements of maintaining the state's political authority.

Recognising these two distinctions and relationships allows us to see that the political actors who represent the state at the highest levels may exercise its legislative supremacy in ways that are inconsistent with or that diminish the state's sovereignty as political authority. And this is precisely what happens when a state privatises its coercive activities, its inherently public functions.

As Dorfman and Harel note, private agents of coercion do not have to defer directly to political masters in the execution of their obligations; rather, they deploy their own reason to determine best practice. This necessarily narrows the scope of the state's political authority. Coercion is now carried out in deference to the authority of the private organisation that employs those who engage in coercion. In this way, privatisation both diminishes the scope of the state's authority and expands the exercise of private authority over the coercion of persons within the state's jurisdiction. The state's ultimate authority over the practice remains, since it has significant influence over the terms of the contract and in practice is closely involved in its execution. In the final analysis, the private use of force is only made possible by the state's licence. Nevertheless, this subtle diminution of the state's authority—of its sovereignty—is real, notwithstanding that it is voluntary.

One aspect of privatisation, observed by Bosworth and Singler in UK immigration control, is that '[t]he contract does additional political work of distancing the Home Office from the practice of deportation.'[16] When too much coercion is used by private agents in executing a deportation, the private contractor and its employees can be blamed.[17] The government does not escape responsibility entirely, since it delegated the use of force to the particular private supplier,[18] but it does put some distance between itself and any negligence or more serious wrongdoing precisely because the coercion is now the result of private force that has been licensed by the state, rather than the force of the state itself. Even if some political responsibility cannot be avoided entirely,[19] this distancing is at odds with the political structure of sovereignty where the state officials who claim the *authority* to coerce are necessarily accountable for its exercise.

This attempt to retreat from the responsibilities of sovereignty is also apparent in the day-to-day practice of deportation studied by Bosworth and Singler. Deportations tend to take place in the early morning and are carried out as discreetly as possible, sometimes on specially chartered planes, so that they remain largely out of the gaze of the ordinary traveller. Bosworth and Singler call the practice 'a mundane spectacle',

[16] Bosworth and Singler, in this volume. See also Federica Infantino, in this volume.

[17] As occurred following the death of Jimmy Mubenga (Bosworth and Singler, in this volume).

[18] See, generally, Dorfman and Harel (n 13) 80.

[19] At the time of writing, a public inquiry into allegations of mistreatment of detainees at the privately run Brook House Immigration Removal Centre is taking place. Its terms of reference include questions about the Home Office's contribution to any wrongdoing: see <https://brookhouseinquiry.org.uk/about/terms-of-reference-2/> accessed 18 November 2021.

the oxymoron ironically casting doubt on the idea that deportation provides 'a spectacle of enforcement' that demonstrates to all the enormity of the sovereign's power.[20] If anything, both the evasion of responsibility for coercion and the discreet character of its execution, connote embarrassment about the sovereign's power.

In themselves these observations about the privatisation of border control tell us nothing about the normative appropriateness of contracting out the state's coercion. What they do tell us is that privatisation is an exercise of the sovereign's legal powers to determine who will control the border that serves to distance government from the responsibilities associated with sovereignty, and which attenuates the domestic political authority that constitutes sovereignty.

This conclusion is reinforced if we consider the implications for sovereignty of the alternative 'moral individualist' position with respect to privatisation. Whereas the statist accounts of Thorburn or Dorfman and Harel draw attention to the weakened state authority entailed in privatisation of border control, normative theorists who favour enforcement by private organisations repudiate the absolute political autonomy of the state that is its sovereignty. For moral individualists, what matters is that justice is done, whether or not the person who does it occupies a public office or defers directly to the hierarchy of public offices through which sovereign state exercises its supreme authority. Indeed, Ashwini Vasanthakumar takes the anti-state argument further, suggesting that the state suffers from 'a blind spot in contexts, such as migration, that implicate the interests of individuals excluded from the institutions of the state and denied a voice in its affairs', so that the state may not be able to 'act justly with respect to outsiders':

> Absent an appropriate institutional framework, such as a robust system of international law and governance or mechanisms that attend to the interests and voices of potential migrants, the state may not be a properly public agent in the context of border control.[21]

Vasanthakumar argues that the involvement of private organisations that have the welfare of migrants among their purposes could 'supplement or correct the state's particular understanding of the public interest'.[22] Whether or not this argument is normatively attractive, it explicitly asserts that the state's political autonomy is not adequate to the task of fully identifying the public interest, when it comes to migrants.[23]

Malcolm Feeley criticises the statist position from a historical rather than an individualist perspective, arguing that statists imagine the state to be 'unitary' in the manner of classical political theory, with public and private roles distinguished clearly. In Feeley's view, this has never been entirely true and is certainly not true today when,

[20] Bosworth and Singler, in this volume.

[21] Ashwini Vasanthakumar, 'Privatising Border Control' (2018) 38 Oxford Journal of Legal Studies 411, 422.

[22] ibid 428. Of course, doing the state's border control work for it may prove to be in tension with the aims of NGOs that are formally committed to migrant welfare: see Anthea Vogl, in this volume.

[23] In this volume, Vasanthakumar further pursues the argument that the autonomous state is inadequate to politically legitimate border control, without some institutional form through which migrants have a say in the border control policies of states of which they are not citizens.

'[t]he state ... now coexists alongside a plethora of *equally significant* actors ... each of them engaged in the policy-making process.'[24] Feeley's argument further confirms the point that, for better or worse, the case for privatisation of coercive state functions entails a diminution of the *supreme* authority of a single sovereign public institution of the sort that characterises sovereignty.

III Privatisation as Endogenous Decay of Sovereignty

Whether border enforcement by private agencies is supported or rejected, privatisation is not compatible with a robust assertion of sovereignty because it entails some degree of qualification or even avoidance of the structure of political authority that is the sovereign state. Crucially, for present purposes, this diminution of sovereignty by privatisation of a core state function cannot be attributed to the globalisation of markets. Certainly, the policy of privatisation has had global influence, and that influence has coincided with the growth of global capital flows, but it does not follow that privatisation is caused by globalisation.[25] Even when privatisation is intended directly to attract foreign capital into an industry, it remains a domestic political choice;[26] one arising from an 'ideology' or 'public philosophy' in which policymakers have 'faith in market mechanisms' as the best, or only, way to deal with the challenge of economic and technological change.[27] The UK is a good example in this respect since it is the home and origin of the policy technique of privatisation that was autonomously adopted by British governments.[28] In the UK, the privatisation of state services has been promoted by domestic political actors, usually on the grounds of efficiency.[29] But in that very moment of claiming efficiency, the privatisation of a core function of the sovereign, such as border control, executes a subtle transformation of the official

[24] Malcolm Feeley, 'The Unconvincing Case against Private Prisons' (2014) 89(4) Indiana Law Journal 1401, 1417 (emphasis added).

[25] Indeed, one of the few empirical studies of the relation concluded, unsurprisingly, that the influence was 'bi-directional': privatisation encouraged foreign direct investment and foreign portfolio investment and, at the same time, increased flows of capital were a spur to privatisation. See Narjess Boubakri, Jean-Claude Cosset, Nassima Debab, and Pascale Valery, 'Privatization and Globalization: An Empirical Analysis' (2013) 37 Journal of Banking & Finance 1898.

[26] It is beyond the scope of this chapter, but arguably the phenomena of globalisation are in any case themselves largely the work of nation states: see Susan Strange, *The Retreat of the State* (CUP 1996) 44–45; William Mitchell and Thomas Fazi, *Reclaiming the State: A Progressive Vision of Sovereignty for the Post-Neoliberal World* (Pluto Press 2017) 119–20.

[27] For a nuanced discussion, see Vanessa Baird and Alan Stone, 'Why Privatization? The Case of German Telecommunications' (1998) 79(1) Social Science Quarterly 193.

[28] Graeme A Hodge, *Privatization and Market Development* (Edward Elgar 2006) 1.

[29] Lacin Idil Oztig, 'Rethinking Sovereignty: The Implications of the Role of Private Security Companies in the Prevention and the Regulation of Unauthorized Flows' (2020) 33(3) Cambridge Review of International Affairs 330, 340. It does not follow that privatisation is necessarily always cost-efficient: see Ole Helby Petersena, Ulf Hjelmarb, and Karsten Vrangbæk, 'Is Contracting out of Public Services still the Great Panacea? A Systematic Review of Studies on Economic and Quality Effects from 2000 to 2014' (2018) 52(1) Social Policy and Administration 130.

conception of the relation between state and citizen; a transformation that avoids the internal political relations of authority and attenuates the state's internal sovereignty.

Privatisation constructs the provision of a good or service like housing, telecommunications, sports facilities, and so on, as a question of value for money and/or consumer choice. This 'new market mode' of governance has 'leached' into the wider public sphere, representing the state as a provider of services to its individual subjects.[30] The relation of citizen and state is remodelled as if it were a market relation between individual consumers and a service provider rather than a political relation between members of a collective association and the representative of their collectivity.[31] Privatisation is an aspect of this domestic transformation of the state—often referred to loosely as neoliberalism—both symptom and cause of the endogenous waning of sovereignty.

Privatisation of a core state function like border control represents the state itself as the consumer of its own functions. The coercive activity of the political association to which all citizens collectively belong (and for which all bear ultimate responsibility) is represented as if it were the provision of a useful service to a consumer. In place of transparent public coercion of non-citizens, our political representatives license private actors to coerce migrants so that the coercion appears to citizens as if it were another service purchased by our representatives in the market. Both the state as a political association, and the citizens that comprise that association, pose as the consumers of our own collective coercion. There is of course a sleight of hand here. At least in so far as it is currently practised, privatisation does not eliminate the state's ultimate control and responsibility; it only undermines the idea that these coercive acts are representative in nature, and belong to the state.[32] To the degree that the state, as the representative of all, appears to be the passive consumer of coercion, rather than its ultimate agent, doubt is cast over whether the state retains the monopoly of legitimate coercion.[33]

The privatisation of coercive border control is, therefore, evidence of an endogenous waning of sovereignty as a mode of government. The state is transformed as coercive force is privatised, as relations of contract and of deference to mediating private interests are substituted for deference to political authority, as those who hold the public offices that comprise the state seek to evade responsibility for coercion that is fundamental to the state's sovereignty.[34] All of this is unrelated to the flow of migrants themselves and is a matter of domestic political choices. This same endogenous decay of sovereignty can be identified in the criminalisation of violations of immigration law.

[30] Wolfgang Streeck, 'Citizens as Customers: Considerations on the New Politics of Consumption' (2012) 27 New Left Review 27, 43.

[31] As Paul Verkuil puts it, in relation to 'efficiency', political accountability provides a 'countervailing principle of democracy': see Paul B Verkuil, *Outsourcing Sovereignty* (CUP 2009) 4.

[32] With respect to the privatisation of the police, see Malcolm Thorburn, 'Reinventing the Nightwatchman State' (2010) 60(2) University of Toronto Law Journal 425.

[33] Oztig (n 29) 339.

[34] On the inherent evasiveness of consumer citizenship, see Streeck (n 30) 44.

IV Criminalising Immigration Violations

The UK Home Office has justified penal enforcement of immigration law on the grounds that unlawful immigration facilitates welfare abuse, undermines minimum wages and fair competition, undermines 'community cohesion', creates a 'pull' for illegal immigration, and leads to more serious crimes, such as terrorism and drug and human trafficking.[35] The evidence that these harms are in fact caused by unlawful immigration is at best controversial.[36] However, here I will assume that there is at least some truth to the Home Office's claims, because my immediate concern is to understand the logic of crimmigration on its own terms. What does this claim about the rationale for the criminal law tell us about the state that makes it?

The harms attributed to unlawful immigration by the Home Office are either harms to the general welfare or to the distribution of that welfare in the form of wages or public services; or the increased risk of serious criminal offences alleged to arise from unauthorised immigration. The purpose of criminalisation is, therefore, to punish behaviour that might result in these harms. Immigration offences appear to be public welfare offences of abstract endangerment, targeting conduct of a type that creates a risk of harm to public welfare in order to pre-empt the harm.

However, it is important to note the high degree of redundancy present in these anticipatory offences.[37] Persons apprehended for most of these offences are very likely themselves to be unauthorised immigrants.[38] They are therefore subject to the state's power to deport them in any case, and they can be detained for that purpose without a criminal conviction. Indeed, deportation appears to be the practical effect of many convictions.[39] Any additional deterrent effect from criminalisation is marginal at best. Alessandro Spena makes the critical point that the fact that conviction leads to expulsion exposes the lack of any real claim to authority in the relationship between the state and the 'offender'.[40] It is worth dwelling on this observation by thinking in a little more detail about sovereign authority.

Where immigration law is a paradigmatic assertion of the rights of the state over the alien, the criminal law is the paradigmatic assertion of the rights of the *state* over its own citizens. Another of way of saying this would be to say that the criminal law asserts the rights of the political association of all citizens (the state) over the individual citizen,[41] and anyone else within the state's jurisdiction. The criminal law consists of commands of the *sovereign*; that is, of the political body that represents the state and which enjoys ultimate lawmaking power.[42] As noted above, sufficient obedience of

[35] Home Office, 'Enforcing the Rules: A Strategy to Ensure and Enforce Compliance with our Immigration Laws' (Borders and Immigration Agency 2007) 11, cited in Ana Aliverti, 'The Wrongs of Unlawful Immigration' (2017) 11 Criminal Law and Philosophy 375.

[36] See Aliverti (n 35).

[37] ibid 389.

[38] Offences of facilitating unauthorised immigration would be an exception, also applicable to nationals and residents and therefore of possible deterrent value.

[39] Aliverti (n 35).

[40] Spena 'The Double-deviant Identity of the Mass-foreigner' (n 4) 313.

[41] This concept of the state is derived from Martin Loughlin, *The Idea of Public Law* (OUP 2003) 58 and 81–86. Loughlin derives it, in turn, from Thomas Hobbes, *Leviathan* (Penguin 1968).

[42] Loughlin (n 41).

the law's subjects to the sovereign's commands is the fundamental condition of the state's *authority*.[43] In so far as the state enjoys this relation of authority with its citizens and subjects—this sovereignty—it forms an autonomous political unit,[44] generating, through the citizens' willing obedience to its commands, enormous *power* to act in pursuit of collective ends.[45] And where one of those commands is disobeyed, punishment is a reassertion of the sovereign's right to obedience over the offender's denial of that right; the practical realisation of the state's sovereignty.[46] In punishing the criminal offender, the sovereign makes good on the state's claim to political authority: that the state alone enjoys a monopoly of legitimate coercion, a critical condition of the state as a political association of all.

However, as Spena points out, where a migrant is liable to administrative expulsion independently of any criminal conviction, the state is not in substance claiming that it has authority over the *unauthorised* migrant such that the breach of immigration rules by the unauthorised migrant is a defiance of that authority.[47] In seeking to expel the person, the state itself declares that it has no expectation of the expelled person's future obedience: the person is not recognised as a subject of that state.[48] Rather than an assertion of its *authority* over the person, the sovereign merely exercises its *power* to expel them,[49] because they are an alien who is within the jurisdiction without any authorisation to be present, and who is, therefore, under no obligation.[50] Spena rightly argues that these offences abuse criminal law by turning it into a facade for administrative measures.[51]

What explains the need for this facade: this misplaced assertion of the state's authority over those whom the state simultaneously denies are subject to it? Spena argues that crimmigration is a sign of weakened sovereignty. He notes Wendy Brown's account of the construction of border walls as a hyperbolic performance of sovereignty that betrays the real decline of political authority:[52]

[43] Drawing on the well-known distinctions of Max Weber, where power is a person's capacity to implement their own will despite resistance, authority is a person's capacity to implement their own will by means of the willing obedience of others to carry out their commands.

[44] Sovereignty is therefore the internal relation of authority that establishes the autonomy of the state with respect to external forces. See Loughlin, The Idea of Public Law (n 41).

[45] For the distinction between power and authority, see n 43.

[46] This thought is derived not from Hobbes but from Malcolm Thorburn, 'Punishment and Public Authority' in Antje du Bois-Pedain and others (eds), *Criminal Law and the Authority of the State* (Hart 2017) 256–63, and Alan Brudner, *The Owl and the Rooster: Hegel's Transformative Political Science* (OUP 2017) 294, who are in turn inspired by Immanuel Kant and GWF Hegel, respectively.

[47] See also Lucia Zedner, 'Is the Criminal Law only for Citizens? A Problem at the Borders of Punishment' in Katja Franko Aas and Mary Bosworth (eds), *The Borders of Punishment: Criminal justice, Citizenship and Social Exclusion* (OUP 2013) 46 and 52.

[48] Note that the sovereign does claim authority to punish an unauthorised migrant who commits a crime that is unrelated to the migrant's unauthorised status. It is only a claim that seeking to expel an unauthorised migrant for any reason is a repudiation of the state's authority over them.

[49] On the power–authority distinction, see n 43 above.

[50] Spena, 'The Double-Deviant Identity of the Mass-foreigner' (n 4) 314.

[51] Alessandro Spena, 'Iniuria Migrandi: Criminalization of Immigrants and the Basic Principles of the Criminal Law' (2014) 8 Criminal Law and Philosophy 635, 654.

[52] Wendy Brown, *Walled States, Waning Sovereignty* (Zone Books 2010) 24.

> While walls provide the scenery, crimmigration provides the script. Both are epiphenomena of a—more theatrical than effective—attempt to re-nationalize the political discourse as a way of compensating for the economic and political uncertainty brought about by globalization; in both cases, states resort to coercion, to brute force, as a substitute for their waning authority.[53]

The state's power is being asserted by crimmigration laws, but in the form of a pretence to sovereignty: a pretence that implies a weakening of the real thing. As we shall see, there is much to recommend this answer. However, as I observed at the beginning, Spena identifies the cause of the declining sovereignty of the state in the process of globalisation, but does not explain why he thinks this external source of limits on the state's sovereignty is the primary or independent source of its internal limits. The criminal law itself gives us good reason to doubt this causal explanation. Border walls are not the only 'scenery' for the waning of sovereign authority, and crimmigration provides only a small part of the 'script'. The specific 'abuse' of the criminal law that Spena describes is practised much more widely than crimmigration law, including in areas with no particular connection to borders or migrants. The waning of the state's authority is not only, or even primarily, found in its handling of unwelcome foreigners. Moreover, investigating this wider jurisdiction will show why crimmigration laws are necessarily 'more theatrical than effective' as a means to 're-nationalize the political discourse'.

V The Exceptionalisation of Normality

Spena observes that, in so far as irregular migrants escape deportation in practice, but are nevertheless committing crimmigration offences by their mere presence, they become 'a category of outcasts', a type of dangerous persons who deserve punishment by virtue of their irregular status.[54] He argues that this punitive approach to irregular migrants is 'xenophobic',[55] and indeed the legitimacy of these laws necessarily entails constructing poor foreigners as a threat. However, as Lucia Zedner notes, migrants are far from alone in being constructed in this way:

> contemporary penal politics ... is prone to identify 'monsters and aliens', not only on our borders but also in our midst.... The antisocial youth, the sex offender, and the would-be terrorist, through their proclivities or conduct, are seen to have breached civic trust and, in so doing, to have placed themselves outside civil society.[56]

Most areas of the criminal law in the UK have been extended in recent years to permit the authorities to identify those who are hostile or indifferent to the norms of the legal order and punish them for that hostility or indifference. Pre-emptive offences of

[53] Spena, 'The Double-deviant Identity of the Mass-foreigner' (n 4) 310.
[54] ibid 312.
[55] ibid.
[56] Zedner (n 47) 48.

preparation, facilitation, and possession have proliferated in relation to assaults, sexual offences, domestic violence, vandalism, public order, terrorism, fraud, and organised crime.[57] These offences create liability for conduct that merely corroborates an ulterior intent to commit an offence, or is merely capable of facilitating an offence. Indeed, the UK has innovated an entire form of liability—the preventive order—through which individuals who are identified by courts as representing a threat of criminal offending are threatened with punishment for highly specific facilitating conduct that remains legal for everyone else.[58]

Many of these offences pre-emptively coerce the non-harmful conduct of people identified in some way as dangerous. They serve to incapacitate persons for their hostility or indifference to the norms of the legal order.[59] These are offences that permit the identification of the disloyal and their punishment for disloyalty.[60] They have been appropriately characterised as 'enemy criminal laws'—offences that aim to neutralise an external threat—as opposed to 'citizen criminal laws' that aim to correct or to communicate with persons subject to the state's authority.[61] These offences assume the future disobedience of those convicted of them; they assume that the state lacks authority over those against whom the criminal law is exercised. In other words, by pre-emptively incapacitating dangerous people for the crimes the state anticipates they will commit, these offences have the characteristics of emergency powers deployed against the state's enemies in times of war; but they have the formal status of normal laws and no emergency is formally declared. These offences tend to make emergency into the permanent and normal condition of society, and this provides the larger 'script' of waning sovereignty.

These enemy criminal laws are the inverse of the much discussed 'normalisation of the state of exception', in which powers taken to deal with an emergency are never withdrawn. These offences have the content of emergency powers but are compliant with the European Convention on Human Rights (ECHR) and are found in ordinary statutes. Rather than normalising the state of exception, these offences 'exceptionalize the state of normality'.[62] The normal order encompasses powers that assume an exceptional challenge to the state's authority.[63] But this challenge comes not from a powerful foreign state or an influential separatist movement, but rather from the quotidian

[57] See Peter Ramsay, *The Insecurity State: Vulnerable Autonomy and the Right to Security in the Criminal Law* (OUP 2012) ch 7.

[58] See Andrew Ashworth and Lucia Zedner, *Preventive Justice* (OUP 2014) ch 4.

[59] Ramsay, *The Insecurity State* (n 57) 191–93.

[60] George Fletcher, *Basic Concepts in Criminal Law* (OUP 1998) 179.

[61] The coinage belongs to the German theorist Günther Jakobs. See Daniel Ohana, 'Günther Jakobs's Feindstrafrecht: A Dispassionate Account' in Markus Dubber (ed), *Foundational Texts in Criminal Law* (OUP 2014) 353–372; Carlos Gomez-Jara Diez, 'Enemy Combatants versus Enemy Criminal Law' (2008) 11(4) New Criminal Law Review 529.

[62] Ramsay, *The Insecurity State* (n 57) 215.

[63] The most striking way in which pre-emptive offences exceptionalise normality is that they formally adhere to the presumption of innocence while subverting it in substance. See Peter Ramsay, 'Preparation Offences, Security Interests, Political Freedom' in Antony Duff and others (eds), *The Structures of the Criminal Law* (OUP 2011) 216–19. On the significance of the presumption of innocence to the state's authority, see Peter Ramsay, 'The Sovereign's Presumption of Authority (Also Known as the Presumption of Innocence)' (2020) LSE Legal Studies Working Paper 15/2020, available at <https://papers.ssrn.com/sol3/papers.cfm?abstract_id=3743730>.

unlawfulness of drug dealers, fraudsters, youth gangs, drunks, football hooligans, vandals, misogynists, and paedophiles.

When the sovereign passes laws that construct the possibility of ordinary crimes as if they were a mortal threat to the state, requiring exceptional measures, it is assuming the permanent weakness of the state as a political association. The sovereign is presenting the normal condition not as one of a commonwealth, in which some citizens may from time to time fail to be obedient to the sovereign's commands, but as one in which citizens are permanently vulnerable to the predation of 'enemies' who need to be incapacitated. These offences seem to confirm Brown's analysis of a weakening of the nation state's authority taking the form of a hyperbolic performance of state power.

However, most of these pre-emptive offences, and the enemies of the state that they seek to incapacitate, have no particular connection to the phenomena of global labour markets and have arisen independently of globalisation. Again, what this wider jurisdiction suggests is that the decline of the state's sovereignty is not something experienced solely, or even primarily, at its external borders that irregular migrants have crossed. Rather, the expansion of crimmigration is another occasion for the *endogenous* waning of sovereignty to manifest itself in the form of criminalisation. The crimmigration offences add little or nothing to the state's capacity to control the border, but they serve to add poor foreigners, preparing to work in low-paid jobs without government authorisation, to the long list of everyday enemies of the state, who are subject to administrative detention dressed up as punishment for wrongdoing.

Crucial to this theory of the endogenous waning of sovereignty is the relative lack of potency of the threats that are invoked to rationalise the exceptionalising of normality. The state's enemies need to be incapacitated not because they are strong but because the state is weak. And if we think about the source of this weakness, we can see why pre-emptive criminalisation, such as that found in crimmigration laws, will only ever amount to what Spena calls a 'more theatrical than effective ... attempt to renationalize political discourse'.[64]

VI The Decay of the Nation

The internal sovereignty of any sovereign state consists in the authority of the political institutions through which its citizens are ruled. The willingness of citizens to obey the laws of the sovereign that represents their association depends to a large degree on the legitimacy of the institutions through which the sovereign represents the state. Legitimacy, in this context, is a social-scientific concept, not a philosophical one. The state's authority is not a question of whether its governing institutions meet the requirement of an abstract philosophical theory, but of whether the authority of those institutions is accepted by those over whom they rule.[65] Without legitimacy, the sovereign and its governing institutions may struggle to achieve willing obedience.

A strong state will, therefore, develop various national traditions and institutions that invest its institutions with legitimacy. This legitimacy often has an ideological

[64] See text at n 53.

[65] For a discussion, see David Beetham, *The Legitimation of Power* (Macmillan 1991) 11–16.

quality; that is, it relies on belief in arguable, partial truths that nevertheless give substance and credibility to the existing sovereign institutions in their claim to represent all citizens. Providing that the ideology is accepted by citizens, then legitimacy in this social-scientific sense will be secured. In the UK, for example, the 'Crown in Parliament' has been legally sovereign for more than three centuries. Parliament was slowly democratised, a process that permitted the UK, by the middle of the twentieth century, to understand itself as a democratic welfare state that sought to uphold the civil liberty of its citizens and ensure an adequate equality of status and material wealth among them.[66] The Crown meanwhile maintained itself as the ceremonial head of a national religion—the unifier of the English, Welsh, and Scottish peoples that made up the United Kingdom—a kingdom that was, for more than a century, the metropolis of a global empire.

It is the decay of these national traditions, especially as it manifests itself in the minds of politicians and other public officials, that has given rise to the current era of exceptionalised normality. Compelling evidence for this decay can be found in a legal case that concerned both the particular threat that is generally regarded as the most serious of those that have been countered with pre-emptive criminalisation, and dangerous persons who were foreign refugees. The government's claim in this case revealed that the official conception of the emergency that requires exceptional measures is one that assumes the most impoverished idea of the nation imaginable.

The *Belmarsh* case was a challenge to a classic emergency power to detain foreign terrorist suspects without trial,[67] a power that the UK government enacted in the wake of the 9/11 attacks in the USA.[68] The statutory power required a derogation from Article 5 ECHR, on the grounds of a 'public emergency threatening the life of the nation': grounds that are set out in Article 15 ECHR. The majority of the House of Lords deferred to the executive's judgement that there was such an emergency. However, Lord Hoffmann dissented, on the basis that the Attorney General had not supplied any evidence of a threat to the life of the nation,[69] and his judgment exposes the underlying assumptions about 'the life of the nation' held by the mainstream of the political class.

The Attorney General had submitted that, 'an emergency could properly be regarded as imminent if an atrocity was credibly threatened by a body such as Al-Qaeda which had demonstrated its capacity and will to carry out such a threat, where the atrocity might be committed without warning at any time'.[70] Lord Hoffmann's objection was

[66] See Thomas H Marshall, *Citizenship and Social Class* (Pluto Press 1987).

[67] *A v Secretary of State for the Home Department* [2004] UKHL 56.

[68] Anti-Terrorism, Crime and Security Act 2001, s 23.

[69] Influential legal commentators (see, eg David Dyzenhaus, 'An Unfortunate Outburst of Anglo-Saxon Parochialism' (2005) 68(4) Modern Law Review 673, 674–75) have interpreted Lord Hoffmann's judgment as contradicting his own earlier ruling, where he endorsed the conventional position that the judiciary should defer to the executive in assessing what is 'in the interests of national security' (*Secretary of State for the Home Department v Rehman* [2001] UKHL 47, [50]. However, in *Rehman*, Lord Hoffmann was also careful to point out that '[w]hat is meant by "national security" is ... a question of law ... subject to appeal' (*Rehman*, [50]). He also observed that the executive was legally required to bring some evidence of a claimed risk to national security (*Rehman*, [54]). On the reading of his *Belmarsh* judgment offered here, Lord Hoffmann was not second-guessing the executive's assessment of the degree of risk to national security, but applying the legal meaning of 'the life of the nation', and finding that the Attorney General had offered no evidence of a threat to it.

[70] *A v Secretary of State for the Home Department* (n 67), [25].

that the Attorney General's submission 'treated a threat of serious physical damage and loss of life as necessarily involving a threat to the life of the nation'.[71] The true position, Lord Hoffmann believed, was that 'the life of the nation is not coterminous with the lives of its people. The nation, its institutions and values, endure through generations.'[72] His judgment waxed patriotic, referring to the Spanish Armada, the aftermath of Dunkirk, and the Provisional IRA as examples of real threats to the life of the nation: threats that were seen off. And he concluded that the Attorney General had not brought adequate evidence of any such threat: '[t]here may be some nations too fragile or fissiparous to withstand a serious act of violence. But that is not the case in the United Kingdom.'[73]

What is compelling for our purposes is that Lord Hoffmann's view was isolated. The majority was content to accept the executive's judgement that a threat to the lives of nationals did indeed amount to a threat to the life of the nation and, implicitly, that the nation was so fragile that it might not withstand a serious act of violence. Both the Attorney General's claim, and the House of Lords' acceptance of it, reduced 'the life of the nation' to the bare lives of its nationals. The institutional coherence of the nation had simply vanished from the thinking of ministers in a government that was particularly keen to criminalise breaches of immigration rules.

Of course, in practice, the government was simply trying to get its preferred policy through the courts while the judicial majority was trying to steer clear of potential political controversy.[74] Nevertheless, the way to achieve these aims was to assume away the institutional life of the nation. Why was this possible? The constitutional institutions and the symbols of national unity that were outlined above have not ceased to function entirely or to provide any legitimacy. They can nevertheless be thought of as *failing* adequately to represent the nation as a unified political association.

Parliament has long been held in widespread public contempt;[75] the monarchy is still esteemed by a majority of British citizens, though to some considerable extent this may be reserved for the person of the Queen herself. Her successor is not popular, and opinion of the wider 'royal family' is mixed.[76] The state religion has been reduced to a rump. The British Empire is long gone. The Union of England and Wales with both Scotland and Northern Ireland is now in a parlous condition. The only national institutions that seem to have a uniting effect across the whole territory are, significantly, those most associated with preserving the lives of nationals: the National Health Service, the fire brigade, and to a lesser extent, the armed forces.[77]

[71] ibid [95].

[72] ibid [91].

[73] Ibid [95].

[74] The majority judgment declared that the detention power was incompatible with the ECHR on the grounds that the particular interference with liberty was disproportionate and discriminated against foreigners. Parliament responded to the judgment with the terrorism Control Order, a key example of a preventive order with the content of an emergency power, but requiring no emergency derogation; an 'ordinary' legal power with the content of emergency power; an exceptionalisation of normality.

[75] Matthew Smith, 'The NHS is the Institution that Brits are Second Most Proud of—After the Fire Brigade' (*YouGov*, 2018) <https://yougov.co.uk/topics/politics/articles-reports/2018/07/04/nhs-british-institution-brits-are-second-most-proud> accessed 18 November 2021.

[76] ibid.

[77] ibid.

The failure of most of these institutions to do the work of representing the British people as a unified nation state represents the decay of that state. In a representative democracy, the failure of the established political parties adequately to represent the electorate, and the disdain with which democratic politics is viewed by ordinary citizens, is a particularly significant aspect of the decay of national life: a phenomenon that is not limited to the UK.[78] The hyperbolic theatrics of crimmigration, and of pre-emptive criminalisation generally, are among the phenomena of an endogenous decline in the life of the nation as an autonomous political association. The state's performance of sovereign power betrays a deficit of sovereign authority, and underlying that deficit is the decay in the nation's political life through the creeping failure of its institutions to represent the people as a unified political association. The performance of sovereign power that is caused by this failure, whether within the territory or at its borders, does not address the causes of this decay of political authority, but only covers it up.

VII Conclusion

I have argued that privatisation of state coercion serves as a means of distancing both government and citizenry from their political responsibilities for the state—a process that is indicative of waning sovereignty—and that there is a comparable political evasiveness in the migration offences which provide a performance of sovereign power that seeks to obscure the decline in sovereign authority. The point I have emphasised is that the source of this declining sovereignty is not external to the state but comes from within.

Of course, much more remains to be said about why migrants are among the targets of a politics whose origin lies in the weakness of the nation state; there is more to be said about the relation of sovereign authority to migration, and about the relation of domestic political authority to the government of labour markets, on the one hand, and to the manipulation of racial and ethnic differences, on the other. I have not sought to argue that global labour flows are unimportant, only that the response to changes in labour markets and labour mobility cannot be understood in isolation from the endogenous weakening of the political authority of states.

References

Aliverti A, 'The Wrongs of Unlawful Immigration' (2017) 11 Criminal Law and Philosophy 375

Ashworth A and Zedner L, *Preventive Justice* (OUP 2014)

Baird V and Stone A, 'Why Privatization? The Case of German Telecommunications' (1998) 79(1) Social Science Quarterly 193

Beetham D, *The Legitimation of Power* (Macmillan 1991)

[78] For a compelling account, see Peter Mair, *Ruling the Void: The Hollowing of Western Democracy* (Verso 2013).

Bosworth M, 'Border Control and the Limits of the Sovereign State' (2008) 17 Social & Legal Studies 199

Boubakri N, Cosset JC, Debab N and Valery P, 'Privatization and Globalization: An Empirical Analysis' (2013) 37 Journal of Banking & Finance 1898

Brown W, *Walled States, Waning Sovereignty* (Zone Books 2010)

Brudner A, *The Owl and the Rooster: Hegel's Transformative Political Science* (OUP 2017)

De Genova N and Peutz N, *The Deportation Regime: Sovereignty, Space, and the Freedom of Movement* (Duke University Press 2010)

Diez CG-J, 'Enemy Combatants versus Enemy Criminal Law' (2008) 11(4) New Criminal Law Review 529

Dorfman A and Harel A, 'The Case against Privatization' (2013) 41 Philosophy & Public Affairs 67

Dyzenhaus D, 'An Unfortunate Outburst of Anglo-Saxon Parochialism' (2005) 68(4) Modern Law Review 673

Feeley M, 'The Unconvincing Case against Private Prisons' (2014) 89(4) Indiana Law Journal 1401

Fletcher G, *Basic Concepts in Criminal Law* (OUP 1998)

Franko Aas K, 'The Ordered and the Bordered Society: Migration Control, Citizenship, and the Northern Penal State' in Aas K F and Bosworth M (eds), *The Borders of Punishment* (OUP 2013)

Gallo ZA, 'Punishment, Authority and Political Economy: Italian Challenges to Western Punitiveness' (2015) 17(5) Punishment & Society 598

Hobbes T, *Leviathan* (Penguin 1968)

Hodge GA, *Privatization and Market Development* (Edward Elgar 2006)

Loughlin M, 'Why Sovereignty?' in Rawlings R, Leyland P, and Young A (eds), *Sovereignty and the Law* (OUP 2013)

— —, *The Idea of Public Law* (OUP 2003)

Mair P, *Ruling the Void: The Hollowing of Western Democracy* (Verso 2013)

Marshall TH, *Citizenship and Social Class* (Pluto Press 1987)

Mitchell W and Fazi T, *Reclaiming the State: A Progressive Vision of Sovereignty for the Post-neoliberal World* (Pluto Press 2017)

Ohana D, 'Günther Jakobs's Feindstrafrecht: A Dispassionate Account' in Dubber M (ed), *Foundational Texts in Criminal Law* (OUP 2014)

Oztig LI, 'Rethinking Sovereignty: The Implications of the Role of Private Security Companies in the Prevention and the Regulation of Unauthorized Flows' (2020) 33(3) Cambridge Review of International Affairs 330

Petersena OH, Hjelmarb U, and Vrangbæk K, 'Is Contracting out of Public Services still the Great Panacea? A Systematic Review of Studies on Economic and Quality Effects from 2000 to 2014' (2018) 52(1) Social Policy and Administration 130

Ramsay P, 'Preparation Offences, Security Interests, Political Freedom' in Duff RA and others (eds), *The Structures of the Criminal Law* (OUP 2011)

— —, *The Insecurity State: Vulnerable Autonomy and the Right to Security in the Criminal Law* (OUP 2012)

— —, 'The Sovereign's Presumption of Authority (Also Known as the Presumption of Innocence)' (2020) LSE Legal Studies Working Paper 15/2020, available at <https://papers.ssrn.com/sol3/papers.cfm?abstract_id=3743730

Smith M, 'The NHS is the Institution that Brits are Second Most Proud of—After the Fire Brigade' (*YouGov*, 2018) <https://yougov.co.uk/topics/politics/articles-reports/2018/07/04/nhs-british-institution-brits-are-second-most-proud>

Spena A, 'Iniuria Migrandi: Criminalization of Immigrants and the Basic Principles of the Criminal Law' (2014) 8 Criminal Law and Philosophy 635

— —, 'The Double-deviant Identity of the Mass-foreigner and the Lack of Authority of the Crimmigrationist State' (2019) (22) 3 New Criminal Law Review 301

Strange S, *The Retreat of the State* (CUP 1996)

Streeck W, 'Citizens as Customers: Considerations on the New Politics of Consumption' (2012) 27 New Left Review, 43

Stumpf J, 'The Crimmigration Crisis: Immigrants, Crime, and Sovereign Power' (2006) 56 American University Law Review 367

Thorburn M, 'Punishment and Public Authority' in du Bois-Pedain A and others (eds), *Criminal Law and the Authority of the State* (Hart 2017)

— —, 'Reinventing the Nightwatchman State' (2010) 60(2) University of Toronto Law Journal 425

Vasanthakumar A, 'Privatising Border Control' (2018) 38 Oxford Journal of Legal Studies 411

Verkuil PB, *Outsourcing Sovereignty* (CUP 2009)

Zedner L, 'Is the Criminal Law only for Citizens? A Problem at the Borders of Punishment' in Franko Aas K and Bosworth M (eds), *The Borders of Punishment: Criminal Justice, Citizenship and Social Exclusion* (OUP 2013)

Legislation

Anti-Terrorism, Crime and Security Act 2001

Cases

A v Secretary of State for the Home Department [2004] UKHL 56

Secretary of State for the Home Department v Rehman [2001] UKHL 47

PART II
LEGITIMACY AND THE RULE OF THE LAW AT THE BORDER

4

Roles and Offices at the Border

Is Privatising Border Control Intrinsically Illegitimate?

*Malcolm Thorburn**

I Introduction

In many jurisdictions, almost every aspect of border control is outsourced to almost every sort of private actor. In the United Kingdom, the United States, and Australia, for example, many aspects of border security have been contracted out to private, for-profit security companies such as G4S and Blackwater.[1] In Italy, the Red Cross, Misericordia d'Italia, and other non-profit non-governmental organisations have been contracted to carry out key border control tasks.[2] In the United Kingdom, the Home Office's so-called 'Compliant Environment' policy requires private citizens to identify and report possible illegal immigrants or face civil proceedings, or even prosecution and punishment.[3] And in the United States, the state has tolerated gun-toting private actors such as the self-styled 'Minutemen' and 'United Constitutional Patriots', who detain would-be migrants at the Mexican border.[4] The forms of privatisation are various,[5] but the general phenomenon is unmistakable: what was thought of as a core

* Professor and Chair in the Legal, Ethical, and Cultural Implications of Technological Innovation, Faculty of Law, University of Toronto. Comments welcome: malcolm.thorburn@utoronto.ca.

[1] On G4S in the UK, see Mattha Busby, 'G4S to Leave Immigration Sector after Brook House Scandal' *The Guardian* (London, 24 September 2019) <https://www.theguardian.com/business/2019/sep/24/g4s-to-leave-immigration-sector-after-brook-house-scandal> accessed 18 November 2021. On private immigration detention facilities in the US, see Alejandro Lazo, 'Private Prisons could See Fortunes Change under Biden Immigration Policy' *Wall Street Journal* (New York, 30 April 2021) <https://www.wsj.com/articles/private-prisons-could-see-fortunes-change-under-biden-immigration-policy-11619800623> accessed 18 November 2021. On the situation in Australia, see Australian Human Rights Commission, 'A Last Resort?—Summary Guide: The Facts about Immigration Detention in Australia' <https://humanrights.gov.au/our-work/last-resort-summary-guide-facts-about-immigration-detention-australia> accessed 18 November 2021.

[2] From 1998, the Red Cross ran the first Italian detention centre on the island of Lampedusa. Until 2014, the Red Cross ran a number of administrative detention centres in Italy. In 2014, the private, for-profit corporation GEPSA won the contract with a bid 30 per cent lower than what the Red Cross had submitted. For more details, see Lydie Arbogast, *Migrant Detention in the European Union: A Thriving Business* (Rosa Luxemburg Stiftung 2016).

[3] See Zedner, in this volume, for discussion.

[4] Paul A Reyes, 'The US–Mexico Border isn't Protected by Militias, it's Patrolled by Domestic Terrorists' (*NBC News*, 22 April 2019) <https://www.nbcnews.com/think/opinion/u-s-mexico-border-isn-t-protected-militias-it-s-ncna997056> accessed 18 November 2021.

[5] I set out three different types of privatisation modalities—contracting out, vouchers, and retreat—in an earlier paper: Malcolm Thorburn, 'Reinventing the Nightwatchman State?' (2010) 60(2) University of Toronto Law Journal 425.

Malcolm Thorburn, *Roles and Offices at the Border* In: *Privatising Border Control*. Edited by: Mary Bosworth and Lucia Zedner, Oxford University Press. © Malcolm Thorburn 2022. DOI: 10.1093/oso/9780192857163.003.0005

aspect of state sovereignty[6] for much of the twentieth century is now more often carried out by non-state entities.

There is already a voluminous literature on the many negative policy outcomes associated with the outsourcing of border control: waste, corruption, incompetence, harm to vulnerable people, arbitrary or discriminatory application of the law, and much more. I will not review these negative policy outcomes here, in part because they receive thorough treatment in several other chapters of this volume. Instead, my focus here is on the current debate in legal theory about whether privatising border control is *intrinsically* illegitimate, whatever the policy consequences. Contemporary legal theory scholarship on this question is divided into two broad camps.

In the first camp—which I shall call the 'statists'—are those who argue that the privatisation of a number of traditionally state-provided services (including border control, policing, war-making, criminal punishment, etc.) is intrinsically illegitimate because it is the state and only the state that has the moral standing to carry them out. I have long advocated a version of this position.[7] The statist position is also supported by legal and political theorists such as Alon Harel, Avihay Dorfman, Chiara Cordelli, and Arthur Ripstein, and it has a long and distinguished pedigree in legal and political thought, particularly in the social contract tradition of Rousseau and Kant.[8] According to the statist account, some activities lose their justification unless they are carried out by the right agents. Granting forgiveness, for example, is not a task that can be performed by just anyone: *I* can forgive those who have wronged *me*, but you (usually) cannot. This remains true even if I am foolish and reprobate, and you are brilliant and kind. The point is that *you* simply do not have the moral standing to forgive those who have wronged *me*. Border control, the statists argue, is like forgiveness in this respect: it is a task that loses its justification if it is carried out by the wrong agent. Since it is the state and only the state that has both the legal and moral standing to determine who shall pass its borders, the actions of private actors in this area, no matter how competent and well-intentioned they might be, are illegitimate.

[6] In 1933, the Montevideo Convention crystallised the idea that the border creates the state: Convention on Rights and Duties of States adopted by the Seventh International Conference of American States (adopted 26 December 1933, entered into force 26 December 1934) LNTS 165, 19, art I: '[t]he State as a person of international law should possess the following qualifications: (a) a permanent population; (b) *a defined territory*; (c) government; and (d) capacity to enter into relations with the other States' (emphasis added). See also *Territorial Dispute (Libyan Arab Jamahiriya/Chad) (Merits)* [1994] ICJ Rep 6, 26, para 52, whereby 'to "define" a territory is to define its frontiers'). In 1910, the Permanent Court of Arbitration affirmed that '[o]ne of the essential elements of sovereignty is that it is to be exercised within territorial limits, and, failing proof to the contrary, the territory is coterminous with the sovereignty' (*Atlantic Coast Fisheries Case (Great Britain, United States)* (1910) RIAA vol IX, 180).

[7] See, eg Malcolm Thorburn, 'Justifications, Powers, and Authority' (2008) 117(6) Yale Law Journal 1070.; Malcolm Thorburn, 'Criminal Law as Public Law' in RA Duff and Stuart Green (eds), *Philosophical Foundations of Criminal Law* (OUP 2010) 21–43; Thorburn, 'Reinventing the Nightwatchman State' (n 5); Malcolm Thorburn, 'Policing and Public Office' (2020) 70(2) University of Toronto Law Journal 248.

[8] The statist view is also central to the landmark decision of the Israeli Supreme Court, HCJ 2605/05 *Academic Center of Law and Business v Minister of Finance* (2009) <http://www.privateci.org/private_pics/Israel_Ruling.pdf> accessed 18 November 2021, on the constitutionality of privatising prisons. In that landmark decision, the Israeli Supreme Court ruled decisively against deprivation of liberty by private actors, on social contract grounds. See, at 23: 'the state, through the various bodies acting in it, is responsible for public security and the enforcement of the criminal law has remained unchanged throughout all those years, and it is a part of the social contract on which the modern democratic state is also based'.

What makes the statist argument about standing especially complex is that it concerns the agency of an artificial corporate person: the state. When talking about natural persons, it is usually quite easy to distinguish those who have standing from others who do not. But when talking about the artificial corporate person of the state, things get more complicated. The basic point here, though, can be expressed fairly simply: if a task must only be carried out by the state in order for it to be legitimate, then those who carry it out must not only act in the state's interest, or at the state's behest; they must be parts of *the state itself*.[9] So, for statists, the crucial question about the privatisation of border control is whether we can still maintain that frontline officials are acting not only in the state's interest or at its behest, but whether they *are* (parts of) *the state itself* as they do so.

The second, rival account of privatisation is provided by those I call 'moral individualists'. This is a large and influential camp in legal philosophy that includes philosophers of state authority such as Joseph Raz, philosophers of criminal law such as John Gardner, philosophers in revisionist just war theory such as Jeff McMahan, and scholars of migration such as Ashwini Vasanthakumar.[10] On this account, any talk of the moral agency of the state is metaphysical nonsense.[11] In the real world, the moral individualists argue, the only moral agents are individual human beings exercising their agency subject to the universal demands of interpersonal morality. Of course, in the real world, people organise their shared lives in ways that often involve moral roles—border control officials among them—that come with extraordinary powers, privileges, and deference. In so far as those roles are morally justified, they should be accompanied by a great number of obligations (to exercise those powers for good reasons, wisely, reasonably, and so on). But, the moral individualists continue, the morally significant aspect of being a border control agent is not that one is a part of the state (and therefore acting in its name), but only that one occupies this morally special role. Any connection between the legitimacy of border control and the status of border agents as public officials is purely contingent.

This chapter is a defence of the statist view about law more generally, and of border control in particular, against the claims of moral individualists. I set out that defence, however, in what might be viewed as a rather peculiar way. I do not simply articulate what I take to be the best case for the statist position and answer the challenges from moral individualists. Instead, I work my account around a critique of Dorfman and Harel's influential statist account as set out by prominent moral individualist and migration scholar Ashwini Vasanthakumar. I do so, in part, to illustrate how the very nature of the dispute between the two camps has been quite frequently—and deeply—mischaracterised. Vasanthakumar's challenge is typical, I believe, of a number of moral

[9] Dorfman and Harel cite Hobbes, who makes this point explicit. The Commonwealth is 'but an artificial man', and state officials are parts of that artificial man: viz, its 'joints': Thomas Hobbes, *Leviathan* (Richard Tuck ed, CUP 1991) 9, cited in Avihay Dorfman and Alon Harel, 'The Case against Privatisation' (2013) 41 Philosophy & Public Affairs 67, 71.

[10] See Vasanthakumar, in this volume, for further elaboration of this account.

[11] The modern origin of this view lies in the work of Jeremy Bentham, who took great pride in identifying ideas (such as natural rights) that he took to be 'nonsense' in moral and political thought. Its contemporary revival is attributable, above all, to Joseph Raz, *The Morality of Freedom* (OUP 1982). I have discussed the intellectual origins of this way of thinking about public authority and the public–private distinction in Thorburn, 'Policing and Public Office' (n 8) 264ff.

individualist critiques of statist positions that portray their critique as though it were a disagreement between two rival answers to the same question. Because Dorfman and Harel frame their discussion in terms of frontline actors' reasons for action, one might think that the intrinsic problem with privatisation is reducible to a set of one-off worries about border agents' reasons. If we see the intrinsic problem of privatisation in this way, we might be tempted to think (with the moral individualists) that it can be solved by regulating the reasons for which frontline border agents carry out their duties.

As I demonstrate below, however, the intrinsic argument against privatisation cannot be solved merely by addressing a series of one-off problems about the reasoning of frontline officials. Instead, the disagreement goes to the very foundations of legal order and the nature of political authority itself. To make this clear, I argue, the statist position ought to be put even more boldly than Dorfman and Harel admit. Instead of their account of public office, which focuses on reasons, I advocate a more robust account, which can be found in the statuses of *fonctionnaire* in French law or of the *Beamter* in German law. The basic point here is that the state is not made up of natural persons, but of interconnected *public offices*, each endowed with a set of powers and privileges and each directed at a set of defining public purposes. When natural persons carry out the duties of a public office, their decisions and acts are properly attributable to their office, not to them personally. Dorfman and Harel's talk of 'fidelity by deference' and 'community of practice' captures some of that picture, but not all of it. Their account leaves out other crucial features of public office: entry into and exit from public offices, for example, should occur only according to certain public legal procedures. Further, not only are those who occupy public office generally trained in a certain ethos of public service, they are also protected from influence by private reasons through devices such as the protection of salary and tenure of office, and prohibitions on participating in outside activities such as unions, political parties, and the like. These features of public office are not designed merely to affect the reasons for which officials act; their ultimate purpose is to define the office, thereby changing the status of frontline officials from independent actors to parts of the state itself.

This chapter proceeds in four sections. In section II, I review some of the better-known examples of privatisation of border security. Since other chapters in this book examine these in much greater detail, I do so only very briefly in order to highlight the novelty of this phenomenon, and to point out the many structurally different ways in which governments have outsourced border security. In section III, I review Dorfman and Harel's statist account of the public nature of border control together with an adjustment to their argument provided by Chiara Cordelli. In section IV, I consider Vasanthakumar's moral individualist argument for some limited privatisation of border control, largely on the grounds that public border control officials are representatives of an alien despotic power exerting unilateral power over migrants. I provide my rejoinder to that claim: legitimate states are not tools for carrying out the partisan will of their citizens; they are institutions whose legitimacy turns on their ability to secure rights and ensure justice within a jurisdiction. Public offices must be secured not only against the private purposes of corporations, but also against the partisan private purposes of populist politicians. The central virtues of legitimate public office, I argue, remain even when officials are dealing with strangers who are not represented within their ranks. Section V concludes by insisting that what is wrong with state-run border security calls for reform from the inside, rather than privatisation.

II Privatised Border Security Today

The privatisation of border control is a fairly recent phenomenon, but the public provision of border control does not have a very long history either. As many scholars have pointed out, although the defence of borders has been a defining feature of state sovereignty at least since the time of the Peace of Westphalia in the mid seventeenth century, it has usually concerned the defence of borders against rival claims of sovereignty, often backed up by invading armies rather than against the migration of alien civilians. In English legal history, statutes concerned with immigration and naturalisation were enacted as specific migration crises erupted—the flight of Huguenots from Louis XIV's France resulted in the Foreign Protestants Naturalization Act 1708, the flight of aristocrats from revolutionary France resulted in the Aliens Act 1793, etc—but there were no general prohibitions on immigration, nor was there any standing public institution with powers to control the flow of immigrants. Indeed, for many years prior to the First World War, there were no passport or visa requirements to cross borders in Europe.[12] In the United States, mounted watchmen of the US Immigration Service began to patrol the border in an effort to prevent illegal crossings as early as 1904, but this was an irregular and poorly funded affair. The main focus of immigration enforcement in the US in the early twentieth century was the enforcement of the racist Chinese Exclusion Act of 1882.[13]

Nowadays, this longer history of national border control seems unimaginably distant. The horrific and deadly measures taken at the borders of many wealthy countries—in the Mediterranean Sea off Italy and Greece, in the South Pacific en route to Australia, on the US–Mexican border, and in many other places around the world—remind us that national borders nowadays are often the loci of massive state coercion usually carried out in the name of national sovereignty.[14] As Vaughan Lowe observes, 'it was the twentieth century that saw the major efforts to turn national boundaries that had been drawn on maps into physical obstacles to travel'.[15] And it is now, at the beginning of the twenty-first century, that we see the 'return of borders' in a new and deadly key.[16]

Across the world, the borders of wealthy countries are hardened against immigration from poorer countries through legislation and coercive enforcement. But that coercive enforcement is complex and very costly. In the late twentieth century, many

[12] The situation is slightly more complicated: passport requirements existed in the early nineteenth century but were abolished in the second half of that century. See, eg Maurice Hartoy, *Histoire des passeports français depuis l'Antiquité jusqu'à nos jours* (H Champion 1937).

[13] 22 Stat 58, Chap 126. A similar racist ban on Chinese immigration was passed in Canada in 1923: the Chinese Immigration Act.

[14] In the EU, where it is a matter of 'Fortress Europe', rather than the sovereignty of a specific country, things are rather more complex.

[15] Vaughan Lowe, *International Law* (OUP 2007) 137.

[16] Michel Foucher, *Le Retour des Frontières* (CNRS Editions 2016).

governments joined the trend of 'reinventing government' by outsourcing a variety of traditional government tasks to private providers.[17] Just as they outsourced policing, the management of prisons, and other expensive and complex coercive enforcement mechanisms to private actors, so too with border control.[18] In Australia, most of the work of immigration control is carried out by private contractors including the operation of all its immigration detention centres.[19] In the United Kingdom, immigration detention is also carried out by large private corporations.[20] And in the United States, roughly 70 per cent of those held in immigration detention are incarcerated in privately run centres.[21]

III The Statist Argument against Privatising Border Control

A Fidelity by Deference

In recent years, many legal scholars have raised questions about the legitimacy of this massive expansion and privatisation of state (or state-sponsored) coercion at the border. An enormous scholarly literature has grown up around these developments, considering the positive and negative effects that it might have on a wide variety of outcomes: waste, corruption, harm to vulnerable people, violations of human rights, and more.[22] In that context, Alon Harel has turned the academic conversation toward the intrinsic worries raised by the privatisation of coercive public services. In a series of articles and a book, Harel, often writing together with Avihay Dorfman, has argued that it is in the very nature of many of the goods the state provides that they simply cannot be provided by private agents. The fact that they are provided by private agents fundamentally transforms the nature of the goods in question, undermining their legitimacy.

[17] 'Reinventing government' was the slogan adopted by the Clinton administration in the early 1990s in their efforts to privatise large swathes of government: see David Osborne and Ted Gaebler, *Reinventing Government: How the Entrepreneurial Spirit is Transforming the Public Sector* (Plume 1993).

[18] In 2013, the United States spent more on immigration control than on all federal criminal law enforcement: Ted Hesson, 'Report: US Spends More on Immigration than all Federal Criminal Enforcement Combined' (*ABC News*, 7 January 2013) <https://abcnews.go.com/ABC_Univision/News/us-spends-immigration-major-federal-criminal-enforcement-combined/story?id=18151143#18> accessed 18 November 2021.

[19] See Global Detention Project, *Country Report: Immigration Detention in Australia: Turning Arbitrary Detention into a Global Brand* (Geneva 2022). <https://www.globaldetentionproject.org/countries/asia-pacific/australia> accessed 1 September 2022. See also Vogl, in this volume.

[20] See Global Detention Project, *Country Report: United Kingdom Immigration Detention Profile* (Geneva 2016). <https://www.globaldetentionproject.org/countries/europe/united-kingdom> accessed 1 September 2022. See also Infantino, in this volume.

[21] See Emily Kassie, 'Detained: How the US Built the World's Largest Immigration Detention System' *The Guardian* 2019. <https://www.theguardian.com/us-news/2019/sep/24/detained-us-largest-immigrant-detention-trump> accessed 1 September 2022. See also Chacón; and Ryo and Peacock, both in this volume.

[22] See, inter alia, Paul Verkuil, *Outsourcing Sovereignty: Why Privatization of Government Functions Threatens Democracy and what we can do about it* (CUP 2007); Martha Minow, 'Public and Private Partnerships: Accounting for the New Religion' (2003) 116 Harvard Law Review 1129; Jody Freeman and Martha Minow (eds), *Government by Contract: Outsourcing and American Democracy* (Harvard University Press 2009).

Dorfman and Harel argue that certain tasks are 'inherently public goods' and therefore ought not to be outsourced. What makes them inherently public, according to Dorfman and Harel, is that their justifying purpose—which, in the case of punishment, is 'the judgment made by the polity concerning the wrongfulness of an act'[23]—is tied inextricably to their being carried out by the state.[24] For hard treatment to serve as criminal punishment, they insist, it must communicate that message of judgement *by the polity*. Put another way, when a private actor goes through the same motions as a state official—say, locking up an offender in a prison cell—it simply constitutes (unjustified) violence, rather than (at least potentially justified) punishment. To be clear, Dorfman and Harel are not suggesting that the state will always punish *well*—conscious of public values, human dignity, etc.—but only that its acts can, at least, constitute criminal punishment. If private actors were to do the same things, they would not constitute criminal punishment of *any* kind: good, bad, or indifferent.

It is not obvious how Dorfman and Harel might extend their argument about inherently public goods and the communicative function of punishment to the area of border control. Political philosopher Chiara Cordelli proposes a more general criterion to do the work here, flowing from the social contract tradition of Rousseau and Kant. Under the rule of law, she suggests, we cannot avoid having our rights and duties authoritatively determined by *someone* (for without this, we do not live under the rule of law).[25] But our claim to dignity as free and equal persons demands that the determination of our rights and duties should not be unilaterally imposed upon us by others. To live at the mercy of someone else's judgement about the determination of our rights and duties is to live under a form of despotism. We cannot each claim to be the authority over our own rights and duties for that would be a return to the state of nature and its own sort of chaotic despotism. The only way to avoid despotism is to ensure that we establish an entity—call it 'the state'—that can make these determinations for us all, in the name of us all. In short, the state arises as a solution to the problem that has been at the centre of political philosophy at least since the time of Rousseau: '[T]o find a form of association which will defend and protect with the whole common force the person and the goods of each associate, and in which each, *while uniting himself with all, may still obey himself alone, and remain as free as before*.'[26] Public officials can act in our collective name, but private contractors can only ever act in their own name. The problem of privatisation, then, cannot be solved merely by regulating the reasons for which frontline agents act, for the problem does not lie in the *reasoning* of private contractors. The real problem here concerns the status of the decision-maker to which we are subject: we need to ensure that, whenever our rights and duties are

[23] Dorfman and Harel (n 9) 69.

[24] In Malcolm Thorburn, 'Judgment, Communication and Coercion: What's Wrong with Private Prisons?' (2015) 2 Critical Analysis of Law 234, I criticised Harel and Dorfman's understanding of what makes punishment an inherently public matter, arguing that the real worry about standing comes from a larger Kantian worry about freedom as independence, rather than the communicative function of punishment. In their 2013 article (n 9), however, they insist (at 90) merely that 'we do not defend the underlying standard justifications of punishment and war used in the main text below. We merely show that given these justifications, it is only the state that can provide these goods.'

[25] Chiara Cordelli, *The Privatized State* (Princeton University Press 2020) 61–62.

[26] Jean-Jacques Rousseau, 'The Social Contract' in *The Social Contract and Discourses* (GDH Cole tr, JM Dent & Sons 1913) 14.

authoritatively determined (as they are in many decisions at the border), this is undertaken in our collective name, by the state.

In order to extend the intrinsic anti-privatisation argument to border control, we need to add one more piece to the puzzle. For one might think that we could solve the problem simply by recourse to a tidy division of labour: the state keeps to itself the power to make general immigration laws in the name of us all but outsources only the enforcement of those laws to private contractors. If that tidy division of labour were possible, then the privatisation of border enforcement might be unproblematic even on the statist account; but it is not possible.[27] As Gillian Metzger and many other privatisation scholars have pointed out, 'the power to implement and apply rules is inseparable from the power to set policy'.[28] At every turn, the application of legal norms to specific instances requires many exercises of judgement, not only in the application of general norms to particular factual settings, but in the interpretation of whether conduct is 'unreasonable', treatment 'unfair', or burdens 'undue'. Frontline officials at the border and elsewhere are constantly called upon to make these sorts of determinations and to act accordingly, affecting our legal rights and duties in innumerable, important ways. It is for this reason that their tasks must be carried out by the state (so that we can understand them to be collectively self-imposed), rather than by private actors.

Once we have established that a function is one that must be carried out by the state, the question that remains is how to make sure that the person charged with doing it is, in fact, acting in the name of the state. It is in answer to this second concern that Harel and Dorfman coin the term 'fidelity by deference': frontline officials show that they are acting in the name of the state simply by the fact that they take on a standing attitude of deference toward their political masters. When they show fidelity by deference, they do things not merely *for* the state, or in the state's *interests*:[29] they can be understood to be instruments through which the state itself exercises its agency. Of course, politicians do not often interfere directly in the affairs of low-level bureaucrats; their influence is to be felt, Dorfman and Harel insist, through the integration of politicians and bureaucrats into a shared community of practice. In a community of practice, 'deference to the state involves collective determination by the deferring agents themselves (qua participants in the requisite practice) concerning what choices deference by them dictates'.[30]

Dorfman and Harel's account turns, first and foremost, on the *reasoning* of frontline officials. What is crucial to their account is that frontline border officials join with other officials (not only bureaucrats, but also elected political officials) to work out a single, shared understanding on matters of public concern. If they were to make decisions for their own private reasons, or where their decisions were constrained by

[27] Legal orders are replete with positions that explicitly blend the power to decide and the power to enforce. An English sheriff, for example, exercises several different types of office. He exercises a judicial office (adjudicating minor matters); he is keeper of the peace, which empowers him to summon citizens to assist in those efforts; and he is a ministerial officer, bound to execute all processes from the King's courts. A 'ministerial office' gives the officer the power to enforce authoritative decisions with coercive force. See William Blackstone, *Commentaries on the Laws of England, Book I* (Callaghan and Company 1884) 331–33.

[28] Gillian E Metzger, 'Privatization as Delegation' (2003) 103 Columbia Law Review 1367, 1395.

[29] Dorfman and Harel (n 9) 73.

[30] ibid 81.

others' private reasons (such as maximising the profits of the corporation for which they work), or even if they were doing their best to pursue the public interest as they conceived it, they would no longer be acting in the state's name. This shared practice whereby officials work together to generate and act according to a shared understanding of the state's purposes is definitive of Dorfman and Harel's account of public office.

B A More Robust Offices Account

Dorfman and Harel's intrinsic argument against privatisation is powerful and important but, I argue here, it is unduly focused on the reasoning of public officials at the price of neglecting other aspects of public office. They suggest, tellingly, that 'it is the integrative practice that makes them officials. Accordingly, it is in principle possible that the private employees of a private firm would be considered, for our purposes, public officials.'[31] But that is to overstate the importance of reasoning, and to underestimate the significance of other features of public office. We cannot so readily make ourselves a part of the state.

At the heart of the idea of office is that there is something real and enduring about an office, irrespective of who might occupy it. In this way, offices are like private property: not only do they have powers and privileges that can be transferred as a unit from one occupant to another, but the decisions made by previous occupants bind future occupants. But offices are also importantly different from private property in several crucial respects, the most important of which is the fact that offices never *belong* to a person to do with as they see fit. Instead, public offices exist only in order to solve the fundamental problem of the state of nature and never to serve the private purposes of their occupants. The reason we are so concerned that offices should serve public purposes rather than private ones is not simply that we want to see public purposes carried out. It is that the only justification for one person to hold coercive power over another in a liberal legal order is to secure the civil condition.[32] To act for private reasons is to do precisely what public offices are designed to preclude.

Clearly, something more than an integrative practice is required to define public offices. Instead, the idea of public office is best understood by examining its purest form in the German idea of the *Beamter* or the French idea of the *fonctionnaire*.[33] Because a public office is not ours to do with as we see fit—it is a position of power over matters that are not entirely our own—we are not entitled to pass it on to whomever we might like. Through the institution of a public procedure for entry into office, the question of who shall fill a given office is transmuted from a matter of one person's unilateral will ('I'll help myself to that office' or 'I'll just pass along this office to my son-in-law, Jared') to a question settled by public procedures. As William Blackstone said of policing, 'it

[31] ibid 88.

[32] Immanuel Kant, *Metaphysics of Morals* (Mary Gregor tr, CUP 1996) MS, AA 06: 345–46 (pagination is to the standard German text from the Akademie-Ausgabe).

[33] Some of what follows in this paragraph is taken from my article, Thorburn, 'Policing and Public Office' (n 7).

is of the utmost importance to have the sheriff appointed according to law, when we consider his power and duty'.[34] So another crucial aspect of public office that Dorfman and Harel's account neglects is this aspect of how one *becomes* a part of the state: it is never through unilateral decisions (such as the hiring of employees by a private company, much less by a private citizen's decision to act in concert with public officials in the name of the state) but only through public procedures that govern entry into the public service.

Many of the other features of public office as they have existed in French or German legal traditions since the nineteenth century—the extensive limits on participation in outside groups such as political parties or trade unions, the protection of employment tenure and salary, the oaths of office that many public officials would have to swear upon entry into office, as well as the extensive training they would undergo to instil in them an ethos of public service—can be seen from one point of view merely as supports to the 'community of practice'; that is, we might think of them merely as ways of encouraging public officials to engage as thoroughly as possible in the community of practice with other officials and to consider matters related to the office only from the public point of view (as set out in their training) and not from any private perspective (that might be encouraged by participation in outside groups). But there is a more robust reading of public office that sees these features as of more than merely instrumental value. These features of office do not merely constrain the individuals who occupy public offices: they define the office itself.[35] It is the network of *offices*—not the network of *officials*—that makes up the state, so the definition of those offices defines the character of the state itself.

IV Vasanthakumar on the New Despotism?

A Migrants at the Mercy of an Alien Bureaucracy?

In a recent article,[36] Ashwini Vasanthakumar rejects Dorfman and Harel's intrinsic argument against the privatisation of border control and insists not only that such privatisation may be permissible, but that in some cases it is desirable. Her argument is a powerful statement of the moral individualist position and its implications for the privatisation of border control, so it is worthy of discussion for that reason alone. But it is also an excellent example of a wider phenomenon among moral individualist accounts of many state functions: rather than recognising that there is a deep-seated disagreement between the two camps on foundational issues, moral individualists frequently treat statist arguments simply as failed moral individualist arguments. So it is worth putting her article into the larger context of this debate between writers

[34] Blackstone (n 27) 331.

[35] Max Weber, Economy and Society (Keith Tribe tr, Harvard University Press 2019), pt 3, ch 6, s 7: Bureaucracy.

[36] Ashwini Vasanthakumar, 'Privatising Border Control' (2018) 38(3) Oxford Journal of Legal Studies 411. I do not mean to suggest that Vasanthakumar's argument parallels Viscount Hewart's critique of the administrative state as set out in his 1929 book of the same name. It is the administrative state that is, once again, in the cross hairs, but accused this time of a very different sort of despotism.

belonging to two competing schools of thought who, more often than not, fail even to recognise the nature of the dispute between them.

Vasanthakumar's position on the privatisation of border control focuses on the core question for all moral individualists: how can we ensure that individuals (in this case, border control agents) act in accordance with the demands of interpersonal morality? In her critique of Dorfman and Harel, she makes clear that she takes them to be engaged in the same moral individualist project as she is. On their account, she argues, '[t]he state is held up as the sole arbiter of the public good, *uniquely capable of ascertaining the public point of view*, and acting so as to preserve the equal freedom of all'.[37] Vasanthakumar assumes that Dorfman and Harel's position is an instrumentalist one: the state has the standing to engage in border control because it is best qualified to do the job well. But, as we have just seen, it is no such thing. Dorfman and Harel are committed statists. Their concern is to establish what is required for us to characterise the acts of a natural person as done in the state's name, *whether or not* that leads to better reasoning on the part of public officials; that is, Dorfman and Harel are trading on the old distinction between constitutive principles (that determine whether something is an example of category X at all) and regulative ones (that determine whether it is a *good* example of category X). To say that someone is acting in the name of the state is not yet to say that he is acting *well* in the name of the state. Of course, being a state agent *tout court* is a necessary condition for being a *good* state agent, but nonetheless these are importantly distinct ideas.

In this way, Vasanthakumar's argument is typical of a larger school of thought that often treats statist arguments as failed moral individualist claims. It is strikingly similar in this respect to John Gardner's moral individualist position in respect of policing. He set out the basics of this world view concisely as follows:

> [M]orality binds police officers on duty just as it binds anyone else. Nobody can evade it by saying: 'I work for the government now'. For morality goes with one wherever life takes one, and is never displaced by the supposed demands of one's work, which always, on the contrary, answer to morality and give one, in themselves, no excuse when one violates it.[38]

In short, the fact that one works for the government—as a soldier, a border guard, or a police officer—is just a role we play in life.[39] Those who occupy these positions are under special obligations, but not because they act in the name of the state. Instead, according to the moral individualists, one's job as a public official is morally significant simply as factual stage-setting. Once again, Gardner puts the point eloquently:

[37] ibid 429 (emphasis added).

[38] John Gardner, 'Criminals in Uniform' in RA Duff, Lindsay Farmer, SE Marshal, Massimo Renzo, and Victor Tadros (eds), *The Constitution of the Criminal Law* (OUP 2013) 117.

[39] In Thorburn, 'Policing and Public Office' (n 7) 259ff, I argue that the role of police officers as public officials is crucial even in England, where the seventh of 'Peel's Principles' state that '[t]he police are the public and ... the public are the police; the police being only members of the public who are paid to give full-time attention to duties which are incumbent on every citizen, in following the interests of community welfare and existence'.

> [T]he moral differences [between public officials and ordinary citizens] as I sketched them are always ordinary moral differences, of a type that we all encounter in our daily lives as we move among our various roles and relationships and try to adapt to their circumstances. As Thorburn anticipates that I will say, being a police officer—and, I would add, a public official of any kind—is just another of those circumstances to adapt to.[40]

In the context of war, this moral individualist position goes by the name of 'revisionist just war theory': the view that, morally speaking, there is nothing more to war than groups of individuals locked in a set of interconnected violent conflicts. For that reason, revisionist just war theorists such as Jeff McMahan, David Rodin, and Helen Frowe insist that soldiers must always act according to the interpersonal morality of their situation. In other words, the moral analysis of war is no different than the moral analysis of two groups of private individuals engaged in fighting. The fact that states go to war with one another, rather than individuals, is just another fact that sets the stage on which individual moral agents must decide how to act.[41] There is no deep sense in which we should think of states themselves as acting through the agency of their soldiers and that, therefore, states might have the moral standing to do things (through their soldiers) that individuals do not. Accordingly, the special status of soldiers, long recognised in international humanitarian law, is one of the great unexplained mysteries, in the eyes of revisionist just war theorists.[42]

How does Vasanthakumar carry out her moral individualist argument in the context of border guards? Like Gardner, she points out (correctly) that everyone, whether or not they work for the government, is answerable to interpersonal morality. Officials must always ask themselves whether the job they have been given is in service of any legitimate public purpose (for example, to be a guard at Auschwitz could never be a public office); they must ask themselves whether the specific orders they have been given are consistent with the public reasons available to the state (for example, the Schießbefehl—the standing order given to East German border guards to shoot escaping citizens on sight—could never be consistent with any public purpose); and they must always consider their own conscience when deciding whether to comply with the demands of their office (it might be legitimate for our country to wage a particular war but we ought still to consider our conscience when deciding whether to serve in that war).

Second, Vasanthakumar argues that, if border agents are trying to cleave as closely as possible to the demands of interpersonal morality, they are more likely to succeed if they act on their own conscience rather than trying to defer to the judgements of their

[40] Gardner (n 39) 118. He adds (at 102): '[T]he special moral position I will be sketching is that of a police officer qua police officer, not that of a police officer qua public servant. In adumbrating this special moral position, I will be assuming, not arguing, that the job of a police officer is and should remain in the public sector. That is what I mean when I say that I will stop short of arguing against the privatization of the police. Nevertheless, I believe that once the special moral position of police officers qua police officers is appreciated, it is a fairly short step to seeing why that job should be kept out of private hands'.

[41] The ur-statement of revisionist just war theory is Jeff McMahan, *Killing in War* (OUP 2009).

[42] I provide a statist explanation for the special status of soldiers in Malcolm Thorburn, 'Soldiers as Public Officials: A Moral Justification for Combatant Immunity' (2019) 32 Ratio Juris 395.

political superiors. This is clearly true where the state has been captured by a partisan interest, or where it suffers from some other pathology. But it is also systematically true, Vasanthakumar argues, where '[t]here is a divergence between the beneficiaries of the good—citizens—and the recipients of its provision—migrants'.[43] In this case, state officials are systematically ill-placed to put the welfare of migrants at the forefront of their reasoning. If we want to ensure that border control agents act in a way that takes the interests of migrants seriously, Vasanthakumar argues, we would do well to free border control agents from 'fidelity by deference' to their political masters.

Privatisation comes into Vasanthakumar's argument as a potential solution to this structural problem in the public administration of border control: '[w]hen the frontline agent is an employee of an organisation whose owners, so to speak, are committed to the welfare of migrants', she suggests, 'the frontline agent is incentivised to attend to migrant welfare'.[44] Thus, not just any kind of privatisation will do. Indeed, privatisation of border control to for-profit companies will likely make the problem worse, by adding the profit motive to the existing problems of partiality against foreigners. But outsourcing border control to organisations that are free of both the profit motive and the partiality of national governments could ensure that border control is carried out in a manner that is maximally respectful of migrants' human rights. Governments might still play a role, she suggests, by ensuring that the appropriate standards are followed, whether by their own officials, or by private contractors, simply by setting out robust *ex post facto* review standards. She writes that, 'the state can stipulate high standards, robust and frequent monitoring, and specialist training of employees',[45] but they should not be guiding decision-making in the fully integrated way contemplated by Dorfman and Harel.

B Public Authority v Populism

Vasanthakumar's argument here is a powerful and important challenge to the statist position. For even if we are fully paid-up statists, there is something troubling about the situation of migrants who are dealt with by officials who represent a group of which they are not members. Central American refugee claimants arriving on the US border, for example, will take little comfort in knowing that the officials who process their claims are part of the US state, acting in the collective name of the people of the United States. As Vasanthakumar suggests, the state might be an instrument of self-rule for citizens, but it looks like just another flavour of despotism to the (foreign) migrant at the border.

Powerful though Vasanthakumar's challenge is, however, it can be answered. The answer comes in two stages. First, we must separate the question of moral standing from the question of who will do best at deciding a particular question. Although in recent years the government of the United States might have done a terrible job of dealing with migrants to that country, it nonetheless remains its job to do; that is, if we

[43] Vasanthakumar (n 36) 427.
[44] ibid.
[45] ibid.

take seriously the statist claim that it is the state and only the state that has the moral standing to deal with certain questions, then the proper way to address concerns about it doing a bad job in certain areas is to reform the state and its procedures, rather than to replace it. Of course, there comes a point where a government does such a poor job that it no longer constitutes a legitimate state at all and some other organisation must step in out of necessity: this is highly controversial, and permissible only in extreme conditions.[46] We can see a parallel to this point in the familial context. It is parents who have the moral standing to make a great many decisions about their children's lives, even when they make the wrong call on many matters—indeed, even when they demonstrably display favouritism among their children. Of course, parents' authority can eventually be overridden where they systematically fail to act as parents at all—in cases of abuse, neglect, etc.—but we do not revoke their moral standing merely for doing their job poorly (such as by favouring one child over another).[47]

Second, and more importantly, we need to keep in mind an important feature of the theory of the state as a network of offices. The key to state legitimacy, on this account, is the fact that it carries out necessary public functions in the name of all, whether or not this is in line with the will of the populace. Although many modern accounts of the state and its legitimacy turn on its democratic credentials[48]—that a state is legitimate in so far as it represents its people's will—this is highly misleading. Democracy is an excellent public procedure for determining who should occupy the office of Member of Parliament or mayor, but this does not mean that public offices should all be aimed at fulfilling the people's will. The account of the state as a network of offices sees the state's most basic role as standing over and above *any* partisan position, determining rights and duties in pursuit of the public purposes that define the justifying conditions of the state's own authority. Rousseau makes a similar point by distinguishing the general will from the will of the people: 'the general will is always right and tends to the public advantage; but it does not follow that the deliberations of the people are always equally correct'.[49] This feature of the modern state is best captured in the recognition that even elected positions (Member of Parliament, Member of Congress, etc.) are offices complete with defining powers and privileges and public purposes that define their role. Although elected representatives have more decision-making power than frontline officials (indeed, deciding on matters of policy is elected officials' stock-in-trade), it is far from an unconstrained discretion. For, much as would-be tyrants such as Donald Trump or Richard Nixon might chafe at the thought (preferring to say, with Louis XIV, '*L'État, c'est moi*'), they are never anything more than temporary occupants of a public office.[50]

[46] The doctrine of humanitarian intervention, which would permit armed intervention to prevent grave violations of human rights, is an object of considerable controversy.

[47] The analogy of parents and children to states and citizens raises a number of difficult questions. It is one that I have considered at length elsewhere. See, eg Thorburn 'Justifications, Powers, and Authority' (n 7) 1072 ff.

[48] Chiara Cordelli, to take one prominent recent example, places democratic self-government at the centre of her account: Cordelli (n 25).

[49] Rousseau (n 27) 25.

[50] Richard Nixon famously said that, 'when the president does it, that means that it is not illegal'. Quoted in 'Excerpts from Interview with Nixon about Domestic Effects of Indochina War' *New York Times* (New York, 20 May 1977) A16. And we all know about Donald Trump.

In short, Vasanthakumar's worry that public officials will be necessarily partisan in favour of the interests of their own nationals, and against the interests of migrants, appears to be based on a populist understanding of the state as a tool of the will of the majority. Although we should always be alive to the worry that governments may be captured by partisan interests, and that one particularly ugly (and currently prevalent) such partisan interest is nativism, we should also recognise that that sort of partisanship is *not* 'baked into' the statist account of the special moral standing of the state to determine rights and duties of those within its jurisdiction.

V Conclusions and Qualifications

In this chapter, I have shown how the statist argument against the privatisation of border control is not simply a misguided version of the moral individualist world view. It arises from a deep disagreement among legal and political theorists on the grounds of legitimate public authority and legal order. If we, along with Rousseau, Kant, and much of the social contract tradition, take the idea of freedom as independence seriously, then the state must play a special and irreducible role in our conception of legitimate legal ordering. What is more, the role assigned to the state in that world view is one that necessarily includes control over the determination of each person's rights and duties within the jurisdiction, according to public reasons that are independent of anyone's partisan interest: even the partisan interest of the population as a whole. One reaction to the ugly bigotry, nativism, and violence toward strangers that has been on display in recent years is Vasanthakumar's plea to outsource border control to non-governmental bodies such as the Red Cross. I fear, though, that this is to sidestep the deeper pathologies at work in many political orders today. The more difficult and more ambitious path lies in determining what principles of self-government are all about. They do not allow for partisanship of any kind, nativist or otherwise.

References

Arbogast L, *Migrant Detention in the European Union: A Thriving Business* (Rosa Luxemburg Stiftung 2016)

Australian Human Rights Commission, 'A Last Resort?—Summary Guide: The Facts about Immigration Detention in Australia' <https://humanrights.gov.au/our-work/last-resort-summary-guide-facts-about-immigration-detention-australia> (Australia 2004)

Blackstone W, *Commentaries on the Laws of England*, Book I (Callaghan and Company 1884)

Busby M, 'G4S to Leave Immigration Sector after Brook House Scandal' *The Guardian* (London, 24 September 2019) <https://www.theguardian.com/business/2019/sep/24/g4s-to-leave-immigration-sector-after-brook-house-scandal>

Cordelli C, *The Privatized State* (Princeton University Press 2020)

Dorfman A and Harel A, 'The Case against Privatisation' (2013) 41 Philosophy & Public Affairs 67

Foucher M, *Le Retour des Frontières* (CNRS Editions 2016)

Freeman J and Minow M (eds), *Government by Contract: Outsourcing and American Democracy* (Harvard University Press 2009)

Global Detention Project, *Country Report: Immigration Detention in Australia: Turning Arbitrary Detention into a Global Brand* (Geneva 2022).

Global Detention Project, *Country Report: United Kingdom Immigration Detention Profile* (Geneva 2016).

Hartoy M, *Histoire des passeports français depuis l'Antiquité jusqu'à nos jours* (H Champion 1937)

Hesson T, 'Report: US Spends More on Immigration than all Federal Criminal Enforcement Combined' (*ABC News*, 7 January 2013) <https://abcnews.go.com/ABC_Univision/News/us-spends-immigration-major-federal-criminal-enforcement-combined/story?id=18151143#18>

Kant I, *Metaphysics of Morals*, Mary Gregor tr (CUP 1996).

Kassie E, 'Detained: How the US Built the World's Largest Immigration Detention System' *The Guardian* 2019.

Lazo A, 'Private Prisons could See Fortunes Change under Biden Immigration Policy' *Wall Street Journal* (New York, 30 April 2021) <https://www.wsj.com/articles/private-prisons-could-see-fortunes-change-under-biden-immigration-policy-11619800623>

Lowe V, *International Law* (OUP 2007)

McMahan J, *Killing in War* (OUP 2009)

Metzger GE, 'Privatization as Delegation' (2003) 103 Columbia Law Review 1367

Minow M, 'Public and Private Partnerships: Accounting for the New Religion' (2003) 116 Harvard Law Review 1129

New York Times (1977) 'Excerpts from Interview with Nixon about Domestic Effects of Indochina War' *New York Times* (New York, 20 May 1977)

Reyes PA, 'The US–Mexico Border isn't Protected by Militias, it's Patrolled by Domestic Terrorists' (*NBC News*, 22 April 2019) <https://www.nbcnews.com/think/opinion/u-s-mexico-border-isn-t-protected-militias-it-s-ncna997056>

Osborne D and Gaebler T, *Reinventing Government: How the Entrepreneurial Spirit is Transforming the Public Sector* (Plume 1993)

Raz J, *The Morality of Freedom* (OUP 1982)

Rousseau J-J, 'The Social Contract' in Cole GDH tr, *The Social Contract and Discourses* (JM Dent & Sons 1913)

Thorburn M, 'Justifications, Powers, and Authority' (2008) 117(6) Yale Law Journal 1070

— —, 'Criminal Law as Public Law' in Duff RA and Green S (eds), *Philosophical Foundations of Criminal Law* (OUP 2010)

— —, 'Reinventing the Nightwatchman State?' (2010) 60(2) University of Toronto Law Journal 425

— —, 'Soldiers as Public Officials: A Moral Justification for Combatant Immunity' (2019) 32 Ratio Juris 395

— —, 'Policing and Public Office' (2020) 70(2) University of Toronto Law Journal 248

Vasanthakumar A, 'Privatising Border Control' (2018) 38(3) Oxford Journal of Legal Studies 411

Verkuil P, *Outsourcing Sovereignty: Why Privatization of Government Functions Threatens Democracy and What We Can Do about It* (CUP 2007)

Weber M, *Economy and Society*, tr K Tribe (Harvard University Press 2019)

Legislation

Convention on Rights and Duties of States adopted by the Seventh International Conference of American States (adopted 26 December 1933, entered into force 26 December 1934) LNTS 165, 19, art I
Chinese Exclusion Act (USA) 22 Stat 58, Chap 126.
Chinese Immigration Act (Canada) RSC, 1927, c 95.

Cases

Academic Center of Law and Business v Minister of Finance HCJ 2605/05 (2009)
Atlantic Coast Fisheries Case (Great Britain, United States) (1910) RIAA vol IX, 180
Libyan Arab Jamahiriya/Chad) (Merits) [1994] ICJ Rep 6

5
Towards Legitimacy at the Border

Ashwini Vasanthakumar

I Introduction

When border guards enter someone's home, grab them, and force them into a van that will take them to a cell in which they will be locked up, this is immigration detention rather than a kidnapping because these guards are state agents acting with legally mandated powers and, therefore, with authority and legitimacy. Or so it is claimed. Border control is now enacted by a range of private actors: non-state actors to whom the state delegates duties and powers to implement its border control policies as frontline decision-makers or agents. Privatisation in border control has invited renewed scrutiny from scholars, advocates, and policymakers, who echo longstanding concerns raised about privatisation in prisons and war: concerns that become more urgent in light of the proliferation of private actors in border control. Implicit in many arguments against privatisation is the assumption that state provision would be better.

Intrinsic arguments against privatisation do not concern themselves with the consequences of privatisation;[1] instead, proponents argue that certain goods are 'inherently public', meaning that they can only be provided by a public authority or agent.[2] In order for intrinsic arguments to preclude privatisation in border control, border control must be an inherently public good; and in order for these arguments to point to the state instead, the state must be a public actor. In this chapter, I challenge this latter claim. Intrinsic arguments persuasively establish the importance of a public agent and I use these accounts to scrutinise the state, arguing against the conclusion these accounts typically reach: I argue that, in the context of border control, the state is deficient as a public agent.

I develop this critique by exploring the principles of legitimacy that apply to border control. I use these principles to assess the state and argue that, absent institutionalised mechanisms of *ex ante* input and *ex post* accountability connecting the state to migrants, the state cannot exercise power over migrants legitimately; or at the very least, it does so with weak legitimacy—migrants are subject to, rather than subjects of, migration control.

[1] Intrinsic arguments are outlined by Avihay Dorfman and Alon Harel, 'The Case Against Privatization' (2013) 41 Philosophy & Public Affairs 67; Avihay Dorfman and Alon Harel, 'Against Privatisation as Such' (2016) 36 Oxford Journal of Legal Studies 400; and Alon Harel, *Why Law Matters* (OUP 2014); Chiara Cordelli, 'Privatization without Profit?' in Jack Knight and Melissa Schwartzberg (eds), Privatization (NOMOS LX 2018) 113–144; Chiara Cordelli, *The Privatized State* (Princeton University Press 2020).

[2] I use the terms political authority, public authority, and public agent interchangeably. Whether or not an entity is a public authority is not only a matter of how it is formally identified or designated.

Ashwini Vasanthakumar, *Towards Legitimacy at the Border* In: *Privatising Border Control*. Edited by: Mary Bosworth and Lucia Zedner, Oxford University Press. © Ashwini Vasanthakumar 2022. DOI: 10.1093/oso/9780192857163.003.0006

The chapter proceeds as follows. In the next section, I provide a brief overview of the actors and processes that constitute border control. In section III, I briefly reconstruct intrinsic arguments and provide a conceptual overview of legitimacy. In section IV, I discuss principles of legitimacy relevant to border control; and in section V, I apply these principles to existing practices of border control. Section VI considers two objections, and section VII concludes with considerations of the role of non-state actors in enhancing legitimacy in border control.

II Privatisation and Border Control

Border control refers to the policies and practices sovereign states articulate and implement with respect to the movement of individuals across their territorial boundaries. I focus on the control of entry by non-citizens. Migrants are individuals seeking entry into a state or who are already present within its territory but are not citizens: this expansive definition, therefore, includes tourists and those travelling for business, those seeking to enter and remain without authorisation, and those seeking to enter with authorisation and eventually acquire membership status. Border control arises at the territorial boundaries of states, in extraterritorial efforts aimed at preventing would-be migrants from arriving at a boundary, and continues, through checks and restrictions, once they enter the state's territory.

States rely on several non-state actors: for-profit corporations, charities, civilian gatekeepers, supranational regulatory agencies, international organisations created by and tasked with upholding international law, and the agents of other states.[3] Note the following about this border control complex: first, there is a great deal of variety amongst non-state actors, a category that includes charities, profit-maximising enterprises, religious bodies motivated by sectarian commitments, and rights-promoting organisations—some of these are not obviously private organisations pursuing self-interested ends. For these reasons, I refer to non-state actors rather than private actors and use privatisation to refer to action by non-state actors in those domains typically reserved for the state.

Second, the relationships between the state and non-state actors, and amongst non-state actors, will vary. In some cases, there are clear lines of delegation and hierarchy between the state and the non-state frontline agent; in others, the state is in a bilateral relationship, notionally between equals; or there is no fixed hierarchy and the relationship between the relevant state and the non-state actor is dynamic and contingent. Consider the variability in the state's relationship to a civilian gatekeeper to whom it delegates monitoring responsibilities on pain of sanction, its relationship to another state with which it partners on border control, and its relationship to a UN body that

[3] These are state actors, in that they are agents appropriately connected to *a* state; however, I use non-state actors to refer to those actors not connected to the relevant state, the border control policies of which are being implemented. Of course, in virtue of the bilateral agreements that are often a precursor for these forms of delegation, the border policies of both states converge; still, I focus on the state that controls immigration as the relevant state and the state to whom it 'externalises' its borders as non-state.

monitors its compliance with international legal obligations but can otherwise do little by way of sanction.

Third, there will not always be a clear or fixed distinction between state and non-state actors[4] in terms of the roles they play and in terms of their constitution. Non-state actors may have close ties to state authorities, may be involved in the formulation of public policy as advisers or consultants, and may be involved in the execution of policy in roles that range from direct providers to monitors. Rather than two binary or discrete categories, the public and the private may better be regarded as two ends of a spectrum.

And finally, there are a host of non-state actors to whom the state does not delegate powers and duties in border control, but who may act to *compensate* for state inaction, for example to provide services that the state has withdrawn from; or to *usurp* the state's authority, for example by acting in contravention of the state's policies to people-smuggle.[5] From the forgoing, a picture emerges of the state as one among many, embedded in a border control complex with a range of non-state actors, in relationships of delegation and deference that may be institutionalised, ad hoc, or in flux.[6]

Intrinsic arguments against privatisation permit non-state actors to play only ancillary roles in providing 'inherently public goods'; by these lights, a border control complex in which non-state actors play a central role will be illegitimate. While intrinsic arguments point to the importance of a public actor—of legitimacy—this public actor need not be the state; indeed, intrinsic arguments provide the resources for appreciating the deficiencies of the state as a legitimate actor as well as the ways in which non-state actors can contribute to legitimacy at the border.

III Intrinsic Arguments against Privatisation

Intrinsic arguments—and here I focus on the accounts provided by Harel and Dorfman, and by Cordelli—generally proceed in two steps. First, they identify some goods as 'inherently public', in that these are goods that can only be provided by a public agent. There are two rationales for why a good is 'inherently public': ontological and axiological.[7] An ontological rationale maintains that, as a matter of conceptual definition, a particular good can only be provided by a public agent. For reasons I elaborate on in section VII, I find this rationale unpersuasive. Instead, I proceed in my analysis with axiological, or functional, rationales: a good is 'inherently public' when it changes the normative status of subjects; only a public provider can provide the good in a way that enshrines subjects' equal freedom.[8]

[4] See Bosworth and Samuel, in this volume.

[5] See Ashwini Vasanthakumar, 'Privatizing Border Control' (2018) 38 Oxford Journal of Legal Studies 411 for a discussion of these other actors and modes of privatisation.

[6] Terry Macdonald, 'Political Legitimacy in International Border Governance Institutions' (2015) 14(4) European Journal of Political Theory 409.

[7] Laura Valentini, 'On the Value of Constitutions and Judicial Review' (2017) 11 Criminal Law and Philosophy 817.

[8] ibid; Cordelli, *The Privatized State* (n 1) 9.

Having deemed a good 'inherently public', intrinsic accounts then identify the appropriate relationship between the public agent who makes rules and the frontline agent who implements these rules through discretionary decision-making. This relationship, described as an 'integrative practice' or bureaucracy, embeds frontline agents into networks or practices that connect them to the public agent, granting these frontline agents access to the public agent's deliberations and subjecting them to public control. In virtue of this relationship, frontline agents do not exercise their individual judgement and discretion, but rather are subject to the public authority's judgement. As a result, when an individual is subject to the frontline agent's discretionary decision-making, that individual is not subject to the private will of another individual but to the will of a public agent. Even when this individual is restricted or burdened in some way, her status as an equal and free agent remains.

Under intrinsic accounts, then, only a public agent can provide certain goods in a way that enshrines the equal freedom of all—for example, criminal punishment—and only when frontline agents remain subject to that public agent's deliberations and control can the frontline agent's provision count as public provision. The trouble with many forms of privatisation becomes apparent: frontline agents are not appropriately connected to public agents. When a private security contractor seizes and detains an individual, that individual is subject to the private will of the contractor: she is neither equal nor free.

Let me note the following features of intrinsic arguments: first, the argument against privatisation is an implication of the argument *for* public authority, typically understood as the state.[9] This positive argument is a justification and defence of a *hypothetical* state: it explains why a public authority is necessary and why individuals have duties to establish such an authority. Without more, however, this argument will not defend any actually existing states; that is, even accepting this account of public authority and inherently public goods will not, by itself, tell us which states, if any, count as a public authority. It is important to keep in mind the hypothetical nature of this defence lest intrinsic arguments be misconstrued as an apologia for, among other things, the nation-state. Such misuse risks using 'ideal theory as ideology';[10] importantly, it misses out on the critical vantage point that such idealised narratives can provide on existing institutions and practices.

Second, these accounts are offered at a level of generality. They do not specify the degree or kind of normative change a good must produce for it to qualify as 'inherently public', or the nature of the control to which frontline agents should be subjected. How encompassing the domain of public action is will depend on how capacious the conception of 'normative change' or of 'control' turns out to be. As proponents of intrinsic accounts clarify, then, they do not argue against all privatisation, and whether or not an agent is 'properly public' is not determined simply by how those agents understand or identify themselves. A state official inappropriately connected to a public decision-maker will not count as a public frontline agent, irrespective of what uniform she dons. And a decision-maker recognised as a public

[9] See, eg Cordelli, *The Privatized State* (n 1).

[10] Charles Mills, 'Ideal Theory as Ideology' in *Black Rights/White Wrongs: The Critique of Racial Liberalism* (OUP 2017) 28–48.

authority will not necessarily be a public agent. What intrinsic accounts seek to establish is the necessity of a public agent for certain goods, and the impossibility of these goods being provided by private actors.

In what follows, I apply intrinsic accounts to the context of border control, an application that proponents of intrinsic accounts do not themselves pursue. Elsewhere, I have scrutinised the argument for an 'integrative practice';[11] here, I focus on the first prong of intrinsic arguments: the need for a 'properly public agent'. For the sake of argument, I grant many of the key claims of intrinsic arguments, using these to critically assess the state. In doing so, my aims are twofold: to show that those who have an 'intuitive dislike'[12] of privatisation have cause for similar misgivings about the legitimacy of the state when it enforces its borders, and to suggest how the state could become a public agent in the context of border control. To do this, I will first provide a brief overview of political legitimacy, connect these debates to intrinsic arguments against privatisation, and then elaborate on some of the requirements of political legitimacy at the border.

IV Political Legitimacy in and beyond the State

Political legitimacy is a virtue of the relationship between an entity that exercises power and those who are subject to that power.[13] I am concerned with legitimacy as a normative concept that tells us when an entity's exercise of power *ought* to be recognised as legitimate.[14] Whether or not an entity's exercise of power ought to be recognised as legitimate will depend on the relationship between the entity and those subject to it, in particular the procedural apparatus that connects them and that constrains the entity's exercise of power.

Political legitimacy is most often theorised within the context of the bounded political community, and these discussions focus on the relationship between a political authority and its political subjects, as well as the way that political authority mediates the relationship amongst political subjects. In the terms of the intrinsic accounts against privatisation, a public agent's exercise of power is politically legitimate because this exercise enshrines the equal freedom of all who are subject to it.

One way to approach the question of political legitimacy in border control is to regard it purely as a domestic phenomenon: if a state is legitimate vis-à-vis its citizens in how it formulates and implements border control, then the state is legitimate in the context of border control. On this approach, border control is a good that the state provides for its citizens; if privatisation raises any concerns about legitimacy, it is

[11] Vasanthakumar, 'Privatizing Border Control' (n 5).

[12] Dorfman and Harel, 'The Case Against Privatization' (n 1) 69.

[13] There is significant conceptual debate about legitimacy. I do not advance a particular conception of political legitimacy, but instead explore it in the context of border control. See, eg David Beetham, *The Legitimation of Power* (Palgrave 1991); Allen Buchanan, *Justice, Legitimacy, and Self-determination* (OUP 2003); Allen Buchanan and Bob Keohane, 'The Legitimacy of Global Governance Institutions' (2006) 20(4) Ethics and International Affairs 405.

[14] De facto legitimacy is when an entity is in fact recognised as exercising power legitimately by those over whom this power is exercised (even when they ought not to treat it as such).

because it interrupts or distorts the relationship between the state and its citizens, for example by corrupting the policymaking process or by limiting the ability of citizens to hold state officials to account.[15]

There are two reasons, however, to reject this conception. The first is that border control does not only involve the state. As I outlined above, border control, although often justified in terms of state sovereignty, is an international and transnational practice: it involves a border control complex. Even if the beneficiaries of border control are citizens of the relevant state, those citizens are subject to the decisions of entities with whom they do not have any institutionalised political relationship. As such, ascertaining the legitimacy of border control will occasion an inquiry into the relationship between citizens and non-state entities, including other states. Second, border control necessarily entails the exercise of power over non-citizens by the relevant state and by non-state actors. Ascertaining the legitimacy of border control will also occasion an inquiry into the relationship between migrants and the various entities who exercise power over them, including the state into whose territory they seek entry. I focus on this latter relationship.

The need to theorise legitimacy beyond the state–citizen relationship arises not only in the context of migration control. Decisions made by one political authority impact those who are not its subjects and who have no say in its decision-making processes. Global problems may be in need of a global body that can coordinate and compel; and transnational or supranational bodies are capable of constraining states and their citizens.[16] The standard, state-based principles and mechanisms of legitimacy will not translate perfectly to the global or transnational domain; what is needed are conceptions of legitimacy and authority relevant to contexts outside the state–citizen relationship, and especially those contexts that are not characterised by clear hierarchies of rule-making, rule interpretation, and rule-taking.

Some have proposed a distinct conception of global political legitimacy that, although related to the standard conceptions, is distinct from and not reducible to them.[17] Consider, for example, Eva Erman's conception of global political legitimacy.[18] Erman understands global political legitimacy as a regulative ideal that identifies when an entity is entitled to exercise political power. An entity can be said to exercise political power when it does so purposefully and systematically: this expands the application of political legitimacy beyond the state and other law-producing and enforcing

[15] The confidentiality of commercial contracts makes it difficult to monitor conflicts of interest between public officials and private contractors, and to hold private contractors to account for abuses.

[16] See, eg Gustaf Arhennius, 'The Boundary Problem' in Folke Tersman (ed), *The Viability and Desirability of Global Democracy* (Filosofiska institutionen, Stockholms Universitet 2007) 14–29; Lars Bergstrom, 'Democracy and Political Boundaries' in Folke Tersman (ed), *The Viability and Desirability of Global Democracy* (Filosofiska institutionen, Stockholms Universitet 2007); Kate MacDonald and Terry MacDonald, 'Liquid Authority and Political Legitimacy in Transnational Governance' (2017) 9(2) International Theory 329; Kate MacDonald and Terry MacDonald, 'Towards a "Pluralist" World Order: Creative Agency and Legitimacy in Global Institutions' (2020) 26(2) European Journal of International Relations 518.

[17] See, eg Macdonald and Macdonald, 'Liquid Authority and Political Legitimacy' (n 16); Buchanan (n 13).

[18] Eva Erman, 'Global Political Legitimacy beyond Justice and Democracy?' (2016) 8(1) International Theory 29. See also Eva Erman, 'A Function-sensitive Approach to the Political Legitimacy of Global Governance' (2020) 50(3) British Journal of Political Science 1001.

entities, but it will not reach those entities whose activities may only incidentally or occasionally have a significant impact on individuals.[19] Erman discusses two contexts in which an entity exercises political power—rule-making and power projection—each of which is regulated by different principles of political legitimacy: 'equal say' and 'public legitimacy', respectively. In contexts of rule-making, political and democratic legitimacy overlap: an entity's exercise of political power over a set of individuals is legitimate in so far as these individuals participate in processes that reaffirm their *political* equality. The 'equal say' principle will call for the right to participate in formal decision-making processes as well as informal fora and will extend this right to all those who are subjected to a decision, which includes those who have a legal obligation to comply with the decision and those who are coerced by the decision. In contexts of power projection, by contrast, political power is exercised through means other than law and policymaking. In this context, a principle of public legitimacy operates: the basic human rights of those subjected to political power should be protected, and they should be able to participate in processes of accountability to hold power-holders to account. The principle of public legitimacy recognises the *moral*, rather than political, equality of those subject to power, and its procedural requirements are therefore thinner.

Note the following features of Erman's dual account of global political legitimacy. Rule-making contexts are characterised by formal decision-making processes focused on formulating and implementing laws and policies, and a core value and function of political legitimacy is to enshrine political equality and enable collective self-determination. Contexts of power projection, on the other hand, arise in the absence of such processes, and a core value and function of political legitimacy is to recognise the moral equality of persons and to protect against domination and abuse. While rule-making contexts are also almost always contexts of power projection, contexts of power projection by definition cannot be rule-making. Second, more than one principle will operate in some contexts, because principles of political legitimacy apply to the *exercise of power* rather than the nature of the relevant entity. Thus, rule-making contexts will be regulated by the 'equal say' principle vis-à-vis those subjected to its rules and by the 'public legitimacy' principle vis-à-vis those who are affected by these rules. The same entity, therefore, may be subjected to different principles: a duality that preserves the salience of collective decision-making without disregarding its impact on those outside the collective. And third, the dual account can accommodate transitions between contexts and identify those contexts where an entity that only projects power ought to, in order to exercise power more legitimately, become rule-making.

[19] Eg, suppose the activities of a corporate entity in Country *A* typically do not affect the interests of citizens in Country *B*. Unexpectedly and unusually, one action of the corporate entity does, in fact, affect important interests of *B*'s citizens. The corporate entity is not subject to principles of political legitimacy; it will be, however, when it purposefully and systematically begins to affect the interests of *B*'s citizens. Of course, this depends, in turn, on how capaciously we understand purposeful and systematic action. This does not concern me, since my focus here is on those entities that straightforwardly exercise political power.

V Legitimacy at the Border

What principles of legitimacy regulate the relationship between the migrant and the state to which she seeks entry? Under Erman's account, the state would straightforwardly seem to be a rule-making context: the state has legislative and executive branches that formulate and enforce immigration rules, that create legal obligations for citizens and migrants, and that are enforced through coercion, especially but not exclusively over migrants. Recall that, in these contexts, Erman argues for an 'equal say' principle: those subjected to the use of force in the implementation of law and policy are entitled to an equal say in the formulation of that law and policy. However, as Erman understands it, the 'equal say' principle aims to establish political equality and enable collective self-determination; giving migrants—by definition, outsiders—a say, much less an equal say, in border control might undermine rather than enable collective self-determination. If the 'public legitimacy' principle is to be applied instead, then border control is legitimate in so far as it does not violate the basic human rights of those subject to it, and in so far as there are mechanisms in place for *ex post* accountability. Recall that the 'public legitimacy' principle operates in those contexts of power projection with the aim of preventing domination and power abuses that prevent individuals from leading autonomous lives. The fundamental commitment in this context is to recognise the moral equality of persons and not to establish political equality amongst members of a self-governing collective. Border control, however, is a context of dense rule-making that deliberately targets and constrains the rights and interests of migrants.

Border control occupies an ambiguous space: it often involves the rule-based use of force against individuals in ways that undermine their ability to lead autonomous lives and yet it is also an exercise in exclusion and self-definition that can enable collective self-determination.[20] There are a few ways this apparent tension can be dissolved: perhaps migrants seeking entry at the border are not coerced, properly understood, and so only the 'public legitimacy' principle applies;[21] or perhaps the democratic inclusion of migrants will not undermine collective self-determination, or the existence of borders.[22] These responses can be understood as attempting to classify border control as requiring *either* the 'equal say' or 'public legitimacy' principle. They maintain the distinction between citizens and migrants in identifying the relevant class of persons who are the beneficiaries of border control and who are subject to coercion, treating border control as a good that is provided for the benefit of citizens and which involves the coercion of migrants. This distinction, however, does not clearly obtain in the context of border control. A state's border control regime, while ostensibly targeting migrants, will also constrain its citizens. For example, intrusive mechanisms that are piloted on migrants are often then extended to citizens more generally, and limiting the rights of

[20] See, eg Sarah Fine, 'The Ethics of Immigration: Self-determination and the Right to Exclude' (2013) 8(3) Philosophy Compass 254.

[21] David Miller, 'Why Immigration Controls are not Coercive: A Reply to Abizadeh' (2010) 38(1) Political Theory 111.

[22] Arash Abizadeh, 'Democratic Legitimacy and State Coercion: A Reply to Miller' (2010) 38(1) Political Theory 121.

foreigners can limit the rights—for example, to family life—of citizens as well.[23] And beyond this, any given citizen is also a would-be migrant.

Rather than regard border control as a good that the state provides to its citizens, I suggest that the relevant good is legitimate migration governance, the beneficiaries of which are would-be migrants: citizens and non-citizens alike.[24] And the context of border control is neither exclusively one of 'rule-making' or 'power projection' but involves both. As a result, the 'equal say' and 'public legitimacy' principles both apply and call for *ex ante* and *ex post* mechanisms that allow for input from migrants in formulating border control policies and accountability for how these policies are implemented. To be clear, this does not entail giving everyone in the world a vote on any given political community's migration and border control policies.[25] Arash Abizadeh reaches a similar conclusion and has argued that in order for a state's border control practices to be democratically legitimate, these practices must result from political processes in which all those subject to these practices, *including non-citizens*, can democratically participate.[26] As Abizadeh clarifies, in response to critics, it is not sufficient that the state democratically accounts for its implementation of laws and policies; instead, those subject to its enforcement must be included in the formulation of these laws and policies.[27] Abizadeh does not specify what particular institutional arrangements this would call for, and leaves open '[w]hether democratic legitimacy requires participation in the literal sense advocated by participatory democrats, or is compatible with representation or other means of institutional articulation'. What matters is that participants 'are able to see themselves as the free and equal authors of the laws to which they are subject'.[28]

The complex combination of actors and institutions that constitute border control allows for *differentiated inclusion*: input and accountability mechanisms can be made available at the state level or at the level of other entities that can channel these down, up, or across to the state.[29] Provided the state is embedded in sufficiently institutionalised relationships with these entities, the perspectives and preferences of migrants can inform state decision-making *without* requiring that migrants participate in collective decision-making as equals with citizens.[30] And so long as these mechanisms of differentiated inclusion allow participants to see themselves as the free and equal authors

[23] Chandran Kukathas, *Immigration and Freedom* (Princeton University Press 2021).

[24] I assume here, without developing this argument further, that every individual benefits from the option to migrate in a way that is politically legitimate, even when they do not have a present intention to exercise that option.

[25] This outcome may be congenial to some cosmopolitans, but I focus on those arguments that establish the importance of bounded political communities and, in particular, the state.

[26] Arash Abizadeh, 'Democratic Theory and Border Coercion: No Right to Unilaterally Control your own Borders' (2008) 36(1) Political Theory 37.

[27] Abizadeh, 'Democratic Legitimacy' (n 22) 128.

[28] ibid 41.

[29] Javier Hidalgo argues that states should subject their migration policies to the control of international organisations that take into account the interests of migrants. Hidalgo focuses, however, on the negative consequences of states' unilateral policymaking and enforcement: Javier Hidalgo, 'The Case for the International Governance of Migration' (2016) 8(1) International Theory 140.

[30] See, eg Felix Bender, 'Enfranchising the Disenfranchised: Should Refugees Receive Political Rights in Liberal Democracies?' (2021) 25(1) Citizenship Studies 56.

of the laws that regulate them, inclusion can take place at levels other than the state;[31] that is, even in those contexts where political legitimacy and democratic legitimacy overlap, mechanisms of democratic legitimacy will be different in the global domain from what is familiar at the domestic level.

Differentiated inclusion allows for collective self-governance by political communities; ensures that migrants have a voice in the policies and practices they confront rather than only by seeking redress; and avoids the binary distinction between citizens and migrants and contexts of rule-making and power projection that do not easily obtain in this and other contexts. In this regard, concern about political legitimacy beyond the state need not be reduced to some purported divide between statists and cosmopolitans.

VI Practices of Legitimacy at the Border

I do not elaborate here on processes of differentiated inclusion; my focus is instead on what the absence of such inclusion means for the legitimacy of existing border control regimes and, in particular, for intrinsic arguments against privatisation that valorise the state. I can, however, make some general observations about differentiated inclusion that follow from the foregoing discussion of political legitimacy. First, in order to achieve legitimacy, differentiated inclusion must be *institutionalised*, in that it is more or less regular, reliable, and robust in the face of changing political and economic priorities. It will not be enough that occasionally and extraordinarily migrants' voices are heeded and inform state policy or practice.[32] This does not mean that institutionalisation will take the same form: at the global and transnational levels, institutionalisation may be more fluid, reliant on norms and deference rather than rules and coercion; and it may be disaggregated, such that participants are included at different moments and different levels. Absent such institutionalisation, however, the state *cannot* be a legitimate entity in the context of border control. This is true even when the state pursues a just border control policy and succeeds in providing migrants with mechanisms of *ex ante* input and *ex post* accountability. The fact that the state unilaterally chooses to implement such procedures—and could therefore unilaterally choose to withdraw these—means that such procedures are not regular, reliable, and robust.[33] In the terms favoured by some intrinsic arguments, migrants are subjected to the unilateral will of the state rather than the omnilateral will of a public agent.[34] Second, the fluidity of this institutionalisation admits of treating political legitimacy as scalar: the greater the institutionalisation *across* the various entities that exercise power and *between* these

[31] It might seem that differentiated inclusion precludes participants from seeing themselves as 'free and equal'. In other contexts, however, differentiated inclusion can be seen as compatible with the moral and political equality of all, eg decision-making in federal constitutional structures.

[32] See, eg Hanna Gros and Samer Muscati, 'Immigration Detainees Hunger Strike Again as Canada Fails to Listen' (*Human Rights Watch*, 26 March 2021) <https://www.hrw.org/news/2021/03/20/immigration-detainees-hunger-strike-again-canada-fails-listen> accessed 26 November 2021.

[33] In Erman's formulation, these would be just policy and practices that are given rather than achieved, where the legitimacy points to the importance of process in securing legitimacy: Erman, 'Global Political Legitimacy beyond Justice and Democracy?' (n 18) 30.

[34] Cordelli, *The Privatized State* (n 1) 9.

entities and those subject to this power, the more legitimate the exercise of power in border control. And finally, this also suggests there may be multiple sources and drivers of institutionalisation: legitimating practices may emerge rather than be given, which is also historically true of many so-called 'inherently public' goods.[35]

Even this sparse set of guidelines provides some measure by which to assess existing practices in border control, in particular, the role of the state. For all the fluidity of possible institutionalised *ex ante* and *ex post* mechanisms, their absence in existing regimes of border control is stark. Migrants have little to no say in the formulation of state immigration policy or the practices by which these policies are implemented.[36] *Ex post* mechanisms are available but unreliable: migrants do not always have guaranteed legal representation in administrative or judicial processes of review, and these processes for redress can be unilaterally reduced by the state. States enjoy wide discretion in determining what constitutes an adequate process for adjudicating migrant rights and what these rights consist of.[37] Even when states are more deferential to international bodies, this does not enhance *migrants'* access to either input or accountability mechanisms since these mechanisms are largely absent even at the international level.[38]

In sum, migrants are subjected to, rather than the subjects of, the institutions and processes of border control. They have little formal influence over the substantive policy goals of state and international actors: for the most part, they have no formal rights to select policymakers, participate in consultations, frame public discourse, or reorganise priorities. And they have few means by which to counter or check these policies when they are being enforced. If we treat migration control as a good the beneficiaries of which are all would-be migrants, then citizens and migrants alike are beneficiaries with a stake in migration governance. Legitimacy at the border cannot be secured by states lacking in *ex ante* input and *ex post* accountability mechanisms.

VII Two Objections

Before concluding, I want to consider two objections to this line of analysis. The first reiterates the agency argument, stipulating that the state alone can provide border

[35] See, eg Sharon Dolovich, 'State Punishment and Private Prisons' (2005) 55(3) Duke Law Journal 437, 450–54.

[36] See, eg Uwe Steinhoff, 'Border Coercion and "Democratic Legitimacy": On Abizadeh's Argument against Current Regimes of Border Control' (2020) 26 Res Publica 281. In some jurisdictions, migrants with certain residency statuses may be able to vote in local, state, or general elections. Those seeking entry, however, are excluded from political decision-making.

[37] See, eg *Department of Homeland Security v Thuraissigiam* 140 S Ct 1959 (2020) on the habeas corpus rights of a migrant in expedited removal proceedings. For discussions of the case and the opinion, see Garrett Epps, 'The Fragility of Immigrants' Constitutional Protections' (*The Atlantic*, November 2019) <https://www.theatlantic.com/ideas/archive/2019/11/fragility-of-immigrants-constitutional-protections/601486/> accessed 24 November 2021; Case Note, 'Leading Case 140: *Department of Homeland Security v Thuraissigiam*' (2020) 134 Harvard Law Review 410.

[38] As Aleinikoff and Zarmore conclude, 'refugees remain largely voiceless': Alexander Aleinikoff and Leah Zarmore, *The Arc of Protection: Toward a New International Refugee Regime* (Stanford University Press 2018) 43.

control;[39] the second points to the ways that existing border control regimes do, in fact, incorporate input and accountability mechanisms. I address these in turn.

Recall, from section III, that intrinsic arguments against privatisation proceed in two steps: they establish that certain goods can only be provided by a public agent, and then they elaborate on how frontline agents or decision-makers should be connected to the public agents. I have not denied that border control should be provided by a public agent; I have only denied that actually existing states can, as currently constituted, be counted as public agents in the context of border control. Proponents of intrinsic arguments may have two responses. The first is to adopt the ontological rationale for when a good is 'inherently public': an enterprise is agent-dependent as a matter of conceptual definition. Examples given include the state and war and punishment, and male relatives and blood feuds.[40] Like these, the response might go, only the state can provide border control. Ontological arguments are largely stipulative. Even if there were broad agreement on the existence of a category of 'state practice', more is needed to tell us why particular practices and agents fall into this category. To argue that only the state can wage war and punish—or in this case, enforce borders—is, without more, to beg the question and to argue by definitional fiat.[41]

A second response is to accept the axiological, or functional, rationale, but to maintain that a state remains a public agent even when it lacks input and accountability mechanisms. For example, no state perfectly administers criminal justice, but this will not necessarily disqualify that state from being a public agent in the domain of punishment. Indeed, as I argued earlier, political legitimacy is a scalar concept, and existing states may be imperfectly public while still counting as public.[42] Scalar concepts still have thresholds, however: at some point, an entity ceases to be legitimate, either as a general matter or with respect to particular goods. This will necessarily call for a line-drawing exercise with disagreement on the threshold conditions that determine when a state, or indeed any actor, slips from being weakly legitimate to being illegitimate. The absence of institutionalised input and accountability mechanisms available to those who are subject to an actor's exercise of power will either be such a threshold condition—I am inclined to say it is—or will significantly weaken that entity's claim to legitimacy. Either way, intrinsic arguments lose their sting. Proponents are reduced to pointing out that the state still qualifies as a public agent and that only it can provide border control, even if it only barely does so on both counts.[43] It is unclear what, morally, turns on the identity of the agent providing the good, and on the normatively salient distinction between a weakly legitimate or illegitimate state and a non-state

[39] See, eg Thorburn, in this volume.

[40] Alon Harel, 'Defending *Why Law Matters*: A Response to Commentaries' (2017) 11 Criminal Law and Philosophy 847.

[41] <John Gardner, 'The Evil of Privatisation' (20 June 2014) 3. Available at SSRN: <https://ssrn.com/abstract=2460655> accessed 26 November 2021. Gardner refers to Hart's 'definitional stop'. To be clear, Harel seems to reject the ontological rationale and the metaphysical claims it would make. He claims to focus on the function that a public agent must perform: Harel, 'Defending *Why Law Matters*' (n 40) 854–55.

[42] See Thorburn, in this volume.

[43] Or, indeed, does not. In the context of punishment, Harel notes that he does not assume all states are legitimate but argues only that for punishment to be legitimate, it must be provided by a (legitimate) state. It is unclear, then, what the normative distinction between an illegitimate state and a non-state actor will be in the context of punishment: Harel, 'Defending *Why Law Matters*' (n 40) 855.

actor.[44] In any event, these objections do not deny that the state might be made a (more) legitimate actor—that is, a public agent—by institutionalising input and accountability mechanisms to regulate its relationship to the migrants it coerces.

This brings me to the second objection, which does not deny the significance of input and accountability mechanisms to the state's legitimacy, but only denies that they are absent from current regimes of border control. Critics might point out that migrants have a number of input mechanisms available to them: they can avail themselves of advocates, such as lawyers, citizen activists, and journalists, who use *their* access to *ex ante* input and *ex post* accountability mechanisms to introduce migrant perspectives and provide migrants with a measure of accountability. I have elaborated on these roles elsewhere to argue that non-state actors can play an ameliorative role with respect to legitimacy in border control.[45] In these roles, non-state actors have been critical in forming better institutions of border control and preventing or mitigating the harm that existing practices can inflict on migrants. And the effectiveness of these non-state actors often depends on the institutional resources and access provided by the state. Providing institutional mechanisms and space to citizens is not the same as providing these to migrants however. And the mediated access that citizens provide is not a substitute for direct and institutionalised access for migrants. Indeed, mediated access raises its own worries about legitimacy and domination.[46] In particular, while advocates aim to minimise the vulnerability of migrants to processes in which they have no say, migrants remain vulnerable to *them*: to whether they will choose to advocate for them, advocate for their interests accurately, and advocate for them in a reliable or stable manner. This is not to understate the value and effectiveness of calls for 'solidarity with migrants', but only to point out that unless this solidarity aims towards institutional change it can, at best, mitigate the illegitimacy at the border in an ad hoc manner; it does not legitimise the state's border control practices.

VIII Conclusion

Privatisation in border control is often criticised for the several negative consequences that follow: for the state, for some of the private actors to which enforcement is delegated, and most significantly, for migrants themselves. Intrinsic arguments against privatisation articulate a deeper set of misgivings about privatisation: that, irrespective of its consequences, it is illegitimate. Typically, intrinsic arguments counsel in favour of the state. In this chapter, I have drawn on intrinsic arguments to critique the state: in the context of border control, I have argued, the state is not a legitimate or public agent because it exercises power over migrants without standing in an appropriate political

[44] Jason Brennan argues that, if punishment can only be provided by a state, and private actors provide some alternative, call it 'schpunishment', which better realises the regulative ideals of punishment, then all things considered 'schpunishment' is morally preferable: Jason Brennan, 'Consequences Matter More: In Defense of Instrumentalism on Private vs Public Prisons' (2017) 11 Criminal Law and Philosophy 801, 812–15.

[45] Ashwini Vasanthakumar, 'Outsourcing Border Control: Public Agency and Action in Migration' in Avihay Dorfman and Alon Harel (eds), *Cambridge Handbook of Privatization* (CUP 2021) 102–16.

[46] ibid 113–16; see also Vogl, in this volume.

relationship to them. Drawing on conceptions of political legitimacy that look beyond the state–citizen relationship, I have identified two features of an appropriate political relationship: mechanisms for *ex ante* input from migrants and mechanisms for *ex post* accountability.

If these mechanisms are absent, then a focus on privatisation is misplaced: at least some of border control's ills lie elsewhere. Nor do these ills pertain to the justifiability of a state's border control policies, or the prior questions of whether and to what extent a state is permitted to exclude migrants from its borders. It is no answer to the question of whether the state is a legitimate actor in the context of border control to insist that it has a prima facie right to exclude. Similarly, that a state pursues a just immigration policy will not make it a legitimate actor: indeed, questions of whether or not state enforcement of border control is legitimate are not beholden to any particular conception of what a just migration policy would be. From the perspective of the migrant grabbed by a border guard, it may be morally irrelevant whether that border guard is a state official or a private contractor.

Indeed, I have suggested two ways in which some non-state actors can enhance legitimacy at the border. First, the presence of non-state actors in existing practices of border control—the border control complex—present opportunities for differentiated inclusion: mechanisms of input and accountability that need not take place at the level of the state but which can nevertheless regulate the state's relationship to migrants so as to better realise political legitimacy. Differentiated inclusion does not seek to establish political equality between migrants and citizens and does not infringe on the latter's collective self-determination. This suggests that the choice between statism and moral individualism is false,[47] and that states can realise political legitimacy with non-citizens without treating them identically to citizens. Second, non-state actors can mitigate the lack of legitimacy in border control. They can use *their* access to input and accountability mechanisms to provide these, in however attenuated and ad hoc a manner, to migrants, and they can help in creating and strengthening mechanisms of differentiated inclusion that regulate the relationship between migrants and the state, among others.

Intrinsic arguments against privatisation provide an ahistorical and idealised defence of political authority, almost always understood as the state. As I have tried to show in this chapter, this 'origin myth' of the state contains the critical resources with which to appraise actually existing states, to identify more morally desirable practices, and to gesture towards the agents and institutions that might help realise these ideals. Without mining these critical resources, intrinsic arguments risk being irrelevant: they criticise privatisation by talking about how the state could be—obfuscating how the state actually is, or indeed has ever been.

[47] See Thorburn, in this volume.

References

Abizadeh A, 'Democratic Theory and Border Coercion: No Right to Unilaterally Control your own Borders' (2008) 36(1) Political Theory 37

— —, 'Democratic Legitimacy and State Coercion: A Reply to Miller' (2010) 38(1) Political Theory 121

Aleinikoff A and Zarmore L, *The Arc of Protection: Toward a New International Refugee Regime* (Stanford University Press 2018)

Arhennius G, 'The Boundary Problem' in Tersman F (ed), *The Viability and Desirability of Global Democracy* (Filosofiska institutionen, Stockholms Universitet 2007)

Beetham D, *The Legitimation of Power* (Palgrave 1991)

Bender F, 'Enfranchising the Disenfranchised: Should Refugees Receive Political Rights in Liberal Democracies?' (2021) 25(1) Citizenship Studies 56

Bergstrom L, 'Democracy and Political Boundaries' in Folke Tersman (ed), *The Viability and Desirability of Global Democracy* (Filosofiska institutionen, Stockholms Universitet 2007

Brennan J, 'Consequences Matter More: In Defense of Instrumentalism on Private vs Public Prisons' (2017) 11 Criminal Law and Philosophy 80

Buchanan A, *Justice, Legitimacy, and Self-determination* (OUP 2003)

— — and Keohane B, 'The Legitimacy of Global Governance Institutions' (2006) 20(4) Ethics and International Affairs 405

Cordelli C, 'Privatization without Profit?' in Knight J and Schwartzberg M (eds), *Privatization* (NOMOS LX 2018)

— —, *The Privatized State* (Princeton University Press 2020)

Dolovich S, 'State Punishment and Private Prisons' (2005) 55(3) Duke Law Journal 437

Dorfman A and Harel A, 'The Case Against Privatization' (2013) 41 Philosophy & Public Affairs 67

— —, 'Against Privatisation as Such' (2016) 36 Oxford Journal of Legal Studies 400

Epps G, 'The Fragility of Immigrants' Constitutional Protections' (*The Atlantic*, November 2019) <https://www.theatlantic.com/ideas/archive/2019/11/fragility-of-immigrants-constitutional-protections/601486/>

Erman E, 'Global Political Legitimacy beyond Justice and Democracy?' (2016) 8(1) International Theory 29

— —, 'A Function-sensitive Approach to the Political Legitimacy of Global Governance' (2020) 50(3) British Journal of Political Science 1001

Fine S, 'The Ethics of Immigration: Self-determination and the Right to Exclude' (2013) 8(3) Philosophy Compass 254

Gardner J, 'The Evil of Privatization' (20 June 2014). Available at SSRN: https://ssrn.com/abstract=2460655

Gros H and Muscati S, 'Immigration Detainees Hunger Strike Again as Canada Fails to Listen' (*Human Rights Watch*, 26 March 2021) <https://www.hrw.org/news/2021/03/20/immigration-detainees-hunger-strike-again-canada-fails-listen>

Harel A, *Why Law Matters* (OUP 2014)

— —

, 'Defending *Why Law Matters*: A Response to Commentaries' (2017) 11 Criminal Law and Philosophy 847

Harvard Law Review, 'Leading Case 140: *Department of Homeland Security v Thuraissigiam*' (2020) 134 Harvard Law Review 410

Hidalgo J, 'The Case for the International Governance of Migration' (2016) 8(1) International Theory 140

Kukathas C, *Immigration and Freedom* (Princeton University Press 2021)

Macdonald K and MacDonald T, 'Liquid Authority and Political Legitimacy in Transnational Governance' (2017) 9(2) International Theory 329
— —, 'Towards a "Pluralist" World Order: Creative Agency and Legitimacy in Global Institutions' (2020) 26(2) European Journal of International Relations 518
Macdonald T, 'Political Legitimacy in International Border Governance Institutions' (2015) 14(4) European Journal of Political Theory 409
Miller D, 'Why Immigration Controls are not Coercive: A Reply to Abizadeh' (2010) 38(1) Political Theory 111
Mills C, 'Ideal Theory as Ideology' in *Black Rights/White Wrongs: The Critique of Racial Liberalism* (OUP 2017)
Steinhoff U, 'Border Coercion and "Democratic Legitimacy": On Abizadeh's Argument against Current Regimes of Border Control' (2020) 26 Res Publica 281
Valentini L, 'On the Value of Constitutions and Judicial Review' (2017) 11 Criminal Law and Philosophy 817
Vasanthakumar A, 'Privatizing Border Control' (2018) 38 Oxford Journal of Legal Studies 411
Vasanthakumar A, 'Outsourcing Border Control: Public Agency and Action in Migration' in Dorfman A and Harel A (eds), *Cambridge Handbook of Privatization* (CUP 2021)

Cases

Department of Homeland Security v Thuraissigiam 140 S Ct 1959 (2020)

6
Privatised Immigration Detention
Morality, Economics, and Transparency

Emily Ryo and Ian Peacock

I Introduction

'I don't know if anybody would be super jazzed to have a detention center in their town. But yeah, the thing that really puts it over for me is the private detention part. That's a part that I really can't get past.'[1] This sentiment, expressed by Brenda Richin, a resident in Evanston, Wyoming, about the prospect of a for-profit private prison company building an immigration detention facility in her town, reflects a growing opposition to a distinct feature of immigration detention: privatisation. In a 2014 nationally representative survey of 1,000 Americans—the only poll of its kind to date—51 per cent of respondents viewed the operation of immigration detention facilities by private organisations as 'sometimes inappropriate' or 'very inappropriate'.[2]

Our goals in this chapter are threefold. First, we discuss the current state of knowledge regarding the origin and nature of privatised detention in the United States. Two-thirds of all immigrant detainees are confined in facilities operated by for-profit private prison companies.[3] This discussion provides a brief overview of the historical and political context in which private prison companies have gained influence, and against which immigrant rights supporters have mobilised. Here we focus on for-profit corporations' ownership and/or operation of facilities in which immigrants facing removal are confined.

Second, we describe the three key anti-privatisation frames advanced by various actors, including immigrant rights advocates, investigative reporters, government watchdogs, political elites, and scholars, in support of detention reform. We call these Morality-Legitimacy, Economic-Instrumental, and Transparency-Accountability Frames. According to Gamson and Modigliani, a frame is 'a central organizing idea or story line that provides meaning to an unfolding strip of events'. It 'suggests what

[1] Samantha Laine Perfas, Jessica Mendoza, and Henry Gass, 'When a Private Prison Company Came to Small-town Wyoming (audio)' (*The Christian Science Monitor*, 2020) <https://www.csmonitor.com/USA/Justice/2020/0824/When-a-private-prison-company-came-to-small-town-Wyoming-audio> accessed 31 August 2021, quoting Brenda Richin.

[2] Peter K Enns and Mark D Ramirez, 'Privatizing Punishment: Testing Theories of Public Support for Private Prison and Immigration Detention Facilities' (2018) 56(3) Criminology 546, 555.

[3] Homeland Security Advisory Council, *Report of the Subcommittee on Privatized Immigration Detention Facilities* (US Department of Homeland Security 2016) 6 <https://perma.cc/CXR8-GRU4> accessed 31 August 2021; Emily Ryo and Ian Peacock, 'A National Study of Immigration Detention in the United States' (2018) 92(1) Southern California Law Review 1, 28.

Emily Ryo and Ian Peacock, *Privatised Immigration Detention* In: *Privatising Border Control.* Edited by: Mary Bosworth and Lucia Zedner, Oxford University Press. © Emily Ryo and Ian Peacock 2022. DOI: 10.1093/oso/9780192857163.003.0007

the controversy is about, the essence of the issue'.[4] The organising ideas or storylines analysed here are aimed at the broader public as well as policymakers, and as we detail below, they appear in a variety of materials such as organisational websites, reports, media-related sources, news articles, and scholarship. Understanding the content of dominant narratives in the public domain is critical for any issue area, given the long line of studies that show that such narratives can help shape public opinion and the course of social movements, structure policy debates, and define research agendas.[5]

Third, we explore the anti-privatisation frames' limitations and possibilities for changing public attitudes and policymaking on privatised detention in particular and immigration detention more generally. Chacón has offered an insightful assessment of some of the major criticisms of private detention facilities,[6] but there is a dearth of empirical evidence that allows us to assess the effectiveness of various anti-privatisation frames. In this section, we develop theoretically informed predictions that we hope will guide future empirical investigations in this area. Developing theory and empirical evidence in this field is a timely and important task. According to a recent survey, a large segment of the American public—about 21 per cent of respondents—thought that privatising prisons and immigration detention centres was neither appropriate nor inappropriate.[7] The researchers concluded: 'This means some segment of the public could be potentially swayed to either support or oppose privatizing these institutions, thereby creating a sizable social movement that could lead to either more private carceral facilities or reform.'[8] This conclusion is bolstered by a large body of research that suggests that, although public opinion is only a part of the story of policymaking, 'overall the finding that opinion influences policy is amazingly robust—most studies show opinion affecting policy regardless of how opinion, policy, and the relationship between them is measured'.[9]

In setting out these three elements, this chapter seeks to provide a context for thinking about the rise of privatised detention in the United States and to develop new lines of inquiry for understanding the evolving contestation over the phenomenon. We also contribute to the rich and growing literature on the impact of framing on immigration-related attitudes, debates, and policy formation.[10] We advance this

[4] ibid.

[5] See, eg Robert D Benford and David A Snow, 'Framing Processes and Social Movements: An Overview and Assessment' (2000) 26(1) Annual Review of Sociology 611; William G Jacoby, 'Issue Framing and Public Opinion on Government Spending' (2000) 44(4) American Journal of Political Science 750; Francesca Polletta and M Kai Ho, 'Frames and their Consequences' in Robert E Goodin and Charles Tilly (eds), *The Oxford Handbook of Contextual Political Analysis* (OUP 2006).

[6] Jennifer M Chacón, 'Privatized Immigration Enforcement' (2017) 52(1) Harvard Civil Rights—Civil Liberties Law Review 1.

[7] Enns and Ramirez (n 2).

[8] ibid 564.

[9] Paul Burstein, 'Public Opinion, Public Policy, and Democracy' in Kevin T Leicht and J Craig Jenkins (eds), *Handbook of Politics: State and Society in Global Perspective* (Springer 2010) 72. See also Saundra K Schneider and William G Jacoby, 'Public Opinion and Public Policy in the United States' in John A Hird (ed), *Policy Analysis in the United States* (Policy Press 2018) 183–204.

[10] See, eg Lynn H Fujiwara, 'Immigrant Rights are Human Rights: The Reframing of Immigrant Entitlement and Welfare' (2005) 52(1) Social Problems 79; Hana E Brown, 'Race, Legality, and the Social Policy Consequences of Anti-immigration Mobilization' (2013) 78(2) American Sociological Review 290; Irene Bloemraad, Fabiana Silva, and Kim Voss, 'Rights, Economics, or Family? Frame Resonance, Political Ideology, and the Immigrant Rights Movement' (2016) 94(4) Social Forces 1647; Chris Haynes, Jennifer L Merolla, and S Karthick Ramakrishnan, *Framing Immigrants: News Coverage, Public Opinion, and Policy*

important line of work by providing a fresh perspective on an issue that has implications not only for immigration policy but also for debates about criminal justice reform.

II Background

Immigration detention plays a central role in immigration enforcement systems around the world. This is certainly true in the United States, which has been described as the 'detention nation'.[11] As is also true of many other countries,[12] privatised immigration enforcement and privatised immigration detention have expanded in the United States over the past few decades. In this section, we briefly describe the origin and expansion of this privatisation, to set the context for understanding the issue frames that define current debates on this form of immigration detention in the United States.

A The Rise of Privatised Immigration Enforcement

From outsourcing the logistics of deportation and policing non-citizens[13] to delegating and monetising non-citizen surveillance,[14] private companies have been closely intertwined with the expanding scale and scope of immigration enforcement. This is true in immigration detention as well, where private prison companies—actors in the business of confining people—have played an important role. The use of privately operated prisons in the United States dates as far back as the colonial times.[15] But the rise of the modern private prison industry can be traced to the 1980s when two major trends converged to expand the scale of prison privatisation.[16] The first trend involved prison overcrowding brought on by the War on Drugs and the concomitant spread of mass incarceration practices. The second trend involved the turn toward neo-liberalism that came to define the Reagan era, which championed limited government and faith in the private sector. Together, these trends breathed life into free market advocates' promotion of prison privatisation as a means of achieving greater efficiency and reducing government bureaucracy in the criminal justice system.

(Russell Sage Foundation 2016); Kim Ebert, Wenjie Lia, and Emily P Estrada, 'Apathy and Color-blindness in Privatized Immigration Control' (2020) 6(4) Sociology of Race and Ethnicity 533.

[11] Emily Ryo, 'Understanding Immigration Detention: Causes, Conditions, and Consequences' (2019) 15 Annual Review of Law and Social Science 97, 99.

[12] Allison Mountz and others, 'Conceptualizing Detention: Mobility, Containment, Bordering, and Exclusion' (2012) 37(4) Progress in Human Geography 522.

[13] See Bosworth and Singler, and Zedner, both in this volume.

[14] See Bigo and Chacón, both in this volume.

[15] James Austin and Garry Coventry, *Emerging Issues on Privatized Prisons* (Bureau of Justice Assistance 2001) 9 <https://perma.cc/RQF6 SM9J> accessed 31 August 2021.

[16] Dae-Young Kim, 'Prison Privatization: An Empirical Literature Review and Path Forward' (2022) 32(1) International Criminal Justice Review 24.

One of the most important private actors that emerged during this period—and which continues to dominate the private prison industry to date—is the Corrections Corporation of America (CCA), which later became CoreCivic.[17] CCA was formed in 1983, and its first contract was with the US Immigration and Naturalization Service (INS), a predecessor agency to the US Immigration and Customs Enforcement (ICE). CCA's first contract was to design, build, and manage a 300-bed immigration detention facility in Houston, Texas, which opened in 1984.[18] The other central private actor in the prison industry was, and continues to be, Wackenhut Corrections Corporation, which later became The GEO Group, Inc. Wackenhut's first contract was also with the INS, to operate a 150-bed immigration detention facility in Denver, Colorado, which opened in 1987.[19] Thus, the INS was 'among the first governmental agencies to take advantage of the emerging market of private prison operators'.[20]

B Expansion and Resistance

The immigrant detainee population has increased steadily over the years. In 2001, the total number of individuals in immigration detention was 204,459; in 2019, the total number of initial book-ins to ICE detention facilities reached 510,854.[21] To maintain this growing system, the Federal Government has relied heavily on the private sector. For example, between 2015 and 2016, about 65 to 67 per cent of immigrant detainees were held in facilities operated by for-profit private prison companies.[22] According to a recent report, 29 per cent of CoreCivic's 2019 revenue came from detention contracts with ICE, which amounted to a total of $574 million.[23] Likewise, about 29 per cent of The GEO Group's 2019 revenue came from detention contracts with ICE, at a total of $708 million in revenue.[24]

To ensure their market dominance and revenues in criminal justice and immigration detention, private prison companies have made substantial political campaign contributions, largely to Republican candidates.[25] In addition, private prison companies have engaged in ongoing lobbying efforts. Disclosure statements filed by CCA and The GEO Group indicate that these companies lobby on issues related to the

[17] See Tuck, in this volume.

[18] Douglas C McDonald, 'Public Imprisonment by Private Means: The Re-emergence of Private Prisons and Jails in the United States, the United Kingdom, and Australia' (1994) 34 British Journal of Criminology 29.

[19] ibid.

[20] Austin and Coventry (n 16) 12.

[21] See Ryo (n 12); US Immigration and Customs Enforcement, *US Immigration and Customs Enforcement Fiscal Year 2019 Enforcement and Removal Operations Report* (US Department of Homeland Security 2019) <https://perma.cc/22ES-S8H9> accessed 31 August 2021. The 'total number of individuals in immigration detention' and the 'total number of initial book-ins to ICE detention facilities' are not equivalents, but our analysis suggests that they are relatively comparable.

[22] Homeland Security Advisory Council (n 3) 6; Ryo and Peacock (n 3) 28.

[23] ACLU, Human Rights Watch, and National Immigrant Justice Center, *Justice-free Zones: US Immigration Detention under the Trump Administration* (American Civil Liberties Union 2020) <https://perma.cc/KWB8-GQWQ> accessed 31 August 2021.

[24] ibid.

[25] Ciara O'Neill, 'Private Prisons: Principally Profit-Oriented and Politically Pliable' (*FollowTheMoney.org*, 2018) <https://perma.cc/L5VU-B3Y8> accessed 20 December 2020.

Department of Homeland Security's (DHS) immigration detention budget and immigration reform legislation, presumably to ensure the continued level of, or expansion in, privatisation and the overall immigrant detainee population.[26]

The expansion of private prison companies' role in immigration detention, however, has not gone unchecked. For example, a recent reform effort has centred around a divestment campaign targeted at banks that provide financial services to private prison companies.[27] In 2019, a number of major banks announced that they would stop financing private prison companies after reports of abusive and dangerous conditions in for-profit prisons and immigration detention facilities garnered widespread public condemnation.[28] In addition, private prison companies have faced growing legal and political challenges. For example, in 2019, Illinois passed House Bill 2040 (HB 2040), becoming the first state to ban the private operation of immigration detention facilities. California followed suit by passing Assembly Bill 32 (AB 32), which came into effect in 2020.[29]

Nonetheless, commentators predict that privatised detention is likely to persist in the United States.[30] The Homeland Security Advisory Council, at the end of the Obama administration, made a similar prognosis, concluding that '[f]iscal considerations, combined with the need for realistic capacity to handle sudden increases in detention, indicate that DHS's use of private for-profit detention will continue'.[31]

III Anti-privatization Frames

The foregoing discussion suggests that there are political openings to question the purported advantages of privatised detention. These mobilisation efforts have been anchored by a specific set of anti-privatisation frames, which provide 'definitions of a situation',[32] or shared understandings of reality. Put another way, frames are social constructions of an issue or phenomenon presented by mass media, activists, political leaders, or other actors and organisations. According to Snow, frames perform three key functions in how we come to understand and engage with various social,

[26] Bethany Carson and Eleana Diaz, 'Payoff: How Congress Ensures Private Prison Profit with an Immigrant Detention Quota' (*Grassroots Leadership*, 2015) <https://perma.cc/PVY5-Q26E> (accessed 31 August 2021).

[27] Danielle C Jefferis, 'Private Prisons, Private Governance: Essay on Developments in Private-sector Resistance to Privatized Immigration Detention' (2019) 15(1) Northwestern Journal of Law and Social Policy 82.

[28] ibid.

[29] ICE, however, awarded long-term contracts to private prison companies in December 2019—two weeks before AB 32 came into effect—to continue the operation of immigration detention facilities in California. Nomaan Merchant, 'Private Prison Industry Backs Trump, Prepares if Biden Wins' (*AP News*, 13 August 2020) <https://apnews.com/article/houston-ap-top-news-prisons-immigration-joe-biden-ca7f6e9fac1f287bb79ae55410112c46> accessed 31 August 2021.

[30] Brett C Burkhardt and Story Edison, 'Correctional Privatization in the United States' in Philip Bean (ed), *Criminal Justice and Privatisation: Key Issues and Debates* (Routledge 2020); Jamile Lartey, 'Think Private Prison Companies are Going Away under Biden? They have Other Plans' (*The Marshall Project*, 2020) <https://perma.cc/M9V8-WTAA> accessed 31 August 2021.

[31] Homeland Security Advisory Council (n 3) 2.

[32] Erving Goffman, *Frame Analysis: An Essay on the Organization of Experience* (Harvard University Press 1974) 10.

economic, and political issues.[33] First, they *focus* our attention on what is, or should be, important or relevant, by demarcating or punctuating certain elements of a phenomenon. Second, they *articulate* a story by drawing together certain salient elements of a phenomenon. Third, frames reconfigure or *transform* our understanding of, and response to, the objects of our attention.

In this section, we delineate three dominant anti-privatisation frames that have emerged in public discourse about privatised detention. As we highlight below, they often draw from and overlap with the longstanding public discourse and scholarship that critique private prisons,[34] though some of the critique is unique to immigration detention.

A Morality-Legitimacy Frame

One of the most enduring frames in the anti-privatised detention discourse is that concerning the morality and legitimacy of this practice. There are at least two central themes here. The first theme emphasises the immorality of profiting from deprivations of personal liberty—or, as depicted by some commentators—'from human misery'.[35] As Lawrence Benito, the executive director of the Illinois Coalition for Immigrant and Refugee Rights, declared: 'Those who seek financial gain by jailing people who are seeking refuge and by tearing apart our families have no business in our state.'[36] The same sentiment undergirds Governor Gavin Newsom's statement at the signing of AB 32: 'These for-profit prisons do not reflect our values.'[37]

The second theme focuses on political legitimacy. As defined by Mark Suchman, legitimacy refers to a 'generalized perception or assumption that the actions of an entity are desirable, proper, or appropriate within some socially constructed system of norms, values, beliefs, and definitions'. [38] Immigrant rights advocates' focus on legitimacy in the context of mobilisation against privatised detention is built on the idea imported from criminal justice, which holds that imprisonment is inherently and uniquely a governmental not private function. That is, 'physical coercion is a core responsibility of the state, one that cannot/should not be handed over to private actors'.[39]

The notion that physical coercion necessary for state-sanctioned confinement cannot and should not be delegated or outsourced to private actors has become

[33] David A Snow, 'Framing and Social Movements' in David A Snow and others (eds), *The Wiley-Blackwell Encyclopedia of Social and Political Movements* (Wiley-Blackwell 2013).

[34] Sharon Dolovich, 'How Privatization Thinks: The Case of Prisons' in Jody Freeman and Martha Minow (eds), *Government by Contract: Outsourcing and American Democracy* (Harvard University Press 2009); Brett C Burkhardt, 'Contesting Market Rationality: Discursive Struggles over Prison Privatization' (2019) 21(2) Punishment & Society 162.

[35] Sarah Lazare, '"Profiting from Misery": Private Prison Corporations Driving Harsh Immigration Policies' (*Facing South*, 2015) <https://perma.cc/9S5L-HY7Z> accessed 31 August 2021.

[36] Cara Yi, 'General Assembly Approves Ban on Private Detention Facilities in Illinois' (*Illinois Coalition for Immigrant and Refugee Rights*, 16 May 2019) <https://perma.cc/V6ES-ES7V> accessed 31 August 2021.

[37] Steve Gorman, 'California Bans Private Prisons and Immigration Detention Centers' (*Reuters*, 11 October 2019) <https://perma.cc/K3Y4-SWWE> accessed 31 August 2021.

[38] Mark C Suchman, 'Managing Legitimacy: Strategic and Institutional Approaches' (1995) 20(3) The Academy of Management Review 571.

[39] Burkhardt (n 31) 167; see also Thorburn, in this volume.

prominent across the criminal–civil divide. For example, the Homeland Security Advisory Council has argued: 'Because legitimate restriction on physical liberty is inherently and exclusively a governmental authority, much could be said for a fully government-owned and government-operated detention model.'[40] For critics, the delegation in immigration detention of this core governmental function to private for-profit companies 'violates our nation's basic guiding principles of justice and fairness'.[41]

B Economic-Instrumental Frame

Private prison companies and proponents of privatisation have justified the rise and expansion of privatisation through claims that private prison companies can deliver the government better services at a lower cost.[42] Supporters argue that private prison companies provide better provision of basic care, educational and substance-abuse programming, and services to confined individuals.[43] They also claim to offer better protection of basic rights of detainees.[44]

The Economic-Instrumental Frame challenges this view. Some point to the lack of competition in an industry where only a few private prison companies dominate the market.[45] Other critics focus on the prevalence of abuse, neglect, and deaths in privately operated detention facilities.[46] Numerous immigrant advocates, investigative reporters, and government watchdogs have long sounded the alarm on dangerous and inhumane conditions of detention in privately operated facilities.[47] According to a recent whistle-blower complaint about a private detention facility in Georgia: 'The conditions in the detention center are squalid, they say, the medical care hideously subpar; they worry that, unless prison authorities do something to shield them from the coronavirus, they'll die.'[48] Consequently, some critics have argued that any cost reduction created by private prison companies comes at the expense of quality of care.[49]

[40] Homeland Security Advisory Council (n 3) 5.

[41] Representative Jimmy Gomez, 'Reps. Gomez, Crow, Jayapal, and Ruiz Lead Colleagues in Calling on Biden Administration to End Private Immigration Detention Centers' (Press Release, 1 February 2021) <https://perma.cc/BMW8-MR6U> accessed 31 August 2021.

[42] Austin and Coventry (n 16).

[43] CoreCivic, 'What We Do' <https://perma.cc/AX6H-Q9HE> accessed 18 September 2021; Curt Bramble and Vernon Jones, *Why Contracting for Performance in Prison and Detention Management is Worth a Closer Look* (Management and Training Corporation 2019) <https://perma.cc/KBD9-P5V6> accessed 18 September 2021.

[44] Bramble and Jones (n 44); Homeland Security Advisory Council (n 3).

[45] Livia Luan, 'Profiting from Enforcement: The Role of Private Prisons in US Immigration Detention' (*Migration Policy Institute*, 2 May 2018)

[46] See, eg ACLU and others (n 24); Center for International Human Rights, *Report on the Role of Private Security Companies in Migrant Detention in the US and their Impact on the Protection of the Rights of Migrants* (Northwestern Pritzker School of Law 2020) <https://perma.cc/MLX6-6GNT> accessed 31 August 2021.

[47] For a recent report, see Committee on Oversight and Reform and Subcommittee on Civil Rights and Civil Liberties, 'The Trump Administration's Mistreatment of Detained Immigrants: Deaths and Deficient Medical Care by For-profit Detention Contractors' (*US House of Representatives*, 2020) <https://perma.cc/Z7LD-HR2F> accessed 31 August 2021.

[48] Jonathan Blitzer, 'The Private Georgia Immigration-detention Facility at the Center of a Whistle-blower's Complaint' (*The New Yorker*, 2020) <https://perma.cc/9WVF-ZVSD> accessed 31 August 2021.

[49] Oliver Hart, Andrei Shleifer, and Robert W Vishny, 'The Proper Scope of Government: Theory and an Application to Prisons' (1997) 112(4) Quarterly Journal of Economics 1127.

Critics of privatised detention who rely on the Economic-Instrumental Frame also emphasise ICE's increased spending on immigration detention and the concomitant rise in annual profits for private prison companies operating immigration detention facilities. As reported by the Migration Policy Institute, a non-partisan think tank:

> In FY 2017, DHS spent approximately $126 per day for each detained noncitizen. As immigration detention costs steadily increased to around $2 billion annually, industry profits soared. Between 2007 and 2014, CoreCivic's overall annual profits grew from about $133 million to $195 million, and GEO Group's profits grew from about $42 million to $144 million yearly.[50]

In addition, critics maintain that the costs of outsourcing detention are much larger than direct payments to private companies. Some scholars argue, for example, that private companies do more than purportedly meet the existing needs of ICE's detention capacity; instead, they work to increase the demand for their services.[51] Furthermore, outsourcing services to private prison companies entails transaction costs, including expenses to monitor and assure contract fulfilment, which are not easily measurable and which do not apply to in-house facilities that are federally operated.[52]

The Economic-Instrumental Frame trades in empirical claims. In 2016, the US Department of Justice Office of the Inspector General found that federal prisons operated by private companies were less safe and secure than their publicly operated counterparts. But research findings on private prisons have not been conclusive,[53] partly because large-scale studies comparing the relative cost and the quality of care of privately operated versus publicly operated prisons remain scarce.[54] Empirical research on these issues is even more scarce and methodologically limited regarding privatised immigration detention.[55] However, emerging research suggests that privately operated facilities may be less safe and secure and have higher levels of grievances than privately operated facilities.[56]

C Transparency-Accountability Frame

The third frame that has gained prominence in public discourse about immigration detention focuses on the lack of transparency and accountability in privatised

[50] Luan (n 46).

[51] Loren Collingwood, Jason L Morin, and Stephen Omar El-Khatib, 'Expanding Carceral Markets: Detention Facilities, ICE Contracts, and the Financial Interests of Punitive Immigration Policy' (2018) 10(4) Race and Social Problems 275.

[52] Richard J Kish and Amy F Lipton, 'Do Private Prisons Really Offer Savings Compared with their Public Counterparts?' (2013) 33(1) Economic Affairs 93.

[53] For a comprehensive review, see Kim (n 17).

[54] Gerald G Gaes, 'Current Status of Prison Privatization Research on American Prisons and Jails' (2019) 18(2) Criminology & Public Policy 269.

[55] Chacón (n 7).

[56] Ryo and Peacock (n 3); Zachary Bauer and Jocelyn M Johnston, 'Who Does It Better? Comparing Immigration Detention Facility Performance in an Intergovernmental and Intersectoral Context' (2020) 80(2) Public Administration Review 244–58.

detention.[57] Transparency in the governance literature generally refers to public availability of information about the operation of organisations, whereas accountability refers to the responsibility of organisations to answer, in some way, about their behaviour and actions.[58] Transparency and accountability are closely related and commonly understood to be mutually reinforcing.[59]

With respect to privatised detention, the calls for transparency and accountability have criticised private prison companies as operating under a veil of secrecy. As one non-profit organisation, the American Friends Service Committee, has stated: 'Unlike public facilities that are subject to state and federal open records laws such as the Freedom of Information Act, private prisons are permitted to operate in secrecy, away from the light of public scrutiny.'[60] In addition, these calls have highlighted the lack of government oversight and failure to impose meaningful sanctions for the private companies' violation of detention standards: 'ICE has systematically failed to hold private prison companies accountable for their inability or unwillingness to comply with ICE detention standards, even where those violations result in death.'[61] The Transparency-Accountability Frame has gained new salience during the COVID-19 pandemic, as ICE in general, and private prison companies in particular, came under growing scrutiny for their failure to track and report infections and to take appropriate steps to protect the detainees and facility staff from the virus.[62]

At the federal level, efforts of policymakers to extend the Freedom of Information Act to cover private prison companies that contract with the Federal Government (including for immigration detention) have failed repeatedly.[63] The latest bill, S. 2773, the Private Prison Information Act, was introduced by Senator Ben Cardin in 2019 but no action is likely to be taken by Congress. By contrast, California recently enacted Assembly Bill 3228 (AB 3228), which responds directly to the focal concern of the Transparency-Accountability Frame. Under AB 3228, individuals may sue private detention facility operators for failing to comply with the standards of care included in the facility contract. Assemblyman Rob Bonta, who authored AB 3228, emphasised the need for accountability in describing the law: 'For-profit private detention centers must be held accountable in the face of egregious human rights violations and harm to the health, safety and welfare of Californians, especially during the COVID-19 pandemic.'[64]

[57] American Friends Service Committee, *The Role of For-profit Prison Corporations in Shaping US Immigrant Detention & Deportation Policies* (American Friends Service Committee 2015) <https://perma.cc/EUN7-NMVA> accessed 31 August 2021; Chacón (n 7).

[58] Christopher Hood, 'Accountability and Transparency: Siamese Twins, Matching Parts, Awkward Couple?' (2010) 33(5) West European Politics 989.

[59] ibid 990.

[60] American Friends Service Committee (n 58).

[61] Katie Shepherd, *Immigrants Detained in California Win the Right to Sue Private Prison Companies* (American Immigration Council 2020) <https://perma.cc/2Z5R-F6LU> accessed 31 August 2021.

[62] Donald Kerwin, *Immigrant Detention and COVID-19: How a Pandemic Exploited and Spread through the US Immigrant Detention System* (Center for Migration Studies 2020) <https://perma.cc/G79D-RJFR> accessed 31 August 2021.

[63] Libbi L Vilher, 'Private Prisons and the Need for Greater Transparency: Private Prison Information Act' (2017) 12(1) Brooklyn Journal of Corporate, Financial, & Commercial Law 213.

[64] Andrea Castillo, 'Detainees at California's For-profit ICE Detention Centers will Soon be Able to Sue over Abuse, Harm' Los Angeles Times (28 September) 2020 <https://www.latimes.com/california/story/

IV Framing Effects

Because frames are used to define problems, identify their causes, and suggest solutions, they are ubiquitous in public discourse.[65] A longstanding body of research based on diverse methodologies, including experiments, surveys, and case and historical studies, shows that frames can shift or change the attitudes and behaviours of their audience.[66] But frames do not operate in a vacuum or on a blank slate. Their effects on social policies are shaped by the social identities of their audience, as well as people's pre-existing values and their views about the policies' intended beneficiaries. In this section, we explore these insights to consider their implications for the three key anti-privatisation frames that we have presented above.

A Identity Salience

Research shows that different social identities can shape attitudes, policy preferences, and behaviours.[67] Social identities refer to psychological constructs that people develop or adopt to define who they are and where they belong based on their group membership(s) including their social class, citizenship, religious affiliation, race, and gender.[68] Identity-based preferences can even result in decision-making that may be inconsistent with the individual's rational economic interests.[69] Studies show that issue framing can increase the salience of certain social identities in at least three ways: (1) by merely mentioning a given social identity; (2) by drawing attention to the identity-based group's interests; and (3) by highlighting threats that affect the identity-based group.[70]

Increasing or decreasing the salience of certain social identities can shape how a frame affects people's attitudes and policy preferences. For example, in an experimental study of identity salience and framing, Diamondfound that priming study subjects with either a non-partisan social identity (parental identity) or a partisan political identity (Republican versus Democrat) prior to being exposed to a climate change frame generated different levels of concern about climate change, engagement

2020-09-28/detainees-at-californias-for-profit-ice-detention-centers-will-soon-be-able-to-sue-over-abuse-harm> accessed 31 August 2021.

[65] Robert M Entman, 'Framing: Toward Clarification of a Fractured Paradigm' (1993) 43(4) Journal of Communication 51.

[66] For a review, see Dennis Chong and James N Druckman, 'Framing Theory' (2007) 10 Annual Review of Political Science 103.

[67] Michael Kalin and Nicholas Sambanis, 'How to Think about Social Identity' (2018) 21 Annual Review of Political Science 239.

[68] Henry Tajfel and John C Turner, 'The Social Identity Theory of Intergroup Behavior' in Stephen Worchel and William G Austin (eds), *Psychology of Intergroup Relations* (Nelson-Hall 1986).

[69] George A Akerlof and Rachel E Kranton, *Identity Economics: How Our Identities Shape Our Work, Wages, and Well-being* (Princeton University Press 2010).

[70] Samara Klar, 'The Influence of Competing Identity Primes on Political Preferences' (2013) 75(4) Journal of Politics 1108.

in pro-climate action, and support for climate change policies.[71] In 2018, Han and Federico examined the role of social identity salience in explaining the policy support effect of news frames about employer-sponsored health insurance coverage of egg freezing for female employees.[72] They found that the frame that made gender salient for the study subjects increased issue polarisation along gender lines. Likewise, the frame that made political partisanship salient increased issue polarisation along partisanship lines.

These studies suggest that making certain social identities more or less salient before or during exposure to anti-privatisation frames may garner increased support for, or opposition to, privatised detention, all else being equal. For example, with respect to the Morality-Legitimacy Frame, in so far as commodification of a system built on 'human misery' is morally repugnant from a religious perspective, the relative persuasiveness of claims about the morality or legitimacy of private detention may depend on activating certain faith-based identities that are associated with progressive causes. We recognise that, given the link between Christian nationalism and nativism, the relationship between religious ideologies and political attitudes is complex. But there are historical examples of reform movements activating certain types of Christian values in service of immigrant-protective policies. For example, Susan Coutin has credited the success of the US sanctuary movement, which aided undocumented Central Americans to activism grounded in religious ethics.[73] Others have highlighted the importance of progressive Christian activists in undermining the Trump administration's zero-tolerance policy against immigrant families apprehended at the US–Mexico border.[74]

In contrast, the success of the Economic-Instrumental Frame may be conditional on making salient people's shared social identity as taxpayers whose financial interests may be at odds with those of private prison companies. In terms of the Transparency-Accountability Frame, ensuring its effectiveness may require underscoring threats to democracy and the rule of law that members of a polity will face when organisations conduct their businesses in secrecy.

These predictions require empirical testing. More broadly, our discussion highlights a new way of thinking about the nature and potential appeal of anti-privatisation arguments. A unifying idea in our foregoing discussion of the anti-privatisation frames is the importance of drawing the public's attention to shared higher-order social identities that transcend partisan identities and the immigrant/non-immigrant dichotomy latent in the privatised detention debate. Overcoming the latent immigrant/non-immigrant dichotomy may be especially important because most members of the public that the anti-privatisation frames target are not immigrants themselves, will

[71] Emily P Diamond, 'The Influence of Identity Salience on Frame Effectiveness: An Experiment' (2020) 41(6) Political Psychology 1133.

[72] Jiyoung Han and Christopher M Federico, 'The Polarizing Effect of News Framing: Comparing the Mediating Roles of Motivated Reasoning, Self-stereotyping, and Intergroup Animus' (2018) 68(4) Journal of Communication 685.

[73] Susan B Coutin, *The Culture of Protest: Religious Activism and the US Sanctuary Movement* (Westview Press 1993).

[74] See, egHarry Bruinius, 'Family Separation: Evangelicals Add their Voices to Opposition' (*Christian Science Monitor*, 18 June 2018) <https://perma.cc/8KGZ-2XNP> accessed 31 August 2021.

not have experienced immigration detention, nor even know individuals who have been detained. This means that activating higher-order social identities that can make immigration detention less distant and abstract may be an important first step in creating a receptive audience that is open to engagement and deliberation about the need to limit or eliminate privatised detention.[75]

B Group-centrism

A longstanding body of research indicates that public opinion on social policy is 'group-centric'.[76] In other words, public opinion is substantially shaped by people's attitudes toward the social group (rather than the social issue at hand) that people perceive as the principal beneficiaries or victims of the policy at stake.[77] Accordingly, the effectiveness of a given issue frame will depend on the extent to which the frame draws the audience's attention towards or away from the policy's perceived beneficiaries or victims. Empirical research across a variety of issue areas provides support for the group-centric theory. For example, in a study about people's attitudes toward campaign finance reform, Grant and Rudolph found that frame effects varied depending on whether the referent group was a liked or a disliked interest group.[78] Moreover, the study showed that the effects of group-centrism were conditioned by the issue frame utilised. Specifically, the effects of group-centrism were smaller when campaign finance was framed as an issue of expression and rights than when it was framed in terms of equality and influence. As Grant and Rudolph explain: 'The situations in which citizens were asked to think of an issue in terms of rights—a term that implies universal entitlement—are precisely the situations in which they were least likely to engage in group-centric thinking.'[79]

Existing research also suggests that it can be easy to activate group-centrism. In Hurwitz and Peffley's survey study, the frame that used the words 'violent *inner-city* criminals' (racially coded condition) resulted in a higher level of support among white respondents for new prisons than poverty programmes, compared to the frame that used the words 'violent criminals' (baseline condition).[80] The study also found that, whereas policy preferences in the control condition were driven by traditional determinants of crime policy attitudes (partisanship, gender, and punitiveness), policy preferences in the racially coded condition were driven by racial attitudes (Black stereotypes and racial fairness evaluations). Hurwitz and Peffley concluded: 'When

[75] Benford and Snow (n 6).

[76] Thomas E Nelson and Donald R Kinder, 'Issue Frames and Group-centrism in American Public Opinion' (1996) 58(4) Journal of Politics 1055.

[77] According to Nelson and Kinder, one reason why public opinion on matters of policy works this way is because focusing on the intended policy beneficiaries or victims serves as an 'efficient heuristic that conveniently reduces the complexity of policy politics to a simple judgmental standard': ibid 1056.

[78] J Tobin Grant and Thomas J Rudolph, 'Value Conflict, Group Affect, and the Issue of Campaign Finance' (2003) 47(3) American Journal of Political Science 453, 469.

[79] ibid 465.

[80] Jon Hurwitz and Mark Peffley, 'Playing the Race Card in the Post-Willie Horton Era: The Impact of Racialized Code Words on Support for Punitive Crime Policy' (2005) 69(1) Public Opinion Quarterly 99–112.

messages are framed in such a way to reinforce the relationship between a particular policy and a particular group, it becomes far more likely that individuals will evaluate the policy on the basis of their evaluation of the group.'[81] Similarly, Brown found that slight differences in the frames used by legislators to mobilise anti-Latino stereotypes were associated with differences in willingness to expand access to welfare benefits to include non-citizens.[82]

What insights can be drawn from this literature to illuminate possible effects of the anti-privatisation frames? First, if these organising ideas are to resonate beyond those who are already opposed to privatised detention, decoupling privatised detention and immigrant detainees in the following way may be important. Immigrant detainees constitute a social group that is likely to trigger a host of negative stereotypes about immigrant criminality,[83] in light of their confinement status. Thus, drawing attention to this group as the principal beneficiaries of eliminating privatised detention may very well backfire. From this standpoint, anti-privatisation arguments that emphasise the broader goal of decarceration that is shared across privatised prison and privatised detention[84] may create a more receptive audience than those arguments that highlight what makes immigration detention and immigrant detainees different or unique (for example, immigration detention as *civil* confinement, from a legal standpoint).[85]

Second, in so far as anti-privatisation frames invariably trigger group-centric evaluations of immigrants or immigrant detainees, research on determinants of public attitudes toward immigrants suggest that certain types of framing are more likely to activate positive rather than negative responses. For example, studies show that accounts that humanise individual immigrants, rather than those that emphasise large numbers of immigrants, elicit greater empathy and sympathy.[86] Likewise, frames that highlight similarities between immigrants and non-immigrants by underscoring their universal life experiences (for example, their roles as parents and children), length of residence in the United States, and deep-rooted social and family ties in the United States can promote concern and inclusivity toward immigrants despite their racial or cultural differences.[87] In brief, the literature on public attitudes toward immigrants, taken together with group-centric research, suggests that the persuasiveness of the anti-privatisation frames that we have described may turn on whether and to what extent the frames can successfully navigate evaluations of immigrants or immigrant detainees—perhaps even more so than the substantive policy issues at stake.

[81] ibid 109.

[82] Brown (n 11).

[83] Jessica T Simes and Mary C Waters, 'The Politics of Immigration and Crime' in Sandra M Bucerius and Michael Tonry (eds), *The Oxford Handbook of Ethnicity, Crime, and Immigration* (OUP 2014) 457–483.

[84] César Cuauhtémoc García Hernández, 'Abolishing Immigration Prisons' (2017) 97(1) Boston University Law Review 245.

[85] See, generally, ibid 250.

[86] Diana C Mutz, *Mass Media and American Attitudes toward Immigration* (Global Shifts Colloquium, University of Pennsylvania 2018) <https://perma.cc/2CY4-JBS4> accessed 31 August 2021.

[87] Haynes, Merolla and Ramakrishnan (n 11); ibid.

C Pre-existing Values

Researchers have long recognised the critical role that people's values and core beliefs play in shaping their decision-making and opinion formation, including on policy issues.[88] As Brewer and Gross have noted: 'When people think about a policy choice, they base their opinions on the connections they draw between the issue and their core beliefs.'[89] Consistent with this idea, studies have found that frames that are resonant with people's existing core values can shift their policy preferences.[90] But conservatives and liberals ascribe to fundamentally different values that translate into diverging political stances on a variety of issues. Studies also demonstrate that, when people are exposed to frames that embody core values that they oppose, they can become even more strident about, and committed to, their pre-existing stance, which results in increased political polarisation.[91]

In this context, 'moral reframing' has been studied as a strategy that can bridge the political divide. According to Feinberg and Willer, 'moral reframing involves arguing in favor of a political position that members of a political group would not normally support in terms of moral concerns that the members strongly ascribe to'.[92] A study by Feygina, Jost, and Goldsmith provides illustrative evidence in support of the effectiveness of moral reframing.[93] This study first showed that system justification tendencies among study participants predicted denial of environmental problems and failure to take pro-environmental action.[94] Next, the study showed that, when environmentalism was reframed as maintaining the 'American way of life' and therefore it was 'patriotic to conserve the country's natural resources', the negative effect of system justification on pro-environmental behaviour disappeared. The reframing produced this result because it portrayed environmentalism as enabling the preservation of the existing social system rather than undermining it, which was a message that worked *with* rather than against system justification. In a similar study, Feinberg and Willer found that reframing pro-environment arguments in the language of purity and sanctity—a

[88] Stanley Feldman, 'Structure and Consistency in Public Opinion: The Role of Core Beliefs and Values' (1988) 32(2) American Journal of Political Science 416; Benford and Snow (n 6). A related body of research that examines the role of people's economic circumstances or interests in shaping attitudes toward immigrants and immigration generally finds little evidence of this relationship: Jens Hainmueller and Daniel J Hopkins, 'Public Attitudes toward Immigration' (2014) 17 Annual Review of Political Science 225.

[89] Paul R Brewer and Kimberly Gross, 'Values, Framing, and Citizens' Thoughts about Policy Issues: Effects on Content and Quality' (2005) 26(6) Political Psychology 929, 930.

[90] See, eg Fuyuan Shen and Heidi Hatfield Edwards, 'Economic Individualism, Humanitarianism, and Welfare Reform: A Value-based Account of Framing Effects' (2005) 55(4) Journal of Communication 795; Bloemraad, Silva, and Voss (n 11).

[91] Philip E Tetlock and others, 'The Psychology of the Unthinkable: Taboo Trade-offs, Forbidden Base Rates, and Heretical Counterfactuals' (2000) 78(5) Journal of Personality and Social Psychology 853.

[92] Matthew Feinberg and Robb Willer, 'Moral Reframing: A Technique for Effective and Persuasive Communication Across Political Divides' (2019) 13(12) Social and Personality Psychology Compass 1, 3.

[93] Irina Feygina, John T Jost, and Rachel E Goldsmith, 'System Justification, the Denial of Global Warming, and the Possibility of "System-sanctioned Change"' (2010) 36(3) Personality and Social Psychology Bulletin 326.

[94] System justification refers to the belief that the system is 'fair, legitimate, beneficial, and stable' and, therefore, the status quo should be maintained (ibid 327).

highly resonant value among conservatives—made such arguments notably more persuasive among conservatives who may otherwise have opposed them.[95]

Of note is that the strength of the moral framing and reframing effects may be conditional on whether and to what extent the audience finds the message source to be credible.[96] As to what constitutes a credible source, the audience must believe that the source is both knowledgeable, and can be trusted to reveal that knowledge.[97] These and other research findings that we have highlighted in this section suggest that moral frames/reframes may be a powerful tool to bridge policy disagreements among citizens: particularly if they are conveyed by a credible and trustworthy source.

These findings have important implications for the anti-privatisation movement. To the extent that immigrant rights advocates' goal is to expand the target audience for the anti-privatisation frames, one important task is to identify the core values of those who have yet to support the anti-privatisation movement. In so far as many members of the public and politicians supporting privatised immigration detention hold conservative economic and racial views,[98] their political stances are likely grounded in such ideals as patriotism, traditionalism, religious and family values, limited government and spending, and personal responsibility.[99] These are, in fact, some of the core beliefs explicitly espoused by the 'Right on Crime' campaign launched by conservative groups to promote criminal justice reform that would reduce mass incarceration.[100]

There may be many ways to reframe anti-privatisation as grounded in these kinds of core conservative values. For example, one approach might highlight the role that private prison companies play in separating families through detention; another could focus on wasteful government spending resulting from the growing number of lawsuits facing private prison companies based on allegations of misconduct, abuse, and deaths in detention.[101] Conversely, attempts to appeal to core values typically associated with liberals (for example, universal human rights and social justice) will likely fail or even backfire among many conservatives.[102]

[95] Matthew Feinberg and Robb Willer, 'The Moral Roots of Environmental Attitudes' (2013) 24(1) Psychological Science 56.

[96] James Druckman, 'On the Limits of Framing Effects: Who can Frame?' (2001) 63(4) Journal of Politics 1041; Christopher Wolsko, Hector Ariceaga, and Jesse Seiden, 'Red, White, and Blue enough to be Green: Effects of Moral Framing on Climate Change Attitudes and Conservation Behaviors' (2016) 65 Journal of Experimental Social Psychology 7.

[97] Druckman (n 97) 1045.

[98] Collingwood, Morin, and El-Khatib (n 52); Enns and Ramirez (n 2).

[99] Carl Takei, 'From Mass Incarceration to Mass Control, and Back Again: How Bipartisan Criminal Justice Reform may Lead to a For-profit Nightmare' (2017) 20(2) University of Pennsylvania Journal of Law and Social Change 125–83; Feinberg and Willer (n 93).

[100] Takei (n 100) 161.

[101] See, generally, Monsy Alvarado and others, '"These People are Profitable": Under Trump, Private Prisons are Cashing in on ICE Detainees' (*USA Today*, 2019) <https://perma.cc/TZ77-BRTA> accessed 31 August 2021.

[102] Bloemraad, Silva, and Voss (n 11); Katerina Linos, Laura Jakli, and Melissa Carlson, 'Fundraising for Stigmatized Groups: A Text Message Donation Experiment' (2021) 115(1) American Political Science Review 14.

V Conclusion

In drawing attention to the importance of understanding anti-privatisation frames as a critical component of the anti-privatisation debate, we do not suggest that political elites or social movement leaders should deploy frames to manipulate popular preferences to serve their own interests. Instead, we follow Chong and Druckman in arguing that '[d]iscussion and debate over the appropriate frames for conceptualizing an issue lead ultimately to common perceptions and judgments about the consequences of a policy'.[103] Our analysis of anti-privatisation frames highlights the limitations of these narratives and the possibilities for alternative narratives that might better attend to important issues such as who the target audience is or should be, who the beneficiaries of the policy reform might be, and which core values might bridge the partisan divide.

These alternative approaches may also help to focus public attention on fundamental issues facing immigration detention, beyond privatisation. Chacón has offered a valuable assessment of some of the central anti-privatisation arguments regarding immigration detention.[104] For example, with respect to existing arguments about the poor conditions of privatised detention, Chacón has argued that private family detention's central problem is not that private family detention might entail worse conditions than public family detention; rather, the core issue is that detention itself is a problem.[105] Likewise, with respect to moral objections to privatised detention, Chacón has noted that, 'the argument implicitly validates the moral standing of the state to administer immigration detention facilities—a concession that might inadvertently encourage the expansion of the public carceral state in certain political moments'.[106]

An empirical investigation of some of the issues that we have highlighted in the previous section may address some of Chacón's critiques that centre around the idea that an exclusive focus on privatisation may inadvertently legitimate state powers to detain, and obscure the often-blurred boundaries that exist between private and public actors in this system. Much like privately operated facilities, many county jails use contracts with ICE as a means of profiting from confining immigrants.[107] Anti-privatisation frames that make salient Americans' faith-based identities or underscore the problem of family separation caused by immigration detention can highlight not only the harms of privatised detention, but also broader goals such as reducing use of immigration detention and improving accountability among public officials who make decisions about whether to enter into contracts with ICE.

Time is ripe for a close consideration of anti-privatization frames and their implications. As pointed out earlier, many Americans' attitudes toward private immigration detention appear to be relatively undeveloped,[108] which suggests that they could

[103] Chong and Druckman (n 67) 120.
[104] Chacón (n 7).
[105] ibid 27–28.
[106] ibid 36.
[107] Emily Ryo and Ian Peacock, 'Jailing Immigrant Detainees: A National Study of County Participation in Immigration Detention, 1983–2013' (2020) 54(1) Law & Society Review 66.
[108] Enns and Ramirez (n 2).

be receptive to different anti-privatisation frames' cues. The potential for significant fluctuations in attitudes toward privatised detention may have increased in recent years, with the growing volume of high-profile investigative reporting of abuses and mistreatment in immigration detention, and increased support for an overhaul of law enforcement agencies in the United States, following the killing of George Floyd. In their study of the feminist movement's efforts to extend jury duty rights to women, McCammon and colleagues[109] found that the movement made significant progress by using frames that exploited the disruption in hegemonic discourse about women's roles brought on by US involvement in the World Wars. Similarly, the unsettled nature of the current US sociopolitical environment may support the emergence of a new opportunity structure for debates and deliberations that are more open to alternative perspectives on immigration detention.

References

ACLU, Human Rights Watch, and National Immigrant Justice Center, *Justice-free Zones: US Immigration Detention under the Trump Administration* (American Civil Liberties Union 2020) <https://perma.cc/KWB8-GQWQ>

Adams C, 'Biden's Order Terminates Federal Private Prison Contracts. Here's what that Means' (*NBC News*, 27 January 2021) <https://perma.cc/WR3V-YMBB>

Akerlof GA and Kranton RE, *Identity Economics: How our Identities Shape our Work, Wages, and Well-being* (Princeton University Press 2010)

Alvarado M and others, '"These People are Profitable": Under Trump, Private Prisons are Cashing in on ICE Detainees' (*USA Today*, 2019) <https://perma.cc/TZ77-BRTA>

American Friends Service Committee, *The Role of For-profit Prison Corporations in Shaping US Immigrant Detention & Deportation Policies* (American Friends Service Committee 2015) <https://perma.cc/EUN7-NMVA>

Austin J and Coventry G, *Emerging Issues on Privatized Prisons* (Bureau of Justice Assistance 2001) <https://perma.cc/RQF6-SM9J>

Bauer Z and Johnston JM, 'Who Does it Better? Comparing Immigration Detention Facility Performance in an Intergovernmental and Intersectoral Context' (2020) 80(2) Public Administration Review 244

Benford RD and Snow DA, 'Framing Processes and Social Movements: An Overview and Assessment' (2000) 26(1) Annual Review of Sociology 61

Blitzer J, 'The Private Georgia Immigration-detention Facility at the Center of a Whistle-blower's Complaint' (*The New Yorker*, 2020) <https://perma.cc/9WVF-ZVSD>

Bloemraad I, Silva F, and Voss K, 'Rights, Economics, or Family? Frame Resonance, Political Ideology, and the Immigrant Rights Movement' (2016) 94(4) Social Forces 164

Bramble C and Jones V, *Why Contracting for Performance in Prison and Detention Management is Worth a Closer Look* (Management and Training Corporation 2019)
<https://perma.cc/KBD9-P5V6>

Brewer PR and Gross K, 'Values, Framing, and Citizens' Thoughts about Policy Issues: Effects on Content and Quality' (2005) 26(6) Political Psychology 929

[109] Holly J McCammon and others, 'Movement Framing and Discursive Opportunity Structures: The Political Successes of the US Women's Jury Movements' (2007) 72(5) American Sociological Review 725.

Brown HE, 'Race, Legality, and the Social Policy Consequences of Anti-immigration Mobilization' (2013) 78(2) American Sociological Review 290

Bruinius H, 'Family Separation: Evangelicals Add their Voices to Opposition' (*Christian Science Monitor*, 18 June 2018) <https://perma.cc/8KGZ-2XNP>

Burkhardt BC, 'Contesting Market Rationality: Discursive Struggles over Prison Privatization' (2019) 21(2) Punishment & Society 162

— — and Edison S, 'Correctional Privatization in the United States' in Bean P (ed), *Criminal Justice and Privatisation: Key Issues and Debates* (Routledge 2020)

Burstein P, 'Public Opinion, Public Policy, and Democracy' in Leicht KT and Jenkins JC (eds), *Handbook of Politics: State and Society in Global Perspective* (Springer 2010)

Carson B and Diaz E, 'Payoff: How Congress Ensures Private Prison Profit with an Immigrant Detention Quota' (*Grassroots Leadership*, April 2015) <https://perma.cc/PVY5-Q26E>

Castillo A, 'Detainees at California's For-profit ICE Detention Centers will Soon be Able to Sue over Abuse, Harm' *Los Angeles Times* (28 September 2020) <https://www.latimes.com/california/story/2020-09-28/detainees-at-californias-for-profit-ice-detention-centers-will-soon-be-able-to-sue-over-abuse-harm>

Center for International Human Rights, *Report on the Role of Private Security Companies in Migrant Detention in the US and their Impact on the Protection of the Rights of Migrants* (Northwestern Pritzker School of Law 2020) <https://perma.cc/MLX6-6GNT>

Chacón JM, 'Privatized Immigration Enforcement' (2017) 52(1) Harvard Civil Rights—Civil Liberties Law Review 1

Chong D and Druckman JN, 'Framing Theory' (2007) 10 Annual Review of Political Science 103

Collingwood L, Morin JL, and El-Khatib SO, 'Expanding Carceral Markets: Detention Facilities, ICE Contracts, and the Financial Interests of Punitive Immigration Policy' (2018) 10(4) Race and Social Problems 275

Committee on Homeland Security, 'Oversight of ICE Detention Facilities: Examining ICE Contractors' Response to COVID-19' (13 July 2020) <https://perma.cc/TDB3-35FV>

Committee on Oversight and Reform and Subcommittee on Civil Rights and Civil Liberties, 'The Trump Administration's Mistreatment of Detained Immigrants: Deaths and Deficient Medical Care by For-profit Detention Contractors' (US House of Representatives, 2020) <https://perma.cc/Z7LD-HR2F>

CoreCivic, 'What we Do' <https://perma.cc/AX6H-Q9HE>

Coutin SB, *The Culture of Protest: Religious Activism and the US Sanctuary Movement* (Westview Press 1993)

Diamond EP, 'The Influence of Identity Salience on Frame Effectiveness: An Experiment' (2020) 41(6) Political Psychology 1133

Dolovich S, 'How Privatization Thinks: The Case of Prisons' in Freeman J and Minow M (eds), *Government by Contract: Outsourcing and American Democracy* (Harvard University Press 2009)

Druckman J, 'On the Limits of Framing Effects: Who can Frame?' (2001) 63(4) Journal of Politics 1041

Ebert K, Lia W, and Estrada EP, 'Apathy and Color-blindness in Privatized Immigration Control' (2020) 6(4) Sociology of Race and Ethnicity 53

Enns PK and Ramirez MD, 'Privatizing Punishment: Testing Theories of Public Support for Private Prison and Immigration Detention Facilities' (2018) 56(3) Criminology 546

Entman RM, 'Framing: Toward Clarification of a Fractured Paradigm' (1993) 43(4) Journal of Communication 51

Feinberg M and Willer R, 'The Moral Roots of Environmental Attitudes' (2013) 24(1) Psychological Science 56

— —, 'Moral Reframing: A Technique for Effective and Persuasive Communication across Political Divides' (2019) 13(12) Social and Personality Psychology Compass 1

Feldman S, 'Structure and Consistency in Public Opinion: The Role of Core Beliefs and Values' (1988) 32(2) American Journal of Political Science 416

Feygina I, Jost JT, and Goldsmith RE, 'System Justification, the Denial of Global Warming, and the Possibility of "System-sanctioned Change"' (2010) 36(3) Personality and Social Psychology Bulletin 326

Fujiwara LH, 'Immigrant Rights are Human Rights: The Reframing of Immigrant Entitlement and Welfare' (2005) 52(1) Social Problems 79

Gaes GG, 'Current Status of Prison Privatization Research on American Prisons and Jails' (2019) 18 Criminology & Public Policy 269

Gamson WA and Modigliani A, 'The Changing Culture of Affirmative Action' (1987) 3 Research in Political Sociology 137

García Hernández C, 'Abolishing Immigration Prisons' (2017) 97(1) Boston University Law Review 245

Goffman E, *Frame Analysis: An Essay on the Organization of Experience* (Harvard University Press 1974)

Gomez J, 'Reps. Gomez, Crow, Jayapal, and Ruiz Lead Colleagues in Calling on Biden Administration to End Private Immigration Detention Centers' (Press Release, 1 February 2021) <https://perma.cc/BMW8-MR6U>

Gorman S, 'California Bans Private Prisons and Immigration Detention Centers' (*Reuters*, 11 October 2019) <https://perma.cc/K3Y4-SWWE>

Grant JT and Rudolph TJ, 'Value Conflict, Group Affect, and the Issue of Campaign Finance' (2003) 47(3) American Journal of Political Science 453

Hainmueller J and Hopkins DJ, 'Public Attitudes toward Immigration' (2014) 17 Annual Review of Political Science 225

Han J and Federico CM, 'The Polarizing Effect of News Framing: Comparing the Mediating Roles of Motivated Reasoning, Self-stereotyping, and Intergroup Animus' (2018) 68(4) Journal of Communication 685

Hart O, Shleifer A, and Vishny RW, 'The Proper Scope of Government: Theory and an Application to Prisons' (1997) 112(4) The Quarterly Journal of Economics 1127

Haynes C, Merolla JL, and Ramakrishnan SK, *Framing Immigrants: News Coverage, Public Opinion, and Policy* (Russell Sage Foundation 2016)

Homeland Security Advisory Council, *Report of the Subcommittee on Privatized Immigration Detention Facilities* (US Department of Homeland Security 2016) <https://perma.cc/CXR8-GRU4>

Hood C, 'Accountability and Transparency: Siamese Twins, Matching Parts, Awkward Couple?' (2010) 33(5) West European Politics 989

Hurwitz J and Peffley M, 'Playing the Race Card in the Post-Willie Horton Era: The Impact of Racialized Code Words on Support for Punitive Crime Policy' (2005) 69(1) Public Opinion Quarterly 99

Jacoby WG, 'Issue Framing and Public Opinion on Government Spending' (2000) 44(4) American Journal of Political Science 750

Jefferis DC, 'Private Prisons, Private Governance: Essay on Developments in Private-sector Resistance to Privatized Immigration Detention' (2019) 15(1) Northwestern Journal of Law and Social Policy 82

Kalin M and Sambanis N, 'How to Think about Social Identity' (2018) 21 Annual Review of Political Science 239

Kerwin D, *Immigrant Detention and COVID-19: How a Pandemic Exploited and Spread through the US Immigrant Detention System* (Center for Migration Studies 2020) <https://perma.cc/G79D-RJFR>

Kim D-Y, 'Prison Privatization: An Empirical Literature Review and Path Forward' (2019) International Criminal Justice Review 1

Kish RJ and Lipton AF, 'Do Private Prisons Really Offer Savings Compared with their Public Counterparts?' (2013) 33(1) Economic Affairs 93

Klar S, 'The Influence of Competing Identity Primes on Political Preferences' (2013) 75(4) Journal of Politics 1108

Lartey J, 'Think Private Prison Companies are Going Away under Biden? They have Other Plans' (*The Marshall Project*, 17 November 2020) <https://perma.cc/M9V8-WTAA>

Lazare S, '"Profiting from Misery": Private Prison Corporations Driving Harsh Immigration Policies' (*Facing South*, 17 April 2015) <https://perma.cc/9S5L-HY7Z>

Linos K, Jakli L, and Carlson M, 'Fundraising for Stigmatized Groups: A Text Message Donation Experiment' (2021) 115(1) American Political Science Review 14

Luan L, 'Profiting from Enforcement: The Role of Private Prisons in US Immigration Detention' (*Migration Policy Institute*, 2 May 2018) <https://perma.cc/PBH7-AX9Z>

McCammon HJ and others, 'Movement Framing and Discursive Opportunity Structures: The Political Successes of the US Women's Jury Movements' (2007) 72(5) American Sociological Review 725

McDonald DC, 'Public Imprisonment by Private Means: The Re-emergence of Private Prisons and Jails in the United States, the United Kingdom, and Australia' (1994) 34 British Journal of Criminology 29

Merchant N, 'Private Prison Industry Backs Trump, Prepares if Biden Wins' (*AP News*, 13 August 2020) <https://apnews.com/article/houston-ap-top-news-prisons-immigration-joe-biden-ca7f6e9fac1f287bb79ae55410112c46>

Mountz A, Coddington K, Catania RT, and Loyd JM, 'Conceptualizing Detention: Mobility, Containment, Bordering, and Exclusion' (2012) 37(4) Progress in Human Geography 522

Mutz DC, 'Mass Media and American Attitudes toward Immigration' (*Global Shifts Colloquium*, University of Pennsylvania 2018) <https://perma.cc/2CY4-JBS4>

Nelson TE and Kinder DR, 'Issue Frames and Group-centrism in American Public Opinion' (1996) 58(4) Journal of Politics 1055

Office of the Inspector General, *Review of the Federal Bureau of Prisons' Monitoring of Contract Prisons* (US Department of Justice 2016) <https://perma.cc/AQF2-L9Q9>

O'Neill C, 'Private Prisons: Principally Profit-oriented and Politically Pliable' (*FollowTheMoney.org*, 7 June 2018) <https://perma.cc/L5VU-B3Y8>

Perfas SL, Mendoza J, and Gass H, 'When a Private Prison Company Came to Small-town Wyoming (audio)' (*The Christian Science Monitor*, 2020) <https://www.csmonitor.com/USA/Justice/2020/0824/When-a-private-prison-company-came-to-small-town-Wyoming-audio>

Polletta F and Kai Ho M, 'Frames and their Consequences' in Goodin RE and Tilly C (eds), *The Oxford Handbook of Contextual Political Analysis* (OUP 2006)

Ryo E, 'Understanding Immigration Detention: Causes, Conditions, and Consequences' (2019) 15 Annual Review of Law and Social Science 97

— — and Peacock I, 'A National Study of Immigration Detention in the United States' (2018) 92(1) Southern California Law Review 1

— — and Peacock I, 'Jailing Immigrant Detainees: A National Study of County Participation in Immigration Detention, 1983–2013' (2020) 54(1) Law & Society Review 66

Shen F and Edwards HH, 'Economic Individualism, Humanitarianism, and Welfare Reform: A Value-based Account of Framing Effects' (2005) 55(4) Journal of Communication 795

Shepherd K, 'Immigrants Detained in California Win the Right to Sue Private Prison Companies' (*Immigration Impact, American Immigration Council*, 2020) <https://perma.cc/2Z5R-F6LU>

Schildkraut DJ, 'Boundaries of American Identity: Evolving Understandings of "Us"' (2014) 17 Annual Review of Political Science 441

Schneider SK and Jacoby WG, 'Public Opinion and Public Policy in the United States' in Hird JA (ed), *Policy Analysis in the United States* (Policy Press 2018)

Simes JT and Waters MC, 'The Politics of Immigration and Crime' in Bucerius SM and Tonry M (eds), *The Oxford Handbook of Ethnicity, Crime, and Immigration* (OUP 2014)

Snow DA, 'Framing and Social Movements' in Snow DA and others (eds), *The Wiley-Blackwell Encyclopedia of Social and Political Movements* (Wiley-Blackwell 2013)

Sparks R and Gacek J, 'Persistent Puzzles: The Philosophy and Ethics of Private Corrections in the Context of Contemporary Penality' (2019) 18(2) Criminology & Public Policy 379

Suchman MC, 'Managing Legitimacy: Strategic and Institutional Approaches' (1995) 20(3) The Academy of Management Review 571

Tajfel H and Turner JC, 'The Social Identity Theory of Intergroup Behavior' in Worchel S and Austin WG (eds), *Psychology of Intergroup Relations* (Nelson-Hall 1986)

Takei C, 'From Mass Incarceration to Mass Control, and Back Again: How Bipartisan Criminal Justice Reform may Lead to a For-profit Nightmare' (2017) 20(2) University of Pennsylvania Journal of Law and Social Change 125

Tetlock PE and others, 'The Psychology of the Unthinkable: Taboo Trade-offs, Forbidden Base Rates, and Heretical Counterfactuals' (2000) 78(5) Journal of Personality and Social Psychology 853

US Immigration and Customs Enforcement, *US Immigration and Customs Enforcement Fiscal Year 2019 Enforcement and Removal Operations Report* (US Department of Homeland Security 2019) <https://perma.cc/22ES-S8H9>

Vilher LL, 'Private Prisons and the Need for Greater Transparency: Private Prison Information Act' (2017) 12(1) Brooklyn Journal of Corporate, Financial, & Commercial Law 213

Wolsko C, Ariceaga H, and Seiden J, 'Red, White, and Blue enough to be Green: Effects of Moral Framing on Climate Change Attitudes and Conservation Behaviors' (2016) 65 Journal of Experimental Social Psychology 7

Yi C, 'General Assembly Approves Ban on Private Detention Facilities in Illinois' (*Illinois Coalition for Immigrant and Refugee Rights*, 16 May 2019) <https://perma.cc/V6ES-ES7V>

PART III
OUTSOURCING OR UNDERMINING STATE AUTHORITY

7

'Because we are Deportable People'

Privatisation, Citizenship, and Race in US All-foreign Prisons

Hallam Tuck

I Introduction

On 20 November 2003, Kurt P Hofmann MD, a surgeon at Meadows Medical Center in Vidalia, Georgia, removed a non-cancerous growth from Luis Alba's neck.[1] After the procedure finished, Hofmann made Alba an appointment for a post-operation evaluation and recommended that he return to the hospital for monthly physiotherapy appointments. Alba never showed up.[2] Instead, what followed was a five-year-long legal battle over access to medical care in the US Federal Bureau of Prisons' privately operated all-foreign prison system.

Medical records published as part of a lawsuit that Alba filed two years later show that he never left McRae Correctional Institution (CI McRae), an all-foreign prison in Telfair County, Georgia, operated by the Corrections Corporation of America (CCA).[3] Instead, he received one post-operation evaluation from Joan Roy, a general practitioner who also served as CI McRae's clinical director. When Alba reported to Susan Montford, CI McRae's health services administrator that he had begun to lose his voice, Montford declined Alba's request to seek follow-up care outside the facility.[4] After nearly two years, Alba was finally taken to a surgical specialist, who found that Alba had 'right vocal fold paralysis', and recommended a surgical procedure which would allow him to recover his voice.[5] Six days later, the CCA-employed health services team denied Alba's request because he had a 'pre-existing condition' and the proposed surgery was an elective procedure that was not covered under the regulations set forth by the Bureau of Prisons (BOP).[6]

On 23 April 2005, Alba filed an administrative grievance arguing that the procedure was not elective, but rather was needed to correct the lack of medical care he had received in the years after the first surgery. Alba also noted wryly that, '[w]hen it is to

[1] *Alba v Montford, Case No CV 305-159 (SD Ga Jul 24, 2006)*, Document 1, 'Report of Operation' 58–60.

[2] ibid, 'Health Services Clinic Notes' 61.

[3] CCA renamed itself CoreCivic in October 2016. See Devlin Barrett, 'Private-prison Firm CCA to Rename itself CoreCivic' *Wall Street Journal* (New York, 28 October 2016) <https://www.wsj.com/articles/private-prison-firm-cca-to-rename-itself-corecivic-1477666800> accessed 14 December 2021.

[4] *Alba v Montford*, 'Health Services Clinic Notes' (n 2) 55.

[5] *Alba v Montford, Case No CV 305-159 (SD Ga Jul 24, 2006)*, Document 1, 'Otolaryngology Report' 48.

[6] *Alba v Montford, Case No CV 305-159 (SD Ga Jul 24, 2006)*, Document 1, 'Utilization Review Conference' 47.

Hallam Tuck, *'Because we are Deportable People'* In: *Privatising Border Control.* Edited by: Mary Bosworth and Lucia Zedner, Oxford University Press. DOI: 10.1093/oso/9780192857163.003.0008

CCA's convenience they use BOP program statements, when it is not convenient for CCA, employees claim that that they do not have to abide by BOP Program statements'.[7] A month later, CI McRae's warden Michael V Pugh denied Alba's grievance.[8] In a final appeal to the Bureau of Prisons' head office in Washington, DC written on 10 June 2005, Alba exclaimed that, '[i]nstead of serving my sentence in a Federal Bureau of Prisons institution, I have been illegally dumped by the BOP into the care of a private, for profit, Corrections Corporation of America facility as a "disposable prisoner" based on my race, national origin, and citizenship'.[9]

CI McRae, the prison where Luis Alba was incarcerated from 2003 to 2007, is one of seven all-foreign 'Criminal Alien Requirement' or CAR facilities. At its peak in 2016, the Bureau of Prisons operated fifteen CAR facilities, housing roughly 22,600 sentenced, non-citizen prisoners.[10] CAR facilities are unique for three reasons. First, they are designed to segregate 'low security criminal alien adult males' from US citizen prisoners in the Bureau of Prisons-run system.[11] Second, CAR facilities are the only privately operated prisons within the federal prison system.[12] Indeed, all CAR facilities are run by one of three private corrections firms: CoreCivic, The GEO Group, and the Management and Training Corporation. Lastly, these all-foreign prisons disproportionately incarcerate Latino men (89 per cent) in general, and Mexican men (72 per cent) in particular.[13]

While practices of outsourced incarceration in the United States have a long history—one that is deeply entwined with structures of racial hierarchy and white supremacy—they have not traditionally fractured along the lines of citizenship or immigration status.[14] Moreover, whereas previous forms of public–private incarceration in the United States extracted value from the labour of prisoners, contemporary privatisation extracts value from the social and biological reproduction of prisoners.[15] Alba's story, and those of thousands of other men in all-foreign prisons, highlights how non-citizens, and in particular Latino men, have become the default subjects of

[7] *Alba v Montford, Case No CV 305-159 (SD Ga Jul 24, 2006)*, Document 1, 'Formal Grievance Appeal Attachment' 17.

[8] ibid 18.

[9] *Alba v Montford, Case No CV 305-159 (SD Ga Jul 24, 2006)*, Document 1, 'Regional Appeal' 10.

[10] Department of Justice Office of the Inspector General (DOJ OIG), *Review of the Federal Bureau of Prisons' Monitoring of Contract Prisons* (US Department of Justice 2016) i <https://oig.justice.gov/reports/2016/e1606.pdf> accessed 14 December 2021.

[11] ibid.

[12] Criminal Alien Requirement prisons are also frequently referred to as Contract Prisons by the Bureau of Prisons: see Bureau of Prisons, 'Contract Prisons' (2021) <https://www.bop.gov/about/facilities/contract_facilities.jsp> accessed 14 December 2021.

[13] Emma Kaufman, 'Segregation by Citizenship' (2019) 132(5) Harvard Law Review 1379.

[14] Rebecca M McLennan, *The Crisis of Imprisonment* (CUP 2008); Alex Lichtenstein, *Twice the Work of Free Labor* (Verso 1995); Angela Davis, *Are Prisons Obsolete?* (Seven Stories Press 2003) 29–33; Michelle Alexander, *The New Jim Crow* (The New Press 2010) 74–75.

[15] I use the term public–private here and throughout the chapter to draw attention to the fundamentally malleable nature of the public/private boundary. No federal prisons are entirely 'public' or 'private': all BOP-run facilities rely on a wide range of contractors for the provision of food, medical, and transport services. See, eg Department of Justice Office of the Inspector General (DOJ OIG), *Audit of the Federal Bureau of Prisons' Contract Awarded to Correct Care Solutions* (US Department of Justice 2019) <https://www.oversight.gov/sites/default/files/oig-reports/a1937_0.pdf> accessed 14 December 2021.

a regime of public–private incarceration premised on extracting financial value from incarcerated life.[16]

This chapter begins to examine the relationship between public–private incarceration, citizenship, and racial difference. In the first section, I examine the origins of all-foreign prisons in the United States, examining how non-citizens came to be the default subjects of public–private incarceration. Tracing the crisis of 'criminal aliens' in concert with the Clinton administration's drive to privatise the Federal Government, I argue that the outsourced, all-foreign prison emerged as the default solution for federal policymakers who were keen to target non-citizens in federal prison but were constrained by an overcrowded prison system and public opposition to increased spending on incarceration. In the second section, I examine attempts to operate private facilities for US citizens at Taft Correctional Institution and Northeast Ohio Correctional Center in 1997. I show how all-foreign prisons succeeded as outsourced facilities precisely because federal policymakers made deliberate choices to exclude non-citizens from a wide range of prison services and BOP oversight. Rationalised by lurid anecdotal references to violent crimes committed by Latino immigrants, these exclusions amounted to a kind of prison welfare chauvinism that mirrored similar efforts to exclude non-citizens from public services in California in 1994. Reflecting Alba's observation that men in CAR prisons are treated as 'disposable prisoners' because of their immigration status, nationality, and racial identity, in the final section I show how practices of public–private confinement shape exclusion in all-foreign prisons. Drawing on research on the 'pains' of imprisonment, I examine how outsourcing shapes specific carceral practices, producing the feeling, as Alba's testimony suggests, that men in CAR prisons are 'disposable' because of their citizenship, race, and ethnicity.[17]

II The 'Criminal Alien Problem' and the Origins of the All-foreign Prison

Although the criminalisation of migration has a long history in the US, the shift towards all-foreign prisons began in the early 1980s with what the scholars Jenna Loyd and Alison Mountz have called the 'Long Mariel Crisis'.[18] The 'Long Mariel Crisis' describes how media coverage and public discourse created a visual and rhetorical spectacle of crisis that outlasted the immediate period of the Mariel boatlift in 1980.[19] Perceptions of crisis, fuelled by the arrival of migrants and asylum seekers from Cuba and Haiti in south Florida, were discursively tied to anxieties about drug trafficking, violent crime, and overburdened public services and healthcare.[20]

[16] Lauren L Martin, 'Carceral Economies of Migration Control' (2021) 45(4) Progress in Human Geography 743.

[17] Hindpal Singh Bhui, 'Foreign National Prisoners: Issues and Debates' in Hindpal Singh Bhui (ed), *Race and Criminal Justice* (Sage Publishing 2009); Jason Warr, 'Foreign National Prisoners and the Pains of Imprisonment' (2016) 16(3) Criminology and Criminal Justice 301; Thomas Ugelvik and Dorina Damsa, 'The Pains of Crimmigration Imprisonment' (2018) 58(5) British Journal of Criminology 1025.

[18] Jenna Loyd and Alison Mountz, *Boats, Borders and Bases* (University of California Press 2018) 61.

[19] ibid 54.

[20] Jonathan Simon, 'Refugees in a Carceral Age' (1998) 10(3) Public Culture 10.

The perceived crisis of 'criminal aliens' fed what the anthropologist Leo Chavez calls the 'Latino threat': a narrative frame in which Latino immigrants are understood as an existential threat to the racial stability of white-dominated American society.[21] A feature-length article in the *New York Times Magazine* published in 1987 breathlessly titled 'Can Miami Save Itself?' portrayed the city as a 'juvenile delinquent' overrun by drugs, violent crime, and simmering racial tension.[22] These problems, according to the *Times*, were to be blamed on the racial turmoil of 1980; precisely, the 'wretched, illegal armada' of Haitian asylum seekers fleeing the Duvalier regime, and the influx of 125,000 Cuban 'Marielitos'.[23] The latter portrayal of recent Cuban emigrants became the stereotype for migrant criminality: as Miami Police Department Lieutenant Mike Gonzalez put it, 'in one year, we got 10,000 additional killers and thieves'.[24]

Critically, the term 'criminal alien' evolved during this period as a term of art with no fixed definition.[25] Federal officials relied primarily on FBI arrest data, which classified offenders based on their country of birth, rather than their immigration status.[26] As a 1987 report prepared by the Government Accountability Office (GAO) put it, 'no one knows how many deportable criminal aliens exist. However, according to the Immigration and Naturalization Service, they are a growing threat to the nation's security'.[27] As Angélica Cházaro has observed, the category of the 'criminal alien' in US immigration law is not fixed, but is rather a shifting signifier, heavily shaped by racial hierarchy, working to justify who may be arrested, detained, and deported. [28] In practice, efforts to target 'criminal aliens' often targeted Mexican men specifically, reflecting Kelly Lytle Hernandez's observation that US border control practices have effectively 'Mexicanized' the unequal social relations emerging from the divide between those who do and those who do not possess legal immigration status.[29]

III 'Simply more Felons than Beds': The Crisis of State Capacity and the Turn to Privatization

In his 1996 State of the Union address, President Bill Clinton famously told the assembled congressional delegates that 'the era of big government is over'.[30] Clinton's 1996 budget proposed a 20 per cent cut to all federal domestic agencies, and the firing of

[21] Leo R Chavez, *The Latino Threat* (University of California Press 2013) 3.

[22] Robert Sherrill, 'Can Miami Save Itself?' *New York Times* (New York, 19 July 1987).

[23] ibid.

[24] ibid.

[25] The term 'criminal alien' has not been defined in federal immigration law. See US Senate Committee on Governmental Affairs, 'Criminal Aliens in the United States', Report 104-48 (1995) 5 <https://www.congress.gov/104/crpt/srpt48/CRPT-104srpt48.pdf> accessed 14 December 2021. The term is generally used to denote a non-citizen who has been convicted of an offence which makes them subject to deportation.

[26] GAO, *Criminal Alien Statistics* (1987) GAO-11-187 44–45.

[27] ibid.

[28] Angélica Cházaro, 'Challenging the Criminal Alien Paradigm' (2016) 63 UCLA Law Review 594, 598.

[29] John Clark, *Hearing before the Subcommittee on Immigration, House of Representatives* (15 July 1997) 91; Kelly Lytle Hernandez, *Migra!* (University of California Press 2010) 19.

[30] President William Clinton, State of the Union Address (1996) <https://clintonwhitehouse4.archives.gov/WH/New/other/sotu.html> accessed 14 December 2021.

100,000 federal employees.[31] Yet, these efforts to reduce the size of government could only go so far: 'there are some areas that the federal government should not leave and should address and address strongly. One of these areas is the problem of illegal immigration. After years of neglect, this administration has taken a strong stand to stiffen the protection of our borders.'[32]

That the Clinton administration focused taxpayer money and federal resources on immigration enforcement while cutting federal aid and welfare spending at every turn is unsurprising. Kitty Calavita's study of the debate over Proposition 187 in California has shown how the targeting of immigrants was linked to the 'crisis of Fordism' reflected in stagnant wages, increasing insecurity, and dismantling of the welfare state.[33] Within this nativist politics, immigrants were framed as a burden on taxpayers through their costly consumption of social services and as a racial threat to the territorial stability of white, suburban society.[34] As anti-immigrant activist Glen Spencer said in 1994, '[w]hat we have in Southern California is not assimilation; it's annexation by Mexico. We took it fair and square, and we're not giving it back.'[35] This logic rationalised the increased exclusion of non-citizens and racial minorities from social services and the intensification of punitive enforcement measures at the US–Mexico border.

As the US prison population surged, growing sixfold from 1980 to 2000, this nativist politics shaped the treatment of non-citizens in federal prisons.[36] Much in the same way that state officials from California baulked at immigrant access to welfare services, federal officials from the state complained about the supposed burden placed on state and federal budgets by the growing number of non-citizens in custody. In 1994, California congressman Gary Condit complained to the House Subcommittee on Immigration that his state spent nearly $50 million annually incarcerating non-citizens.[37] At the same hearing, Florida Representative Tom Lewis fumed that, 'incarceration costs the taxpayer between $800 million and $1.5 billion keeping these criminals aliens in our overcrowded prisons. We clothed them, housed them, and fed them, we put them through the drug treatment and job training programs to make them better citizens, then we deported them.'[38] Lewis' logic connected citizenship and deportability to a kind of less eligibility: non-citizens in federal prison did not

[31] National Performance Review, *A Brief History of the NPR*, Government Printing Office (1997) <https://govinfo.library.unt.edu/npr/library/papers/bkgrd/brief.html> accessed 14 December 2021.

[32] Clinton, 'State of the Union Address' (n 30).

[33] Proposition 187 was a 1994 ballot initiative in California that aimed to establish a citizenship screening system that would exclude non-citizens from State-run public services. Kitty Calavita, 'The New Politics of Immigration' (1996) 43(3) Social Problems 285.

[34] ibid 300.

[35] Ruth S Adams and others, 'Immigration: Proposition 187, Five Years Later' (*Bulletin of the American Academy of Arts and Sciences*, 2000) <https://www.amacad.org/news/immigration-proposition-187-five-years-later> accessed 14 December 2021.

[36] Nazgol Ghandnoosh, 'US Prison Population Trends' (*The Sentencing Project*, 2019) <https://www.sentencingproject.org/publications/u-s-prison-population-trends-massive-buildup-and-modest-decline/> accessed 14 December 2021.

[37] Gary Condit, *Hearing before the Subcommittee on Immigration, House of Representatives* (23 February 1994) 156.

[38] Thomas F Lewis, *Hearing before the Subcommittee on Immigration, House of Representatives* (23 February 1994) 142.

deserve proper housing, rehabilitation, or care precisely because they were eligible to be deported.

The solution to this perceived crisis of criminal aliens was to dramatically expand the scope of immigration enforcement, thereby bringing the process of deportation directly into state and federal prisons. In a 1995 radio address, Clinton told listeners that, 'criminal aliens should move directly from the prison to the plane and right out of the country without passing go'.[39] He also explicitly tied the consequence of deportation to any interactions with the criminal justice system: 'When an illegal alien enters our criminal justice system, the process shouldn't end until they leave our country. If they are found innocent, they should be deported immediately. If they are found guilty, they should be deported immediately after they do their time.'[40] This commitment expanded the existing infrastructure of the Institutional Hearing Program (IHP), a specialised court process created in 1986 by the Reagan administration to expedite deportation proceedings for non-citizens in federal prisons. Specific measures targeting 'criminal aliens' were combined with a broader programme of immigration enforcement, passed in 1996, that dramatically expanded the grounds for deportation while shrinking the avenues available to contest removal, and making lawful permanent resident status far more precarious.[41]

The Clinton administration projected a clear image of the state's crimmigration powers: as dangerous criminal aliens threaten US citizens, the integration of deportation and criminal punishment was to become so seamless that immigrant prisoners would barely touch the ground between their incarceration and removal from the United States. As Emma Kaufman has observed, this shift towards targeting non-citizens in criminal custody transformed the prison system from a 'a site of corrections, in which the implicit aim was to reform prisoners and return them to the polity, into an institution dedicated to finding and sorting foreigners'.[42]

This shift away from rehabilitation and towards exclusion brought material changes to federal prison policy that reflected the differential treatment of non-citizen prisoners.[43] In 1994, a DC Circuit Court ruling confirmed that non-citizens were ineligible for placement in halfway houses because they were considered to be 'flight risks'.[44] In 1996 and 1998, the Bureau of Prisons issued policy memos that excluded non-citizens from a wide range of rehabilitative services.[45] These policy changes also

[39] William Clinton, 'Radio Address to the Nation' (6 May 1995) <https://clinton.presidentiallibraries.us/items/show/12973> accessed 14 December 2021.

[40] ibid.

[41] See Illegal Immigration Reform and Immigration Responsibility Act 1996 <govinfo.gov/content/pkg/PLAW-104publ208/pdf/PLAW-104publ208.pdf> accessed 14 December 2021. See also The Antiterrorism and Effective Death Penalty Act 1996 <https://www.congress.gov/bill/104th-congress/senate-bill/735> accessed 14 December 2021; Jennifer M Chacón, 'Overcriminalizing Immigration' (2012) 102 Journal of Criminal Law & Criminology 613.

[42] Kaufman, 'Segregation by Citizenship' (n 13) 1388.

[43] ibid 1411–12.

[44] *United States v Smith*, 27 F.3d 649, 668 (DC Cir 1994). See also BOP, *Program Statement 7310.04*, 10<https://www.bop.gov/policy/progstat/7310_004.pdf> accessed 14 December 2021.

[45] Department of Justice Office of the Inspector General (DOJ OIG), *Community Corrections Center Program Audit Results* (US Department of Justice 1995) <https://oig.justice.gov/reports/BOP/a9608/au9608p1.htm> accessed 14 December 2021. See also GAO, *Eligibility and Capacity Impact Use of Flexibilities to Reduce Inmates' Time in Prisons* (2012) GAO-12-320, 32.

exempted non-citizen prisoners from placement closer to their families in the United States.

Beyond foreignness, race played a critical role in suturing together the logics of punishment and deportation and rationalising the differential treatment of non-citizens. Much like Calavita's and Chavez's observations that concerns of the use of the welfare system by immigrants in California were narrated as a Latino 'invasion', the threat posed by 'criminal aliens' in federal prisons was clearly understood in racial terms. Stricter measures towards non-citizens in prison custody were rationalised by spectacular anecdotes of the violent crimes committed by immigrant men from Mexico. In an effort to attack the Clinton administration's record on immigration and crime in Congress in 1999, Republican Congressman Elton Gallegly told the story of Jose Zavalla, a Mexican man who had been convicted of rape three times and returned to the community in California each time, rather than being deported.[46] Zavalla's story, Gallegly argued, demonstrated the need for a stronger commitment to the identification and removal of non-citizens in federal prisons: 'we are catching hundreds and hundreds of criminal aliens that should not even be in this country. We do not need to import criminals. We have enough of our own.'[47]

As part of the broader trend towards mass incarceration, however, the Clinton administration struggled to reconcile incarcerating an increasing number of immigrants with the goal of ending the era of big government. In response to the near-exponential growth of prison populations during the period after 1980, courts put pressure on state and federal officials to reduce overcrowding.[48] Moreover, the 1996 laws overwhelmed the IHP's system of dedicated immigration courts within federal prisons, leading to damaging reports by the GAO that suggested that the IHP was failing to identify and deport a large majority of non-citizens in federal prisons.[49] Yet, while voters supported putting more and more people in prison, they frequently baulked at the idea of having to pay the costs of prison construction and operation.[50] Pressing to lock up more non-citizens while at the same time reducing the size and cost of the federal government, the Clinton administration and Congress turned to the use of privately operated facilities.

The growth of privately operated prisons, as Ruth Wilson Gilmore has observed, depended on the notion that expanding prison capacity through private contracts avoided the need for state borrowing or the expansion of public payrolls.[51] In 1999, Congress obligated the Federal Bureau of Prisons to begin the procurement process for two 'Criminal Alien Requirement' facilities designed to hold 'low security criminal alien men'.[52] By June of the following year, the Bureau of Prisons had issued contracts

[46] Elton Gallegy, *Hearing before the Subcommittee on Immigration, House of Representatives* (15 July 1997) 61.

[47] ibid.

[48] Stephen Raher, 'The Business of Punishing' (2010) 13(13) Richmond Journal of Law and the Public Interest 215.

[49] GAO, *Criminal Aliens* (1997) GAO/T-GGD-97-154. GAO, *Criminal Aliens* (1998) GAO/GGD-99-3. GAO, *Criminal Aliens* (1999) GAO/T-GGD-99-47.

[50] Bernard McCarthy, 'Coping with Crowding' (1989) 13(2) American Journal of Criminal Justice 245.

[51] Ruth Wilson Gilmore, *Golden Gulag* (University of California Press 2007) 122–25.

[52] BOP, *Notice of Intent to Prepare a Draft Environmental Impact Statement (DEIS) for Housing Criminal Alien Population in Non-federal Low-security Correctional Facilities* (The Federal Register 1999) <https://

for two all-foreign facilities to the Corrections Corporation of America: Cibola County Correctional Facility in New Mexico, and California City Correctional Facility in California.[53] A report published by the Department of Justice in 1999 trumpeted the role played by these new all-foreign facilities in helping the Clinton administration to achieve the goal of reducing prison overcrowding through contract confinement.[54] Perhaps more importantly, these CAR facilities brought racially disproportionate migration control into the heart of the federal prison system. As Assistant Director John L Clark testified in 1997, these facilities were 'targeted at the Mexican citizens' by design.[55] Clark's testimony made explicit the oft-implicit connection between exclusion along the lines of immigration status and exclusion along the lines of race: in practice, targeting 'criminal aliens' in federal prison meant targeting Latino men.[56]

IV Privatization for All?

When the BOP began the procurement process for the first Criminal Alien Requirement prison in 1999, it was not the Bureau's only private contract.[57] In the late 1990s, the Bureau of Prisons had begun experimenting with privatisation for US citizens at two facilities in California and Ohio, in addition to at least four other privately contracted facilities operated through intergovernmental agreements.[58] This begs a broader question: how did non-citizens become the singular subjects of public–private incarceration within the federal prison system?

All-foreign prisons emerged from an unsettled period of 'turf battles' in which federal agencies and congressional leaders fought over the shape and scale of the federal prison and immigration detention system.[59] From the beginning of 'mandatory detention' policies in 1981 until the late 1980s, there was significant debate between the White House, the Department of Justice, the BOP, and the Immigration and Naturalization Service (INS) over which agency should be responsible for immigration detention.[60] Unlike the federal prison system, the BOP and the INS had a

www.federalregister.gov/documents/1999/04/23/99-10337/notice-of-intent-to-prepare-a-draft-environmental-impact-statement-deis-for-housing-criminal-alien> accessed 14 December 2021.

[53] BOP, *Contract J1PCc-006-California City, California* (contract award document) (Federal Bureau of Prisons 2000); *Contract J1PCc-007-Cibola County, New Mexico* (contract award document) (Federal Bureau of Prisons 2000).

[54] Department of Justice, *Annual Report: Detention and Incarceration* (US Department of Justice 1999) V-9 <https://www.justice.gov/archive/ag/annualreports/ar99/Chapter5.pdf> accessed 14 December 2021.

[55] Clark (n 29).

[56] Hernandez (n 29) 19.

[57] Judith Greene, 'Bailing out Private Prisons' (*The American Prospect*, 19 December 2001) <https://prospect.org/features/bailing-private-jails/> accessed 14 December 2021.

[58] From 1986 to 1989, the Federal Bureau of Prisons opened four privately contracted so-called 'dedicated Institutional Hearing Program' prisons. While these facilities were not explicitly all-foreign, they were clear predecessors to the CAR system. See Kathleen Hawk Sawyer, *Hearing before the Subcommittee on International Law, Immigration, and Refugees* (23 February 1994) Serial No 37 167–68 <https://books.google.es/books?id=gIEAcQqPG94C&redir_esc=y> accessed 14 December 2021. See also Ingrid Eagly and Steven Shafer, 'The Institutional Hearing Program' (2020) 54(4) Law and Society Review 813.

[59] Kaufman, 'Segregation by Citizenship' (n 13) 1394.

[60] Loyd and Mountz (n 18) 92–96.

relatively long track record of contracting with private firms to operate immigration detention facilities.

From the early 1980s, public sector unions mounted vocal opposition to private confinement. At the American Federation of State, County and Municipal Employees (AFSCME) convention in June 1984, union members adopted a resolution that opposed the contracting of incarceration, resolving that privatisation 'creates an inherent conflict of interest between the desire for profits and the desire to rehabilitate inmates'.[61] Yet this opposition only went so far. The resolution also noted the established precedent set by the BOP and INS's use of contractors to house non-citizens and called for federal subsidies for states and local governments to construct new publicly run facilities.

When the Clinton administration began the National Performance Review in 1993, organised labour put significant pressure on federal elected officials and civil servants to resist privatisation.[62] Key among these groups was the American Federation of Government Employees' Council of Prison Locals. Both AFSCME and the Council of Prison Locals were key opponents of the Capital District Revitalization Act, passed in 1997, which obligated the BOP to place sentenced prisoners from the District of Columbia in privately operated, low-security facilities.[63] Organized labour spent millions of dollars, and conducted dozens of campaigns, contesting the spread of privately operated federal prisons.[64] Although, frequently, these labour groups were massively outspent by private contractors, their resistance played a key role in shaping federal policy.[65] Interviewed about the role played by organised labour, prominent anti-privatisation activist Judith Greene mentioned how the AFGE opposed wholesale privatisation, but had little to say about the expansion of the all-foreign prison system.[66] Greene felt strongly that union officials had struck a tacit deal with federal administrators after 1999, rendering no opposition to contracts that locked up immigrants.[67]

After 1997, BOP experiments with privatisation for US citizen prisoners were marked by highly publicised scandals. Congress obligated the BOP to procure and operate Taft Correctional Institution (CI Taft) under contract with Wackenhut in 1997 as a 'demonstration project' used to evaluate and compare outsourced incarceration at Taft with three other BOP-run facilities.[68] For the advocates of privatisation in the

[61] AFSCME, 'Contracting out of Correctional Institutions' (1984) 26th Convention, Resolution no 147 <https://www.afscme.org/about/governance/conventions/resolutions-amendments/1984/resolutions/147-contracting-out-of-correctional-institutions> accessed 14 December 2021.

[62] AFSCME, 'Privatization of Prisons' (1996) 32nd Convention, Resolution no 20 <https://www.afscme.org/about/governance/conventions/resolutions-amendments/1996/resolutions/20-privatization-of-prisons> accessed 14 December 2021.

[63] AFSCME, 'Opposing Prison Privatization' (1998) 33rd Convention, Resolution no 44 <https://www.afscme.org/about/governance/conventions/resolutions-amendments/1998/resolutions/44-opposing-prison-privatization> (accessed 14 December 2021).

[64] Thomas Michael Kelly, *The Politics of Prison Privatization* (2019) (PhD Thesis, University of California Berkeley) 15–16 <https://escholarship.org/content/qt3qj7q63d/qt3qj7q63d.pdf?t=q0navt> accessed 14 December 2021.

[65] ibid.

[66] Interview with Judith Greene, Executive Director, Justice Strategies (telephone, 24 March 2021).

[67] ibid.

[68] Harley Lappin and others, *Evaluation of the Taft Demonstration Project* (Federal Bureau of Prisons 2005).

White House and Congress, the decision to contract out Taft marked the first step towards fulfilling Clinton's promise to remain tough on crime while also slashing federal payrolls.[69]

Yet the cost savings promised by privatisation never materialised. A study by the National Institute of Corrections in 1999 found that CI Taft's contract was more expensive than comparable BOP facilities, specifically due to the costs of staffing and providing medical care to prisoners.[70] On 14 November 1999, hundreds of prisoners at Taft rioted in protest over poor conditions. One prisoner, Nathaniel Osuorji, wrote to Prison Legal News to contest the one-sided depiction of the 1999 riot in the local media.[71] Taft, as Osuorji put it, was a 'prison for profit' that was built to make money, rather than rehabilitate prisoners. Osuorji pointed out that Taft offered no vocational, educational, or similar programmes that were provided to prisoners of the same classification in BOP-run facilities: 'Inmates are simply wasting away without gaining any of the special skills they will need for post-release survival.'[72] Echoing the 1999 report, a BOP study published in 2005 found that the potential savings available through privatisation were outweighed by the extra costs associated with monitoring and administering the contract.[73]

Like CI Taft, the 1997 Revitalization Act set a timeline for the closure of prison facilities operated by the District of Columbia, and obligated the BOP to house sentenced District of Columbia prisoners in privately contracted facilities.[74] In May 1997, CCA opened the Northeast Ohio Correctional Center (NEOCC) in Youngstown, Ohio, housing 900 medium- and high-security prisoners from the District of Columbia. Almost immediately, the facility encountered a series of problems with understaffing, security, and poor medical care.[75] By the end of May, prisoners had begun to protest about the lack of basic necessities, health screenings, and other services by refusing to obey count.[76] Despite these issues, the BOP renewed its contract with CCA in September, increasing the total bed space at NEOCC to 1,700.[77] In February 1998, two prisoners, Derrick Davis and Bryson Chisley, were stabbed to death by other prisoners. Davis bled to death while awaiting attention because the facility was so short-staffed that there was no officer on the floor.[78] A Department of Justice inquiry into the

[69] Pam Belluck, 'As more Prisons go Private, States Seek Tighter Controls' *New York Times* (New York, 15 April 1999) <https://timesmachine.nytimes.com/timesmachine/1995/11/24/058823.html?pageNumber=1> accessed 14 December 2021.

[70] Julianne Nelson, *Taft Prison Facility: Cost Scenarios*. National Institute of Corrections (1999).

[71] Prison Legal News, 'Riot at Private Prison' (June 2000) *Prison Legal News* 4 <https://www.prisonlegalnews.org/news/2000/jun/15/riot-at-private-prison/> accessed 14 December 2021.

[72] ibid.

[73] Scott Camp and Dawn M Daggett, *Comparing Private and Public Prisons Using Operational Data* (Federal Bureau of Prisons 2001). See also Lappin and others (n 68).

[74] National Capital Revitalization and Self-Government Improvement Act 1997, Sec 11201 Bureau of Prisons <https://www.govinfo.gov/content/pkg/COMPS-10833/pdf/COMPS-10833.pdf> accessed 14 December 2021.

[75] Barry Yeoman, 'Steel Town Lockdown' (*Mother Jones*, May/June 2000) <https://www.motherjones.com/politics/2000/05/steel-town-lockdown/> accessed 14 December 2021.

[76] Department of Justice Corrections Trustee, *Inspection and Review of the Northeast Ohio Correctional Center* (US Department of Justice 1998) <https://www.justice.gov/archives/ag/report-attorney-general-inspection-and-review-northeast-ohio-correctional-center> accessed 14 December 2021.

[77] ibid.

[78] See Yeoman (n 75).

failures at the facility found that, 'in response to a perceived emergency need for contract prison beds, the District of Columbia rushed into an abbreviated procurement process which minimized competition [resulting in] a flawed contract, at a somewhat inflated price, with weak requirements on the contractor and minimal provisions for enforcement'.[79]

The cloud of negative publicity produced by CI Taft and NEOCC made privately contracted confinement an albatross around the BOP's neck. Despite internal opposition, the BOP awarded Cornell Corrections a contract for a new low-security facility to house sentenced District of Columbia prisoners in 1998 as per the obligations set out in the 1997 District of Columbia Revitalization Act.[80] When Cornell Corrections began construction in Philipsburg, Pennsylvania a year later, the proposal was immediately met by legal challenges from the state attorney general, and from local citizens' groups.[81] Notably, the legal challenge made by local citizens' groups was directly funded by the American Federation of State, County, and Municipal Employees.[82]

A memo prepared by BOP counsel shows that, in the wake of the cost overruns at CI Taft and the scandals at NEOCC, the BOP replaced sentenced District of Columbia prisoners with non-citizens at the planned facility in Pennsylvania.[83] By 2003, when both legal challenges had been resolved, Cornell pressed the Bureau to consider design changes to the facility, and the substitution of a different prisoner population, to 'reduce the costs associated with the [construction] delay'.[84] The proposed changes provide critical insight into how the public–private relationship shaped the creation of the prison. Rather than a three-building facility designed to house a range of prisoners with varied needs, Cornell proposed a massive, one-building facility where people could be warehoused in a single large space to reduce costs.[85] While the BOP rejected this initial proposal out of hand, they eventually agreed to a design for a two-building facility. Moreover, BOP officials agreed to replace all District of Columbia prisoners with 'criminal aliens'. BOP assistant general counsel Mary Carney wrote that:

> the original population was expected to be very expensive because DC inmates require a great deal of programming … The substitution of criminal aliens for many of the DC male inmates and the entire [youth offenders] program … was expected to lead to even lower per diem rates than in the original proposal.[86]

Besides the lack of programming, outsourced facilities for non-citizens were cheaper to operate because they were not held to the same regulatory standards as BOP-run facilities. BOP-run facilities are regulated by criteria set forth in 'program

[79] See Corrections Trustee (n 76) ch III.

[80] Mike Buckso, 'Texas Firm to Operate Pa.'s First Private Prison in Clearfield' *Pittsburgh Post-Gazette* (Pittsburgh, 30 April 2006) <https://www.post-gazette.com/uncategorized/2006/04/30/Texas-firm-to-operate-Pa-s-1st-private-prison-in-Clearfield/stories/200604300138> accessed 14 December 2021.

[81] Yeoman (n 75).

[82] Buckso (n 80).

[83] Mary E Carney, *Philipsburg Contract Issues* (Department of Justice Internal Memorandum 2004). On file with author.

[84] ibid 9.

[85] ibid.

[86] ibid 10.

statements'.[87] These regulations set forth clear standards for healthcare, educational programming, rehabilitative services, and more. While BOP-run facilities may fail to live up to these standards, the fact that these rules exist set a clear standard of operations. Among eight contracts for all-foreign facilities, none contained language holding contractors to the rules set forth in BOP program statements.[88] As Donna Mott, a former employee in the BOP's privatisation management unit, stated: 'If you put in specificity exactly like BOP program statements then it is basically going to cost the contractor the same amount to operate their facility as it does a bureau facility, which then takes the draw for private contracting off the table—because the draw is that it costs the government less money.'[89]

Overall, the decision to replace sentenced US citizen prisoners with non-citizen prisoners in the plans for the Philipsburg facility shows how the privately operated, all-foreign prison emerged as a contingent solution to the problems faced by federal political and administrative officials, private contractors, and local governments. The integration of the logics of migration control and punishment within a privately operated facility allowed politicians to project the image of being tough on 'criminal aliens' while simultaneously being seen to reduce the size and cost of the Federal Government. In practice, BOP decisions to restrict non-citizen access to a wide range of prison services, and the exemption of all-foreign facilities from the same regulations applied to BOP facilities, made all-foreign facilities significantly cheaper to operate. Yet cost was predicated on the foreign racial identities of prison subjects: the incarceration of 'criminal aliens' was rendered available for private contractors precisely because of the drive expressed by the Clinton administration and the House Subcommittee on Immigration to treat non-citizens differently.

V Practices of Public-private Incarceration and the 'Pains' of All-foreign Prison

In this section, I examine how practices of public–private incarceration come to shape how men in US all-foreign prisons understand who does and who does not belong. I draw on the testimonies of thirty-two men incarcerated at CI North Lake, a CAR prison in Northern Michigan, interviewed in collaboration with the grass-roots advocacy group No Detention Centers in Michigan. I also conducted mail correspondence with twelve men incarcerated in three other CAR prisons.[90] This data is contextualised

[87] For a list of all BOP program statements, see BOP, 'BOP Policies' (2021) <https://www.bop.gov/PublicInfo/execute/policysearch?todo=query> accessed 14 December 2021.

[88] Contract and proposal documents for eight CAR facilities were obtained by Stephen Raher, an attorney with the Prison Policy Initiative, via Freedom of Information Act request. Raher has kindly shared these documents with me, and made many of the documents available online at <https://app.box.com/s/e541c0a813751fdf2e09> accessed 14 December 2021.

[89] Donna Mott, in Seth Wessler, 'Separate Unequal and Deadly' (*Type Investigations*, 27 January 2016) <https://www.typeinvestigations.org/investigation/2016/01/27/separate-unequal-deadly/> accessed 14 December 2021.

[90] Mail-based correspondence is an established method in correctional settings, where other forms of research are difficult. See Mary Bosworth and others, 'Doing Prison Research: Views from Inside' (2005) 11(2) Qualitative Inquiry 249.

through analysis of three previous studies of conditions in CAR facilities conducted between 2013 and 2016, and analysis of contract documents obtained by public records request.[91]

My goal in describing how the public–private relationship shapes conditions of confinement is not to compare these facilities to those run by the BOP. Rather, my aim is to show how privately operated confinement has become a tool of the prison welfare chauvinism articulated by the Clinton administration and the House Subcommittee on Immigration.[92] In this section, I show how outsourced confinement puts into practice Congressman Lewis' 1994 assertion that immigrant prisoners are not worth being clothed, housed, and fed, because they will eventually be deported. In turn, I suggest that this neglect functions as a key mode of exclusion along the lines of citizenship and racial difference and constitutes a key feature of the pain of all-foreign imprisonment in the United States.

VI Prison Housing and Overcrowding

The spaces in which non-citizens are incarcerated, and the ways in which they are coerced into inhabiting those spaces, demonstrate how the public/private boundary shapes conditions of confinement in CAR prisons. On a basic level, the financial structure of contracts between the BOP, local governments, and private contractors incentivise overcrowding. Contract records from ten CAR facilities procured by the BOP between 1999 and 2019 show how both federal officials and private contractors are rewarded financially for increasing the density of CAR facilities as much as possible.[93] Each contract has a 'fixed incremental unit price' structure, meaning that the BOP pays a flat monthly fee when the number of prisoners held in the contracted facility is below a certain point, and then pays an increased 'unit price per inmate day' fee when the average number of prisoners housed during a monthly period exceeds the set threshold.[94] All contracts maintained by the BOP for the incarceration of federal prisoners specify the 'rated capacity' of the contracted facility, referring to the number of prisoners that the designated facility can safely incarcerate.[95] The flat monthly fee paid by the BOP is generally set at a percentage threshold of the contracted facility's overall 'rated capacity'.

In the first two CAR contracts signed by the BOP on 9 June 2000 with the Corrections Corporation of America, the fixed price threshold was set at 95 per cent of rated capacity. At the Cibola County facility in New Mexico, 95 per cent of rated capacity meant an average monthly prisoner population of 961, for which the BOP paid roughly $1.7 million per month.[96] At the California City Facility in California,

[91] ACLU, *Warehoused and Forgotten* (June 2014) <https://www.aclu.org/sites/default/files/assets/060614-aclu-car-reportonline.pdf> accessed 14 December 2021; DC Corrections Information Council, *Rivers Correctional Institution Inspection Report* (2017). See also Wessler (n 89); note re contract documents (n 88).

[92] See, eg Condit (n 37); Clinton, 'Radio Address to the Nation' (n 39).

[93] See note re contract documents (n 88).

[94] See, eg BOP, *Contract PCC-0009-Reeves County, Texas* (Federal Bureau of Prisons 2006).

[95] ACLU (n 91).

[96] Federal Bureau of Prisons, '*Contract J1PCc-006-California City, California*' (n 53) 2.

that meant an average monthly prisoner population of 2,189, for which the BOP paid roughly $4 million per month.[97] Both contracts had a three-year base period, meaning that because of the fixed-price structure of the contract, the BOP was on the hook for $206 million whether or not the agency ever actually used these facilities.

This contract structure creates financial pressures to keep each CAR facility as densely occupied as possible. An American Civil Liberties Union (ACLU) investigation in 2014 found that each of the five CAR facilities in Texas regularly operated beyond their 100 per cent 'rated capacity'. Financial documents filed by CCA with the Securities and Exchange Commission in 2006 listed the 'design capacity' at Eden County Detention Center in Texas to be 1,225 prisoners.[98] However, the covering letter submitted by CCA vice president Damon Hininger to the BOP contracting office on 4 August 2006 confidently projected that the facility would be able to run at a 115 per cent rated capacity of 1,558 beds. To accommodate the 333 additional beds, Hininger promised that CCA would 'convert the existing 96 bed segregation unit to general population and build a new 136 bed segregation unit'.[99] Interviews conducted by the ACLU years later found that prisoners who were transferred to Eden were regularly held in the segregation unit during their intake period, while the facility waited for space to open up in general population.[100] CCA also forced prisoners to sleep in spaces not designed as prison cells. William, another prisoner at Eden in 2014, said: 'I sleep in a hallway with about 80 inmates. I sleep right next to the bathroom so it's like I'm sleeping in the toilet. I feel like my head is in the toilet.'[101]

While all-foreign prisons are certainly not the only overcrowded penal facilities in the United States, the testimonies of men in CAR prisons suggest that overcrowded conditions fuel perceptions of exclusion based on immigration status and race. For Andres, a prisoner at CI Giles W Dalby in Texas born in Mexico, immigration status and race were preconditions for overcrowding. He was forced to live in a cell where 'you might be brushing your teeth and there is someone taking a shit a foot away' precisely because he did not have immigration status.[102] For Alejandro, a prisoner at CI McRae in Georgia, the fact that it was 'too crowded' was a sign of how private prison contractors made money from the incarceration of Latino men: 'For them, we're just dollar signs.' While the 'we' claimed by Alejandro clearly referred to Spanish-speaking, Latino prisoners in McRae, 'them' was ambiguous, referring both specifically to CoreCivic, and more broadly to federal officials vested with the authority to make decisions about immigration status.

Alejandro's observation also reflects a broader sentiment that came through in nearly all the interviews that I conducted. Whether conditions were worse in contract prisons was often immaterial. Rather, men in these facilities drew direct connections between their race and immigration status, and the ways in which financial value was

[97] Federal Bureau of Prisons, '*Contract J1PCc-007-Cibola County, New Mexico*' (n 53) 2.

[98] Corrections Corporation of America, *Securities and Exchange Commission Form 10-K* (2005) 10 <http://ir.corecivic.com/static-files/0c7d04b7-35ac-4326-b88c-95a6e870cdad> accessed 14 December 2021.

[99] Corrections Corporation of America, *Proposal Vol 1: RFP PCC-0010* (proposal document 2005) 2.

[100] ACLU (n 91) 77.

[101] ibid 78.

[102] Letter from Andres to author (11 August 2021) on file with author. All names used in this chapter are pseudonyms.

extracted from their incarceration. In this sense, the 'pain' of overcrowding was not simply that private confinement was worse than public. Rather, for men like Andres and Alejandro, overcrowding came to signify the ways in which they were subject to extractive financial practices because of their foreign racial identities.

VII Medical and Mental Care

For decades, the provision of medical care has been one of the largest drivers of the rising expense of incarceration within the federal prison system.[103] For both public administrators and private contractors, outsourced incarceration delivers value by reducing the costs associated with providing care in custody.[104] Yet, the drive to reduce expenditures shaped the process of keeping men in CAR prisons alive. In Luis Alba's case, this relationship was clear-cut. On 13 February 2004, Corrections Corporation of America published an investor brief advertising the value generated by a 5.8 per cent reduction in the 'variable costs per compensated man-day' at CI McRae.[105] These savings were achieved by 'stronger expense controls in food and medical care' and lower medical costs reflecting 'contract modifications that eliminated or decreased responsibility for medical expenses'.[106] By refusing to pay for medical care—like the treatment needed to help Alba regain the use of his voice—CCA delivered value to shareholders, and to the Federal Government.

Medical neglect remains a ubiquitous feature of the CAR system, only exacerbated by the spread of the COVID-19 pandemic. A group of prisoners at North Lake Correctional Institution, a GEO-operated prison in Baldwin, Michigan, described a harrowing experience whereby a cellmate with severe COVID symptoms collapsed, and was left lying on the floor of their shared cell for hours in the middle of the night, while they tried to call the medical staff.[107] The sick man only received emergency care five hours after he collapsed because the facility did not have medical staff available to respond immediately.[108]

In turn, difficulties in accessing medical care exacerbated the perception that men in CAR prisons were being neglected so that the BOP and private contractors could turn a profit. Medical neglect, ostensibly for the purpose of profit, came to be a primary mode of exclusion differentiating between US citizens in BOP custody and non-citizens in privately operated facilities. Raul, a prisoner at CI McRae in early 2020, suffered a massive heart attack after contracting COVID-19 in custody. When I asked him about the medical situation there, he connected the lack of care directly to the differential treatment of Latino prisoners: 'for [CoreCivic], it's just a business decision ... but it means that the Spanish-speaking guys suffer'.[109]

[103] GAO, *Bureau of Prisons: Better Planning and Evaluation Needed to Understand and Control Rising Inmate Health Care Costs* (2017) GAO-17-379 <https://www.gao.gov/assets/gao-17-379.pdf> accessed 14 December 2021.

[104] Wessler (n 89).

[105] *Alba v Montford, Case No CV 305-159 (SD Ga Jul 24, 2006)*, Document 1, 'Company Update' 67.

[106] ibid.

[107] Transcript of No Detention Centers in Michigan Call (5 May 2020).

[108] ibid.

[109] Interview with Raul, 25 March 2021.

David, a prisoner at CI North Lake, interviewed in April 2020, put it bluntly:

> because we are immigrants, they don't treat us right... This is my sixth prison. I've never seen stuff like this. You know, I feel—whoever built this place, they built this place really wrong.... Because we are deportable people, that's why they're doing what they're doing with us. One of the CO's told me that the Constitution of the United States, it don't protect us, because we're not from here. And I told him that we're on American soil, we should be protected. He told me no. That's why they're doing what they're doing with us.[110]

For David, the unprecedented lack of care at CI North Lake, caused by outsourcing, was directly connected to the foreign racial identities of the men incarcerated there. In turn, this testimony identified an additional 'pain' of all-foreign imprisonment. Beyond simply engendering conditions of neglect, prisoners in all-foreign prisons contested practices of public–private private incarceration as clear tools of racial, ethnic, and national exclusion.

VIII Conclusion

On 2 February 2008, a panel of three judges from the US Court of Appeals for the Eleventh Circuit struck down Luis Alba's final appeal against the Corrections Corporation of America.[111] While the court acknowledged the facts of Alba's mistreatment, the panel concluded that, because he was incarcerated in a privately operated prison, Alba's claim should not have been filed as a federal suit, but instead as a state medical malpractice against a private entity.[112] It is not clear how much this decision mattered to him personally: Alba had long since been deported to Colombia, and was no longer in regular contact with the court.[113] This ending neatly reflects the interlocking prison-to-deportation circuitry promised by President Clinton in 1995. Rather than 'passing go' and returning to American society, or indeed seeing the conclusion of his legal case, Alba was deported to a country where he had not lived for decades.[114]

This chapter has examined the evolution of privately contracted confinement within the federal prison system, and shown how non-citizens, and particularly Latino men, have come to be the default subjects of outsourced confinement. As concerns about 'criminal aliens' gripped the public after 1980, federal officials took steps to target and exclude non-citizens within the federal prison system. Often, the drive to exclude non-citizens reflected a racially motivated drive to exclude Latino immigrants from

110 Transcript of No Detention Centers in Michigan Call (19 April 2020).
111 *Alba v Montford*, 517 F3d 1249 (11th Cir 2008).
112 ibid.
113 ibid.
114 Clinton, 'Radio Address to the Nation' (n 39).

public services, echoing Emma Kaufman's observation that citizenship has increasingly come to 'mean race' in practice.[115]

Drawing directly on the testimonies of men in CAR prisons, this chapter has also begun to explore how prisoners negotiate practices of public–private confinement as a condition of their immigration status, nationality, and race. In both how they are housed, and the services and care that are offered to them, non-citizen prisoners in all-foreign facilities become sources of financial value, and in turn frequently experience deprivation or neglect. Yet rather than comparing contract facilities to nominally public BOP facilities, this analysis has shown how experiences of deprivation and neglect structure how prisoners understand and negotiate their own relationship to or exclusion from the US public. Irrespective of whether contract confinement is better or worse than 'public' prison, the financial dehumanisation embodied in public–private practices of incarceration has become a de facto tool of exclusion along lines of race, immigration status, and citizenship. This constitutes a key feature of the 'pain' of all-foreign imprisonment in the United States.

References

ACLU, *Warehoused and Forgotten* (June 2014) <https://www.aclu.org/sites/default/files/assets/060614-aclu-car-reportonline.pdf>

Adams RS, Bean FD, Chavez LR, and Zhou M, 'Immigration: Proposition 187, Five Years Later' (*Bulletin of the American Academy of Arts and Sciences*, 2000) <https://www.amacad.org/news/immigration-proposition-187-five-years-later>

AFSCME, 'Contracting out of Correctional Institutions' (1984) 26th Convention, Resolution no 147 <https://www.afscme.org/about/governance/conventions/resolutions-amendments/1984/resolutions/147-contracting-out-of-correctional-institutions>

— —, 'Privatization of Prisons' (1996) 32nd Convention, Resolution no 20 <https://www.afscme.org/about/governance/conventions/resolutions-amendments/1996/resolutions/20-privatization-of-prisons>

— —,'Opposing Prison Privatization' (1998) 33rd Convention, Resolution no 44 <https://www.afscme.org/about/governance/conventions/resolutions-amendments/1998/resolutions/44-opposing-prison-privatization>

Alexander M, *The New Jim Crow* (The New Press 2010)

Barrett D, 'Private-prison Firm CCA to Rename itself CoreCivic' *Wall Street Journal* (New York, 28 October 2016) <https://www.wsj.com/articles/private-prison-firm-cca-to-rename-itself-corecivic-1477666800>

Belluck P, 'As more Prisons go Private, States Seek Tighter Controls' *New York Times* (New York, 15 April 1999) <https://timesmachine.nytimes.com/timesmachine/1995/11/24/058823.html?pageNumber=>

Bhui HS, 'Foreign National Prisoners: Issues and Debates' in Hindpal Singh Bhui (ed), *Race and Criminal Justice* (Sage Publishing 2009)

BOP, *Program Statement 7310.04* (US Department of Justice 1998) <https://www.bop.gov/policy/progstat/7310_004.pdf>

[115] Emma Kaufman, 'When Citizenship Means Race' in Mary Bosworth, Alpa Parmar, and Yolanda Vasquez (eds), *Race, Criminal Justice and Migration Control* (OUP 2018) <http://doi.org/10.1093/oso/9780198814887.001.0001>.

— —, *Notice of Intent to Prepare a Draft Environmental Impact Statement (DEIS) for Housing Criminal Alien Population in Non-federal Low-security Correctional Facilities* (The Federal Register 1999) <https://www.federalregister.gov/documents/1999/04/23/99-10337/notice-of-intent-to-prepare-a-draft-environmental-impact-statement-deis-for-housing-criminal-alien>

— —, *Contract J1PCc-007-Cibola County, New Mexico* (contract award document) (Federal Bureau of Prisons 2000)

— —, *Contract J1PCc-006-California City, California* (contract award document) (Federal Bureau of Prisons 2000)

— —, *Contract J1PCc-006-California City, California* (contract award document) (Federal Bureau of Prisons 2000)

— —, *Contract J1PCc-007-Cibola County, New Mexico* (Federal Bureau of Prisons 2000)

— —, *Contract PCC-0009-Reeves County, Texas* (Federal Bureau of Prisons 2000)

— —, 'BOP Policies' (2021) https://www.bop.gov/PublicInfo/execute/policysearch?todo=query

— —, 'Contract Prisons' (2021) <https://www.bop.gov/about/facilities/contract_facilities.jsp>

Bosworth M, Campbell D, Demby B, Ferranti SM, and Santos M, 'Doing Prison Research: Views from Inside' (2005) 11(2) Qualitative Inquiry 249

Buckso M, 'Texas Firm to Operate Pa.'s First Private Prison in Clearfield' *Pittsburgh Post-Gazette* (Pittsburgh, 30 April 2006) <https://www.post-gazette.com/uncategorized/2006/04/30/Texas-firm-to-operate-Pa-s-1st-private-prison-in-Clearfield/stories/200604300138>

Calavita K, 'The New Politics of Immigration' (1996) 43(3) Social Problems 285

Camp S and others, *Comparing Private and Public Prisons Using Operational Data* (Federal Bureau of Prisons 2001)

Carney ME, *Philipsburg Contract Issues* (Department of Justice Internal Memorandum 2004) (on file with author)

Chacón JM, 'Overcriminalizing Immigration' (2012) 102 Journal of Criminal Law & Criminology 613.

Chavez LR, *The Latino Threat* (University of California Press 2013)

Cházaro A, 'Challenging the Criminal Alien Paradigm' (2016) 63(594) UCLA Law Review 598

Clark J, *Hearing before the Subcommittee on Immigration, House of Representatives* (15 July 1997)

Clinton W, 'Radio Address to the Nation' (6 May 1995) <https://clinton.presidentiallibraries.us/items/show/12973>

— —, 'State of the Union Address' (23 January 1996) <https://clintonwhitehouse4.archives.gov/WH/New/other/sotu.html>

Corrections Corporation of America, *Securities and Exchange Commission Form 10-K* (2005) 10 <http://ir.corecivic.com/static-files/0c7d04b7-35ac-4326-b88c-95a6e870cdad>

— —, *Proposal Vol 1: RFP PCC-0010* (proposal document 2005)

Condit G, *Hearing before the Subcommittee on Immigration, House of Representatives* (23 February 1994)

Davis A, *Are Prisons Obsolete?* (Seven Stories Press 2003)

DC Corrections Information Council, *Rivers Correctional Institution Inspection Report* (DC Corrections Information Council 2017)

Department of Justice, *Annual Report: Detention and Incarceration* (US Department of Justice 1999) <https://www.justice.gov/archive/ag/annualreports/ar99/Chapter5.pdf>

Department of Justice Corrections Trustee, *Inspection and Review of the Northeast Ohio Correctional Center* (US Department of Justice 1998) <https://www.justice.gov/archives/ag/report-attorney-general-inspection-and-review-northeast-ohio-correctional-center>

Department of Justice Office of the Inspector General (DOJ OIG), *Community Corrections Center Program Audit Results* (US Department of Justice 1995) <https://oig.justice.gov/reports/BOP/a9608/au9608p1.htm>

— —, *Review of the Federal Bureau of Prisons' Monitoring of Contract Prisons* (US Department of Justice 2016) <https://oig.justice.gov/reports/2016/e1606.pdf>

— —, *Audit of the Federal Bureau of Prisons' Contract Awarded to Correct Care Solutions Prisons* (US Department of Justice 2019) <https://www.oversight.gov/sites/default/files/oig-reports/a1937_0.pdf>

Eagly I and Shafer S, 'The Institutional Hearing Program' (2020) 54(4) Law and Society Review 813

Gallegy E, *Hearing before the Subcommittee on Immigration, House of Representatives* (15 July 1997)

GAO, *Criminal Alien Statistics* (GAO 1987) GAO-11-187

— — *Criminal Aliens* (1997) GAO/T-GGD-97-154.

— — *Criminal Aliens* (1998) GAO/GGD-99-3.

— — *Criminal Aliens* (1999) GAO/T-GGD-99-47

— — *Eligibility and Capacity Impact Use of Flexibilities to Reduce Inmates' Time in Prisons* (2012) GAO-12-320

— —, *Bureau of Prisons: Better Planning and Evaluation Needed to Understand and Control Rising Inmate Health Care Costs* (GAO 2017) GAO-17-379 <https://www.gao.gov/assets/gao-17-379.pdf>

Ghandnoosh N, 'US Prison Population Trends' (*The Sentencing Project*, 17 September 2019) <https://www.sentencingproject.org/publications/u-s-prison-population-trends-massive-buildup-and-modest-decline/>

Gilmore Wilson R, *Golden Gulag* (University of California Press 2007)

Greene J, 'Bailing out Private Prisons' (*The American Prospect*, 19 December 2001) <https://prospect.org/features/bailing-private-jails/>

Hernandez KL, *Migra!* (University of California Press 2010)

Kaufman E, 'When Citizenship Means Race' in Bosworth M, Parmar A, and Vasquez Y (eds), *Race, Criminal Justice and Migration Control* (OUP 2018) http://doi.org/10.1093/oso/9780198814887.001.0001

— —, 'Segregation by Citizenship' (2019) 132(5) Harvard Law Review 1379.

Kelly TM, *The Politics of Prison Privatization* (PhD thesis, University of California Berkeley 2019) <https://escholarship.org/content/qt3qj7q63d/qt3qj7q63d.pdf?t=q0navt>

Lappin, H and others, *Evaluation of the Taft Demonstration Project* (Federal Bureau of Prisons 2005)

Lewis TF, *Hearing before the Subcommittee on Immigration, House of Representatives* (23 February 1994)

Lichtenstein A, *Twice the Work of Free Labor* (Verso 1995)

Loyd J and Mountz A, *Boats, Borders and Bases* (University of California Press 2018)

Martin LL, 'Carceral Economies of Migration Control' (2021) 45(4) Progress in Human Geography 743.

McCarthy B, 'Coping with Crowding' (1989) 13(2) American Journal of Criminal Justice 245

McLennan RM, *The Crisis of Imprisonment* (CUP 2008)

Mott D, in Wessler S, 'Separate Unequal and Deadly' (*Type Investigations*, 27 January 2016) <https://www.typeinvestigations.org/investigation/2016/01/27/separate-unequal-deadly>

National Performance Review, *A Brief History of the NPR* (Government Printing Office 1997) <https://govinfo.library.unt.edu/npr/library/papers/bkgrd/brief.html>

Nelson J, *Taft Prison Facility: Cost Scenarios* (National Institute of Corrections 1999)

Prison Legal News, 'Riot at Private Prison' (June 2000) Prison Legal News 4 <https://www.prisonlegalnews.org/news/2000/jun/15/riot-at-private-prison/>

Raher S, 'The Business of Punishing' (2010) 13(13) Richmond Journal of Law and the Public Interest 215

Sawyer KH, *Hearing before the Subcommittee on International Law, Immigration, and Refugees* (23 February 1994), Serial No 37 <https://books.google.es/books?id=gIEAcQqPG94C&redir_esc=y>
Sherrill R, 'Can Miami Save Itself?' *New York Times* (New York, 19 July 1987)
Simon J, 'Refugees in a Carceral Age' (1998) 10(3) Public Culture 10
Ugelvik T, and Damsa D, 'The Pains of Crimmigration Imprisonment' (2018) 58(5) British Journal of Criminology 1025
US Senate Committee on Governmental Affairs, 'Criminal Aliens in the United States', Report 104-48 (1995) <https://www.congress.gov/104/crpt/srpt48/CRPT-104srpt48.pdf>
Warr J, 'Foreign National Prisoners and the Pains of Imprisonment' (2016) 16(3) Criminology and Criminal Justice 301
Yeoman B, 'Steel Town Lockdown' (*Mother Jones*, May/June 2000) <https://www.motherjones.com/politics/2000/05/steel-town-lockdown/>

Cases

Alba v Montford, Case No CV 305-159 (SD Ga Jul 24, 2006)
United States v Smith, 27 F.3d 649, 668 (DC Cir 1994)

Statutes

Illegal Immigration Reform and Immigration Responsibility Act 1996
The Antiterrorism and Effective Death Penalty Act 1996
National Capital Revitalization and Self-Government Improvement Act 1997, Sec 11201 Bureau of Prisons <https://www.govinfo.gov/content/pkg/COMPS-10833/pdf/COMPS-10833.pdf>

8

The Marketisation of 'Legitimate' Violence

Inducing Deportation through Public–Private Cooperation

Federica Infantino[*]

I Introduction

Immigration detention and deportation are increasingly employed as forms of border and migration control. Representative of two of the most coercive actions states may take, they also routinely involve non-state actors. Analysing the day-to-day implementation of immigration detention and deportation thus raises questions about state capacity to control migration and borders.[1] In this chapter, I explore detention for the purpose of expulsion.

There is a large body of scholarship that sees immigration detention and deportation as instruments of border and migration control.[2] Primarily theoretical, much of this work draws on Foucault's writings on governmentality and biopolitical power,[3] and on Agamben's writings on the state of exception and 'the Camp'.[4] Another set of scholars questions the day-to-day practices of detention and deportation[5] and the role of private companies, most notably in the UK;[6]

[*] I would like to thank Myriam Cherti, Sarah Spencer, Bastian Vollmer, and especially Mary Bosworth for supporting the empirical part of this research. I would like to thank the editors for their comments on the draft versions of this chapter.

[1] Antje Ellermann, *States Against Migrants: Deportation in Germany and the US* (CUP 2009).

[2] Diego Bigo, 'Globalized (In)Security: The Field and the Ban-opticon' in Diego Bigo and Anastassia Tsoukala (eds), *Terror, Insecurity, and Liberty: Illiberal Practices of Liberal Regimes after 9/11* (Routledge 2008); Nicholas De Genova and Nathalie Peutz, *The Deportation Regime. Sovereignty, Space, and the Freedom of Movement* (Duke University Press 2010); Vicki Squire, *The Contested Politics of Mobility: Borderzones and Irregularity* (Routledge 2010); William Walters, 'Deportation, Expulsion, and the International Police of Aliens' (2002) 6(3) Citizenship Studies 265–92.

[3] Michael Foucault, *Dits et ecrits 1954–1988; Tome 2: 1970–1975* (Editions NRF Gallimard 1994).

[4] Giorgio Agamben, *Homo Sacer: Il potere sovrano e la nuda vita* (Einaudi 1995).

[5] Mary Bosworth, *Inside Immigration Detention* (OUP 2014); Mathilde Darley, 'Le pouvoir de la norme. La production du jugement et son contournement dans les lieux d'enfermement des étrangers' (2010) 34(2) Déviance et Société 229; Ellermann (n 1); Nicolas Fischer, 'The Detention of Foreigners in France: Between Discretionary Control and the Rule of Law' (2013) 10(6) European Journal of Criminology 692; Alexandra Hall, '"These People could be anyone": Fear, Contempt (and Empathy) in a British Immigration Removal Centre' (2010) 36(6) Journal of Ethnic and Migration Studies 881; Carolina Kobelinsky, *L'accueil des demandeurs d'asile. Une ethnographie de l'attente* (Editions du Cygne 2010); Chowra Makaremi, 'Waiting Zone' in Julia Creet and Andreas Kitzmann (eds), *Memory and Migration: Multidisciplinary Approaches to Memory Studies* (University of Toronto Press 2011).

[6] Christine Bacon, *The Evolution of Immigration Detention in the UK: The Involvement of Private Prison Companies* (RSC Working Paper No 27) (2005); see also Bosworth and Singler, in this volume.

Federica Infantino, *The Marketisation of 'Legitimate' Violence* In: *Privatising Border Control*. Edited by: Mary Bosworth and Lucia Zedner, Oxford University Press. © Federica Infantino 2022. DOI: 10.1093/oso/9780192857163.003.0009

these scholars have focused on the experience of detainees and their views of state practices.[7]

As others have argued, immigration detention and deportation are not just meant to keep people out but also to produce a docile workforce[8] whose lives are characterised by their 'deportability'.[9] The stated goal of detention—to facilitate the removal of foreigners from the territory—remains largely symbolic.[10] Detention and deportation, in this view, are part of a range of strategies that aim to strengthen and make more visible the policing of borders.[11] Border guards, walls, and military forces contribute to the so-called border spectacle[12] designed to appease public anxieties over immigration, rather than necessarily to diminish clandestine passages and irregular migration.[13]

In this chapter, I build on the 'practice perspective' to analyse empirical evidence on how public–private cooperation plays out in the implementation of detention and deportation policies. Practice is treated as 'the place to study the nature and transformation of our research object'.[14] As I will show, the achievement of deportation remains a key objective for those in the public and private sectors. Cooperation between them also helps individuals make sense of their day-to-day work.[15] The marketisation of public action requires conformity to market rules and norms[16] and affects how people make sense of goals and how to achieve them. Targets, the meeting of contractual requirements, and economic efficiency, rather than the rule of law, define their day-to-day practices. The rule of law tends to be seen as a constraint weighing on the capacity of states to control migration and borders.[17] To analyse responses to these constraints, I will show how the state uses its cooperation with private companies to achieve its aims. This perspective aims to contribute to debates about the privatisation of migration and border control by focusing on organisational responses to achieve the deportation of undesirable foreigners.

[7] Guy J Coffey and others, 'The Meaning and Mental Health Consequences of Long-term Immigration Detention for People Seeking Asylum' (2010) 70(12) Social Science & Medicine 2070; Melanie Griffiths, 'Out of Time: The Temporal Uncertainties of Refused Asylum Seekers and Immigration Detainees' (2014) 40(12) Journal of Ethnic and Migration Studies 1991.

[8] Julien Jeandesboz, 'Violence, Capture and Apparatus' in Yolande Jansen, Robin Celikates, and Joost De Bloois (eds), *The Irregularization of Migration in Contemporary Europe: Detention, Deportation, Drowning* (Rowman & Littlefield 2014) 87–95.

[9] De Genova and Peutz (n 2).

[10] Peter Andreas, *Border Games: Policing the US–Mexico Divide* (Cornell University Press 2000).

[11] Virginie Guiraudon and Christian Joppke (eds), *Controlling a New Migration World* (Routledge 2001).

[12] Ruben Andersson, *Illegality Inc: Clandestine Migration and the Business of Bordering Europe* (California University Press 2014).

[13] Andreas (n 10).

[14] Theodore R Schatzki, Karin Knorr, and Eike von Savigny, *The Practice Turn in Contemporary Theory* (Routledge 2001) 2.

[15] Cynthia E Coburn, 'Framing the Problem of Reading Instruction: Using Frame Analysis to Uncover the Microprocesses of Policy Implementation in Schools' (2006) 43(3) American Educational Research Journal 343; Martha S Feldman, 'Social Limits to Discretion: An Organizational Perspective' in Keith Hawkins (ed), *The Uses of Discretion* (OUP 1992) 163–83.

[16] Nikolas Rose, 'Governing "Advanced" Liberal Democracies' in Aradhana Sharma and Akhil Gupta (eds), *The Anthropology of the State* (Blackwell Publishing 2006) 144–62; Nikolas Rose and Peter Miller, 'Political Power beyond the State: Problematics of Government' (1992) 43(2) British Journal of Sociology 179.

[17] Guiraudon and Joppke (n 11).

This analysis draws on research I conducted in 2016 in two UK immigration detention centres. The chapter starts by describing the research design and methodology used in the empirical part of the project. I focus on the background, tasks, and skills of private and public employees and managers by paying particular attention to the ways in which they understand the purposes to which organisational action is bent. Then, I show how the state uses public–private cooperation to achieve its goals. I suggest that the state delegates violence to private actors, even though the use of 'legitimate' violence or coercion lies at the core of state sovereignty. While private companies undertake the state's coercive action and, with it, accept the responsibilities and blame that might result, state actors concentrate their efforts on 'induced deportations', in which they secure migrants' agreement to leave by advising, persuading, and threatening.

II The Methodology of the Empirical Research

This chapter builds on interviews and observations I conducted in 2016 with Home Office officials and with private security staff of two immigration removal centres (IRC) in the UK: IRC Colnbrook and IRC Brook House. As with almost all removal centres in the UK, these institutions are run by private sector security firms, on behalf of the Home Office: at the time of my visits these were Mitie and G4S.[18] The Home Office staff monitored the contract and passed information to the detained population about their immigration and asylum cases.

Within the immigration detention estate, Brook House and Colnbrook are distinctive: they are among the largest centres in the country; they are the closest to the London airports; and they are built to secure, Category B prison standards. 'It looks like a prison' was the first sentence that Robert,[19] the Mitie manager at Colnbrook, said to me. Fences topped with barbed wire; CCTV cameras; walls; bars on the windows; specific rituals, such as passing through security gates, and opening and closing gates; enclosed routes for entering; the architectural design of wings, cells, corridors, passages: all of these realise the security and confinement objectives of these premises. As a result, 'the most problematic cases tend to go to Brook [and] Colnbrook for managing purposes', one G4S worker stated.

Over a period of six months, I interviewed Home Office and private security staff in their offices and observed the frontline staff in the centres. I also observed Home Office Contact Officers conducting face-to-face interactions with detainees. To refine my understanding of Brook House, I conducted additional interviews with G4S frontline staff at Tinsley House, which is located nearby and run under the same contract; together these two institutions constitute IRC Gatwick.

I interviewed two high-ranking Home Office civil servants. One, whom I refer to as John, was retired, and another, Franck, was then Deputy Director of Detention Operations. I interviewed John in his house on the outskirts of London. John has long-term work experience in UK border enforcement. At the age of eighteen, he started

[18] In 2020, after years of negative publicity following a BBC exposé of staff violence, G4S opted not to bid for a contract renewal at Brook House, and, since then, it has been operated by Serco.

[19] This is not his real name. I have given all research participants pseudonyms.

his career at the frontline as a border guard at Heathrow airport and ended up taking management positions in the Home Office immigration and border enforcement policy areas. Currently, John is a private consultant and owner of his own consultancy firm. I interviewed Franck in his office in London. He has worked for the Home Office for more than thirty years in different areas including policing, prisons, immigration, and passports.

Obtaining permission to conduct ethnographic research in migration control and security settings is a subject of academic debate.[20] There is considerable reluctance to open doors to external observers in border control enforcement areas. Explaining strategies for obtaining access matters, given that it may inspire and enable further research on the topic, or help researchers struggling with methodological and ethical issues.[21] It also strengthens the scientific quality of academic research, which relies on the explanation of the conditions of data gathering, for both qualitative and quantitative data.[22] As Goffman[23] noted in one of his rare writings about the tricks of the trade in empirical research, fieldwork divides into three general problems, which he defines as getting into, staying in, and getting out of a place. Following Goffman, I will explain the conditions of data gathering by focusing on how I got into the fieldwork settings and how I established myself there. In other words, what kind of rapport I developed with respondents, what factors facilitated relationships, and what difficulties I encountered.

To get into the fieldwork settings, I turned to academics who had established contacts with the private service providers and government officials or who had conducted research previously. Thanks to these contacts and introductions, I conducted preliminary interviews during which I managed to obtain access to the centres. Being introduced by academics who had already done research with the interviewees facilitated access, given that it ensured a relationship based on initial trust. I always had to explain the aims and scope of my research. While in the centres, I asked the private service providers' managers to put me in contact with the Home Office, given that they were aware of my research and had authorised it.

Once I obtained formal permission, I still needed to be accepted by the workers. The key word I found I had to use to refer to my work was 'shadowing'. The managers introduced me as somebody who was there to shadow every worker. That term made my presence understandable because shadowing is the practice each newcomer to the organisation undertakes to acquire the skills and practical knowledge to carry out their job. The managers provided a positive image of me, which facilitated my interaction with the staff. In Colnbrook, I saw the email that Ben, the Home Office manager, had sent about me and my research. The email said that I 'was pleasant' and noted that 'she

[20] Karine Côté-Boucher, Federica Infantino, and Mark B Salter, 'Border Security as Practice: An Agenda for Research' (2014) 45(3) Security Dialogue 195; Marieeke de Goede, Esmé Bosma, and Polly Pallister-Wilkins, *Secrecy and Methods in Security Research: A Guide to Qualitative Fieldwork* (Routledge 2019); Barak Kalir, Christin Achermann, and Damian Rosset, 'Re-searching Access: What do Attempts at Studying Migration Control Tell us about the State?' (2019) 27(S1) Social Anthropology 5.

[21] Pauline Maillet, Allison Mountz, and Keegan Williams, 'Researching Migration and Enforcement in Obscured Places: Practical, Ethical and Methodological Challenges to Fieldwork' (2016) 18(7) Social & Cultural Geography 927.

[22] Stéphane Beaud and Florence Weber, *Guide de l'enquête de terrain* (La Découverte 1998).

[23] Erving Goffman, 'On Fieldwork' (1989) 18(2) Journal of Contemporary Ethnography 123.

is looking at various aspects of immigration detention'. Once Ben authorised my research and introduced me, my interaction with the staff was facilitated. However, that was just the beginning. It took time, daily contact, and lunches together to build relationships with the staff. Home Office Contact Officers would always display a caring attitude towards me by explaining to detainees that I was not part of the Home Office, meaning that I could not give them any kind of information about their situation, or by ensuring that all security measures were in place during face-to-face interactions. Managers and frontline staff from the Home Office and the private security companies were surprised at my interest in detention and my desire to spend time in the centres.

In contrast, some private service providers' frontline employees took confrontational or even threatening attitudes towards me. While I was in the area where the deportation of some detainees was taking place, for example, one employee of the company then providing the escorting service, Tascor, asked me aggressively: 'How come you are not wearing an identity pass? And if you are mixed with a resident?' Some staff felt under surveillance because a short part of my fieldwork took place directly after the broadcast of the BBC1 *Panorama* documentary *Undercover: Britain's Immigration Secrets*,[24] shot secretly by one G4S employee at Brook House. I had to explain that my research was not connected to the documentary. However, given my concern that the peculiarity of the moment might have biased the data gathering and made it difficult to build rapport with respondents, I shortened the period of empirical research in Brook House. Instead, I took the opportunity to observe the ways in which the scandal was dealt by the Home Office and G4S, most notably the implications for contract renewal and the effects on the Home Office. That particular moment offered an excellent opportunity to observe the advantages of outsourcing for the state.

III Working in Detention: Tasks, Skills, Sense-making

Staff use specific terms to describe the inhabitants of detention centres. These places are populated by detainees, called 'residents' by those (private sector) workers who oversee their 'custody', 'care', and 'security', and by other (public sector) employees who are the 'interface' with the bureaucratic organisations that make decisions on their cases. The term 'residents' conceals a myriad of different circumstances and situations. At the time of my fieldwork, for example, according to the Home Office high-ranking personnel, 50 per cent of detainees were so-called Foreign National Offenders, ie non-British citizens who were to be deported after serving their sentences in prisons. The rest of the 'residents' included immigrants of precarious residency status who were requested to report regularly to Home Office reporting centres, and others who had been arrested during raids conducted by Immigration Enforcement in private homes. Irregular status can result from a variety of situations: from rejected asylum seekers to students overstaying their visa. According to G4S and Mitie workers, the nationalities in the centre reflected the targets of the Home Office's raids, an excellent

[24] See <https://www.bbc.co.uk/programmes/b094mhsn> accessed 14 December 2021. The documentary is available at <https://www.youtube.com/watch?v=_fp0QLDKgME> accessed 14 December 2021.

example of how immigration enforcement means policing the borders within national territories.[25]

The Home Office staff who work in an immigration removal centre play no role in immigration or asylum decisions. Those decisions are made by case workers, who never meet detainees face to face. In detention, Home Office staff include the 'pre-departure team' known as Home Office Contact Officers because they have direct interactions with detainees. These people serve paperwork. They are the link between the caseworker and the detainee. Usually, they do not know why somebody is in detention. Before or after meetings, when I asked about the background of the detainees, I found that they rarely knew the answer, although often they were kind enough to find out, once we returned to their offices.

These Home Office employees perform their tasks routinely and follow the instructions of the caseworkers who, in turn, never meet the detainees in person. The lack of knowledge on—or indeed interest in—the reasons underlying their detention and their personal situations was profoundly dehumanising for the men in detention. It also facilitated what Hughes refers to as 'skills learning',[26] which in the sites I studied consisted primarily of learning to maintain emotional distance from the detained population. As Gabriel, a Home Office Contact Officer in Colnbrook, put it, the main skill required for this job was to 'remain focused, no emotions get involved'. The abrogation of frontline officers' selves, a costly and probably unachievable endeavour,[27] is key for working in immigration detention.

Working in the office shielded most of the contact officers from the destabilising effect of interacting with detainees. The appeal of their job, they said, lay in its association with the state: 'you work for the government'. It came with solid career prospects, as after just two-and-a-half years a person could apply to become a manager. Many considered their position in the IRC to be temporary, an idea that helped make their work more bearable.

Home Office Contact Officers in Colnbrook worked in an open space. They shared a common room but usually ate lunch at their desks. Although initially resembling the workspace of any form of business or public administration, the bars at the window, and the security rituals to reach this workplace, including gates, keys, and badges, reminded everyone of the detention setting.

Following Elster,[28] like other organisations which allocate benefits or sanctions, these non-penal institutions of confinement dispense 'local justice' by using broader principles of justice to justify their day-to-day practices. To make sense of their job, Home Office Contact Officers relied on ideas about individual responsibility, fairness, and objectivity. 'These places shouldn't exist, [because] people should simply comply with the rules', David, one contact officer, said, and all his colleagues agreed. That sentence was repeated to me on multiple occasions. Irregular immigration status was, in these terms, presented as an individual responsibility. The avowed lack of knowledge

[25] Ana Aliverti, *Policing the Borders within* (OUP 2021).

[26] Everett C Hughes, *The Sociological Eye: Selected Papers* (Transaction Books 1971).

[27] Mary Bosworth, 'Affect and Authority in Immigration Detention' (2019) 21(5) Punishment & Society 542.

[28] Jon Elster, *Local Justice: How Institutions Allocate Scarce Goods and Necessary Burdens* (Russell Sage Foundation 1992).

about why people were in detention sustained this framework of individual responsibility. No worker placed detention or the deservingness of sanctions under question.

In their interactions with detainees, Home Office staff felt detainees encountered suffering, mental and physical unease, and frustration. Like Gabriel, most tried to maintain distance. Fewer showed understanding, like Amar, who chatted and laughed with detainees while trying to comfort them. Whatever approach they took in their interactions, all emphasised their lack of culpability. They were not the decision-makers they said, repeating sentences like, 'I don't make the decisions', 'It's not me, it's the caseworker', and so on.

The contract monitoring team makes up the other section of the Home Office on-site staff. In that group of employees, the immigration delivery manager supervises the contract delivery. While the contract forms the basis of the relationship between the Home Office and the private security providers, its delivery involves a series of services, ranging from the selection and provision of food to the presentation of detainees for the meetings with Home Office Contact Officers or their removal within certain time frames. As in the outsourcing of visa procedures, profits ensure the cooperation of non-state actors.[29] However, as in the case of carriers, fines drive compliance with the requirements that the state dictates.[30]

Like the Home Office employees, private security staff are divided into those who work directly with detainees 'on the frontline', such as the Detainee Custody Officers (DCOs) and the Detainee Custody Managers (DCMs), and others who predominantly remain in their offices: the Senior Management Team (SMT). The SMT are further subdivided by their responsibilities for specific departments called Operations, Residence, Regimes, Technical Facilities, and so on. The Centre Manager is the most senior private security employee and bears ultimate responsibility for successfully delivering the contract.

Running a detention centre and managing the population of detainees relies on the potential use of violence. Every worker must pass through training on the use of force. The Home Office employees are trained in self-protection instead, which is delivered by the private service provider. As observed by Bosworth and by Hall,[31] most frontline workers (DCOs and DCMs) have few educational qualifications beyond secondary school. Many were previously employed in the army or in other uniformed areas of work like the police or the fire brigade. They say that their choice to work in detention is due to the career prospects; with time they hope they might be promoted.

Senior managers were previously employed in the public sector, mostly in prisons. Private security companies tend to employ such people because they are used to custodial settings and have the skills and know-how required to handle situations of confinement and violence, and because of their contacts in the public sector, which

[29] Frederica Infantino, *Outsourcing Border Control: Politics and Practice of Contracted Visa Policy in Morocco* (Palgrave Macmillan 2016).

[30] Virginie Guiraudon, 'European Integration and Migration Policy: Vertical Policy-making as Venue Shopping' (2000) 38(2) Journal of Common Market Studies 251.

[31] Mary Bosworth, 'Working in this Place Turns you Racist: Staff, Race, and Power in Detention' in Mary Bosworth, Alpa Parmar, and Yolanda Vázquez (eds), *Boundaries of Belonging: Race, Migration and Criminal Justice* (OUP 2017) 214–28; Alexandra Hall, *Border Watch: Cultures of Immigration, Detention and Control* (Pluto Press 2012).

facilitate the public–private cooperation and business development. Managers cited the prospect of higher salary levels as a reason for leaving the public sector. Employee transfer, one of the mechanisms that accounts for organisational isomorphism,[32] diffuses the prison model to the immigration detention setting. Skills and know-how that come from prisons are valued, Franck made clear: 'detention is akin to prison', he said, so 'the skills required are akin to prison service'. Former employees of the prison sector constructed their understanding of policy implementation in immigration detention through the lens of their pre-existing beliefs and practices. They borrowed ideas and ways of doing things from the specific knowledge and experience of prison settings and used them in immigration detention, just like the training that will be discussed below. From a day-to-day organisational perspective, immigration detention and prisons become similar even though, from legal and institutional points of view, their aims are different.

Managers and high-ranking civil servants made sense of their work and understood the organisational objective of immigration detention in shared terms. Specifically, they often relied on principles about the just use of public goods in improving effectiveness and economic efficiency; targets must be achieved with minimum expense. Their discourse was informed by New Public Management, a term which refers to a series of reforms from the 1980s onwards aimed at improving the efficiency and performance of public sector organisations[33] through market-based modes of regulation. Franck exemplified the managerial and target-based understanding of the objectives of organisational action. From his office in London, he defined the objective of his job as being to 'enable an increase of removals from the UK'. The achievement of targets dominates policy implementation. In his words, '

the main challenge involved in this job is effecting the removal, especially because they are able to legally challenge the decisions to remove, and those legal challenges can go over the steps of the aircraft'.

The achievement of quantitative targets, often referring to KPIs (Key Performance Indicators), dominated the understanding of the objectives of day-to-day implementation. So, too, from the offices in London to the detention centres, collective sense-making supported the understanding of the purpose of organisational action to be the achievement of deportation. As Ben, the Mitie Manager in Colnbrook, noted, 'we have Home Office pressure to remove quickly'. Public action is guided by the achievement of quantitative targets that are hindered by what Franck termed, using management vocabulary, as 'a very high attrition rate, when you book a flight and an escort for that person and then something happens, a legal challenge'. The discrepancy between the number of flights booked and the actual removals remained. Targets were not achieved, while expenses increased.

The costs involved in deportations that rarely occur are widely debated in the press, even though, as Bosworth and Singler suggest, such matters do little to erode the system itself.[34] The 'failure' to implement deportation is meaningful to actors on

[32] Paul J DiMaggio and Walter W Powell, 'The Iron Cage Revisited: Institutional Isomorphism and Collective Rationality in Organizational Fields' (1983) 48(2) American Sociological Review 147.

[33] Christopher Pollitt and Colin Talbot (eds), *Unbundled Government: A Critical Analysis of the Global Trend to Agencies, Quangos and Contractualisation* (Routledge 2004).

[34] See Bosworth and Singler, in this volume.

the ground. First, it means that the state is not capable of controlling migration and borders; in other words, it is seen as a failure of sovereignty. Second, the failure of deportation has a cost that hinders the accomplishment of economic efficiency, a principle that, as we have seen above, guides the understanding of these organisations' practices.

Two elements deserve mention. First, the key role of targets that legitimise public policies and are the main focus of policy assessment; second, the predominance of 'governance by numbers' over rule by law, according to which power is impersonal and incarnated in the 'machine of government'.[35] In detention, I found that the rule of law was widely viewed as a constraint over the capacity to achieve targets. Staff from the public and private sectors routinely criticised 'legal challenges', in similar terminology that was used at all levels. Most of their day-to-day work revolved around anticipating whether detainees would use any legal pathways to contest the removal decisions that underlined their detention and whether that resistance would be successful. They also worried about whether it would be time-consuming, since the decision to release detainees tends to be dictated by the time involved in legal processes that would prolong detention and increase costs. As Franck put it, 'we have a number of legal firms out there that promote fighting all the ways to win'. As Mitsilegas argues, legal assistance, on this view, is disconnected from the rule of law.[36] It is cast as an unwanted impediment to state sovereignty, exemplified by the achievement of deportation. Franck's words offered an important framing exercise in which the problem of failed deportations was ascribed to 'legal challenges' that resulted in flights leaving almost empty, therefore considerably increasing costs.[37]

In fact, not all failed deportations were caused by legal challenges. Instead, during the period of my research, the escorting company Tascor routinely failed to collect detainees who had agreed to depart. From the beginning of my fieldwork in the centres, Home Office officers on the ground defined the problem of failed deportations by emphasising the non-compliance of the subcontractor. In Colnbrook, Andrew, one Home Office member of staff, offered an alternative frame to Franck's emphasis on legal challenges by claiming: '

We have big problems with Tascor, they don't meet the contractual requirements, because removals fail; they don't have enough staff. The company is in trouble. For us, it is a lot of work, before and after.'

Failed pickup of detainees prolonged periods of detention, causing stress and frustration, as is shown in the following meeting between Gabriel and a detainee:

> Detainee from Latvia: 'Yesterday, nobody came to pick me up.'
> Contact Officer: 'Because there is a subcontractor.'
> Detainee from Latvia: 'There must be a release, I can't stay here.'
> Contact Officer: 'It's not under Home Office control.'

[35] Alain Supiot, *Governance by Numbers: The Making of a Legal Model of Allegiance* (Hart 2017).
[36] See Mitsilegas, in this volume.
[37] See Ryo and Peacock, in this volume; see also Abigail C Saguy, *What's Wrong with Fat?* (OUP 2013); David A Snow and others, 'Frame Alignment Processes, Microbilization, and Movement Participation' (1986) 51(4) American Sociological Review 464.

IV Outsourcing Violence?

In the UK, the outsourcing of government functions is not restricted to the context of immigration nor it is novel in the context of immigration detention. It is part of the widespread marketisation of public functions that has developed since the 1980s. Subcontracting is one of its forms. In detention centres, private companies provide the personnel for the surveillance of confinement. According to John:

> Immigration officers here weren't really seen as enforcement. They were mostly civil servants. There was a gap, if you have not got the police or the military. We didn't have uniforms, we weren't trained in restraining people. So, we use private sector companies and we give them a detention authority.

Detention and removal are carried out by private contractors. State actors tend to associate two kinds of advantages with the decision to outsource: saving time and financial/human resources while also reassigning the responsibilities of policy implementation. As Franck noted:

> We don't have to employ staff, there is no capture of resources and time for the provision of the service.... There have been many advantages of using the private sector providers. They have skills, they carry a lot of the risk of providing the service, it's a transfer of low-level management risk so if bad things happen in the centre, the Home Office you know...

Also, the reputational cost of failure does not bear on the Home Office. In the wake of the scandal at Brook House, following the BBC *Panorama* exposé in 2017, the G4S Director at Brook House had to resign and Franck had to reply to a series of enquiries. The delivery of the contract guides the relationship between the Home Office and the private service providers. According to Franck, the output rather than the process is the criterion on which to assess the outsourcing of detention and deportation. As Franck noted:

> A contract is output-based: you are there to deliver a service; you are not paid for the mechanics of how the service is to be delivered. So, outsourcing has its place. It's criticised because it's cheap and you don't get good quality. In my sector, it works.

The delivery of the contract is an organisational priority. A specific team of Home Office staff in the centres monitors the delivery of the contract. The contract permits the private security guard to use violence, if 'necessary' and 'proportionate', when handing over the detainee to the escort agent who takes them to their flight. If centre staff are unable to successfully deliver the detainee to the escort agent, the company is fined, the removal fails, and the costs of detention increase.

When individuals refuse to comply with a deportation order, non-state actors are allowed to use force on them. These uses of force are planned in formal meetings that assess the risks involved. I witnessed one such risk-assessment meeting. At the end of the meeting, Robert, a Detainee Custody Manager in Colnbrook, spoke on the phone with Ben, the Home Office manager, about my presence: 'She is here', he said, 'she saw a lot'. The objective of the risk-assessment meeting was clearly the (re)allocation of responsibility. It involved Mitie personnel, two Home Office Contact Officers, and the medical staff, whose role was key in assessing the medical conditions that might or might not allow for the use of force. 'I have done the meeting to cover my back', Robert stated. To describe his role, he said:

> [the] Oscar 1[38] role is risk assessment. I'm paid for this, minimize the risk ... logical and simple approach ... can be stressful. I need to be quick with the action.

The use of violence that might be required to meet the contract requirements is an extremely sensitive area. According to Philip, a G4S employee with a background in the prison service, 'immigration is different. If somebody dies in prison, fine, but if somebody dies in detention, people will say: you are keeping people under shaky laws.' In the event of deaths, the legitimacy of detaining irregular migrants is put under further public scrutiny. During detention, private companies are expected to detect risks of self-harm and suicide, and also to assess these risks at the moment of the removal. Each time somebody considers a detained person to pose a risk of suicide or self-harm, the service providers' staff open an ACDT file (Assessment, Care in Detention and Teamwork). The ACDT file systematises the collection of information while defining the signals of risk. The collection of information is key. 'Care and Custody' staff do not just supervise daily needs and activities in the centre; they also shape the ways in which detainees are handled, because they are turned into informants.

The removal apparatus[39] builds on architectural settings as well. On the one hand, workers at the frontline tended to agree that a prison-like setting was not conducive to the smooth management of detention. It exacerbated tensions and frustrations among detainees. On the other hand, most staff considered the high-security design of Colnbrook and Brook House to be appropriate for specific types of detainees, namely the Foreign National Offenders, who, according to most workers, should not be mixed with other detainees. Above all, the setting was suitable for facilitating removal. Rebecca, a G4S worker at Tinsley House—adjacent to Brook House, with a smaller capacity and a different outlook—connected the spatial characteristics of the building to the achievement of deportation:

> Isolating is easier in Brook House. Here, I would say, removal fails because the potential is of 130 people involved, and you risk your staff injured, the detainee injured and it's a lot of paperwork. Removal from association to effect the removal is easier in Brook House. You meet the contract without accidents.

[38] Oscar 1 refers to a DCM role in every immigration removal centre. The Oscar 1 oversees the running of the institution and all operational matters. They report to the SMT.

[39] Michel Foucault, *Dits et ecrits 1954–1988; Tome 2: 1970–1975* (Editions NRF Gallimard 1994) 299.

Like any other street-level organisation, staff in detention centres seek compliant, co-operative, and non-confrontational behaviours.[40] Implementing organisations need to maximise cooperation.[41] Presenting detainees to the escorts and achieving the objective of deportation seldom rely on detainees' consent, which both state and private organisations nonetheless aim to obtain. While the use of overt violence is outsourced to the private service providers, state actors concentrate their efforts on the achievement of swifter and less burdensome 'voluntary' returns, through a series of strategies discussed in the next section.

V Matters of State: Persuading, Threatening, and Advising

The problematic claims, and manipulative formulation, of the idea that returns 'home' are 'voluntary' are well known,[42] as are the limits of voluntariness, and its entanglement with coercion.[43] In the UK, there exist a series of official 'voluntary' return schemes for rejected asylum seekers, foreign national prisoners, illegal entrants, and overstayers.[44] Implementing personnel use the idea of 'voluntary' return to indicate the achievement of deportations with the consent of detainees. A series of organisational 'routines', understood as patterns of action engaged in by more than one person in response to a common stimulus,[45] are meant to induce people to depart voluntarily. Some, John recalled, draw on what Yanow[46] would define as local knowledge at organisational peripheries: 'We tried to be very close with the refugees' group and the communities on this, to try and see if there is anything we could do that would encourage people to go back voluntarily.'

Direct contact and face-to-face interactions are crucial to state persuasion. Pre-departure teams offer detainees the opportunity to leave from the very first contact, which typically takes place at the so-called induction meeting.[47] From that point onwards, Home Office Contact Officers never stop repeating to the detained population that, 'we can help you go home'. One instruction for frontline personnel consists in offering 'help' to go 'home' in every conversation. As Franck claimed:

> We communicate the inevitability of removal; all conversations start with 'when you go home'. Getting people in the mindset that you're going home, not that you are

[40] Michael Lipsky, *Street-level Bureaucracy: Dilemmas of Individuals in Public Services* (Russell Sage Foundation 1980).

[41] Murray Edelman, *The Symbolic Uses of Politics* (University of Illinois Press 1964).

[42] Kalir, Achermann, and Rosset (n 20).

[43] Stephan Dünnwald, 'Voluntary Return' in Martin Geiger and Antoine Pécoud (eds), *Disciplining the Transnational Mobility of People* (Palgrave Macmillan 2013).

[44] Frances Webber, 'How Voluntary are Voluntary Returns?' (2011) 52(4) Race & Class 98.

[45] Martha S Feldman, 'Social Limits to Discretion: An Organizational Perspective' in Keith Hawkins (ed), *The Uses of Discretion* (OUP 1992) 163–84.

[46] Dvora Yanow, 'Translating Local Knowledge at Organizational Peripheries' (2004) 15(1) British Journal of Management 9.

[47] Pre-departure teams also try to solve paperwork issues that might hinder the deportation process.

> going to be released. Getting people in the state of mind [that] I don't want to stay in this detention centre, I want to go home.

However, for many people in detention, 'home' is the UK, and therefore the very idea they are being 'returned' is misleading. Also, when the proposed alternative to 'agreeing' to leave is an indefinite period in a detention centre, the term 'voluntary' loses its meaning. Contact Officers used to explain the pathway to removal, and the existence of specific thresholds:

> The removal will happen soon or later. If you refuse now, you will have an escort next time and you will arrive in your country in handcuffs. If you depart voluntarily you will have a one-year ban from re-entering the UK. If we put you on a plane, it is a ten-year ban.

Under these circumstances, their eventual departure is perhaps best understood as an 'induced deportation'; one based on persuasion to obtain their consent rather than voluntary return.

At the time of my fieldwork in Colnbrook, the Home Office was piloting a project in which specific teams of staff focused exclusively on induced deportations. According to Franck, the aims of these teams were:

> To sit and engage with detainees, promote voluntary return, explaining the situation to people, removing low-level obstacles to departure. Some removals fail because the detainee does not have his property. You can put somebody on a flight but it takes four people and restraining belts. Explaining that there are various thresholds about removals. So, if you go early and buy your own ticket, your ban to the UK will only be for a year; if we put you on a plane, it is ten years, and getting that message across.
>
> When it comes to inducing deportations by advising, persuading, and threatening, state actors need direct contact with the detainees. In John's view, they were:
>
> More likely to achieve voluntary departure because you built a relationship with the person and you can say I know everything you have said, we have been through all this, the appeal, and I'm telling you now, I'm sorry … if you have a relationship with somebody that you have built over a period of time and you are still dealing with them until the end, then they will be more likely to accept what you say than if somebody new comes in, in a different uniform, and says 'come on', we are going to the airport now.

The bureaucratic jargon calls direct interactions that are aimed at inducing deportation 'engaging' with detainees. Governing at a distance, via the contract and the redirection of certain responsibilities, entails a series of advantages. However, to achieve their organisational objective, state officials reduce distance and promote direct contact with detainees.

Provision of training and certificates is also used as a tool of persuasion to leave. Franck explained:

> We use activities, education, training to give something usable and transferable: 'here's something you can take with you at home.' Removing resistances. We can give you skills. From a department perspective, it's removing blockages not giving hope: that is not our job.

Providing training is a practice borrowed from prisons, where training is aimed at reintegrating the prisoners into society. In immigration detention, by contrast, it is used to promote reintegration into the 'home' society. To further justify the use of training as an incentive to leave, Franck noted that in Australia, the private service provider Serco uses training as well. When asked if these strategies were useful, one G4S employee, Martin, said, 'training provides a sense of achievement, it's not an official diploma but they can still put it on the CV, it proves they have done something.' It is not only outsourced violence but also and especially persuasion with which staff attempt to overpower resistance and legal appeals against deportation.

VI Conclusions

In this chapter, I have analysed state and non-state practices of immigration detention and deportation to show 'what is happening there'.[48] This endeavour builds on critical approaches in security and border studies[49] to promote public scrutiny and reappraisal of the privatisation of border control. Such a practice perspective matters, because it takes into account several consequences that detained foreigners experience every day.

As I have demonstrated, detention and deportation policy implementation follows the lines of market-based modes of regulation. These are most visible in the involvement of private actors in the enactment of states' sovereignty and in the predominance of the principles of economic efficiency and targets over adherence to the rule of law. The marketisation of public action in this domain affects the understanding of organisational purposes. It makes sense of and justifies deportation, which is regarded as the target, while strengthening the understanding of the rule of law as a constraint on state capacity to meet its targets.

The analysis of day-to-day practice shows that, while governing at a distance, through the contract and private companies, public organisations also play an active, direct role in carrying out induced deportations through a combination of persuasion, threats, and advice. Induced deportations can, therefore, be characterised as an organisational response to the constraints weighing on state capacity to control borders and migration. Induced deportations attempt to expel foreigners through obtaining their consent, and thereby nullifying the different forms of legal and physical resistances that set the limits to state's authority. In so doing, the practice of violence is shifted to non-state actors instead.

From the point of view of deportable foreigners, the bureaucratic distance from the decision-makers denies them the opportunity to explain their cases and seek redress.

[48] Bosworth, *Inside Immigration Detention* (n 5).

[49] See also Bigo, in this volume.

Deportable foreigners are placed at a distance from everything but obtaining their consent to leave. Lipsky[50] has defined street-level bureaucracies as 'agencies whose workers interact and have wide discretion over the dispensation of benefits or the allocation of public sanctions'. The organisational conditions in which immigration detention and deportation policies are put into action separates the decision-making process from direct contact. It can therefore be characterised as the condition of 'halved street-level bureaucracies'.[51]

Direct contact serves not only the objective of communication between decision-makers and their subjects, but also and especially for gathering information useful to decision-makers. Direct contact is, in other words, used to achieve deportations, despite outsourcing to private companies and bureaucratically engineered distance from decision-makers. In the context of widespread adoption of the idea of 'voluntary' returns, further research could examine the recourse to induced deportations and the bureaucratic strategies to make detainees leave, as well as the role of private companies in diffusing practices of immigration detention and deportation in the different national contexts in which they operate.

The privatisation of detention and deportation, most notably the outsourcing of 'legitimate' violence by the state, entails the achievement of a series of objectives, such as blame avoidance, the redirection of responsibilities, and the dilution of liabilities. The state concentrates its resources on combating resistances and circumventing legal constraints by making undesirable foreigners leave voluntarily. Meanwhile, it redirects to private companies the time- and resource-consuming, most problematic tasks in the implementation of detention and deportation policies. In a policy area characterised by symbolism and systematic 'failure', the analytical focus on the day-to-day organisational attempts to deport people reveals the uses of privatisation as a means to strengthen state capacity. The state gives away parts of its authority to achieve goals and to enhance its capacity to govern.

References

Agamben G, *Homo Sacer: Il potere sovrano e la nuda vita* (Einaudi 1995)

Aliverti A, *Policing the Borders within* (OUP 2021)

Andersson R, *Illegality, Inc: Clandestine Migration and the Business of Bordering Europe* (California University Press 2014)

Andreas P, *Border Games: Policing the US–Mexico Divide* (Cornell University Press 2000)

Bacon C, *The Evolution of Immigration Detention in the UK: The Involvement of Private Prison Companies* (RSC Working Paper No 27) (2005)

Beaud S and Weber F, *Guide de l'enquête de terrain* (La Découverte 1998)

Bigo D, 'Globalized (In)Security: The Field and the Ban-opticon' in Bigo D and Tsoukala A (eds), *Terror, Insecurity, and Liberty: Illiberal Practices of Liberal Regimes after 9/11* (Routledge 1998)

Bosworth M, *Inside Immigration Detention* (OUP 2014)

[50] Lipsky (n 40) xi.

[51] Infantino (n 29).

— —, 'Working in this Place Turns you Racist: Staff, Race, and Power in Detention' in Bosworth M, Parmar A, and Vázquez Y (eds), *Boundaries of Belonging: Race, Migration and Criminal Justice* (OUP 2017)

— —, 'Affect and Authority in Immigration Detention' (2019) 21(5) Punishment & Society 542

Coburn CE, 'Framing the Problem of Reading Instruction: Using Frame Analysis to Uncover the Microprocesses of Policy Implementation in Schools' (2006) 43(3) American Educational Research Journal 343

Coffey GJ, Kaplan I, Sampson CR, and Tucci, MM, 'The Meaning and Mental Health Consequences of Long-term Immigration Detention for People Seeking Asylum' (2010) 70(12) Social Science & Medicine 2070

Côté-Boucher K, Infantino F, and Salter MB, 'Border Security as Practice: An Agenda for Research' (2014) 45(3) Security Dialogue 195

Coutin SB, *Legalizing Moves: Salvadoran Immigrants' Struggle for US Residency* (The University of Michigan Press 2003)

Darley M, 'Le pouvoir de la norme. La production du jugement et son contournement dans les lieux d'enfermement des étrangers' (2010) 2 Déviance et Société 229

De Genova NP, 'Migrant "Illegality" and Deportability in Everyday Life' (2002) 31(1) Annual Review of Anthropology 419

— — and Peutz, N, *The Deportation Regime: Sovereignty, Space, and the Freedom of Movement* (Duke University Press 2010)

DiMaggio PJ and Powell WW, 'The Iron Cage Revisited: Institutional Isomorphism and Collective Rationality in Organizational Fields' (1983) 48(2) American Sociological Review 147

Dünnwald S, 'Voluntary Return' in Geiger M and Pécoud A (eds), *Disciplining the Transnational Mobility of People* (Palgrave Macmillan 2013)

Edelman M, *The Symbolic Uses of Politics* (University of Illinois Press 1964)

Ellermann A, *States Against Migrants: Deportation in Germany and the US* (CUP 2009)

Elster J, *Local Justice: How Institutions Allocate Scarce Goods and Necessary Burdens* (Russell Sage Foundation 1992)

Feldman MS, 'Social Limits to Discretion: An Organizational Perspective' in Hawkins K (ed), *The Uses of Discretion* (OUP 1992)

Fischer N, 'The Detention of Foreigners in France: Between Discretionary Control and the Rule of Law' (2013) 10(6) European Journal of Criminology 692

Foucault M, *Dits et ecrits 1954–1988; Tome 2: 1970–1975* (Editions NRF Gallimard 1994)

Goede M de, Bosma E, and Pallister-Wilkins P, *Secrecy and Methods in Security Research: A Guide to Qualitative Fieldwork* (Routledge 2019)

Goffman E, 'On Fieldwork' (1989) 18(2) Journal of Contemporary Ethnography 123

Griffiths M, 'Out of Time: The Temporal Uncertainties of Refused Asylum Seekers and Immigration Detainees' (2014) 40(12) Journal of Ethnic and Migration Studies 1991

Guiraudon V, 'European Integration and Migration Policy: Vertical Policy-making as Venue Shopping' (2000) 38(2) Journal of Common Market Studies 251

— — and Joppke C (eds), *Controlling a New Migration World* (Routledge 2001)

Hall A, '"These People could be anyone": Fear, Contempt (and Empathy) in a British Immigration Removal Centre' (2010) 36(6) Journal of Ethnic and Migration Studies 881.

— —, *Border Watch: Cultures of Immigration, Detention and Control* (Pluto Press 2012)

Hughes EC, *The Sociological Eye: Selected Papers* (Transaction Books 1971)

Infantino F, *Outsourcing Border Control: Politics and Practice of Contracted Visa Policy in Morocco* (Palgrave Macmillan 2016)

Jeandesboz J, 'Violence, Capture and Apparatus' in Jansen Y, Celikates R, and de Bloois J (eds), *The Irregularization of Migration in Contemporary Europe: Detention, Deportation, Drowning* (Rowman & Littlefield 2014)

Kalir B, 'Between "Voluntary" Return Programs and Soft Deportation' in Vathi Z and King R (eds), *Return Migration and Psychosocial Wellbeing: Discourses, Policy-making and Outcomes for Migrants and their Families* (Routledge 2017)

— —, Achermann C, and Rosset D, 'Re-searching Access: What do Attempts at Studying Migration Control Tell us about the State?' (2019) 27(S1) Social Anthropology 5

Kobelinsky C, *L'accueil des demandeurs d'asile. Une ethnographie de l'attente* (Editions du Cygne 2010)

Lipsky M, *Street-level Bureaucracy: Dilemmas of Individuals in Public Services* (Russell Sage Foundation 1980)

Maillet P, Mountz A, and Williams K, 'Researching Migration and Enforcement in Obscured Places: Practical, Ethical and Methodological Challenges to Fieldwork' (2016) 18(7) Social & Cultural Geography 92

Makaremi C, 'Waiting Zone' in Creet J and Kitzmann A (eds), *Memory and Migration: Multidisciplinary Approaches to Memory Studies* (University of Toronto Press 2011) 68–92

Pollitt C and Talbot C (eds), *Unbundled Government: A Critical Analysis of the Global Trend to Agencies, Quangos and Contractualisation* (Routledge 2004)

Rose N, 'Governing "Advanced" Liberal Democracies' in Sharma A and Gupta A (eds), *The Anthropology of the State* (Blackwell Publishing 2006)

— — and Miller P, 'Political Power beyond the State: Problematics of Government' (1992) 43(2) British Journal of Sociology 179

Saguy AC, *What's Wrong with Fat?* (OUP 2013)

Schatzki TR, Cetina KK, and von Savigny E, *The Practice Turn in Contemporary Theory* (Routledge 2001)

Snow DA, Rochford Jr EB, Worden SK, and Benford RD, 'Frame Alignment Processes, Microbilization, and Movement Participation' (1986) 51(4) American Sociological Review 464

Squire V, *The Contested Politics of Mobility: Borderzones and Irregularity* (Routledge 2010)

Supiot A, *Governance by Numbers: The Making of a Legal Model of Allegiance* (Hart 2017)

Walters W, 'Deportation, Expulsion, and the International Police of Aliens' (2002) 6(3) Citizenship Studies 265

Webber F, 'How Voluntary are Voluntary Returns?' (2011) 52(4) Race & Class 98

Yanow D, 'Translating Local Knowledge at Organizational Peripheries' (2004) 15(1) British Journal of Management 9

9

A Mundane Spectacle? (In)visibility, Normalisation, and State Power in the UK's Migrant Escorting Contract

Mary Bosworth and Samuel Singler

I Introduction

The privatisation of the UK deportation system has intensified over the past two decades. Each year, multiple companies assist in thousands of deportations authorised by the Home Office. In this chapter, we draw on six months of fieldwork carried out in 2019 and early 2020 to explore how the British deportation system works in practice. Our research included non-participant observation of, and unstructured conversations with, Home Office staff and privately contracted detainee custody officers (DCOs) charged with moving foreign national citizens around the immigration estate, and removing them from the UK. Drawing on that work, we map the contours of this system, from the food provided in the vans to the airport, to the detainee custody officers tasked with removing people, and the security companies who protect the private contractors when they arrive in Kabul, Mogadishu, and Baghdad. As we will show, the messy, everyday, nature of deportation is often hard to explain or understand, and the impact of its privatisation is not straightforward. Despite contracting out much of the logistics of enforced removal, the state remains present in the figure of the border force agent or immigration enforcement officer at the port, in the immigration officer on a charter flight, and in the human rights monitors who scrutinise all stages of the process. It is also the state—via the Detainee Escort and Population Management Unit (DEPMU)—that authorises, cancels, and delays movements.

The UK government enforced the removal of 6,778 people during the year ending March 2020 (ie before the COVID-19 pandemic). This sum included those who were deported and others who were administratively removed. Although 'deportation' is commonly used to include both populations, and nowadays both face a ten-year ban on re-entry, legally the causes of their expulsion are distinct. In UK law, 'deportation' refers to removals enacted on the basis of section 5 of the 1971 Immigration Act, which allows for the deportation of individuals whose removal is 'conducive to the public good', such as foreign criminal offenders. The basis for 'administrative removals' is section 10 of the 1999 Immigration and Asylum Act, and this category refers mainly to the enforced removal of individuals who are in breach of the Immigration Rules.

Over the same period there were 10,421 'voluntary returns', another complex category that includes those forced to leave who may be escorted to the airport but permitted

Mary Bosworth and Samuel Singler, *A Mundane Spectacle? (In)visibility, Normalisation, and State Power in the UK's Migrant Escorting Contract* In: *Privatising Border Control*. Edited by: Mary Bosworth and Lucia Zedner, Oxford University Press.
 DOI: 10.1093/oso/9780192857163.003.0010

to board without being accompanied by escorts.[1] The entry ban for those who leave 'voluntarily' is shorter than for those whose departure is enforced. More than one in four (28 per cent, or 4,742 men and women) of those returned in either fashion are recorded in the report as 'foreign national offenders'. In 2019, the top five nationalities of those forced to leave were all from Eastern Europe: Albania, Romania, Poland, Ukraine, and Lithuania.[2]

From a legal perspective, deportation and removal mark out the limits of foreigners' legal rights, while symbolically establishing and putatively protecting those of the citizens.[3] As political theorists Bridget Anderson, Matthew Gibney, and Emanuela Paoletti observe, deportation:

> also affirms citizenship's normative qualities [as it] establishes, in a particularly powerful and definitive way, that an individual is not fit for citizenship or even further residence in the society in question.... Deportation thus shows the citizenry not simply as a community of law, but also as a community of value.[4]

Notwithstanding a rich and developing field of 'deportation studies',[5] largely outside criminology, we know little about the practices of the process of forced expulsion. Most empirical accounts, quite understandably, concentrate on the experiences of those made to leave.[6] Conceptually too, scholars have tended to focus on the implications of expulsion for migrants, as evident in Nicholas De Genova's work on the deportation regime and his concept of 'deportability'.[7]

This approach has left significant gaps in our understanding of the practice of enforced removals and its constitutive parts. As William Walters has observed, 'the plane is not a black box or mere instrument but a problem space with its own material and social specificities'.[8] However, in all countries, deportation 'operates in the shadows. Acquiring systematic information about the policy is a challenge for the researcher'.[9]

[1] Home Office, *Immigration Statistics, Year Ending March 2020: How Many People are Detained or Returned?* (Home Office 2020). Available at <https://www.gov.uk/government/publications/immigration-statistics-year-ending-march-2020/how-many-people-are-detained-or-returned> accessed 28 July 2020; see also Infantino, in this volume.

[2] Home Office, *Annual Report and Accounts 2019–2020 (for the Year Ended 31 March 2020)* HC 334 (Home Office 2020) <https://www.gov.uk/government/publications/home-office-annual-report-and-accounts-2019-to-2020> accessed 25 November 2021.

[3] Or at least, those of most citizens: since the British Nationality and Status of Aliens Act 1914, the government has been able to strip the British citizenship of those with dual nationality, on the grounds of national security. In 2014, the Immigration Act expanded this power to allow the Home Secretary to revoke citizenship even if it rendered the naturalised person stateless, if they were satisfied that the deprivation was 'conducive to the public good'. See Lucia Zedner, 'Citizenship Deprivation, Security and Human Rights' (2014) 18(2) European Journal of Migration and Law 222.

[4] Bridget Anderson, Matthew Gibney and Emanuela Paoletti, 'Citizenship, Deportation and the Boundaries of Belonging' (2011) 15(5) Citizenship Studies 547, 548.

[5] Susan Bibler Coutin, 'Deportation Studies: Origins, Themes and Directions' (2015) 41(4) Journal of Ethnic and Migration Studies 671.

[6] See, eg Shahram Khosravi, *After Deportation: Ethnographic Perspectives* (Palgrave Macmillan 2018).

[7] Nicholas De Genova, 'Spectacles of Migrant "Illegality": The Scene of Exclusion, the Obscene of Inclusion' (2013) 36(7) Ethnic and Racial Studies 1180; Nicholas De Genova and Nathalie Peutz (eds), *The Deportation Regime: Sovereignty, Space, and the Freedom of Movement* (Duke University Press 2010).

[8] William Walters, 'Deportation, Expulsion, and the International Police of Aliens' in De Genova and Peutz (eds) (n 7) 69–100.

[9] William Walters, 'The Flight of the Deported: Aircraft, Deportation, and Politics' (2016) 21(2) Geopolitics 435, 446.

Such barriers to research have left scholars unable to evaluate theoretical claims against empirical evidence.

This chapter, which draws on our material from the first ethnographic study of immigration detainee transportation and deportation in the UK, seeks to fill some of these gaps. In fleshing out the 'infrastructure'[10] required to forcibly eject people, we seek to inform debates over (in)visibility, normalisation, and legitimacy, while exploring in more detail the relationship between the private sector and the sovereign state. As the COVID-19 pandemic both toughens state borders and changes the nature of mobility and its control, making sense of the increasingly complex field of border control practices is ever more urgent. Yet, scholarship on deportation remains distanced from the escorting practices carried out in planes, ports, and vans. Here we start the process of bringing them together.

II Abstraction, Empirics, and Obstacles to Access

Focusing on migrants' experiences during and after the deportation process, authors across a range of social sciences have produced important insights into the impacts of deportation, people's agency in resisting and shaping the removal process, and the complex legal frameworks used to carry out and legitimise deportations, as well as to challenge them.[11] Empirical accounts of these phenomena inform key theoretical concepts like 'deportability', which, Nicholas De Genova argues, renders 'undocumented migrant labour a distinctly disposable commodity'.[12]

In addition to research into the experiences of deportation and deportability, scholars have focused on the external dimensions of this form of border control. Michael Collyer, for example, points to the centrality of international agreements and inter-state hierarchies of power in the practice of deportation, to raise questions about state sovereignty and to challenge understandings of deportation as a unilateral act of state power.[13] In a similar view, Barry Hindess claims deportation as merely one component in 'the international regime of population management'.[14]

More recently, Ashwini Vasanthakumar[15] and Federica Infantino[16] have noted, albeit from quite different perspectives, that the reliance by states on the private sector for facilitating border control raises important questions about the power of the sovereign state more generally, along with normative questions about outsourcing (see also this volume). For Tendayi Bloom, the private sector increasingly mediates the relationship

[10] William Walters, 'Aviation as Deportation Infrastructure: Airports, Planes, and Expulsion' (2018) 44(16) Journal of Ethnic and Migration Studies 2796.

[11] Coutin (n 5).

[12] Nicholas de Genova, 'Migrant "Illegality" and Deportability in Everyday Life' (2002) 31 Annual Review of Anthropology 419, 438.

[13] Michael Collyer, 'Deportation and the Micropolitics of Exclusion: The Rise of Removals from the UK to Sri Lanka' (2012) 17(2) Geopolitics 276.

[14] Barry Hindess, 'Citizenship in the International Management of Populations' (2000) 43(9) American Behavioral Scientist 1486, 1496.

[15] Ashwini Vasanthakumar, 'Privatising Border Control' (2018) 38(3) Oxford Journal of Legal Studies 411.

[16] Federica Infantino, *Outsourcing Border Control: Politics and Practice of Contracted Visa Policy in Morocco* (Palgrave Macmillan 2016).

between non-citizens and the state, generating the 'business of noncitizenship',[17] or what Ruben Andersson has described elsewhere as an 'illegality industry'.[18]

Beyond these wide-ranging theoretical debates, many of which appear in the pages of this volume, there has been limited empirical research into the process of deportation, as states and their private sector counterparts have been reluctant to allow independent researchers access to study this process.[19] These obstacles are familiar to scholars of security and border research more generally[20] and have led to a field of study marked out by high levels of abstraction. Such matters stand in some contrast to border sites where, as Karine Côté-Boucher, Federica Infantino, and Mark Salter point out, 'as border security policies and programmes are enacted, they lose their abstraction—through their everyday practices, the wide-ranging actors involved in securing borders give practical meaning to border security'.[21]

It took many years to obtain permission for this study, and there were numerous false starts when personnel in the Home Office and in the private sector changed and the project was considered too sensitive. The fieldwork was largely suspended by the COVID-19 pandemic, until the summer of 2021. However, between September 2019 and March 2020, the two authors engaged in many hours of qualitative research, observing, and informally discussing with Home Office and private security workers the nature and quality of their jobs. This research included observations of two charter flights, three 'scheduled' flights, and multiple visits to the operation centres for 'in-country' and overseas escorting (ICE and OSE), the vehicle bases which send out vans and buses to collect people for deportation, and classroom training for new and existing DCOs.

Detailed field notes were taken during each period of fieldwork and shared between the two authors. They included descriptions of sites and conversations with research participants as well as personal reflections about the research experience. All participants were informed about our status as researchers, and agreed to our note-taking. They have all been given pseudonyms, allowing us to use their testimonies without identifying them. Finally, during fieldwork we were also given various handbooks and reports from the Home Office and the contractor. These have been supplemented with additional (unpublished) statistics, official published reports, and some historical material. While much more work remains to be done, sufficient material has been gathered to analyse everyday practices of deportation.

Rather than assessing the relative shift of power from the state to private companies, we sought to examine the nature of the relationship between the various actors in the process, in keeping with the qualitative nature of our study. In so doing, we critically

[17] Tendayi Bloom, 'The Business of Noncitizenship' (2015) 19(8) Citizenship Studies 892.

[18] Ruben Andersson, *Illegality, Inc: Clandestine Migration and the Business of Bordering Europe* (University of California Press 2015).

[19] Although, see Antje Ellermann, *States against Migrants: Deportation in Germany and the United Kingdom* (CUP 2007); Barak Kalir, 'The Uncomfortable Truth about Luck: Reflections on Getting Access to the Spanish State Deportation Field' (2019) 27(S1) Social Anthropology 84; Barak Kalir and Leike Wissink, 'The Deportation Continuum: Convergences between State Agents and NGO Workers in the Dutch Deportation Field' (2016) 20(1) Citizenship Studies 34.

[20] Marieke de Goede, Esmé Bosma, and Polly Pallister-Wilkins (eds), *Secrecy and Methods in Security Research: A Guide to Qualitative Fieldwork* (Routledge 2020).

[21] Karine Côté-Boucher, Federica Infantino, and Mark Salter, 'Border Security as Practice: An Agenda for Research' (2014) 45(3) Security Dialogue 195, 198.

assessed the productive effects of the public–private partnership that underpins the British deportation process. Following our examination of the everyday practices of deportation below, in the final section we explore how specific aspects of the deportation process depoliticise,[22] legitimise,[23] and commodify[24] forced removal. To begin, however, we place current practices in a historical context.

III Privatising Border Control in the UK: A Brief History of the Present

Although it had earlier antecedents,[25] the modern UK deportation regime began to take shape in the latter half of the twentieth century, with the 1962 and 1968 Commonwealth Immigrants Acts. Passed in the context of a waning British Empire, these Acts expanded the system of immigration control to include a vast number of former British subjects in Commonwealth countries. As Bob Hepple noted at the time, 'legislative action was taken to narrow down the category of those who are deemed to "belong" to the UK'.[26] The power to deport non-citizens, with its attendant implications for notions of belonging, was fully enacted by the 1971 Immigration Act, which remains the main legal basis for deportation today. The British Nationality Act 1981 further restricted access to citizenship.[27]

In 1970, fledgling security company Securicor, which had been employed in Heathrow and Manchester airports to oversee a few rooms in the terminals for holding those denied entry, was given a contract for a new detention unit at Harmondsworth.[28] Shortly thereafter they were employed to do the same in the first Gatwick Airport terminal, known as the Beehive, and in a suite of rooms within the grounds of Dover Castle. Additional sites of immigration detention were slowly added over the next few decades. In 2001, under New Labour Prime Minister Tony Blair, detention centres were relabelled as immigration removal centres (IRCs) and asylum seekers were decanted into them from prisons where they had previously been held. It was at this point that Britain's immigration detention system really took off.[29] During this period, the number of deportations and administrative removals also crept up, with a concomitant rise in attention to them in the media and in parliamentary debates.

[22] Jonathan Darling, 'Privatising Asylum: Neoliberalisation, Depoliticisation and the Governance of Forced Migration' (2016) 41(3) Transactions 230.

[23] Matthew J Gibney, 'Is Deportation a Form of Forced Migration?' (2013) 32(2) Refugee Survey Quarterly 116; Walters, 'Deportation, Expulsion, and the International Police of Aliens' (n 8).

[24] Bloom (n 17).

[25] Eg, powers of detention and deportation in the UK date to the Aliens Act of 1793, the Removal of Aliens Act in 1848, and the 1905 Aliens Act: Walters, 'Deportation, Expulsion, and the International Police of Aliens' (n 8); Robin Cohen, 'Shaping the Nation, Excluding the Other: The Deportation of Migrants from Britain' in Jan Lucassen and Lars Lucassen (eds), *Migration, Migration History, History: Old Paradigms and New Perspectives* (Peter Lang Publishing 1997) 351–73.

[26] Bob Hepple, 'Immigrants Act 1968' (1968) 31(4) The Modern Law Review 424, 425.

[27] Daniel Wilsher, *Immigration Detention: Law, History, Politics* (CUP 2012); Colin Yeo, *Welcome to Britain: Fixing Our Broken Immigration System* (Biteback Publishing 2020); Nadine El-Enany, *(B)ordering Britain: Law, Race and Empire* (University of Manchester Press 2020).

[28] Mary Bosworth, *Inside Immigration Detention* (OUP 2014).

[29] Christine Bacon, *The Evolution of Immigration Detention in the UK: The Involvement of Private Prison Companies: An RSC Working Paper* (Oxford Refugee Studies Centre 2005) 39; Wilsher (n 27).

From the early 1960s, MPs asked regular questions about the deportation of Commonwealth citizens, their numbers, and the crimes for which they were expelled. Politicians were evidently somewhat concerned about the treatment of former British subjects, both at the point of entry and while awaiting return. They also occasionally discussed the merits of different sites of detention. For the most part, however, very little can be found in official records of how the process of expulsion worked. We thus have limited historical records of who was employed to force people out of the country, how and where they operated, or what was it like to be removed.

It was not until 1993, when Joy Gardner died following an attempt to deport her to Jamaica by officers from the Metropolitan Police's 'Alien Deportation Group', that the practicalities of how people were treated when they were deported began to emerge. In the early hours of 28 July, reports indicate, a group of police officers and immigration staff arrived at Ms Gardner's address to deport her. When she refused to go, the officers grappled with her, applied a body belt, and gagged her with four metres of masking tape.[30] A few days later, she was dead.

Even as the specific unit responsible for her death was disbanded, and the use of 'mouth restraints' was suspended and then discontinued, the police continued to support the immigration authorities in removing foreign citizens.[31] Slowly, however, they were superseded by the private sector who, in any case, had been assisting administrative removals from immigration detention centres since the 1980s.[32] Today, the police no longer carry out deportations, assisting instead with identifying those subject to deportation, through Operation Nexus, and working closely with Immigration Enforcement operations in the community and at ports and airports.[33]

The Immigration and Asylum Act 1999—which defined a detainee custody officer and their powers, and required them to have a 'certificate of authorisation' from the Secretary of State—began a general 'reform' of the system under New Labour, which also led to its expansion. In 2000, the Home Office signed a contract with Loss Prevention International to manage deportation. This company worked alongside Wackenhut UK, who already held the contract for detainee transportation and short-term holding facilities. One year later, in 2001, as part of the rebranding of detention centres as 'removal centres', the UK began using charter flights to enforce large-scale departures. Although the Public Accounts Committee raised concerns about 'flaws in its contractual arrangements with Wackenhut UK for moving and escorting arrested immigration offenders', which prevented the swift enforcement of removal

[30] Amnesty International, *United Kingdom: Cruel, Inhuman or Degrading Treatment during Forcible Deportation*, index no EUR 45/05/94 (1994) <https://www.amnesty.org/download/Documents/180000/eur450051994en.pdf> accessed 31 August 2020; Ryan Erfani-Ghettani, 'The Defamation of Joy Gardner: Press, Politics and Black Deaths in Custody' (2015) 56(3) Race & Class 102.

[31] See, eg then Home Secretary Michael Howard, MP's statement on the outcome of an internal review, made on 12 January 1994, available at HC Deb 12 January 1994, vol 235, col 212–13W <https://api.parliament.uk/historic-hansard/written-answers/1994/jan/12/deportation> accessed 17 December 2021.

[32] In a discussion at Westminster Hall, on 24 May 2000, Mr Charles Wardle, Conservative MP for Bexhill and Battle, and the Labour Minister of State for the Home Office, Mrs Barbara Roche, described the historical antecedents to the privatised overseas escort business in the UK: HC Deb 24 May 2000, vol 350, col 256–63WH <https://publications.parliament.uk/pa/cm199900/cmhansrd/vo000524/hallindx/00524-x.htm> accessed 25 November 2021.

[33] Ana Aliverti, 'Benevolent Policing? Vulnerability and the Moral Pains of Border Controls' (2020) 60(5) The British Journal of Criminology 1117.

decisions,[34] in 2005 the government awarded the full contract for what is now called 'in-country escorting' (ICE) and 'overseas escorting' (OSE) to G4S, which had acquired Wackenhut just three years earlier. Since then the contract has changed hands three more times, once after another death following the use of force, and, more recently, following a standard retendering process.

In 2010, Jimmy Mubenga died on a British Airways plane to Angola as a result of the restraints applied to him by G4S escort agents, who were enforcing his deportation. According to evidence provided at the inquest three years after his death, he was:

> Handcuffed in the rear stack position and restrained in a seat by the DCOs ... in all probability, [for] between 30 and 40 minutes ... Mr Mubenga had died by the time the LAS crew reached him. Accordingly, when a defibrillator was applied, Mr Mubenga was showing asystolic meaning he was in complete cardiac arrest.[35]

Although G4S lost the escorting contract to Reliance—which was awarded it the following year and, shortly thereafter, bought out by Capita and renamed Tascor—the escorting system continued unabated. As we document below, only the physical techniques of restraint and their method of instruction were altered by this tragedy. On 14 December 2017, Mitie reported that they had been awarded a ten-year contract at an estimated cost to the public of £525 million:

> Mitie will be responsible for escorting immigration detainees, both within the UK and overseas, on removal flights to detainees' home countries. The contract, which will start in May 2018, also includes the management of a number of fixed facilities throughout the UK, including airport holding rooms, reporting centres, and two short term holding facilities.[36]

In addition to their contract for Heathrow IRCs, this new deal made them the 'market leader' in immigration enforcement, a position that is all the more striking given that their first contract, to run IRC Campsfield House outside Oxford (£27 million over five years), had been awarded only six years earlier, in February 2011.

As this brief historical overview demonstrates, the responsibility for deportation and removal has been narrowing from multiple service providers to just one, as earlier ad hoc arrangements were revoked and reorganised under New Labour's neo-liberal march towards efficiency. And yet it remains profoundly difficult to expel someone, even if they have exhausted all their legal remedies.[37] While Mitie holds the

[34] Public Accounts Committee, *Thirty-fourth Report, Session 2005–06* (House of Commons 2006) 5 <https://publications.parliament.uk/pa/cm200506/cmselect/cmpubacc/620/62002.htm> accessed 24 September 2020.

[35] Karon Monaghan, *Report by the Assistant Deputy Coroner Karon Monaghan QC under the Coroner's Rules 1984, Rule 43: Inquest into the Death of Jimmy Kelenda Mubenga* (IAPDC 2013) <https://www.42br.com/_files/content/42br-Mubenga.pdf> accessed 30 May 2022.

[36] Mitie, 'Press Release: Mitie Awarded Contract with the Home Office' (14 December 2017) <https://news.mitie.com/news/mitie-awarded-contract-with-the-home-office> accessed 24 September 2020.

[37] Matthew J Gibney, 'Asylum and the Expansion of Deportation in the United Kingdom' (2008) 43(2) Government and Opposition 146.

deportation contract, they too cannot force people out without help. Instead, as we shall set out in more detail below, they depend on numerous other providers to make deportation possible; even then, flights usually fail. The diffusion of the system into the hands of a complex network of public and private actors makes it both more difficult and more important to understand how exactly this system operates, and what this 'dispersal of the state' does to sovereign power.[38]

IV Everyday Practices of Deportation

The everyday practices of deportation, characterised by mundane contractual arrangements over shift patterns, uniforms, health and safety, and airside passes, as well as refresher courses in the use of force, delays in traffic, and time spent awaiting boarding, contrast markedly with theoretical accounts of deportation as a 'spectacle of enforcement'.[39] Not only is much of the detail of deportation banal, but the vast majority of attempts to expel people are unsuccessful. Time spent observing deportations and their preparation reveals multiple failures and inconsistencies. These include cancellations, delays, and even on occasion the retrieval of someone unlawfully expelled. Rather than a 'spectacularly visible' enactment of the UK border, most deportations are shielded from view not only by secrecy but also by the humdrum nature of their constitutive parts. The division of labour between the private and public sectors assists in this regard, as does the range of subcontractors involved. Such matters, as we will argue further below, also play an important role in normalising this practice by embedding it across a wide range of businesses, locations, and personnel.

The first and most basic element that must be in place for someone to be deported is a deportation order. This can only be issued by a state agent: an immigration case worker. Other official paperwork from the state is also necessary for a deportation order to be fulfilled, including evidence of the person's identity and nationality and a travel document. Once this material is in order, the Home Office sets a date for departure.

At this point, matters are handed over to staff in the Detainee Escorting and Population Management Unit (DEPMU) within the Home Office, to keep track of and order the various movements required to deliver someone to the plane. Private sector agents—referred to as 'escorts' but known officially as 'detainee custody officers' (DCOs)—receive instruction from DEPMU to collect people from a prison or IRC and take them to the airport. They sit next to them on the flight and hand them over at the other end to immigration authorities or to the police in the country to which they are being forcibly returned.

DCOs are trained in specific methods of restraint by members of the public sector HM Prison and Probation Service's 'National Tactical Response Group' (NTRG). The training course, known with unintentional irony by the acronym 'HOMES',[40] was designed after the death of Jimmy Mubenga to minimise the risk of death during use

[38] John Clarke, 'Dissolving the Public Realm? The Logics and Limits of Neo-liberalism' (2004) 33(1) Journal of Social Policy 27.

[39] De Genova, 'Spectacles of Migrant "Illegality"' (n 7) 1181.

[40] Named after the Home Office, *Home Office Manual for Escorting Safely* (Home Office 2014).

of force on deportees on vans and on planes. During a one-week residential course, DCOs are taught a series of manoeuvres designed to enforce compliance. These are accompanied by videos and worksheets, and are described in some detail in a manual that DCOs retain. Techniques range from applying a 'guiding hold', in which two officers flank a detainee and hold his or her elbows and wrists, to inflicting pain through the 'mandibular angle technique' in which they apply a pressure point behind the ear.[41] All the 'approved techniques, including their application in different positions have been risk assessed by independent medical advisors'.[42] New recruits also learn how to apply a waist restraint belt, which has been designed in partnership with the Prison Service and Deenside Ltd, 'a UK based manufacturer of civil and military protective equipment used by police, prisons and military throughout the world'.[43]

DCOs who enforce removals do not act alone. Many flights include a paramedic, subcontracted by Mitie from another company: currently Aeromed, who characterise themselves as 'one of the UK's leading suppliers of travel and event related medical services'.[44] Originally established to assist with 'international medical repatriation', the website proclaims that 'clinical excellence' and 'the high quality treatment' of their patients is 'their primary concern'. Aeromed staff assess deportees as 'fit to fly', and administer medication on the journey. Since 2015, they have also offered basic medical care at the Kent Intake Unit in Dover, which holds asylum seekers arriving from France on small boats.

For the purposes of deportation, paramedics accompany the DCOs to collect people from prison and detention. They are handed and must read the medical notes of the person being removed. They may also be entrusted with additional medicine to administer to the individual during the flights and upon their arrival in the country to which they are being deported; it is not uncommon for someone to be issued with a few months' worth of pills upon arrival.

Airline tickets are arranged through a separate contract between the Home Office and Carlson Wagonlit Travel, also known as 'CWT Solutions'. Billed as a 'travel management company', CWT promises to help its customers 'design a programme that fits your needs', and that it 'will stand with you to drive adoption of it. We'll also deliver key metrics and reports that show your leadership you made the right choice'.[45] They work closely with Mitie administrative staff, known as 'setters' and 'checkers', who arrange and rearrange flight schedules around the world.

CWT are not always necessary, as Mitie sometimes uses charter flights. For these they work with an array of companies, including Titan Airways, 'specialists in bespoke air-charter travel, [who] fly passengers and cargo worldwide with passion and care'.[46]

[41] William Walters, 'The Microphysics of Power Redux' in Phillipe Bonditti, Didier Bigo, and Frédéric Gros (eds), *Foucault and the Modern International: Silences and Legacies for the Study of World Politics* (Palgrave Macmillan 2017) 57–76; Home Office, *Home Office Manual for Escorting Safely: Redacted Version—Physical Restraint Techniques* (Home Office 2014) <https://assets.publishing.service.gov.uk/government/uploads/system/uploads/attachment_data/file/567631/HOMES_Redacted_Manual.pdf> accessed 2 October 2020, ch 7.

[42] ibid 11.

[43] See <https://www.deenside.co.uk> accessed 30 May 2022.

[44] See <https://www.iprs-aeromed.com> accessed 30 May 2022.

[45] See <https://www.mycwt.com/uk/en/travel-management/getting-started/> accessed 30 May 2022.

[46] See <https://www.titan-airways.com> accessed 30 May 2022.

Titan's planes fly from hangars at Stansted Airport and may be rented elsewhere from companies such as XLR Executive Jet Centre in Birmingham. These flights may be scheduled early in the morning, so that business travellers are not disturbed, and the vans transporting people to the airport encounter minimal traffic. In these cases, detainees are extracted from IRCs in the middle of the night. To transport them to the airport, Mitie hires buses and drivers from Rotala Passenger Transport among other companies.[47]

The state physically re-enters the process at the point of departure, in the form of Border Force and Immigration Enforcement staff at the airport. On charter flights the list of state agents grows as many of these trips are observed by members of the Independent Monitoring Boards (IMB), and occasionally by staff from HM Inspectorate of Prisons. An immigration officer travels too, to answer final questions from those being deported, and to observe the handover of these people to state counterparts abroad. HM Prison and Probation Service staff from NTRG may also attend, to monitor the application of the HOMES techniques they have earlier taught the DCOs.

For scheduled flights, Mitie uses its own fleet of vans stored at Vehicle Bases (VBs) located adjacent to IRCs. In addition to carrying out ICE moves from prisons to IRCs, and between different IRCs or to various courts, the vans can also be used by OSE staff to transport detainees to airports for removal. Depending on the airport, they may drive on to the tarmac, allowing staff to escort the detainee up the backstairs and straight onto the plane.

Before that happens, one of the DCOs, designated as the 'point of contact', 'team leader', or 'senior', checks everyone in, and meets with the airline dispatcher. This person also usually speaks to the captain who makes the final decision to allow boarding. The Home Office's 'engagement team' have taken over regular meetings with the airlines; previously this was part of the contractor's responsibilities.

Escort staff provide basic snacks to detainees in the vans. Whereas under the previous contract with Tascor people had been offered sandwiches, Mitie staff give detainees a white paper bag containing a 'Daily Croissant' manufactured in Albania,[48] a packet of crisps, and a bottle of water. Sandwiches were messy, we were told by various staff members: 'Detainees used to squash them underfoot. They prefer the croissants.' Whatever form it takes, Harry[49] explained during an ICE move from a prison to an IRC, 'having food in the back just makes things easier for us. Sometimes the guys we pick up maybe haven't eaten all morning, and obviously if they get hungry, they get irritated.... I'd be ecstatic if someone offered me unlimited crisps!'

Staff have reported supplementing onboard snacks with food they purchase at the airport for those being removed on scheduled flights, or transported between facilities, although the company does not encourage this practice, and we have not observed this ourselves. Rather when we saw staff buying snacks before boarding, they did not share them with the person being deported. The charter flight provides a hot meal to everyone after take-off. The waist restraint belts on detainees are loosened,

[47] See <http://www.rotalaplc.com/about-us/rotala-plc-overview.html> accessed 30 May 2022.
[48] See <https://www.elka-sa.com/our-brands/daily/> accessed 30 May 2022.
[49] Not his real name. All participants have been given pseudonyms.

but not removed, to allow for a cumbersome eating experience. DCOs are offered hot drinks; detainees are not.

Detainees are meant to be 'risk assessed' prior to their collection. A risk-assessment document is produced by the Home Office and is part of the batch of paperwork given to the team leader along with the person's travel document. It is usually based on records of their behaviour in prison and detention, and thus includes 'security incident reports' filled in by public and private sector workers along with general information about their health conditions. The precise 'risk' that is being assessed is never made entirely explicit, although escort agents are most concerned about compliance and behaviour during the flight.

Finally, Mitie relies on external risk assessment too, for up-to-date information about their flight destination. When we were doing the fieldwork, they used two different companies for this: VPI and Pilgrims. While the former offer online information about current 'threat levels', the latter provide manpower for Mitie staff upon arrival. Pilgrims are used only in a few destinations which are considered particularly unsafe, for example Baghdad, Kabul, and Mogadishu. The safety of deportees following their forced return is, in contrast, guaranteed by the UK government through Memoranda of Understanding (MOUs) with receiving states in which the UK receives 'specific assurances that [deportees] would be treated in line with human rights standards'.[50] The effectiveness of these MOUs has been questioned, with critics dismissing them as 'a diplomatic mechanism for circumventing ECHR protections and 1951 Geneva Convention (Relating to the Status of Refugees) prohibitions'.[51] Nonetheless, these guarantees by the state remain a necessary component of the deportation system.

As these examples demonstrate, the state and the private sector coalesce and sometimes separate in governing and executing the complicated process of enforcing departures. These removals operate both in the public eye and, at other times, in secret. Such (in)visibility complicates assessments of the relationship between the state and private companies.

From the perspective of the state, for example, momentarily politicising deportation practices such as charter flights can be a useful part of an attempt to appear tough on migration and 'take back control of our borders', as Home Secretary Priti Patel put it in reaction to the English Channel migrant crossings in August 2020.[52] Yet, equally, such actions can backfire, when lawyers succeed in obtaining judicial review.[53] The state, at those moments, appears to be weak.

[50] See, eg Foreign & Commonwealth Office (FCO), 'Memoranda of Understanding on Deportations with Assurances' (FCO 2013) <https://www.gov.uk/government/collections/memoranda-of-understanding-on-deportations-with-assurances> accessed 17 December 2021.

[51] Derek McGhee, 'Deportation, Detention & Torture by Proxy: Foreign National Terror Suspects in the UK' (2008) 29(1) Liverpool Law Review 99, 109; see also David Anderson with Clive Walker, *Deportation with Assurances* (Cm 9462, 2017) <https://assets.publishing.service.gov.uk/government/uploads/system/uploads/attachment_data/file/630812/59541_Cm_9462_Print.pdf> accessed 17 December 2021.

[52] BBC, 'MPs Launch Inquiry into Increase in Channel Migrant Crossings' (*BBC News*, 7 August 2020) <https://www.bbc.co.uk/news/uk-politics-53685918> accessed 31 August 2020.

[53] BBC, 'Asylum-seeker Returns Flight is Halted by Legal Challenges' (*BBC News*, 27 August 2020) <https://www.bbc.co.uk/news/uk-england-kent-53905550#:~:text=A%20plane%20due%20to%20remove,France%20and%20Germany%20by%20plane> accessed 25 September 2020.

The private contractors generally try to keep a low profile, boarding detainees at the back of the plane, and removing their Mitie-branded high-visibility jackets as soon as they can. During a field visit to the Luton short-term holding facility, one DCO, Fraser, commented on the hazards of visibility for contract staff:

> When we go out into the terminal, to get the boarding passes, the families of detainees see us in these Care and Custody uniforms and of course they come over to talk and to shout. It's really uncomfortable, and I keep telling Mitie 'why can't the uniforms be less noticeable?'

Allowing the vans on to the tarmac at Luton Airport makes it possible to escort detainees more quickly and discreetly into the Mitie-operated holding room.

This view explains the appeal of charter flights, despite their considerable expense and the organisational and practical effort required to pull them off. Yet, even as the invisibility of charter flights renders them 'much easier than commercial flights in terms of the public eye and that', as Avni put it, they can be more challenging in other ways. 'Detainees kick off on charters', she noted, in a view our observations upheld, 'but they don't always on commercial flights'. Under the cover of darkness, men (and some women) are hauled up the backstairs of a plane, shrieking and writhing, with nobody other than the Human Rights monitors to witness—if they are in attendance—let alone intervene; all the other staff, whether public or private sector, are united in their goal to remove them. Although difficult for individual officers, and certainly for those being deported, such attempts at resistance have little effect on the outcome of a charter flight. In contrast, on a commercial flight DCOs have to negotiate, not only with the person being removed, but with the captain, cabin crew, and, increasingly, with members of the public.

Accessing and observing these everyday details is crucial to understanding how 'order can come from disorder',[54] and thus how competing motivations and logics within the deportation system combine to produce overarching political effects, such as the depoliticisation,[55] legitimisation,[56] and commodification[57] of forced removal. While 'forms of routinisation' in any workplace may 'lead to a forgetting of the contested origins of political discourses, structures, and processes',[58] the minimal impact that high failure rates seem to have on the economic resources devoted to deportation, and enduring state support for this practice, demand further analysis if we are to understand the productive effects of outsourcing deportation. It is to this issue that we now turn.

[54] Jason Dittmer, 'Geopolitical Assemblages and Complexity' (2014) 38(3) Progress in Human Geography 385, 392.

[55] Darling (n 22).

[56] Gibney, 'Is Deportation a Form of Forced Migration?' (n 23); Walters, 'Deportation, Expulsion, and the International Police of Aliens' (n 8).

[57] Bloom (n 17).

[58] Bob Jessop, 'Repoliticising Depoliticization: Theoretical Preliminaries on some Responses to the American Fiscal and Eurozone Debt Crises' (2014) 42(2) Policy & Politics 207, 216.

V Privatisation, Depoliticisation, and Sovereign Power

In 2020, the National Audit Office reported that each year between January 2015 and December 2019, the Home Office had cancelled approximately 42,600 airline tickets, incurring a net cost of £14 million.[59] According to figures shared with us by the private contractor, between January 2019 and August 2020, 4,706 overseas escort moves failed; of these, the vast majority were cancelled by the Home Office (4,646), and only 60 failed due to errors attributed to the private company. Over this same period 2,209 people were escorted on scheduled flights, and a further 907 were taken on charter flights.[60]

What to make of these figures depends very much on the lens through which they are viewed. For those concerned with the punitive impact of enforced removal, the relatively modest scale of deportations may be good news. For others, who support this form of border control, the opposite would be true. For our purposes, the failure rates reveal two key facets of the deportation process which, in turn, crystallise the impact of privatisation: it is the Home Office who stops the flights, although it is Mitie who must manage the failure. While this outsourcing of failure is no doubt politically expedient, it is notable that it does not disrupt the logic or the practicalities of deportation. Instead, failure is built into the system through a confidential service level agreement (SLA) between the Home Office and Mitie.

The SLA outlines parameters for assessing whether there has been a breach of the escorting contract. We were told by a senior member of the Home Office that, 'there is a performance target of 95–97 per cent each month for the service supplier and financial penalties vary according to their OSE and ICE performance'. An incomplete move will not necessarily be in breach of the contract, if the Home Office is satisfied Mitie has demonstrated 'best endeavours' in attempting to do it. This step contributes towards the depoliticisation[61] of deportation and to its legitimation.

The routine, administrative character of deportation is actively constructed through the everyday enactment of contracting arrangements between the Home Office and Mitie, and it is evident in the accounts of DCOs and other Mitie staff asked to reflect upon the nature of their work. One Mitie employee, Edward, commented, 'I try not to think too hard about what it is [my unit] as a whole, does. I just focus on my own tasks'. For him, the bureaucratic and contractual specifics of his work obscures (or perhaps shields him from thinking about) the broader political and moral implications of his contribution to the deportation system.

[59] National Audit Office, *Immigration Enforcement* HC 110 (2020) 38 <https://www.nao.org.uk/wp-content/uploads/2020/06/Immigration-enforcement.pdf> accessed 18 September 2020.

[60] Personal communication.

[61] The extent to which the contract depoliticises Mitie's role in the deportation system became evident in different ways during the COVID-19 pandemic. With the numbers of ICE jobs severely limited, the Home Office tasked Mitie DCOs with food and medicine delivery jobs instead. Within the company, the senior management team redeployed those previously set to enforcing removal on a plane to driving vans and staffing holding centres. A regular number were sent to Dover to assist with transporting arrivals from small boats across the English Channel. From Mitie's perspective, the exact nature of contracted jobs was immaterial: what mattered was that the company managed to complete these delivery jobs successfully enough to retain its previous levels of contract fulfilment.

Nonetheless, among DCOs, there is some variation in how officers treat those whom they are removing. Some are more compassionate than others; most are fairly indifferent; still others are explicitly racist, misogynist, and aggressive. All are aware that their job is controversial; some are more bitter about that than others. One DCO reported 'pangs of guilt' due to her work, while her colleague explained that although he feels bad for detainees, 'you can't start feeling that way with this job. You have to stay numb.' Indeed, many report considerable levels of job satisfaction. They like the travel, 'meeting different people every day', the frequent-flyer miles they earn, and the thrill of visiting new places. While extensive industrial action with the main union suggests otherwise, one manager went so far as to claim that 'people don't work here for the money. They value happiness more, and that's what this job gives you.' The disjuncture between this statement and the coercion required to force people out of the country invites further reflection, and is the topic of our writing elsewhere.

In focusing on the SLA, Mitie staff present themselves as morally neutral economic agents working to a contract. Even resistance can be explained away. 'I tell them, you will do what you will do', Cameron commented, when asked about how he felt about applying force, 'and I will do what I will do ... It's horrible, his situation', he acknowledged; '[w]e're all just people, so it's difficult to think why this happens. But I think he knows it's just our job. It's not our fault.'

Given the large number of private actors involved in the various steps of deportation, and the consequent obscuring of accountability and legitimacy within the system, at first it might seem that it is Mitie, not the British state, that is sovereign at the border. However, this conclusion overlooks the practical importance of the state authority that still underpins every ICE and OSE move that Mitie carries out. The state—or, as the escort company tellingly refers to them as, the 'customer'—remains in charge.

The sustained significance of sovereign power to the everyday practices of deportation becomes most evident whenever a problem arises relating to the official paperwork that DCOs must carry for each individual detainee. No deportation can occur without a deportation order signed by an immigration official, and no detainee transport can begin without a valid IS91 document issued by the Home Office. The IS91 grants the authority to detain an individual under immigration powers. Mitie DCOs are willing to let scheduled moves grind to a halt or be cancelled entirely if a valid IS91 is not produced by those handing over detainees. During an ICE detainee pickup at a prison in Wales, a smooth handover was halted when prison officers failed to produce a valid IS91 for the individual being collected. The prison officers contested the importance of the document, arguing that they did have a prisoner movement order, 'so who needs an IS91?'. Nonetheless, Mitie DCOs refused to accept the man into their custody until the correct document was produced by prison officers.

This incident, and many others like it, reveal the sustained centrality of sovereign power that underpins the entire deportation infrastructure. Even as the visibility of the Home Office in the everyday practice of deportation has decreased significantly—and, as we have shown, is often deliberately minimised—the privatisation of deportation has not eliminated the sovereign power of the British state at its borders. This does not mean that deportation no longer constitutes a 'border spectacle',[62] but rather

[62] De Genova, 'Spectacles of Migrant "Illegality"' (n 7).

that the British state is better able to control when to politicise deportation by making it visible, and when to depoliticise and normalise it through keeping deportation practices in the shadows. In this way, as Infantino puts it, the privatisation of deportation allows the British state to 'govern *through* the distance'.[63]

VI Conclusion: The Business of (In)visible Borders

As the role of private actors in the enactment of border control across the globe continues to expand, it is increasingly important to make sense of the impact of privatisation on sovereign power. Privatisation, however, is a complicated process, characterised by the 'dispersal' of the state.[64] The sheer complexity of the system lends itself to multiple interpretations, and it is not always easy to assess their relative merits.

In much of the literature on deportation there is a split between macro-level theorising, focused on interrogating the overarching logic of deportation and border enforcement from the perspective of the state[65] and micro-level theorising, which calls for more detailed analysis of 'the specific types of activities, relationships and circulations which produce human mobility'.[66] Whereas the former focuses on broad political motives and outcomes, the latter is more interested in specific practices, techniques, and relationships. Grand narratives of neo-liberalisation, spectacle, and what Walters terms the 'global security hypothesis'[67] are common at the macro level, while an acknowledgement of complexity and contingency through the adoption of the 'assemblage' metaphor[68] characterises much micro-level theorising.

In this chapter we have shown how attentiveness to everyday detail can help synthesise these accounts by showing when and why a certain level of analysis is relevant in explaining the particularities of deportation practices. Although much more empirical work remains to be done, our findings above already show how privatisation renders migrant escorting and deportation into a complex network of commodity exchange involving not only the state and the private provider of escorting services, but also a large number of other private companies.

It would be mistaken, however, to assume that the state is no longer involved in or responsible for the everyday practices of deportation. Rather, as we have shown, in the UK context, privatisation has allowed the state more control over the selective (in)visibilisation of migrant escorting and forced removal through processes of

[63] Infantino, *Outsourcing Border Control* (n 16) 4, emphasis in original.

[64] Clarke (n 38).

[65] De Genova, 'Migrant "Illegality" and Deportability in Everyday Life' (n 12); Neil Brenner and Stuart Elden, 'Henri Lefebvre on State, Space, Territory' (2009) 3(4) International Political Sociology 353.

[66] Lauren Martin, 'Discretion, Contracting, and Commodification: Privatisation of US Immigration Detention as a Technology of Government' in Deirdre Conlon and Nancy Hiemstra (eds), *Intimate Economies of Immigration Detention: Critical Perspectives* (Routledge 2017) 32–50, 36.

[67] William Walters, 'Rezoning the Global: Technological Zones, Technological Work and the (Un-) making of Biometric Borders' in Vicki Squire (ed), *The Contested Politics of Mobility: Borderzones and Irregularity* (Routledge 2011) 51–73.

[68] Keith Woodward and John Paul Jones, 'On the Border with Deleuze and Guattari' in Henk Van Houtum, Oliver Kramsch, and Wolfgang Zierhofer (eds), *B/ordering Space* (Ashgate Publishing 2005) 235–48.

routinisation and the normalisation of failure; in effect, a detailed empirical examination of deportation practices uncovers the operation of 'depoliticisation as a tool of government',[69] limiting opportunities for the political contestation of forced removal. Key to repoliticising deportation, then, is reclaiming the political and contestable nature of these practices through first-hand knowledge of the everyday inner workings of this system.

References

Aliverti A, 'Benevolent Policing? Vulnerability and the Moral Pains of Border Controls' (2020) 60(5) British Journal of Criminology 1117

Amnesty International, *United Kingdom: Cruel, Inhuman or Degrading Treatment during Forcible Deportation*, index no EUR 45/05/94 (Amnesty International 1994) <https://www.amnesty.org/download/Documents/180000/eur450051994en.pdf>

Anderson B, Gibney M, and Paoletti E, 'Citizenship, Deportation and the Boundaries of Belonging' (2011) 15(5) Citizenship Studies 547

Anderson D and Walker C, Deportation with Assurances (Cm 9462, 2017) <https://assets.publishing.service.gov.uk/government/uploads/system/uploads/attachment_data/file/630812/59541_Cm_9462_Print.pdf>

Andersson R, *Illegality, Inc: Clandestine Migration and the Business of Bordering Europe* (University of California Press 2014)

Bacon C, *The Evolution of Immigration Detention in the UK: The Involvement of Private Prison Companies: An RSC Working Paper* (Oxford Refugee Studies Centre 2005)

BBC, 'MPs Launch Inquiry into Increase in Channel Migrant Crossings' (*BBC News*, 7 August 2020) <https://www.bbc.co.uk/news/uk-politics-53685918>

— —, 'Asylum-seeker Returns Flight is Halted by Legal Challenges' (*BBC News*, 27 August 2020) <https://www.bbc.co.uk/news/uk-england-kent-53905550#:~:text=A%20plane%20due%20to%20remove,France%20and%20Germany%20by%20plane>

Bloom T, 'The Business of Noncitizenship' (2015) 19(8) Citizenship Studies 892

Bosworth M, *Inside Immigration Detention* (OUP 2014)

Brenner N and Elden S, 'Henri Lefebvre on State, Space, Territory' (2009) 3(4) International Political Sociology 353

Clarke J, 'Dissolving the Public Realm? The Logics and Limits of Neo-liberalism' (2004) 33(1) Journal of Social Policy 27

Cohen R, 'Shaping the Nation, Excluding the Other: The Deportation of Migrants from Britain' in Lucassen L and Lucassen J (eds), *Migration, Migration History, History: Old Paradigms and New Perspectives* (Peter Lang Publishing 1997)

Collyer M, 'Deportation and the Micropolitics of Exclusion: The Rise of Removals from the UK to Sri Lanka' (2012) 17(2) Geopolitics 276

Côté-Boucher K, Infantino F, and Salter MB, 'Border Security as Practice: An Agenda for Research' (2014) 45(3) Security Dialogue 195

Coutin SB, 'Deportation Studies: Origins, Themes and Directions' (2015) 41(4) Journal of Ethnic and Migration Studies 671

Darling J, 'Privatising Asylum: Neoliberalisation, Depoliticisation and the Governance of Forced Migration' (2016) 41(3) Transactions 230

[69] Darling (n 22) 233.

De Genova N, 'Migrant "Illegality" and Deportability in Everyday Life' (2002) 31 Annual Review of Anthropology 419

— —, 'Spectacles of Migrant "Illegality": The Scene of Exclusion, the Obscene of Inclusion' (2013) 36(7) Ethnic and Racial Studies 1180

— — and Peutz N (eds), *The Deportation Regime: Sovereignty, Space, and the Freedom of Movement* (Duke University Press 2010)

Dittmer J, 'Geopolitical Assemblages and Complexity' (2014) 38(3) Progress in Human Geography 385

El-Enany N, *(B)ordering Britain: Law, Race and Empire* (University of Manchester Press 2020)

Ellermann A, *States against Migrants: Deportation in Germany and the United Kingdom* (CUP 2007)

Erfani-Ghettani R, 'The Defamation of Joy Gardner: Press, Politics and Black Deaths in Custody' (2015) 56(3) Race & Class 102

Foreign & Commonwealth Office (FCO), 'Memoranda of Understanding on Deportations with Assurances' (FCO 2013) <https://www.gov.uk/government/collections/memoranda-of-understanding-on-deportations-with-assurances>

Franko Aas K, *Globalization and Crime* (SAGE Publications 2007)

Gibney MJ, 'Asylum and the Expansion of Deportation in the United Kingdom' (2008) 43(2) Government and Opposition 146

— —, 'Is Deportation a Form of Forced Migration?' (2013) 32(2) Refugee Survey Quarterly 116

de Goede M, Bosma E, and Pallister-Wilkins P (eds), *Secrecy and Methods in Security Research: A Guide to Qualitative Fieldwork* (Routledge 2013)

Gray A, 'G4S Loses Deportation Contract to Reliance' *Financial Times* (London, 2010) <https://www.ft.com/content/7d238186-e3ab-11df-b6a6-00144feabdc0>

Hepple B, 'Immigrants Act 1968' (1968) 31(4) The Modern Law Review 424

Hiemstra N and Conlon D, 'Beyond Privatization: Bureaucratization and the Spatialities of Immigration Detention Expansion' (2017) 5(3) Territory, Politics, Governance 252

Hindess B, 'Citizenship in the International Management of Populations' (2000) 43(9) American Behavioral Scientist 1486

Hirschler S, 'Brexit, Immigration and Expanded Markets of Social Control' (2017) 16(4) Safer Communities 176

Home Office, *Fairer, Faster, Firmer: A Modern Approach to Immigration and Asylum* (Cm 4018, 1998) <https://assets.publishing.service.gov.uk/government/uploads/system/uploads/attachment_data/file/264150/4018.pdf>

— —, *Home Office Manual for Escorting Safely: Redacted Version—Physical Restraint Techniques* (Home Office 2014) <https://assets.publishing.service.gov.uk/government/uploads/system/uploads/attachment_data/file/567631/HOMES_Redacted_Manual.pdf>

— —, *How Many People are Detained or Returned?* (Home Office 2019) <https://www.gov.uk/government/publications/immigration-statistics-year-ending-december-2018/how-many-people-are-detained-or-returned>

— —, *Annual Report and Accounts 2019–2020 (for the Year Ended 31 March 2020)* HC 334 (Home Office 2020)

— —, *Immigration Statistics, Year Ending March 2020: How Many People are Detained or Returned* (Home Office 2020) <https://www.gov.uk/government/publications/immigration-statistics-year-ending-march-2020/how-many-people-are-detained-or-returned>

Infantino F, *Outsourcing Border Control: Politics and Practice of Contracted Visa Policy in Morocco* (Palgrave Macmillan 2016)

— —, *Schengen Visa Implementation and Transnational Policymaking: Bordering Europe* (Palgrave Macmillan 2019)

Jessop B, 'Repoliticising Depoliticization: Theoretical Preliminaries on some Responses to the American Fiscal and Eurozone Debt Crises' (2014) 42(2) Policy & Politics 207

Kalir B, 'The Uncomfortable Truth about Luck: Reflections on Getting Access to the Spanish State Deportation Field' (2019) 27(1) Social Anthropology 84

— — and Wissink L, 'The Deportation Continuum: Convergences between State Agents and NGO Workers in the Dutch Deportation Field' (2016) 20(1) Citizenship Studies 34

Khosravi S, *After Deportation: Ethnographic Perspectives* (Palgrave Macmillan 2018)

Lewis P and Taylor M, 'G4S Security Company Loses Bid to Renew Deportee Contract' *The Guardian* (London, 29 October 2010) <https://www.theguardian.com/uk/2010/oct/29/g4s-security-loses-deportee-contract>

Martin L, 'Discretion, Contracting, and Commodification: Privatisation of US Immigration Detention as a Technology of Government' in Conlon D and Hiemstra N (eds), *Intimate Economies of Immigration Detention: Critical Perspectives* (Routledge 2017)

McGhee D, 'Deportation, Detention & Torture by Proxy: Foreign National Terror Suspects in the UK' (2008) 29(1) Liverpool Law Review 99, 109

Mitie, 'Press Release: Mitie Awarded Contract with the Home Office' (14 December 2017) <https://news.mitie.com/news/mitie-awarded-contract-with-the-home-office>

Monaghan K, *Report by the Assistant Deputy Coroner Karon Monaghan QC under the Coroner's Rules 1984, Rule 43: Inquest into the Death of Jimmy Kelenda Mubenga* (IAPDC 2013) <https://www.42br.com/_files/content/42br-Mubenga.pdf>

Mitchell H, *Deportation and Administrative Removal* Briefing Paper 8.42 (Migration Watch 2006)

National Audit Office, *Immigration Enforcement* HC 110 (2020) <https://www.nao.org.uk/wp-content/uploads/2020/06/Immigration-enforcement.pdf>

Public Accounts Committee, *Public Accounts—Thirty-fourth Report, Session 2005–06* (House of Commons 2006) <https://publications.parliament.uk/pa/cm200506/cmselect/cmpubacc/620/62002.htm>

Salter MB, 'To Make Move and Let Stop: Mobility and the Assemblage of Circulation' (2013) 8(1) Mobilities 7

Vasanthakumar A, 'Privatising Border Control' (2018) 38(3) Oxford Journal of Legal Studies 411

Walters W, 'Deportation, Expulsion, and the International Police of Aliens' in Peutz N and De Genova N (eds), *The Deportation Regime: Sovereignty, Space, and the Freedom of Movement* (Duke University Press 2010)

— —, 'Rezoning the Global: Technological Zones, Technological Work and the (Un-) making of Biometric Borders' in Squire V (ed), *The Contested Politics of Mobility: Borderzones and Irregularity* (Routledge 2011)

— —, 'The Flight of the Deported: Aircraft, Deportation, and Politics' (2016) 21(2) Geopolitics 435

— —, 'The Microphysics of Power Redux' in Bonditti P, Bigo D, and Gros F (eds), *Foucault and the Modern International: Silences and Legacies for the Study of World* (Palgrave Macmillan 2017)

— —, 'Aviation as Deportation Infrastructure: Airports, Planes, and Expulsion' (2018) 44(16) Journal of Ethnic and Migration Studies 2796

Wilsher D, *Immigration Detention: Law, History, Politics* (CUP 2012)

Woodward K and Jones JP, 'On the Border with Deleuze and Guattari' in Van Houtum H, Kramsch O, and Zierhofer W (eds), *B/ordering Space* (Ashgate Publishing 2005)

Yeo C, *Welcome to Britain: Fixing Our Broken Immigration System* (Biteback Publishing 2020)

Zedner L, 'Citizenship Deprivation, Security and Human Rights' (2014) 18(2) European Journal of Migration and Law 222

Legislation

Aliens Act 1793
Aliens Act 1905
British Nationality and Status of Aliens Act 1914
British Nationality Act 1981
Removal of Aliens Act 1848

PART IV
PRACTICES OF PRIVATISATION AT THE BORDER

10

Outsourcing Deterrence

The Humanitarian Border, Asylum Seekers, and Non-Government Organisations in Australia

Anthea Vogl

I Introduction

In 2012, Khodayar Amini, a thirty-year-old Hazara man, came to Australia by boat to seek asylum. Upon arrival, the Australian government incarcerated him for five months in immigration detention centres on Christmas Island and in Darwin in the Northern Territory. He was then granted a temporary visa to live in the community while his protection claim was being assessed. In 2014, he was redetained for approximately eleven months following a dispute with the Department of Transport in South Australia in relation to his driver's licence fee.[1] In 2015, Amini was once again released from detention on a temporary visa and permitted to reside in the community while awaiting the resolution of his claim. After his release, he regularly expressed a fear of redetention to his friends, who described him as wise, logical, and a good cook.[2]

In October 2015, Amini committed suicide by self-immolation. Directly before his death, his fear of redetention for a third time was acute, due to a recent telephone call with his Australian Red Cross caseworker. Amini had been calling for medical assistance for a severe and persistent cough. The exchange during that phone call became the basis of an allegation that Amini had breached Australia's Asylum Seeker Code of Behaviour (the 'Code of Behaviour') for 'harassing, intimidating or bullying' the caseworker.[3] One of the possible consequences for breaching the Code of Behaviour is redetention. The Red Cross reported the incident to the Department of Immigration and Border Protection.[4] The report was made in accordance with the Red Cross's contractual reporting obligations, as one of the non-government organisations delivering the government's outsourced asylum seeker welfare programme. The Department recorded the incident as a breach of the Code. In September 2015, police charged Amini with the Commonwealth offence of using a carriage service to threaten or

[1] Abdul Karim Hekmat, 'The Death of Khodayar Amini' *The Saturday Paper* (Melbourne, 24 October 2015) <https://www.thesaturdaypaper.com.au/news/immigration/2015/10/24/the-death-khodayar-amini/14456052002536> accessed 25 March 2021.

[2] Michelle Bui and others, 'Perpetual Insecurity: The Weaponisation of Mental Suffering' (*Deathscapes*, 2018) <https://www.deathscapes.org/case-studies/perpetual-insecurity/> accessed 17 September 2021.

[3] Government of Australia Department of Immigration and Border Protection, 'Code of Behaviour for Subclass 050 Bridging (General) Visa Holders' (Form 1444i) (Commonwealth of Australia, 2015) <https://immi.homeaffairs.gov.au/form-listing/forms/1444i.pdf> accessed 17 September 2021.

[4] Bui and others (n 2).

Anthea Vogl, *Outsourcing Deterrence* In: *Privatising Border Control*. Edited by: Mary Bosworth and Lucia Zedner, Oxford University Press. © Anthea Vogl 2022. DOI: 10.1093/oso/9780192857163.003.0011

intimidate his Red Cross caseworker. Amini correctly believed that the Red Cross's report to the Department and a criminal charge against him put him at immediate risk of redetention. He had been scheduled to appear before a local criminal court on 10 November and killed himself on 15 October.[5]

In the months before committing suicide, Amini had written numerous messages and social media posts about the harm he had suffered under Australia's refugee policies. In a final video call directly before his death, he asked a close friend and a refugee advocate to contact Australia's public television broadcasters to publicise his suicide, and to convey the injustices he had experienced in Australia. Amini specifically requested that the media be told 'that the Red Cross, the police and the Immigration Department had killed him'.[6] His friend and refugee advocate explained, '[h]is instructions were clear and his messages were targeted ... he wanted people to know what happened to him'.[7] One day before his death, Amini wrote:

> Humanity is not a slogan; every human being has the right to live. Living shouldn't be a crime anymore. Red Cross, Immigration and the Police killed me with their slogans of humanity and cruel treatments.[8]

Amini's experience of relying for his welfare on a government-contracted NGO, which was also required to police and report on any breach of his immigration conditions, is common for asylum seekers released from immigration detention. In Australia, government-funded income support, accommodation, and casework support to asylum seekers is delivered almost exclusively by NGOs that have 'won' contracts for service provision in a competitive tender process.[9] The NGO providers are also contractually required to police and enforce the Code of Behaviour, which is the instrument that led to Amini being reported by his caseworker to the Department. As a result, core aspects of the management and enforcement of immigration laws and policies, as they apply to asylum seekers in the community, fall to non-government employees and organisations.

This chapter explores the implications of outsourcing asylum seeker welfare, surveillance, and reporting functions to NGOs. It examines what is enabled by the direct participation of these NGOs in migration and border control via government contracts, and the significance of their private yet not-for-profit 'humanitarian' status. In particular, I analyse the outsourcing to government-contracted NGOs as an example of what William Walters has identified as 'humanitarianization of the border'.[10] I argue

[5] Hekmat (n 1).

[6] Bui and others (n 2).

[7] ibid.

[8] Hekmat (n 1).

[9] Following Gerard and Weber, I use the term 'government-contracted NGO' to describe the nature of these organisations' participation and to distinguish them from organisations undertaking volunteer work at the border, or work independent of government funds: Alison Gerard and Leanne Weber, '"Humanitarian Borderwork": Identifying Tensions between Humanitarianism and Securitization for Government Contracted NGOs Working with Adult and Unaccompanied Minor Asylum Seekers in Australia' (2019) 23 Theoretical Criminology 266.

[10] William Walters, 'Foucault and Frontiers: Notes on the Birth of the Humanitarian Border' in Ulrich Bröckling, Susanne Krasmann, and Thomas Lemke (eds), *Governmentality: Current Issues and Future Challenges* (Routledge 2011) 147.

that the Australian government's reliance upon NGOs to manage the internal border exemplifies the alliance between care and control in humanitarian interventions at the border.[11] Further, I argue that the NGOs are co-opted and captured by the government as direct partners in immigration control and deterrence, even as they are informed by their own mandates of care, welfare, and asylum seeker support. This partnership operates by virtue of direct contracting with government, mandatory participation in surveillance and reporting, and the implementation of inadequate welfare services, which by design, deprive asylum seekers in the community of a subsistence standard of living. This kind of capture not only has a net-widening effect on the actors involved in migration control, and on sites of discretionary power and decision-making for asylum seekers; it also functions to control and constrain the capacity of NGOs to contest or resist state policy objectives, and instead—especially with the Code of Behaviour—involves them in the enforcement of sovereign borders as a condition for providing care.

The chapter focuses on the role of government-contracted NGOs in enforcing internal borders, rather than humanitarian interventions at or beyond the territorial border. With the exception of Gerard and Weber's two recent empirical studies,[12] research on the role of humanitarian organisations in enforcing Australia's internal borderscape is limited, despite a long history of outsourcing to NGOs.[13] The chapter first outlines the growing body of work on humanitarian borders, tracing how humanitarian interventions enable and expand state securitisation objectives. It then turns to the mix of migration law, policy, and contractual relations that structure NGOs' participation in the management of Australia's internal border. It examines the terms of the Code of Behaviour, and the role of government-contracted NGOs in policing asylum seekers under it. Finally, it presents the design and detail of welfare services that contracted NGOs provide *and* deny under the Status Resolution Support Services (SRSS). The inadequate financial assistance available and narrow eligibility criteria entail that the programme, by design, denies a subsistence standard of living and operates as a strategy of asylum seeker deterrence and border control. Crucially, the use of NGOs neutralises the punitive and exclusionary aspects of this work and provides a veneer of preserving life and dignity to a regime ultimately orientated towards punishment and removal.[14]

The outsourcing I examine here involves NGOs playing quite a different role to the humanitarian organisations addressed by Valsamis Mitsilegas. Mitsilegas focuses

[11] See, eg Polly Pallister-Wilkins, 'The Humanitarian Politics of European Border Policing: Frontex and Border Police in Evros' (2015) 9 International Political Sociology 53; Adrian Little and Nick Vaughan-Williams, 'Stopping Boats, Saving Lives, Securing Subjects: Humanitarian Borders in Europe and Australia' (2017) 23 European Journal of International Relations 533; Gerard and Weber (n 9).

[12] Gerard and Weber (n 9); Leanne Weber, 'From State-centric to Transversal Borders: Resisting the "Structurally Embedded Border" in Australia' (2019) 23 Theoretical Criminology 228.

[13] Although, see also Rebecca Field, Donna Chung, and Caroline Fleay, 'The Influence of Policy, Cultural and Historical Contexts on Social Work and Human Service Practice Responses with People Seeking Asylum in Germany and Australia' (2021) 15 Ethics and Social Welfare 294. On privatisation in Australia generally, see Sara Dehm, 'Outsourcing, Responsibility and Refugee Claim-making in Australia's Offshore Detention Regime' in Siobhan McGuirk and Adrienne Pine (eds), *Asylum for Sale: Profit and Protest in the Migration Industry* (PM Press 2020) 159–188.

[14] Walters (n 10) 145.

on NGOs, citizens, and commercial carriers engaging in migrant search and rescue operations, in defiance and disruption of state sovereignty and migrant prevention policies.[15] Nonetheless, both chapters highlight a similar phenomenon, namely state attempts to capture and control the activities of humanitarian and non-government organisations. These strategies range from direct criminalisation to the implementation of soft codes to govern the actions of private actors. In Australia, capture is achieved through the creation of contractual relationships with private NGOs, which step into the gap left by the government's active withdrawal from the provision of welfare to asylum seekers. Kox and Starring rightly note that in each instance, the state seeks to disarm 'humanitarian organizations for unauthorized migrants by either responsibilizing or criminalizing them'.[16] Lucia Zedner investigates the state's 'responsibilisation' of private citizens in another context still. She considers the legitimacy of border control functions undertaken by private actors, who are required to police immigration status as part of the UK's 'hostile environment' policy, with failure to comply again punishable by fines and imprisonment.[17] Questions about the regulation and oversight of private and privatised power, and the proliferation of new sites of migration control *as a result* of privatisation, run through this volume, and the examination of NGOs' participation in Australia's internal border regime that follows.

II The Expanding Humanitarian Border

Humanitarian organisations, with missions to provide care and preserve life, may simultaneously produce forms of migration control that cause harm and legitimise restrictive migration policies.[18] As Bosworth has argued, humanitarianism plays an increasingly central role in expanding state penal power within and beyond territorial borders,[19] as well as in legitimising border controls, including policies that enact the violent and sometimes deadly exclusion of non-citizens.[20] This phenomenon has been especially evident in relation to interdiction and 'rescue' operations of people migrating by boat, undertaken by both state and non-state actors. As Moreno-Lax has observed in the EU, 'through narratives of "rescue", maritime interdiction of "unlawful" migrants is laundered into an ethically sustainable strategy of border governance'.[21] She notes, 'instead of being considered a problematic (potentially lethal) means of control, it is re-defined into a lifesaving device'.[22] Similarly, successive Australian

[15] See Mitsilegas, in this volume. See also Sergio Carrera and others, *Policing Humanitarianism: EU Policies against Human Smuggling and their Impact on Civil Society* (Hart Publishing 2019).

[16] Mieke Kox and Richard Staring, '"If you don't have Documents or a Legal Procedure, you are Out!" Making Humanitarian Organizations Partner in Migration Control' (2020) European Journal of Criminology 1.

[17] Zedner, in this volume.

[18] Walters (n 10); Kox and Staring (n 16) 2.

[19] Mary Bosworth, 'Penal Humanitarianism? Sovereign Power in an Era of Mass Migration' (2017) 20 New Criminal Law Review 39.

[20] Little and Vaughan-Williams (n 11).

[21] Violeta Moreno-Lax, 'The EU Humanitarian Border and the Securitization of Human Rights: The "Rescue-Through-Interdiction/Rescue-Without-Protection" Paradigm' (2018) 56 Journal of Common Market Studies 119.

[22] ibid.

governments' humanitarian slogan of 'saving lives at sea' is explicitly used to limit the rights of asylum seekers and deny access to refugee protection and Australian territory. The humanitarian framing of the policy, discouraging would-be asylum seekers from 'risking their lives' travelling by boat, is also used to legitimise the militarisation of maritime borders and Australia's aggressive refugee 'boat turn-back' policies.[23] The government's ostensible concern with preserving life sits cynically alongside Australia's other border control measures, not least offshore detention and the well-documented cruel and inhumane conditions associated with it.[24]

That border policing and humanitarianism are not separate domains of action informed Walters' identification of the border itself 'as a space of humanitarian government' roughly a decade ago.[25] For Walters, the regulation of borders is marked by the exercise of humanitarian power as a strategy of government, and is 'connected to the actualization of new spaces of authority and control' in relation to migration.[26] This reading draws on colonial and post-colonial analyses of humanitarianism, and specifically on Fassin's analysis of it as a form of governance that justifies state intervention in the name of 'universalized' human life and dignity.[27] Or, as Chimni observes, humanitarianism is 'the ideology of hegemonic states in the era of globalisation' that 'mobilizes a range of meanings and practices to establish and sustain global relations of domination'.[28]

Recurring themes in a fast-growing literature on humanitarian borders include the ways in which state and non-state humanitarian interventions function to control and contain those seeking to cross borders; non-state actors as directly participating in the securitisation of migration; and the unique capacity for humanitarianism to recast migration control as promoting human life and welfare.[29] The role of government-contracted NGOs in enforcing Australia's internal border is a clear instance of the intertwining of care, policing, and control, whereby their participation involves both the provision of care (to at-risk groups, namely asylum seekers) and control (of risks to the border, also asylum seekers).[30] Pallister-Wilkins notes that states' own border-policing operations equally contain a humanitarian element, such that the logics of care and securitisation are intertwined rather than opposed.[31] This observation accurately describes Australia and the EU's 'saving lives at sea' deterrence rhetoric, as well

[23] Sydney Morning Herald, 'Saving Lives Trumps Politics, Says Gillard' *Sydney Morning Herald* (Sydney 19 August 2012) <https://www.smh.com.au/politics/federal/saving-lives-trumps-politics-says-gillard-20120819-24g0i.html> accessed 4 March 2021.

[24] Ben Doherty and Daniel Hurst, 'UN Accuses Australia of Systematically Violating Torture Convention' *The Guardian* (London, 10 March 2015) <https://www.theguardian.com/australia-news/2015/mar/09/un-reports-australias-immigration-detention-breaches-torture-convention> accessed 4 March 2021.

[25] Walters (n 10) 138.

[26] ibid 139.

[27] Didier Fassin, 'Humanitarianism: A Nongovernmental Government' in Michel Feher, Gaëlle Krikorian, and Yates McKee (eds), *Nongovernmental Politics* (Zone Books 2007).

[28] BS Chimni, 'Globalization, Humanitarianism and the Erosion of Refugee Protection' (2000) 13 Journal of Refugee Studies 243, 244.

[29] See, eg Pallister-Wilkins, 'The Humanitarian Politics of European Border Policing' (n 11); Little and Vaughan-Williams (n 11); Gerard and Weber (n 9); Ana Aliverti, 'Benevolent Policing? Vulnerability and the Moral Pains of Border Controls' (2020) 60 The British Journal of Criminology 1117.

[30] Pallister-Wilkins, 'The Humanitarian Politics of European Border Policing' (n 11) 66.

[31] ibid.

as the paternalistic overtones of the Code of Behaviour, which the government benignly explains as 'describing' Australian values to asylum seekers even as breaching the Code poses the threat of reincarceration.

Australia has a long history of governmental, as well as charitable and religious organisations implementing racialised controls and exclusions in the name of 'care' and protection.[32] Indeed, discourses of welfare and care played a central role in the dispossession of Aboriginal and Torres Strait Islander people and removal of Indigenous children from their families.[33] While race as a basis for exclusion is not made explicit in Australia's deterrence regime and the capture of NGOs within it, Boochani and Tofighian argue that Australia's border regime is rooted in Australia's legacy of colonial violence, racism, and the dispossession of Aboriginal and Torres Strait Islander peoples.[34] Silverstein has argued that humanitarian narratives in relation to both border control and settler colonialism rely on a conception of Australia as a nation of 'white saviours' and on the benevolent care (and control) of white policymakers.[35] Tracing instances of humanitarian governance in Australia as exercises of a possessive, white sovereignty,[36] as Silverstein does, highlights the centrality of race in acts of control *and* care at the border.

The focus of the remainder of this chapter is on the structural aspects of outsourcing to NGOs, rather than how these obligations are navigated by NGOs and the asylum seekers who are reliant on them. Research on personnel who enforce border controls has highlighted the diverse ways in which individuals negotiate conflicting mandates of exclusion and care of people in their custody.[37] Gerard and Weber have demonstrated that NGOs' day-to-day delivery of the SRSS in Australia compels compliance with 'extreme forms of securitization [of migration]' as well as creating opportunities for resistance.[38] Research on 'border work' in practice highlights the dynamic nature of the border and identifies spaces of humanitarian governance not as fixed,[39] but as zones marked by frameworks that are being actively negotiated, and potentially resisted.[40]

[32] Irene Watson, 'In the Northern Territory Intervention: What is Saved or Rescued and at what Cost?' (2009) 15 Cultural Studies Review 45.

[33] Leigh Boucher and Lynette Russell, *Settler Colonial Governance in Nineteenth-century Victoria* (ANU Press 2015).

[34] Omid Tofighian, 'Introducing Manus Prison Theory: Knowing Border Violence' (2020) 17 Globalizations 1138.

[35] Jordana Silverstein, 'Refugee Children, Boats and Drownings: A History of an Australian "Humanitarian" Discourse' (2020) 17 History Australia 728.

[36] Aileen Moreton-Robinson, 'The Possessive Logic of Patriarchal White Sovereignty: The High Court and the *Yorta Yorta* Decision' (2004) 3(2) Borderlands E-Journal 1<https://eprints.qut.edu.au/7690/> accessed 17 September 2021.

[37] See, especially, Mary Bosworth, 'Affect and Authority in Immigration Detention' (2019) 21 Punishment & Society 542; Aliverti (n 29).

[38] Gerard and Weber (n 9) 280.

[39] Weber, 'From State-centric to Transversal Borders' (n 12).

[40] Walters (n 10) 148.

III Government-contracted NGOs and the Internal Deterrence Regime

Walters emphasises that while humanitarian borders are concentrated along geographic frontiers or globalisation 'fault lines' where 'the Global North and Global South confront one another in a very concrete, abrasive way', their incidence is not geographically or otherwise determined.[41] Rather, such borders target the routes of travel and mobility forged by migrants and non-citizens themselves, as well as by state action and the political interventions of NGOs.[42] This observation holds true for the emergence of humanitarian borders *within* the territory of wealthy industrialised states like Australia, as deterrence regimes move inwards, to manage or expel asylum seeker populations already within state territory.[43] The participation of government-contracted NGOs takes place within state territory, in relation to what Yuval-Davis, Wemyss, and Cassidy describe as 'everyday bordering' and Weber has identified as the 'structurally embedded border', whereby border controls infiltrate the 'fabric of everyday life' and the internal bordering regime operates alongside externalised border controls.[44]

The law and policies that govern asylum seekers in Australia after they are *released* from detention constitute an internal regime of systemic and racialised punishment, which forms part of the government's overall strategy of deterrence.[45] The government's current policy approach to asylum seekers who arrive by boat is to release the majority of this population from otherwise mandatory detention on a discretionary and case-by-case basis. Accordingly, as at March 2021, only 367 asylum seekers who arrived by boat were incarcerated in immigration detention, while 12,194 were living in the community, waiting for their refugee claims to be assessed.[46] This approach has seen a gradual but resolute shift of the locus of deterrence initiatives from closed detention centres into the broader community.[47] This has included imposing an enduring temporary status on asylum seekers, who are granted serial, short-term bridging visas while their claims are being assessed, with no guarantee of renewal. These bridging visas may last for as little as one to six months.[48] The uncertainty caused

[41] ibid 146.

[42] ibid 147–48.

[43] See also Kox and Staring (n 16).

[44] Leanne Weber, *Policing Non-citizens* (Routledge 2013); Nira Yuval-Davis, Georgie Wemyss, and Kathryn Cassidy, 'Everyday Bordering, Belonging and the Reorientation of British Immigration Legislation' (2018) 52 Sociology 228; Weber, 'From State-centric to Transversal Borders' (n 12).

[45] Anthea Vogl, 'Crimmigration and Refugees: Bridging Visas, Criminal Cancellations and "Living in the Community" as Punishment and Deterrence' in Peter Billings (ed), *Crimmigration in Australia: Law, Politics, and Society* (Springer 2019) 149–71.

[46] Department of Home Affairs, 'Immigration Detention and Community Statistics Summary' (Australian Border Force, 31 March 2021) <https://www.homeaffairs.gov.au/research-and-stats/files/immigration-detention-statistics-31-march-2021.pdf> accessed 7 April 2021.

[47] Lisa Hartley and Caroline Fleay, '"We are like Animals": Negotiating Dehumanising Experiences of Asylum-seeker Policies in the Australian Community' (2017) 36 Refugee Survey Quarterly 45; Anthea Vogl and Elyse Methven, 'Life in the Shadow Carceral State: Surveillance and Control of Refugees in Australia' (2020) 9 International Journal for Crime, Justice and Social Democracy 61.

[48] Australian Human Rights Commission, *Lives on Hold: Refugees and Asylum Seekers in the 'Legacy Caseload'* (Australian Human Rights Commission 2019) 59 <https://humanrights.gov.au/our-work/asy

by short-term visas is compounded by extended processing delays.[49] This prolonged limbo, alongside the withdrawal of welfare and support services, has led to severe mental health deterioration and chronic suicidal ideation in this group, which Procter and others have analysed as creating a 'lethal sense of hopelessness'.[50] Although not quite so brazenly named, the resulting internal borderscape for asylum seekers recalls key aspects of the UK's hostile environment policy—now renamed the compliant environment policy.[51]

The government-contracted NGOs competitively tender to deliver asylum seeker services and operate within this system of deterrence and 'everyday bordering'. In 2014, the SRSS replaced two previous programmes: the Asylum Seeker Assistance Program and the Community Assistance Support Program.[52] Broadly speaking, each programme was or is directed towards people unable to meet their basic needs while awaiting the outcome of visa applications. Until 2011, the Australian Red Cross was the only national provider of outsourced support.[53] However, from 2012, other groups were able to tender and there are now eight organisations delivering the SRSS across Australia. The largest providers include Settlement Services International, Adult Multicultural Education Services, and Life Without Barriers.[54] Smaller providers include NGOs such as CatholicCare Tasmania and Mercy Care (South Australia).

The competitive tender process and contractual obligations to the Department of Home Affairs distinguish these NGOs from volunteer-based or financially independent organisations involved in service provision to non-citizens, or migration management generally. Most of the NGOs currently delivering the SRSS also provide other government- and non-government-funded settlement and humanitarian services.[55] While each organisation has a distinct mission and mandate, and not all operate explicitly as 'humanitarian' organisations, they each describe their work as allowing refugees and migrants to overcome barriers to social and economic life, helping them access 'the rights we enjoy as human beings',[56] or as providing aid or support to refugees seeking to 'settle', live, or prosper in Australia.[57] The government funding allocated to these organisations is substantial, particularly for NGOs operating in urban

lum-seekers-and-refugees/publications/lives-hold-refugees-and-asylum-seekers-legacy> accessed 17 September 2021 .

[49] ibid 44.

[50] Nicholas G Procter and others, 'Lethal Hopelessness: Understanding and Responding to Asylum Seeker Distress and Mental Deterioration' (2018) 27 International Journal of Mental Health Nursing 448.

[51] See Zedner, in this volume.

[52] Refugee Council of Australia, 'Starving them Out: Destitution of People Seeking Asylum in Australia' (*Refugee Council of Australia Brief*, May 2018) 2 <https://www.refugeecouncil.org.au/starving-them-out/> accessed 28 March 2021. The two foregoing programmes operated from 1992 to 2005, and 2005 to 2013, respectively.

[53] As of 2018, the Red Cross no longer holds an SRSS contract with the Federal Government.

[54] Department of Home Affairs, 'Status Resolution Support Services' (6 July 2021) <https://immi.homeaffairs.gov.au/what-we-do/status-resolution-service/status-resolution-support-services> accessed 17 September 2021.

[55] ibid.

[56] See, eg Life Without Barriers, 'About Us' (*Life Without Barriers*, 2021) <https://www.lwb.org.au/about-us/> accessed 17 September 2021.

[57] See Settlement Services International, 'About Us' (*Settlement Services International*,undated) <https://www.ssi.org.au/about-us> accessed 17 September 2021.

areas. For example, for the period from September 2014 to June 2022, the Life without Barriers contract was worth over AU$220 million, and over AU$124 million for Settlement Services International.[58] As the following sections demonstrate, the NGOs' provision of services and support is constrained, if not entirely determined, both by their contractual terms and by the design of the SRSS welfare programme, which is itself a feature of the post-detention deterrence regime.

A Government-contracted NGOs and the Code of Behaviour

The Code of Behaviour is the instrument that Amini's Red Cross caseworker alleged he had breached when reporting his behaviour to the Department of Immigration and Border Protection ('the Department'). Introduced by the Liberal–National Coalition government in December 2013,[59] the Code applies exclusively to all so-called 'unauthorised maritime arrivals' (UMAs) who apply for or seek to renew a bridging visa.[60] This means that, in order to access a visa and be released from otherwise mandatory detention, this group of asylum seekers must sign the Code. Thereafter they are bound by a 'list of expectations' about how to behave at all times while in Australia. If the Code's provisions are deemed to be breached, income support may be reduced or stopped, an existing bridging visa may be cancelled, or an asylum seeker may be detained in onshore or offshore detention.

The Code itself is less than one page long. It is prefaced by approximately one-and-a-half pages described as 'Supporting Information', directly addressed to asylum seekers with headings such as 'Why do I need to sign the Code of Behaviour?' The supporting information includes the following sweeping statement:

> By signing the code you agree to behave according to values that are important to the Australian society while working towards the resolution of your immigration status.

The Code does not explicitly elaborate on these 'values'. It does, however, note that Australia is 'a free and democratic country where men and women are equal' and where people are expected 'not to abuse or threaten others'.

In considering the role of NGOs in enforcing the Code, there are several points to make about the Code's terms, which apply to asylum seekers in an explicitly discriminatory manner and significantly exceed the scope of the criminal law. The substantive content of the Code is brief. It contains six 'expectations' in point form, which stipulate that asylum seekers:

- 'must not disobey any Australian laws', including Australian road laws
- 'must not make sexual contact with another person without that person's consent'

[58] AusTender, 'Contract Notice CN2616652-A14, CN2616622-A9' (Department of Home Affairs) <https://www.tenders.gov.au/Cn/Show/9aee07e9-b062-4a03-836a-66b4340ea991> accessed 17 September 2021.

[59] Government of Australia Department of Immigration and Border Protection (n 3).

[60] Bridging visas temporarily regularise the legal status of people awaiting the resolution of a visa application, or removal/departure from Australia.

- 'must not take part in, or get involved in any kind of criminal behaviour in Australia'
- 'must not harass, intimidate or bully any other person or group of people or engage in any anti-social or disruptive activities that are inconsiderate, disrespectful or threaten the peaceful enjoyment of other members of the community'
- 'must not refuse to comply with any health undertaking' provided by the Department of Immigration and Border Protection or Chief Medical Officer
- 'must co-operate with all reasonable requests' of the Department of Immigration and Border P12 rotection.

As a result, asylum seekers are not only forbidden from disobeying Australian law (to which they are of course already subject), they must also comply with additional behavioural standards that do not apply to the community at large. The expectation prohibiting 'anti-social or disruptive activities' is notable both for its breadth and the explanatory text that accompanies it, which states that such activities include 'persistently irritating someone', 'spreading rumours', 'spitting or swearing in public', or 'other actions that other people might find offensive'. Weber and Powell note that these expectations do not merely target pre-criminal behaviour, but represent 'a shift from pre-crime to sub-crime' as a catalyst for punishment.[61] As a result of these extraordinary requirements, the minutest aspects of asylum seekers' lives are subject to surveillance and made punishable by the Code.

Data gathered via a series of freedom of information (FOI) requests reveals that government-contracted NGOs are at the centre of the operation of the Code and visa cancellations flowing from it. Although the text of the Code is silent on who can police or report on 'breaches', the Department stated, in response to a FOI request in 2015, that it expected to receive allegations through 'a range of sources', including 'members of the public', 'service providers', 'police services', and 'other government agencies'.[62] Further, redacted contracts between the Department and SRSS providers, released under FOI requests in 2017 and 2021, revealed the NGOs' mandatory reporting duties in relation to Code breaches. Crucially, the contracts confirm that NGO caseworkers must make the Department 'aware of any breaches of the Code'.[63] The contracts also set out that providers must assist asylum seekers to 'understand and comply with their obligations under the Code' and ensure they 'understand the importance of their responsibility' for 'adhering to acceptable standards of behaviour in the community, including those stipulated in the Code'.[64]

The NGOs' mandatory reporting requirements are reflected in data on how the Code is operating. In late 2017, the Department partially fulfilled a further FOI request seeking details of the Code's implementation, which included a question relating to the sources of allegations under the Code. The data released included a table of 499

[61] Leanne Weber and Rebecca Powell, 'Crime, Pre-crime and Sub-crime: Deportation of "Risky Non-citizens" on Character Grounds as "Enemy Crimmigration"' in John Pratt and Jordan Anderson (eds), *Criminal Justice, Risk and the Revolt against Uncertainty* (Palgrave Macmillan 2020) 245–272.

[62] Anthea Vogl and Elyse Methven, 'We will Decide who Comes to this Country, and how they Behave: A Critical Reading of the Asylum Seeker Code of Behaviour' (2015) 40 Alternative Law Journal 175.

[63] Department of Immigration and Border Protection, 'Contract for the Provision of SRSS' (freedom of information requests FA 21/05/01201, 2021; FA 17/06/00046, 2017).

[64] ibid.

alleged breaches of the Code over approximately two years. It listed the 'source', 'nature', and 'outcome' of allegations and provided the most comprehensive data to date about the Code's operation.[65] One of the major and unanticipated findings from this data was that NGO providers and caseworkers were, by far, the predominant source of reports to the Department of asylum seekers breaching the Code and/or Australian criminal laws. Specifically, the released data reveals that more than two-thirds (68 per cent) of allegations under the Code originated from the humanitarian organisations providing asylum seekers with resettlement services and assistance (SRSS providers).[66] The next highest source was the 'National Allegation Assessment Team Dob-in Line', which enables community members to 'dob', meaning to anonymously tell authorities of Code breaches. This line was responsible for 9 per cent of allegations. Police only accounted for 5 per cent of allegations. Further statistical analysis demonstrated that where an SRSS Provider was the source of an allegation, a large majority of allegations resulted in 'either the cancellation of a visa or a finding that the Code itself had been breached' (84 per cent).[67]

The final relevant aspect of the NGOs' role is work they undertake to discipline asylum seekers found to be in breach of the Code. In 163 instances, the outcome of a Code breach was not visa cancellation but rather referral for counselling or a 'discussion' with an SRSS caseworker or a departmental officer.[68] Further data is required to understand the nature of these 'discussions' and exactly how the humanitarian border's care/control nexus is operating in these encounters. However, the NGOs' disciplining role gives rise to yet another site of discretionary regulation and punishment for asylum seekers, with no public oversight or review of how caseworkers' discretion is exercised. Indeed, the Department's annual reports confirm that counselling sessions and discussions with SRSS providers are aimed at 'reinforc[ing] expected behavioural standards'.[69] They also confirm that SRSS caseworkers are contractually required to provide 'comprehensive' orientation services that provide information about rules, laws (including the Code), and 'appropriate public behaviour', involving NGOs once again in migration control in so far as they must 'educate' clients about the conditionality of their status.[70] Notably, these sessions are also required to cover welfare and health-related information such as the location of local doctors, pharmacies, libraries, and public park and recreation areas.

NGOs contracted by the state to provide care and welfare services while simultaneously participating in the enforcement of the Code is an example of the humanitarian border in action. The NGOs must agree to 'reinforce' a Code that is an explicitly punitive, extrajudicial regulation of refugee behaviour consistent with colonial, civilising

[65] For an account of the Code as an instrument of crimmigration and in breach of fundamental principles of natural justice, see Vogl (n 45).

[66] Meg Randolph and others, *Australia's Asylum Seeker Code of Behaviour: A Statistical Analysis* (Research Brief No 15) (Border Crossing Observatory, July 2019) <https://www.monash.edu/__data/assets/pdf_file/0007/1872061/research-brief-15-FINAL-MR.pdf> accessed 17 September 2021.

[67] ibid.

[68] Vogl and Methven, 'Life in the Shadow Carceral State' (n 47) 69.

[69] Department of Immigration and Border Protection, *Annual Report 2015–16* (Commonwealth of Australia, 2016) 51 <https://www.homeaffairs.gov.au/reports-and-pubs/Annualreports/dibp-annual-report-2015-16.pdf> accessed 17 September 2021.

[70] Department of Immigration and Border Protection, 'Contract for the Provision of SRSS' (n 63).

discourses, and targeting a racialised 'other'.[71] These contractual duties must be agreed to in order to provide welfare services and support to those living in the community. If 'education' fails, and a breach is suspected, it must be reported to the Department, where it will be assessed by departmental officers in the absence of basic procedural safeguards. Where a breach is found, reporting can result in a client's return to indefinite detention or termination of the very income support the NGO is contracted to provide.

Walters observes that humanitarian participation is part of the regime of border control rather than separate from it.[72] Indeed, it is only because of outsourcing to NGOs that the Department can indirectly manage 'clients' and place them under surveillance in a manner not possible without the NGOs' involvement. Long-time refugee advocate Pamela Curr reports that many asylum seekers fear that caseworkers will report disclosures of their problems to the Department:

> If [asylum seekers] have an agency that's looking after them and they go to that agency and say, 'I'm feeling suicidal, I want to jump in front of a train, I can't sleep, I've got voices in my head'—all the marks of mental ill health—those agencies will notify the immigration department, and the next thing you know, the department will rock up and cart them off to detention.[73]

As such, asylum seekers may interact with caseworkers *as if* they were interacting with independent practitioners and without awareness of mandatory reporting requirements. In Gerard and Weber's study of the SRSS, research participants reported concerns that some asylum seekers 'were unaware of how entangled their service providers were within government networks of surveillance and securitization'.[74] Amini's final message to the Australian public, by contrast, demonstrates that some asylum seekers are fully aware of their caseworkers' reporting and surveillance role. In both scenarios, government-contracted NGOs are 'intrinsic to the policing network of the state',[75] but they fulfil this role without the same visibility or accountability mechanisms that apply to state agencies or actors.

As the next section outlines, the contracted NGOs are asylum seekers' primary source of welfare, information, and casework assistance. However, every encounter with these organisations is also a site of surveillance, and each meeting could eventuate in a report to the government of breaches of the Code or visa conditions. Asylum seekers are required to actively negotiate the dual role that their SRSS providers play, in supporting their needs at the same time as policing and potentially disciplining them. Further, they must do this in the context of systemic withdrawal of support and assistance *implemented by* the NGOs as per their contractual duties, and while awaiting the determination of their protection claims.

[71] Vogl and Methven, 'Life in the Shadow Carceral State' (n 47) 69.
[72] Walters (n 10).
[73] Rob Stott, 'A Refugee Committed Suicide at Brisbane Airport and Barely anyone Noticed' (*BuzzFeed*, 2 November 2015) <https://www.buzzfeed.com/robstott/a-refugees-public-suicide-and-the-system-that-let-him-down> accessed 14 February 2019.
[74] Gerard and Weber (n 9) 277.
[75] ibid 282.

B Government-contracted NGOs and the Provision/Denial of Welfare Services

The contracted NGOs provide the only government-funded welfare support available to asylum seekers who arrived by boat and are living in the community. As a result, these organisations are people's principal point of contact with the state and state-funded services beyond the immediate question of their migration status, which is still managed by the Department. This service delivery takes place primarily via the SRSS programme, which, as noted, provides 'temporary needs-based support' to persons awaiting the resolution of their immigration status.[76] The support outsourced under the SRSS may include limited financial support, casework support, and, in certain instances, access to torture counselling and trauma counselling services.[77]

While the government-contracted NGOs are cast only as *providers* of services, they are also required, as Gerard and Weber highlight, to refuse welfare and other assistance, in line with government policy.[78] This active refusal of care and assistance is central to the 'work' of these NGOs, which are responsible for conducting eligibility assessments that are then referred to the Department, as well as for terminating SRRS support if circumstances change or an asylum seeker's behaviour affects their eligibility.[79] There are six different 'bands' of SRSS eligibility. The first five apply to unaccompanied minors, those being held in community detention,[80] or those transitioning out of closed detention. The majority of resources are provided under the sixth band, which covers asylum seekers living in the community while awaiting resolution of their protection visas.[81]

The extremely meagre level of support available to those who *do* qualify for SRSS financial assistance is itself a form of deterrence, as it makes day-to-day subsistence-level existence extremely difficult.[82] The SRSS fortnightly payment is indexed to Australia's national unemployment payment but falls short of it by 11 per cent.[83] This is a measure that is both directly and symbolically punitive, especially as Australia's national base welfare payment has been repeatedly assessed as far below the poverty

[76] Department of Home Affairs, 'Status Resolution Support Services' (n 54).

[77] John van Kooy, 'An Unnecessary Penalty: Economic Impact of SRSS Changes' (Refugee Council of Australia 2018) <https://www.refugeecouncil.org.au/srss-economic-penalty/> accessed 28 March 2021. Asylum seekers with valid bridging visas have access to Medicare, Australia's national health care programme, alongside SRSS services.

[78] Gerard and Weber (n 9).

[79] Van Kooy (n 77) 5.

[80] Under Australian law, community detention allows primarily children and families to be released from closed detention under a 'residence determination', while they remain formally detained under Australian law: Migration Act 1958 (Cth), s 197AB.

[81] Parliament of Australia Legal and Constitutional Affairs Committee, '2017–18 Additional Estimates, Question on Notice No 99' (Home Affairs Portfolio Question Number AE18/104, 26 February 2018) <https://www.aph.gov.au/api/qon/downloadestimatesquestions/EstimatesQuestion-CommitteeId6-EstimatesRoundId2-PortfolioId20-QuestionNumber99> accessed 17 September 2021.

[82] Refugee Council of Australia (n 52).

[83] In practice, this amounts to as little as AU$35 per day, for a single adult without accommodation support: van Kooy (n 77) 3.

line.[84] Due to the need to access both work and community assistance, most asylum seekers live in major Australian cities where the cost of living is much higher than the national average, rendering the income payment especially inadequate.

The criteria to access SRSS support are narrow, strictly applied, and have been limited by a series of punitive reforms implemented from 2017 onwards. In 2018, radical changes to the programme introduced the category of 'job-ready' asylum seekers. As a result, those who were assessed as job-ready were no longer eligible for financial assistance, regardless of whether they had current employment or any form of income.[85] Under the reforms, overall eligibility for support for people living in the community was determined on the basis of 'vulnerability', and original assessments were carried out by the contracted NGOs under extremely short timelines, and submitted to the Department for oversight and review.[86] Vulnerability assessments considered four factors, each of which is striking for its extra criteria, in addition to 'ordinary' vulnerability. For example, only single parents with *pre-school* aged children and pregnant women *with* complications were defined as vulnerable and therefore outside of the expectation to find work due to being 'job-ready'.[87]

These changes were jointly implemented by the NGOs and the Department. Those deemed 'not vulnerable' by their NGO provider were given just seven to ten days to transition off SRSS support and payments.[88] Under the reforms, asylum seekers with negative decisions regarding their protection claims are also ineligible for assistance, even where judicial review proceedings are in train. While approximately 13,300 people were receiving SRSS payments in February 2018,[89] by 31 August 2020, the number had dropped to 4,057 individuals receiving a similar level of support.[90]

Two further ineligibility criteria, introduced in 2017, are noteworthy for their punitive quality. One ineligibility rule requires SRSS payments to be stopped if an asylum seeker engages in any post-secondary school education on a full-time basis, including where an asylum seeker has won a tertiary scholarship; and another applies if more than AU$1,000 is transferred to an overseas or domestic bank account over a twelve-month period.[91] The Refugee Council of Australia received reports of people being declared ineligible for the programme 'because they had transferred small amounts of money overseas, for example AUD50, many years ago'.[92] However, the policy was reportedly clarified so debts could only be incurred from 2017, when 'SRSS providers were first notified of the policy'.[93]

[84] Melbourne Institute of Applied Economic & Social Research, *Poverty Lines: Australia. March Quarter 2018* (University of Melbourne 2018) <https://melbourneinstitute.unimelb.edu.au/__data/assets/pdf_file/0010/2844487/Poverty-lines-Australia-March-Quarter-2018.pdf> accessed 17 September 2021.

[85] Van Kooy (n 77) 5.

[86] Refugee Council of Australia (n 52) 7.

[87] ibid (emphasis added).

[88] ibid. The Department also used its own information to review assessments.

[89] Van Kooy (n 77) 5.

[90] Senate Legal and Constitutional Affairs Legislation Committee, '2020–21 Budget Estimates' (Parliament of Australia, Evidence of Justine Jones, Acting First Assistant Secretary, Immigration Integrity and Community Protection Division, 19 October 2020) 125. The award of status, deportation, or repatriation also account for the decline in numbers.

[91] Refugee Council of Australia (n 52) 6.

[92] ibid.

[93] ibid 8.

The humanitarian border, as it operates in relation to the Code and the delivery of SRSS services, enables new forms of border control. Some of the effects of outsourcing to not-for-profit NGOs follow the effects of the privatisation of immigration enforcement more generally. For example, the Australian government's own secrecy and lack of accountability in relation to its treatment of refugees and asylum seekers is further enabled by the outsourcing to these humanitarian organisations. The non-disclosure clauses in each of the NGO contracts also impede direct qualitative research with these organisations.[94] Accessing accurate data about how the SRSS is operating is best described as somewhere between difficult and impossible. As the Refugee Council has noted, 'the Department of Home Affairs has consistently denied access to detailed SRSS data, SRSS providers are contractually restricted from sharing information and there is no public reporting under the SRSS program'.[95] Critically, in tracing the involvement of the NGOs in the *refusal* of care at the humanitarian border, 'there is no information on the number of new applications that are being refused'.[96]

Alongside the suppression of information facilitated by private outsourcing, the multiplicity of NGOs involved in the SRSS further diffuses and widens border control and enforcement for asylum seekers, while impeding the ability of advocates to map, assess, and contest this. The geographic and organisational dispersal of the eight NGOs, which are located across Australia, also affects their ability to organise in relation to their clients' needs or respond to proposed policy reforms. Moreover, contractual and funding relationships, and the *competitive* tender process, constrain the independence of the NGOs and co-opt them into the migration control apparatus on a cyclical basis. The competitive tender process means the NGOs are in direct and ongoing competition for available funding, which comes to the fore each time contracts are due for renewal. As such, organisations are not only bound by existing contractual terms, but their willingness to perform and adhere to standards set by government may affect their capacity to secure future funding. Where 'client' well-being is directly harmed by government policy, government-contracted NGOs acting as advocates or openly contesting policy may put their own financial viability at immediate risk.[97]

The unpredictability of how the SRSS operates is yet another form of insecurity that must be navigated by asylum seekers living in the community. Regular reforms to the design of the SRSS, and level of assistance available under it, are implemented at the discretion of the executive government, and achieved via policy and contractual amendments, since the programmes are not expressed within any legislation.[98] While contractual terms provide some degree of standardisation and statement of private obligations, systematic changes to the programmes do not require legislative reform or parliamentary oversight.[99] The non-legislative nature of the SRSS, and the privatisation of programme design, is critical when thinking through the motivations for and implications of outsourcing. The alternative—of providing financial support via Australia's federal unemployment agency or via departmental avenues—would limit

[94] See Weber, 'From State-centric to Transversal Borders' (n 12).
[95] Van Kooy (n 77) 3.
[96] ibid.
[97] Gerard and Weber (n 9) 279–80.
[98] Refugee Council of Australia (n 52) 2.
[99] ibid.

the discretion afforded by contracting out these services, or at the very least, enable greater public oversight of and accountability for reforms. As with privatisation generally, the SRSS facilitates the government's discretion in revising how programmes operate, who administers them, and, of course, who may access information about them and on what terms.

IV Conclusion

Immigration regulation is marked by its tendency to 'push deeply inward into domestic arenas while also reaching out beyond our territorial borders'.[100] These movements outward and inward have not only merited a re-examination of immigration law as a tool for exercising sovereignty; the outsourcing and privatisation of these functions has resulted in an increasing cast of actors and organisations shaping, interpreting, and enforcing border and immigration controls. The increasing involvement of corporations, charities, and humanitarian organisations in migration control has revealed what Bosworth, Franko, and Pickering describe as the 'flexibility of punishment and how easily it is unhinged from the state and its territory'—both geographically and administratively.[101] This chapter has explored the outsourcing of core asylum seeker welfare, surveillance, and reporting functions to government-contracted NGOs, and the implications of this development for the operation of Australia's internal bordering practices and general deterrence regime. It has addressed two key elements of the government-contracted NGOs' work, namely the implementation and oversight of a welfare regime orientated toward deterrence and deprivation via the SRSS, and their role in enforcing the extraordinary Code of Behaviour.

In outsourcing the provision of welfare, as well as the policing and enforcement of state laws, the Australian government has created new sites of discretion and control over the lives of asylum seekers. In contrast to other sites of privatisation, which also generate new sites of decision-making, discretion, and administration, the participation of NGOs enables a form of governance, marked by simultaneous care and migration control objectives. As a contractual condition for providing welfare assistance, NGOs must both police and report on asylum seekers in their care. Equally, by stepping into the welfare role vacated and outsourced by the government, they are bound to observe and enforce conditions that have been appraised as 'starving out' asylum seekers and deploying deprivation as a means of deterrence. The state's co-option of organisations into partnerships to regulate internal borders exemplifies the care/control nexus involved in humanitarian governance at the border. It aims to achieve what Pallister-Wilkins describes as the transformation of border regulation from work concerned with 'stopping, defending and securing territory' to work concerned with saving or securing lives.[102]

[100] Lori A Nessel, 'Instilling Fear and Regulating Behavior: Immigration Law as Social Control' (2016) 31 Georgetown Immigration Law Journal 525, 526.

[101] Mary Bosworth, Katja Franko, and Sharon Pickering, 'Punishment, Globalization and Migration Control: "Get them the Hell out of Here"' (2018) 20 Punishment & Society 34.

[102] Polly Pallister-Wilkins, 'Humanitarian Borderwork' in Cengiz Günay and Nina Witjes (eds), *Border Politics* (Springer International 2017) 86.

The humanitarian border, as it operates in relation to the delivery of welfare and the Code of Behaviour in Australia, enables new forms of migration control, surveillance, and policing of the internal border. At the same time, the outsourcing of welfare and policing to government-contracted NGOs captures them as direct partners in migration management and control. Asylum seekers' responses to state migration policies, however, alongside day-to-day acts of solidarity *and* compliance, also shape the operation of internal (humanitarian) borders.[103] Further 'micro-level' theorising[104] is needed to understand the multifaceted effects of outsourcing for asylum seekers dependent on privatised welfare, as well as for avenues of resistance, and the regulation of internal borders and state sovereignty.

References

Aliverti A, 'Benevolent Policing? Vulnerability and the Moral Pains of Border Controls' (2020) 60 The British Journal of Criminology 1117

AusTender, 'Contract Notice CN2616652-A14, CN2616622-A9' (Department of Home Affairs) <https://www.tenders.gov.au/Cn/Show/9aee07e9-b062-4a03-836a-66b4340ea991>

Australian Human Rights Commission, *Lives on Hold: Refugees and Asylum Seekers in the 'Legacy Caseload'* (Australian Human Rights Commission 2019) <https://humanrights.gov.au/our-work/asylum-seekers-and-refugees/publications/lives-hold-refugees-and-asylum-seekers-legacy>

Bosworth M, 'Penal Humanitarianism? Sovereign Power in an Era of Mass Migration' (2017) 20 New Criminal Law Review 39

— —, 'Affect and Authority in Immigration Detention' (2019) 21 Punishment & Society 542

— —, Franko K, and Pickering S, 'Punishment, Globalization and Migration Control: "Get them the Hell out of Here"' (2018) 20 Punishment & Society 34

Boucher L and Russell L, *Settler Colonial Governance in Nineteenth-century Victoria* (ANU Press 2015)

Bui M and others, 'Perpetual Insecurity: The Weaponisation of Mental Suffering' (*Deathscapes*, 2018) <https://www.deathscapes.org/case-studies/perpetual-insecurity/>

Carrera S and others, *Policing Humanitarianism: EU Policies against Human Smuggling and their Impact on Civil Society* (Hart 2019)

Chimni BS, 'Globalization, Humanitarianism and the Erosion of Refugee Protection' (2000) 13 Journal of Refugee Studies 243

Dehm S, 'Outsourcing, Responsibility and Refugee Claim-making in Australia's Offshore Detention Regime' in McGuirk S and Pine A (eds), *Asylum for Sale: Profit and Protest in the Migration Industry* (PM Press 2020)

Department of Home Affairs, 'Immigration Detention and Community Statistics Summary' (Australian Border Force, 31 March 2021) <https://www.homeaffairs.gov.au/research-and-stats/files/immigration-detention-statistics-31-march-2021.pdf>

— —, 'Status Resolution Support Services' (6 July 2021) <https://immi.homeaffairs.gov.au/what-we-do/status-resolution-service/status-resolution-support-services>

[103] Weber, 'From State-centric to Transversal Borders' (n 12).

[104] See Bosworth and Singler, in this volume.

Department of Immigration and Border Protection, 'Code of Behaviour for Subclass 050 Bridging (General) Visa Holders' (Form 1444i) (Commonwealth of Australia 2015) <https://immi.homeaffairs.gov.au/form-listing/forms/1444i.pdf>

— —, *Annual Report 2015–16* (Commonwealth of Australia 2016) <https://www.homeaffairs.gov.au/reports-and-pubs/Annualreports/dibp-annual-report-2015-16.pdf>

— — 'Contract for the Provision of SRSS' (freedom of information requests FA 21/05/01201, 2021; FA 17/06/00046, 2017).

Doherty B and Hurst D, 'UN Accuses Australia of Systematically Violating Torture Convention' *The Guardian* (London, 10 March 2015) <https://www.theguardian.com/australia-news/2015/mar/09/un-reports-australias-immigration-detention-breaches-torture-convention>

Fassin D, 'Humanitarianism: A Nongovernmental Government' in Feher M, Krikorian G, and McKee Y (eds), *Nongovernmental Politics* (Zone Books 2007)

Field R, Chung D, and Fleay C, 'The Influence of Policy, Cultural and Historical Contexts on Social Work and Human Service Practice Responses with People Seeking Asylum in Germany and Australia' (2021) 15 Ethics and Social Welfare 294

Gerard A and Weber L, '"Humanitarian Borderwork": Identifying Tensions between Humanitarianism and Securitization for Government Contracted NGOs Working with Adult and Unaccompanied Minor Asylum Seekers in Australia' (2019) 23 Theoretical Criminology 266

Hartley L and Fleay C, '"We are like Animals": Negotiating Dehumanising Experiences of Asylum-seeker Policies in the Australian Community' (2017) 36 Refugee Survey Quarterly 45

Karim Hekmat A, 'The Death of Khodayar Amini' *The Saturday Paper* (Melbourne, 24 October 2015) <https://www.thesaturdaypaper.com.au/news/immigration/2015/10/24/the-death-khodayar-amini/14456052002536>

Kox M and Staring R, '"If you don't have Documents or a Legal Procedure, you are Out!" Making Humanitarian Organizations Partner in Migration Control' (2020) European Journal of Criminology 1

Life Without Barriers, 'About Us' (*Life Without Barriers*, 2021) <https://www.lwb.org.au/about-us/>

Little A and Vaughan-Williams N, 'Stopping Boats, Saving Lives, Securing Subjects: Humanitarian Borders in Europe and Australia' (2017) 23 European Journal of International Relations 533

Melbourne Institute of Applied Economic & Social Research, *Poverty Lines: Australia. March Quarter 2018* (University of Melbourne 2018) <https://melbourneinstitute.unimelb.edu.au/__data/assets/pdf_file/0010/2844487/Poverty-lines-Australia-March-Quarter-2018.pdf>

Moreno-Lax V, 'The EU Humanitarian Border and the Securitization of Human Rights: The "Rescue-Through-Interdiction/Rescue-Without-Protection" Paradigm' (2018) 56 Journal of Common Market Studies 119

Moreton-Robinson A, 'The Possessive Logic of Patriarchal White Sovereignty: The High Court and the *Yorta Yorta* Decision' (2004) 3(2) Borderlands E-Journal 1 <https://eprints.qut.edu.au/7690/>

Nessel LA, 'Instilling Fear and Regulating Behavior: Immigration Law as Social Control' (2016) 31 Georgetown Immigration Law Journal 525

Pallister-Wilkins P, 'The Humanitarian Politics of European Border Policing: Frontex and Border Police in Evros' (2015) 9 International Political Sociology 53

— —, 'Humanitarian Borderwork' in Günay C and Witjes N (eds), *Border Politics* (Springer International 2017)

Parliament of Australia Legal and Constitutional Affairs Committee, '2017–18 Additional Estimates, Question on Notice No 99' (Home Affairs Portfolio Question Number AE18/104, 26 February 2018) <https://www.aph.gov.au/api/qon/downloadestimatesquestions/EstimatesQuestion-CommitteeId6-EstimatesRoundId2-PortfolioId20-QuestionNumber99>

Procter NG, Kenny MA, Eaton H, and Greech C, 'Lethal Hopelessness: Understanding and Responding to Asylum Seeker Distress and Mental Deterioration' (2018) 27 International Journal of Mental Health Nursing 448

Randolph M, Vogl A, Methven E, and Weber L, *Australia's Asylum Seeker Code of Behaviour: A Statistical Analysis* (Research Brief No 15) (Border Crossing Observatory, July 2019) <https://www.monash.edu/__data/assets/pdf_file/0007/1872061/research-brief-15-FINAL-MR.pdf>

Refugee Council of Australia, 'Starving them Out: Destitution of People Seeking Asylum in Australia' (*Refugee Council of Australia Brief*, May 2018) <https://www.refugeecouncil.org.au/starving-them-out/>

Senate Legal and Constitutional Affairs Legislation Committee, '2020–21 Budget Estimates' (Parliament of Australia, Evidence of Justine Jones, Acting First Assistant Secretary, Immigration Integrity and Community Protection Division, 19 October 2020)

Settlement Services International, 'About Us' (*Settlement Services International*, undated) <https://www.ssi.org.au/about-us>

Silverstein J, 'Refugee Children, Boats and Drownings: A History of an Australian "Humanitarian" Discourse' (2020) 17 History Australia 728

Stott R, 'A Refugee Committed Suicide at Brisbane Airport and Barely anyone Noticed' (*BuzzFeed* 2 November 2015) <https://www.buzzfeed.com/robstott/a-refugees-public-suicide-and-the-system-that-let-him-down>

Sydney Morning Herald, 'Saving Lives Trumps Politics, Says Gillard' *Sydney Morning Herald* (Sydney, 19 August 2012) <https://www.smh.com.au/politics/federal/saving-lives-trumps-politics-says-gillard-20120819-24g0i.html>

Tofighian O, 'Introducing Manus Prison Theory: Knowing Border Violence' (2020) 17 Globalizations 1138

van Kooy J, *An Unnecessary Penalty: Economic Impact of SRSS Changes* (Refugee Council of Australia 2018) <https://www.refugeecouncil.org.au/srss-economic-penalty/>

Vogl A, 'Crimmigration and Refugees: Bridging Visas, Criminal Cancellations and "Living in the Community" as Punishment and Deterrence' in Billings P (ed), *Crimmigration in Australia: Law, Politics, and Society* (Springer 2019)

— — and Methven E, 'We will Decide who Comes to this Country, and how they Behave: A Critical Reading of the Asylum Seeker Code of Behaviour' (2015) 40 Alternative Law Journal 175

— — and Methven E, 'Life in the Shadow Carceral State: Surveillance and Control of Refugees in Australia' (2020) 9 International Journal for Crime, Justice and Social Democracy 61

Walters W, 'Foucault and Frontiers: Notes on the Birth of the Humanitarian Border' in Bröckling U, Krasmann S, and Lemke T (eds), *Governmentality: Current Issues and Future Challenges* (Routledge 2011)

Watson I, 'In the Northern Territory Intervention: What is Saved or Rescued and at what Cost?' (2009) 15 Cultural Studies Review 45

Weber L, 'From State-centric to Transversal Borders: Resisting the "Structurally Embedded Border" in Australia' (2019) 23 Theoretical Criminology 228

— — *Policing Non-citizens* (Routledge 2013)

— — and Powell R, 'Crime, Pre-crime and Sub-crime: Deportation of "Risky Non-citizens" on Character Grounds as "Enemy Crimmigration"' in Pratt, J and Anderson, J (eds), *Criminal Justice, Risk and the Revolt against Uncertainty* (Palgrave Macmillan 2020)

Yuval-Davis N, Wemyss G, and Cassidy K, 'Everyday Bordering, Belonging and the Reorientation of British Immigration Legislation' (2018) 52 Sociology 228

Legislation

Migration Act 1958 (Cth), s 197AB

11

Outsourcing the Border Within

Private Citizens as Border Guards, State Sovereignty, and Civil Peace

Lucia Zedner[*]

I Introduction

The state's sovereign power to criminalise, police, and punish within its jurisdiction extends to the limits of its territory. The policing of borders, no less than policing itself, is the state's primary preserve. Even if some public services are delegable without detriment to state authority,[1] some core functions are so central as to be inalienable.[2] Policing is one such function, even to the limits of the state's sovereign territory, where it is pursued through ever tougher immigration laws and border controls.[3] Despite this forceful assertion of state sovereignty, in the UK as elsewhere, much border control has long been privatised. Today, security companies play a major role in border policing, immigration detention, escort services, and deportation.[4] The contracting-out of border policing attracts much academic interest,[5] and raises questions about the state exercise of sovereign power at the very margins of its jurisdiction.[6]

More complex questions arise in respect of newer modes of outsourcing. In the 2000s, the UK government began to co-opt civil society organisations and private individuals as partners in immigration control.[7] This form of outsourcing relies not on contract, but on the imposition of positive obligations on civil society organisations

* With thanks to Mary Bosworth and Samuel Singler for very helpful comments, and to all the workshop participants for their insights and suggestions.

1 Daniel Philpott, 'Sovereignty' in *Stanford Encyclopedia of Philosophy* (2003) <https://plato.stanford.edu/entries/sovereignty> accessed 21 December 2021.

2 Malcolm Thorburn, 'Reinventing the Nightwatchman State' (2010) 60 University of Toronto Law Journal 425.

3 John C Torpey, *The Invention of the Passport: Surveillance, Citizenship and the State* (CUP 2018) ch 1.

4 Ruben Andersson, 'Profits and Predation in the Bioeconomy of Border Controls' (2018) 30(3) Public Culture 413;Federica Infantino, *Outsourcing Border Control: Politics and Practice of Contracted Visa Policy in Morocco* (Palgrave Macmillan 2016).

5 Ashwini Vasanthakumar, 'Privatising Border Control' (2018) 38(3) Oxford Journal of Legal Studies 411; Lacin Idil Oztig, 'Rethinking Sovereignty: The Implications of the Role of Private Security Companies in the Prevention and the Regulation of Unauthorized Flows' (2020) 33(3) Cambridge Review of International Affairs 330; Daniel L Stageman, 'The Punishment Marketplace: Competing for Capitalized Power in Locally Controlled Immigration Enforcement' (2019) 23(3) Theoretical Criminology 394.

6 Alan James, 'The Practice of Sovereign Statehood in Contemporary International Society' (1999) 47(3) Political Studies 457.

7 Home Office, *Enforcing the Deal: Our Plans for Enforcing the Immigration Laws in the United Kingdom's Communities* (Home Office 2008) <http://data.parliament.uk/DepositedPapers/Files/DEP2008-1595/DEP2008-1595.pdf> accessed 16 November 2021.

Lucia Zedner, *Outsourcing the Border Within* In: *Privatising Border Control*. Edited by: Mary Bosworth and Lucia Zedner, Oxford University Press. © Lucia Zedner 2022. DOI: 10.1093/oso/9780192857163.003.0012

and private citizens to monitor immigration status and report irregularities.[8] Private citizens, including employers, landlords, health and charity workers, teachers, and professors, are now legally required to collaborate in checking immigration status to ascertain migrants' right to work, rent, and to access health, welfare, and education.[9] These controls operate informally away from the border and are dispersed throughout society,[10] prompting the insight that today, 'borders are everywhere'.[11]

This chapter explores the role of private citizens in 'outsourcing the border within' to explore its implications for state–citizen relations, state sovereignty, and civil order. It first examines the interior network of controls created by the UK government's 'Hostile Environment' policy, in particular the co-option of private citizens to identify and report on immigration irregularities. It explores the political drivers of these recent developments, and examines their form and significance to ask what is, and what should be, the role of the state vis-à-vis non-citizens,[12] and whether imposing duties on private citizens to police immigration status can be defended. It next considers whether citizens obligated to enforce immigration checks act as agents of the state or as private actors and, if so, on whose authority they police. The chapter then traces the official shift to the so-called 'Compliant Environment', to consider the role of private citizens in compelling compliance. It suggests that the hurdles to entry thus created are more, not less, difficult for migrants to surmount. Finally, attention turns to the legal and ethical implications of co-opting private citizens in the policing of immigration. The chapter concludes by observing that, although citizens are called upon to fulfil public policing functions, the finding of the UK courts that they do so not as agents of the state, but as private actors for whom the state is not liable, constitutes a serious relinquishing of state sovereignty, injurious to social trust and civil peace.

II The Hostile Environment

Migrants contribute to economic prosperity,[13] cultural diversity, and a more cosmopolitan society. While the wealthy and highly educated are welcomed, others are

[8] Home Office, *Enforcing the Deal* (n 7); Gallya Lahav, 'Immigration and the State: The Devolution and Privatization of Immigration Control in the EU' (1998) 24(4) Journal of Ethnic and Migration Studies 675.

[9] Ana Aliverti, 'Enlisting the Public in the Policing of Immigration' (2015) 55(2) British Journal of Criminology 215.

[10] Aliverti, 'Enlisting the Public in the Policing of Immigration' (n 9); Vasanthakumar (n 5); Alpa Parmar, 'Arresting (Non)Citizenship: The Policing Migration Nexus of Nationality, Race and Criminalization' (2020) 24(1) Theoretical Criminology 28.

[11] Chris Rumford, 'Citizens and Borderwork in Europe' (2008) 12(1) Space and Polity 1; Arjen Leerkes, James D Bachmeier, and Mark A Leach, 'When the Border is "Everywhere": State-level Variation in Migration Control and Changing Settlement Patterns of the Unauthorized Immigrant Population in the United States' (2013) 47(4) Immigration Migration Review 910.

[12] Lucia Zedner, 'Is the Criminal Law only for Citizens? A Problem at the Borders of Punishment' in Katja Franko Aas and Mary Bosworth (eds), *The Borders of Punishment: Migration, Citizenship, and Social Exclusion* (OUP 2013) 43

[13] See, eg OECD, 'Is Migration Good for the Economy?' <https://www.oecd.org/migration/OECD%20Migration%20Policy%20Debates%20Numero%202.pdf> accessed 16 November 2021.

shunned and excluded.[14] In the face of rising migration, recent UK governments have promoted a deliberate 'Hostile Environment' policy designed to deter refugees and asylum seekers. While private sector involvement in immigration dates back to the first immigration centres in the 1970s, only in the 2000s did the UK government begin co-opting civil society organisations and private individuals as partners to reinforce immigration controls,[15] as the Labour government imposed ever more stringent conditions on those seeking UK citizenship.[16] Attitudes towards migration hardened further from 2010 when the Conservative-led coalition government determined to deter illegal immigrants by making life so difficult as to prompt their 'voluntary' departure.[17] The then Home Secretary Theresa May declared, '[t]he aim is to create, here in Britain, a really hostile environment for illegal immigrants'.[18] New laws limited access to housing, employment, health services, and other essentials of everyday life (including bank accounts and driving licences) for those lacking documentation. Enforcement relied increasingly on the systematic co-option of private individuals tasked with verifying the immigration status of employees, tenants, patients, and students. These statutory obligations (of which, more below) were accompanied by informal injunctions addressed to all citizens to report suspected illegal immigrants.[19]

The Hostile Environment policy was exemplified by the Home Office initiative 'Operation Vaken' (2013), in which vans bearing the slogan 'Go home or face arrest' toured areas of London with high migrant populations.[20] The billboards warned irregular migrants that they faced 'a near and present danger of their being arrested' and invited the general public to send text messages reporting 'illegals' within their community.[21] Although Operation Vaken was withdrawn following public outcry, it set the tenor of a resolutely inhospitable environment that relied not only on the strict enforcement of border controls by immigration officials but also on the dispersal of controls throughout civil society. The following section analyses more prominent instances of this systematic outsourcing, whose effect, it will suggest, was to make border guards of private citizens.

[14] Mary Bosworth, 'Border Control and the Limits of the Sovereign State' (2008) 17(2) Social and Legal Studies 199, 202–04; see also Mary Bosworth and Mhairi Guild, 'Governing through Migration Control' (2008) 48(6) The British Journal of Criminology 703.

[15] Home Office, *Enforcing the Deal* (n 7).

[16] See, eg Lucia Zedner, 'Security, the State and the Citizen: The Changing Architecture of Crime Control' (2010) 13(2) New Criminal Law Review 379; Catherine Dauvergne, *Making People Illegal: What Globalization Means for Migration and Law* (CUP 2008); Jef Huysmans, *The Politics of Insecurity: Fear, Migration and Asylum in the EU* (Routledge 2006).

[17] Home Affairs Committee, *Immigration Policy: Basis for Building Consensus: Second Report of Session 2017–19* (HC 500, 2019) 20 <https://publications.parliament.uk/pa/cm201719/cmselect/cmhaff/500/500.pdf> accessed 16 November 2021.

[18] Laura Hood, 'Hostile Environment' (*The Conversation*, 26 April 2018) <https://theconversation.com/hostile-environment-the-uk-governments-draconian-immigration-policy-explained-95460> accessed 16 December 2021.

[19] HM Government, 'Report an Immigration or Border Crime' <https://www.gov.uk/report-immigration-crime> accessed 16 November 2021; Ana Aliverti, *Policing the Borders within* (OUP 2021) 188.

[20] Simon Hatterstone, 'Why was the Scheme behind May's "Go Home" Vans called Operation Vaken? *The Guardian* (London, 26 April 2018) <https://www.theguardian.com/commentisfree/2018/apr/26/theresa-may-go-home-vans-operation-vaken-ukip> accessed 16 December 2021.

[21] Home Office, Operation Vaken: Evaluation Report (Home Office 2013) 2 <https://assets.publishing.service.gov.uk/government/uploads/system/uploads/attachment_data/file/254411/Operation_Vaken_Evaluation_Report.pdf> accessed 16 December 2021.

III Enlisting Citizens as Border Guards

The outsourcing of border control is by no means confined to the UK. In the US, for example, employers have long been required to verify the immigration status of prospective employees.[22] In Australia, Weber observes that, '[r]esponsibility for migration policing is ... projected onto the population at large', by requiring employers to conduct visa checks and by inviting 'voluntarily provided "community information"' via a so-called 'Dob-in Service'.[23] Its effect was to produce forms of 'structurally embedded' migration policing, creating a 'ubiquitous border' throughout society.[24] In the UK, the Hostile Environment policy introduced a network of micro border controls exercised by private citizens required to check passports and paperwork, and report those with doubtful immigration status to the authorities. Affecting every aspect of daily life, from housing and employment to education and health, these controls rendered it ever more difficult for undocumented migrants to remain in the UK. Those in breach of immigration laws faced the threat of prosecution, detention, and, ultimately, deportation. In practice, it cast the net of control far beyond the ostensible target of undocumented migrants, as wary citizens subjected those with 'foreign' names, accents, or appearance to unwarranted suspicion and needless checks.[25] Significantly, the policy also subjected private citizens to scrutiny and sanctions for failure to fulfil the new obligations, burdening, above all, those who were themselves members of migrant communities.[26] The effect was radically to extend an existing trend towards creating positive obligations in criminal law,[27] which rendered citizens who failed to comply punishable by fines and imprisonment, raising the question whether outsourcing via the imposition of positive obligations constitutes a diminution of state power or its extension.

First, let us explore the range of statutory duties imposed, to consider the various ways in which private citizens have been co-opted. Recent legislation imposes multiple duties on health workers to police migrant access to the National Health Service (NHS). The Immigration Act 2014 (IA 2014), section 38 obliged health workers to enforce an 'immigration health charge', payable by those not 'ordinarily resident' in the UK, for non-emergency hospital treatment. In 2017, further regulations extended charging to community health services, and in 2018, doubled the fee payable. GPs and their staff had to carry out routine document checks on all prospective patients

[22] Immigration Reform and Control Act 1986: see Jennifer M Chacón, 'Privatized Immigration Enforcement' (2017) 52 Harvard Civil Rights–Civil Liberties Law Review 1, 8–9.

[23] Leanne Weber, Amanda Wilson, and Jenny Wise, 'Cops and Dobbers: A Nodal Cartography of Onshore Migration Policing in New South Wales' (2013) 46(1) Australian & New Zealand Journal of Criminology 32, 42.

[24] ibid 47; see also Leanne Weber, *Policing Non-citizens* (Routledge 2013) ch 6.

[25] See Aliverti, *Policing the Borders within* (n 19) 187.

[26] Franck Düvell, Myriam Cherti, and Iryna Lapshyna, 'Does Immigration Enforcement Matter? Irregular Immigrants and Control Policies in the UK' (COMPAS University of Oxford 2018) 30 <https://www.compas.ox.ac.uk/wp-content/uploads/DIEM-Irregular-Immigrants-and-Control-Policies-in-the-UK.pdf> accessed 16 November 2021.

[27] Andrew Ashworth, *Positive Obligations in the Criminal Law* (Hart 2013); Liora Lazarus, 'Positive Obligations and Criminal Justice: Duties to Protect or Coerce?' in Lucia Zedner and Julian V Roberts (eds), *Principles and Values in Criminal Law and Criminal Justice* (OUP 2012) 135.

accessing non-emergency care. One commentator suggests the intention was to effect a '"cultural change" where doctors and nurses will become happy immigration enforcers'.[28] Predictably, many health professionals were far from happy, protesting that they were 'docs not cops' and that there should be 'no borders in the NHS'.[29] Health workers resisted the statutory duty to identify and impose charges on non-citizens as a contravention of their professional commitment to treat all on the basis of need, not immigration status.[30]

Disquiet about the co-option of health workers was intensified by the 2016 agreement which gave UK Immigration Enforcement (IE) the power to issue 'tracing requests' on named individuals, obliging NHS staff to supply ordinarily confidential data.[31] Despite promises that such data sharing would cease,[32] the duty to share patient data continues.[33] During the COVID-19 pandemic, this obligation generated concerns that fear of being reported inhibited undocumented migrants from seeking healthcare, rendered them more vulnerable to the virus, hindered its containment, and increased risks to public health.[34] Concern that NHS complicity with Immigration Enforcement deterred migrants from seeking medical care provoked one harried health official to protest, '[w]e have long warned that NHS charging and data-sharing fundamentally undermines people's trust in the NHS. As healthcare workers that trust is absolutely vital to our work.'[35]

Health workers are not the only citizens subject to such obligations. Since the late 1990s, UK employers have been obliged to undertake 'right to work' checks, and since 2008, employers found in breach are liable to civil penalties up to £10,000 per illegal worker.[36] Whereas the test was previously whether an employer 'knowingly' employed someone illegally,[37] the Immigration Act 2016 (IA 2016), section 35(3) expanded the duty to require checks where the employer has 'reasonable cause to believe' an employee is disqualified by reason of immigration status. The government defended this extension on the grounds 'that some employers are deliberately not checking whether their employees have the right to work. The Government believes that these employers

[28] Corporate Watch, 'The Hostile Environment: Turning the UK into a Nation of Border Cops' (*Corporate Watch*, 8 April 2017) <https://corporatewatch.org/the-hostile-environment-turning-the-uk-into-a-nation-of-border-cops-2/> accessed 16 December 2021.

[29] The 'Docs not Cops' campaign was established and championed by healthcare workers: see <http://www.docsnotcops.co.uk/> accessed 30 May 2022.

[30] Düvell, Cherti, and Lapshyna (n 26) 22.

[31] Sharing of NHS data is not ordinarily lawful, however, s 261(5)(e) of the Health and Social Care Act 2012 permits disclosure in connection with the investigation of a criminal offence.

[32] Denis Campbell, 'NHS will no Longer have to Share Immigrants' Data with Home Office' *The Guardian* (London, 9 May 2018) <https://www.theguardian.com/society/2018/may/09/government-to-stop-forcing-nhs-to-share-patients-data-with-home-office> accessed 16 December 2021.

[33] May Bulam, 'Home Office still Using NHS Patient Data for Immigration Enforcement despite Suggesting it would End Practice' *The Independent* (London, 3 February 2019) <https://www.independent.co.uk/news/uk/home-news/home-office-nhs-data-sharing-immigration-enforcement-a8761396.html> accessed 16 December 2021.

[34] Liberty, 'Hostile Environment Risks Public Health during Coronavirus Outbreak' (*Liberty*, 16 March 2020) <https://www.libertyhumanrights.org.uk/issue/hostile-environment-risks-public-health-during-coronavirus-outbreak/> accessed 16 December 2021.

[35] Dr Jessica Potter, quoted in ibid.

[36] Home Office, Enforcing the Deal (n 7) 14.

[37] Immigration, Asylum and Nationality Act 2006, s 21.

are not knowingly employing illegal workers, because they are choosing not to know.'[38] Section 35 was intended to facilitate prosecution of those employing undocumented persons, punishable by fines or up to five years' imprisonment. Research suggests that overly cautious employers have unfairly restricted access to jobs by limiting vacancies to applicants with British passports, even though this practice is illegal.[39] Penalising employers for hiring undocumented workers has driven migrants into shadow labour markets, notwithstanding widespread public concern about worker exploitation, the health and safety risks of illegal working, and an official commitment to eradicating modern slavery.[40]

The outsourcing of border controls also occurs in many other sectors. Teachers are obliged to monitor their pupils, and university staff must monitor overseas students or risk their university's 'trusted sponsor status', essential to securing student visas.[41] Academics must now report regularly on student attendance and share email communications with UK Visas and Immigration.[42] In the financial sector, section 40 IA 2014 requires bank and building society employees to carry out 'status checks' to prevent 'disqualified persons' from opening bank accounts and, since 2016, to make quarterly checks on existing account holders.[43] Across the public sector, similar duties are imposed upon individuals in their professional roles. For example, DVLA[44] officials must carry out immigration checks in respect of driving licences (section 46 IA 2014), and registrars have a duty to report suspicious or 'sham' marriages and civil partnerships (section 56 IA 2014). These border control duties are extensive, yet private actors may be ill-disposed to carry out such checks or lack professional expertise or training to fulfil them effectively.[45] All these schemes have been beset by faulty decision-making; official errors result in individuals being falsely identified as 'disqualified persons' and wrongly denied access to services.[46] In consequence, migrants and all those who simply appear to be 'foreign' may face unwarranted suspicion and needless checks, which beset every aspect of their daily lives. Given the unfair burdens thus imposed, the following section poses questions concerning the standing of private actors to

[38] Immigration Act 2016, Explanatory Notes, 'Policy Background' <https://www.legislation.gov.uk/ukpga/2016/19/notes/division/3/index.htm> accessed 16 December 2021.

[39] Home Affairs Committee (n 17) 21.

[40] Virginia Mantouvalou, 'The UK Modern Slavery Act 2015 Three Years on' (2018) 81(6) Modern Law Review 1017.

[41] Alexander Topping, 'Universities being Used as Proxy Border Police, say Academics' *The Guardian* (London, 2 March 2014) <https://www.theguardian.com/education/2014/mar/02/universities-border-police-academics> accessed 16 December 2021.

[42] Formerly the UK Border Agency.

[43] Immigration Act 2016, sch 7.

[44] Driver and Vehicle Licensing Agency.

[45] Liberty, *A Guide to the Hostile Environment* (Liberty 2019) 9 <https://www.libertyhumanrights.org.uk/issue/report-a-guide-to-the-hostile-environment/> accessed 16 December 2021.

[46] Independent Chief Inspector of Borders and Immigration, *An Inspection of the 'Hostile Environment' Measures Relating to Driving Licences and Bank Accounts* (ICBI 2016) 6 <https://assets.publishing.service.gov.uk/government/uploads/system/uploads/attachment_data/file/567652/ICIBI-hostile-environment-driving-licences-and-bank-accounts-January-to-July-2016.pdf> accessed 30 May 2022; Independent Chief Inspector of Borders and Immigration, *An Inspection of the 'Right to Rent' Scheme* (ICBI 2018) 40 <https://www.gov.uk/government/publications/an-inspection-of-the-right-to-rent-scheme> accessed 30 May 2022.

police and explores how these questions have been resolved by the courts in recent cases in respect of the fundamental need to put a roof over one's head.

IV On whose Authority do Private Citizens Monitor Immigration Status?

Like many of the services already discussed, housing is essential to enable people to live in dignity and full enjoyment of their rights. Nonetheless, 'right to rent' checks, introduced by section 21 IA 2014, jeopardise this basic need by requiring landlords to verify the immigration status of prospective tenants. Failure to fulfil these checks may result in penalties of up to £3,000 per disqualified tenant, and non-payment risks criminal prosecution.[47] IA 2016, section 39[48] replaced the existing civil penalty scheme with new criminal offences that penalise landlords for failure to report an existing tenant who is disqualified or whose 'leave to remain' has expired. Landlords failing to fulfil these obligations risk a fine, and default can lead to up to five years' imprisonment.[49] Rates of prosecution appear low, but are impossible to ascertain as the Home Office does not keep records of offender occupation type.[50] Yet, the impact on landlords and prospective tenants is significant.

The 'right to rent' duty increases the risk of racial discrimination. In 2017, the Mayor of London, Sadiq Khan, wrote, 'I am concerned that it presents the very real risk that people who have a legal right to be in this country, including British citizens from black and minority ethnic communities, will be discriminated against in the rental market.'[51] A 2018 survey revealed that 44 per cent of landlords were less likely to let to those without British passports and 53 per cent were less likely to rent to someone with time-limited permission to stay in the UK, even if they had the right to rent.[52] The outcome is a rental market in which it 'takes BME people and migrants up to twice as long to find a home to rent as a white British person'.[53] As one NGO objected, '[t]he Government hasn't considered the concerns of landlords who don't want to become border guards.'[54] While prejudice toward migrants and ethnic minority citizens is hardly new, the threat of sanctions further inclines landlords to discriminate.

[47] Immigration Act 2014, s 23.

[48] Amending Immigration Act 2014, s 33A.

[49] Immigration Act 2016, Explanatory Notes (n 38), s 39.

[50] Nor does the Home Office collect statistics on removals of those disqualified following right to rent checks: Noora Mykkanen and Tom Simcock, *The Right to Rent Scheme and the Impact on the Private Rented Sector* (Residential Landlords Association 2018) 13.

[51] Mayor of London/London Assembly, 'The "Right to Rent" Scheme and Racial Discrimination within the Private Rental Sector' (22 March 2017) <https://www.london.gov.uk/questions/2017/1749> accessed 16 November 2021.

[52] ibid 9; Richard Ekins, 'The High Court's "Right to Rent" Decision is a Travesty' (*The Spectator*, 2 March 2019) <https://www.spectator.co.uk/article/the-high-court-s-right-to-rent-decision-is-a-travesty> accessed 16 November 2021.

[53] Note, BME refers to Black and Minority Ethnic people. Mayor of London/London Assembly (n 51) 19; The Joint Council for the Welfare of Immigrants, 'Right to Rent' (*JCWI* 2020) <https://www.jcwi.org.uk/right-to-rent> accessed 16 November 2021.

[54] The Joint Council for the Welfare of Immigrants (n 53).

Where landlords seek to avoid sanction by discriminating against those whom they believe to be foreign nationals, these tenants fall prey to unregulated, unsafe, and otherwise substandard housing.[55] In 2019, the Joint Council for the Welfare of Immigrants (JCWI) brought a legal challenge that led to a High Court ruling that the right to rent scheme was unlawful on the grounds it had a 'disproportionately discriminatory effect', even though it had 'little or no effect' on the control of immigration.[56] The ruling was controversial because it exacerbated existing constitutional tensions around the role of the judiciary, particularly in the realm of human rights. In the press, one critic deplored the judgment as an 'unavoidably political one of whether the right to rent scheme was justified', which was 'not a fit question for a court to decide' and regretted the tendency of 'courts to stray into the political realm'.[57] This reaction is symptomatic of a growing legal dispute about state sovereignty and judicial power: some criticise 'interventionism' by judges in the parliamentary prerogative to determine policy,[58] while others insist that judicial review is essential to ensure accountability and uphold the rule of law.[59]

In 2020, the government challenged the right to rent decision, and the Court of Appeal upheld the Home Secretary's appeal.[60] The Court did not deny that, as a result of the scheme, 'those who had a right to rent, but did not have British passports ... were the subject of discrimination on the basis of their actual or perceived nationality'.[61] However, it found such discrimination to be 'proportionate to the legitimate aim' of identifying unlawful migrants and therefore held the scheme was justified.[62] Significantly, the Court held that 'any discrimination is exclusively that of landlords as private citizens for which the state bears no responsibility'.[63] It elaborated that, '[a]lthough the Scheme requires them to perform checks ... that does not make landlords agents of the state for these purposes: they engage in discrimination in implementing a statutory scheme as private citizens'.[64] The Court's finding that landlords carrying out border checks do so not as agents of the state and therefore the government is not responsible for their decisions, raises the obvious question: in whose name do they act? If landlords are not acting as agents of the state, it is unclear in what capacity and with what standing they carry out immigration checks. To argue, as the Court did, that if, 'landlords are choosing to discriminate in the way suggested then

[55] David Bolt, *An Inspection of the 'Right to Rent' Scheme* (HMSO 2018) <https://assets.publishing.service.gov.uk/government/uploads/system/uploads/attachment_data/file/695273/An_inspection_of_the_Right_to_Rent_scheme.pdf> accessed 16 November 2021.

[56] *R (on the application of Joint Council for the Welfare of Immigrants) v SSHD* [2019] EWHC 452 (Admin) [123].

[57] Ekins, 'The High Court's "Right to Rent" Decision is a Travesty' (n 52).

[58] Policy Exchange, 'Judicial Power Project' <https://judicialpowerproject.org.uk/> accessed 16 November 2021.

[59] Owen Bowcott, 'UK Needs Judges to Limit Government Power, Says Lord Kerr' *The Guardian* (London, 19 October 2020)<https://www.theguardian.com/law/2020/oct/19/uk-needs-judges-to-limit-government-power-says-lord-kerr> accessed 16 November 2021.

[60] *SSHD v Joint Council for the Welfare of Immigrants* [2020] EWCA Civ 542.

[61] ibid [66].

[62] ibid [151]; Richard Ekins, 'The Court of Appeal's Powerful "Right to Rent" Judgment' (*The Judicial Power Project*, 4 May 2020) <https://judicialpowerproject.org.uk/the-court-of-appeals-powerful-right-to-rent-judgment/> accessed 16 November 2021.

[63] *SSHD v Jount Council* (n 60) [80].

[64] ibid [148]. The JCWI immediately announced their intention to take their appeal to the Supreme Court.

they are not acting within their postulated "authority" at all'[65] leaves unanswered the question of on whose authority landlords impose right to rent checks. If the authority of landlords to check immigration status is uncertain, surely so too is their standing to demand that tenants furnish their passports. This uncertainty leaves the legitimacy of the entire scheme in question.

The discriminatory impact of right to rent checks has rendered migrant access to housing more difficult, leaving many in precarious shelter or homeless. Yet, the imperatives of immigration control have also made border guards of individuals working with rough sleepers or volunteering for homeless charities. Outreach workers for some of the largest UK homeless charities, including Thames Reach and St Mungo's, have been implicated in immigration control, sharing information about rough sleepers, and even carrying out joint street patrols with Immigration Enforcement (IE) teams.[66] Here too the courts have intervened.

In 2017, following an action for judicial review, the High Court in *Gureckis*[67] found that rough sleeping was not an 'abuse' of EU freedom of movement rights and held that the Home Office policy of detaining and removing rough sleepers was discriminatory and unlawful. Although the judgment led to the halting of joint IE patrols with homeless charities, data sharing between charity workers and the state continued, in 2018, under a new government initiative, the Rough Sleeping Support Service (RSSS). The Home Office attempted to refute claims that charity workers 'were "secretly" sending rough sleepers' personal information to the Home Office' and denied that the Service was 'designed to undertake enforcement action', but acknowledged that immigration enforcement 'may be considered on a case-by-case basis'.[68] Continued reliance on charity workers sharing information about rough sleepers without consent led the rights organisation Liberty to brand the RSSS, 'a secret scheme to turn homelessness outreach workers into border guards, oxymoronically called the "Rough Sleeping Support Service" '.[69] In the view of Liberty and other rights organisations, the RSSS was an initiative designed 'to co-opt ... charities into the delivery of immigration control'.[70]

Here again, the question of whether charity workers acted independently or as agents of the state was contested. Problematic protocols dispensed with the requirement for charity workers to secure consent to share personal information with RSSS on the dubious grounds that they were engaged in 'carrying out a specific task in the public interest laid down by law. The task in question would be delivering immigration

[65] *SSHD v Joint Council* (n 60) [163].

[66] Liberty, *A Guide to the Hostile Environment* (n 45) 51 <https://www.libertyhumanrights.org.uk/issue/report-a-guide-to-the-hostile-environment/> accessed 30 May 2022.

[67] *Gureckis, R (on the Application Of) v SSHD* [2017] EWHC 3298 (Admin) [106], [113]–[114].

[68] Home Office, *Factsheet: Rough Sleeping Support Service* (Home Office 2019) <https://homeofficemedia.blog.gov.uk/2019/07/10/factsheet-rough-sleeping-support-service/> accessed 16 November 2021.

[69] Liberty, 'How the Home Office is Turning Homeless Workers into Border Guards' (*Liberty*, 12 July 2019) <https://www.libertyhumanrights.org.uk/issue/how-the-home-office-is-turning-homeless-workers-into-border-guards/> accessed 16 November 2021.

[70] Public Interest Law Centre, 'Rough Sleeping Support Service and Migrant Rough Sleeper Rights' (*PILC*, 25 September 2019) <https://www.pilc.org.uk/news/story/rough-sleeping-support-service-and-migrant-rough-sleeper-rights/> accessed 16 November 2021.

controls.'[71] Designating information sharing as a 'public task' evaded the need for consent and yet undermined the privacy rights of rough sleepers. It prompted Liberty to declare, '[i]f any document more aptly demonstrates the breadth of Home Office ambition to turn everyone in society into agents of immigration enforcement, we have yet to see it.'[72] However, the primary concern of the homeless charity St Mungo's was less that their workers were entangled in immigration control, and more with the serious 'reputational risk' this imposed on their organisation.[73]

In 2020, following critical media scrutiny, the RSSS was relaunched with a new stipulation that charities should henceforth secure 'fully informed consent' by requiring rough sleepers to sign a form that acknowledged deportation as a possible outcome before they consented to receiving help. The new consent form states that 'the service is not intended to identify or locate immigration offenders', but blandly notes the 'possibility that you may be required to leave the UK.'[74] Emphasising the vulnerability of rough sleepers, one barrister observed, '[t]he person giving them this form is not someone who has Home Office or Border Force written on their tabard. It is somebody who they've turned to for help.'[75] The Home Office rejoinder that, '[t]he purpose is to resolve their status and identify any additional support they may need'[76] does little to conceal the fact that volunteers and charity workers are thereby rendered complicit in triggering a process that may lead to deportation.

In sum, while landlords making 'right to rent' checks have been held to act solely as 'private citizens', by contrast, homeless charity workers sharing information with RSSS are deemed to be engaged in a 'public task' on behalf of the state. Why the question of whether individuals engaged in border controls are acting as private citizens or as agents of the state attracts such inconsistent responses remains unclear. One cynical but plausible answer is that the state seeks either to assert its authority or to disassociate itself by outsourcing border control to private actors expediently according to the vested interests at stake. Whatever the case, the result is further to blur the lines between public and private exercise of border controls.[77]

[71] Liberty, 'Home Office Rough Sleeping Support Service Information Sharing Proposal' FOI MGLA290519-3560 (26 June 2019) <https://www.pilc.org.uk/wp-content/uploads/2019/09/MGLA290519-3560-FOI-response.pdf> accessed 16 November 2021.

[72] Liberty, 'How the Home Office is Turning Homeless Workers into Border Guards' (n 69).

[73] Liberty, 'Email Communication from St Mungo's to the Home Office (03 May 2019)' FOI MGLA290519-3560 (26 June 2019) <https://www.pilc.org.uk/wp-content/uploads/2019/09/MGLA290519-3560-FOI-response.pdf> accessed 16 November 2021.

[74] Mark Townsend and Aaron Walawalkar, 'Home Office Revives Plan to Deport Non-UK Rough Sleepers' *The Guardian* (London, 27 March 2021) <https://www.theguardian.com/uk-news/2021/mar/27/home-office-revives-plan-to-deport-non-uk-rough-sleepers> accessed 16 November 2021.

[75] ibid.

[76] Liberty, 'Home Office Signs up Charities to Scheme that could Lead to Deportation of Rough Sleepers' (27 March 2021) <https://libertyinvestigates.org.uk/articles/home-office-signs-up-charities-to-scheme-that-could-lead-to-deportation-of-rough-sleepers/> accessed 16 December 2021.

[77] For further discussion of statist and non-statist accounts of border control, see Thorburn, in this volume.

V From the Hostile Environment to the Compliant Environment

The Hostile Environment was a major factor in the ongoing scandal concerning treatment of the 'Windrush generation' of Commonwealth immigrants who had arrived in the UK before the 1970s, and who had the right to live in the UK, but lacked documentation to prove it. Failings in Home Office data and other egregious errors led many of the Windrush generation to suffer exclusionary practices and, in at least sixty-three documented cases, wrongful deportation after decades living and working in the UK.[78] Public outrage that longstanding UK residents were threatened with deportation without adequate notice or capacity to contest the decision,[79] was intensified by the fact that delegating immigration checks to private citizens made it impossible to assess the true impact of the policy or the number of individuals adversely affected.[80] Public outcry prompted the government to commission an independent review,[81] and the then Home Secretary, Sajid Javid, to promise a 'fairer, more compassionate' immigration system.[82]

In 2018, the UK government announced a shift to the 'Compliant Environment', acknowledging that the term 'hostile' was 'unhelpful and … does not represent our values as a country'.[83] Journalist Laura Hood observed, '[t]he latest change in language from "hostile" to "compliant" aimed to detoxify policies that are reaching deeper and deeper into everyday life, drawing ordinary people into the roles of border guards.'[84] Although the move to talk of 'compliance' appears to be significant, the term is ubiquitous in immigration control, and it is doubtful how much this rhetorical shift changes in practice.[85] While sustained protests brought an end to Immigration Enforcement

[78] House of Lords Library, *Research Briefing: Impact of 'Hostile Environment Policy Debate on 14 June 2018'* (House of Lords Library 2018) <https://lordslibrary.parliament.uk/research-briefings/lln-2018-0064/> accessed 16 December 2021; Aliverti, *Policing the Borders within* (n 19) ch 6.

[79] Home Affairs Committee (n 17) 21.

[80] Baroness Williams of Trafford acknowledged, 'it is not possible for the Government to accurately estimate the number of individuals who have been impacted by these measures' <https://www.parliament.uk/written-questions-answers-statements/written-question/lords/2018-04-23/HL7145> accessed 16 November 2021.

[81] Wendy Williams, *Windrush Lessons Learned Review* (HC 2020, 93) <https://assets.publishing.service.gov.uk/government/uploads/system/uploads/attachment_data/file/876336/6.5577_HO_Windrush_Lessons_Learned_Review_LoResFinal.pdf> accessed 16 December 2021.

[82] Amelia Gentleman, 'Sajid Javid Plans "Fairer, More Compassionate" Immigration System' *The Guardian* (London, 6 June 2018) <https://www.theguardian.com/uk-news/2018/jun/06/sajid-javid-plans-fairer-more-compassionate-immigration-system> accessed 16 December 2021.

[83] Dulcie Lee, 'Javid Ditching "Hostile" was Wise, but "Compliance" won't Humanise the Home Office' (*New Statesman*, 1 May 2018) <https://www.newstatesman.com/politics/2018/05/sajid-javid-home-secretary-office-compliant-hostile-environment> accessed 16 December 2021.

[84] Georgie Wemyss, '"Compliant Environment": Turning Ordinary People into Border Guards' (*The Conversation*, 20 Nov 2018) <https://theconversation.com/compliant-environment-turning-ordinary-people-into-border-guards-should-concern-everyone-in-the-uk-107066> accessed 16 December 2021.

[85] In 2020, a public inquiry into the hostile environment policies and their compliance with the public sector equality duty (under s 31 of the Equality Act 2006) was launched by the Equality and Human Rights Commission, *Assessment of Hostile Environment Policies* (EHRC 2020) <https://www.equalityhumanrights.com/en/inquiries-and-investigations/assessment-hostile-environment-policies> accessed 16 November 2021.

officials' access to NHS non-clinical personal data in 2018,[86] health workers are still required to check the immigration status of those seeking hospital care.[87] Elsewhere, practices of 'everyday bordering' continue to require employers, landlords, bank officials, and charity workers to verify immigration status in their daily interactions with prospective employees, tenants, clients, and the general public.[88] The claim that the ending of the Hostile Environment constituted an important 'cultural change'[89] is undermined by the fact that ordinary citizens remain subject to wide-ranging obligations to police immigration status.[90]

Although the Compliant Environment suggests willing acquiescence, it is enforced by draconian consequences for non-compliance. Private individuals, by virtue of their role or profession, are still required to identify and report possible illegal immigrants or face civil proceedings, or even prosecution and punishment. Migrants too must fulfil reporting requirements, furnish passports and papers on demand, and conform to other strictures imposed by a complex array of immigration laws. Official promises of a 'more compassionate' approach[91] mask the exclusionary impact of the multiple micro-hurdles that a citizen army of border guards must place in the path of those whose only wish is to comply. In December 2020, for example, new immigration rules gave officials discretion to refuse or cancel permission to remain in the UK 'where ... a person has been rough sleeping',[92] a move that provoked protests, not least for its failure to acknowledge the widespread loss of jobs and homes during the COVID-19 pandemic. Rather than ushering in a less antagonistic approach to immigration, the Compliant Environment fails on its own terms; sold as enabling greater conformity with immigration laws, it has made it more difficult for migrants to regularise their status, not less.

VI Implications for the Rule of Law and Civil Peace

The co-option of private citizens as agents of immigration control raises fundamental questions about the exercise of state sovereign power at the border and beyond—first, concerning *accountability* and *transparency*. Co-opting citizens as border guards may allow for more effective, economical immigration control but it achieves efficiency by circumventing the constraints of regulation and accountability that limit and guide

[86] Including protests by Doctors of the World, Docs not Cops, and the National AIDS Trust.

[87] Peter Pannier, 'NHS Data-sharing U-turn is Welcome—But More to do to Scrap the 'Hostile Environment' (*Open Democracy*, 1 May 2018) <https://www.opendemocracy.net/en/ournhs/data-sharing-u-turn-is-welcome-but-more-to-do-to-scrap-hostile-environment-in-n/> accessed 16 December 2021.

[88] Wemyss (n 84).

[89] Caroline Nokes (Minister for Immigration), HC Deb 12 July 2018, col 1119 <https://www.theyworkforyou.com/debates/?id=2018-07-12b.1112.5#g1117.0> accessed 16 November 2020.

[90] Ashworth (n 27).

[91] Peter Walker, 'Priti Patel Promises "Compassionate" Home Office after Windrush Scandal', *The Guardian* (London, 21 July 2020) <https://www.theguardian.com/uk-news/2020/jul/21/priti-patel-promises-compassionate-home-office-after-windrush-scandal> accessed 16 November 2021.

[92] Rules 9.21.1 and 9.21.2 in *Statement of Changes to the Immigration Rules* (HC 2020, 813) <https://assets.publishing.service.gov.uk/government/uploads/system/uploads/attachment_data/file/928751/CCS001_CCS1020373376-001_Statement_of_changes_in_Immigration_Rules_-_HC_813__PRINT_.pdf> accessed 16 December 2021.

the conduct of state actors. Venue shopping is a well-known means of seeking a more propitious legal environment in which to achieve policy goals; delegating police powers to private citizens acting in the community is another such example.[93] Co-opting citizens as informers spins the immigration surveillance web throughout civil society, but the promotion of 'remote control' immigration policy[94] detaches liability from state officials, freeing them of responsibility for the decisions of third-party actors. Regulatory oversight, reporting requirements, and scrutiny of public officials is largely lost when discretionary decision-making passes to private citizens.[95] Their low visibility combines with extensive discretion to obscure how citizens make immigration checks, against whom, and on what grounds. The difficulty of establishing how citizens exercise their powers raises the risk that rules are inappropriately, or over-extensively, applied.

Secondly, outsourcing has occurred with little regard for *fairness* and *impartiality*. The state seems largely indifferent to the knowledge, capacity, competence, or motivation of private citizens to perform their immigration duties justly and lawfully. There are no background checks, training, or accreditation, and little guidance to ensure citizens are equipped to undertake the tasks assigned. In consequence, discriminatory attitudes, overt prejudice, and unconscious bias may incline citizens to act against those who simply appear 'foreign'. Citizens fearful of sanctions for non-compliance may discriminate by relying on crude indicators of accent, appearance, or family name to refuse tenancies and employment to a larger population of 'visible minorities'[96] than those who are formally the targets of immigration laws. Some citizens, motivated by hostility to migrants as undeserving of access to housing, social, or healthcare services, take the opportunity to overcomply. Others evade reporting obligations by resorting to informal, extralegal arrangements that offer few protections, and promote a clandestine market in illegal employment, housing, and other services. Illicit migrants, those yet to regularise their status, and even those lawfully resident, risk being denied healthcare; or consigned to unregulated jobs in conditions barely distinguishable from modern slavery; or housed in substandard, unsafe accommodation. These divergent practices of overcompliance and evasion compound the wider tendency of the Compliant Environment to foster social division and inequality.

Thirdly, co-option has profound implications for *citizenship*. Enlisting the public in policing immigration has been said to enhance qualities of citizenship, instil civic responsibility and civic values, and 'to recuperate the coherence of citizenship and nationhood'.[97] But, as Aliverti observes, although it 'conveys expectations about the duties that come with being a good citizen—including the active cooperation in law enforcement' and appeals to ideas of social cohesion, it does so 'by mobilizing the exclusionary side of citizenship'.[98] Citizen compliance is secured by threat of sanctions

[93] Virginie Guiraudon and Gallya Lahav, 'A Reappraisal of the State Sovereignty Debate: The Case of Migration Control' (2000) 33 Comparative Political Studies 163, 177.

[94] ibid 185.

[95] Chacón (n 22) 9.

[96] Düvell, Cherti, and Lapshyna (n 26) 20.

[97] James Walsh, 'Report and Deport: Public Vigilance and Migration Policing in Australia' (2020) 24(2) Theoretical Criminology 276, 278.

[98] Aliverti, 'Enlisting the Public in the Policing of Immigration' (n 9) 226.

rather than any attempt to engender a positive commitment to state immigration policy. No wonder that, rather than embracing their role as 'active citizens', Düvell and colleagues found that 'employers and landlords have developed diverse practices to prevent detection and have to some extent become resilient to the threat of enforcement actions'.[99] Enlisting individuals may be an attempt to responsibilise citizens to engage in practices of control and to collaborate with state enforcement officials.[100] However, punishing failure to comply promotes an environment prone to suspicion and fear, not only for those formally targeted but also those citizens tasked with enforcement, many of whom are themselves from minority backgrounds.

Fourthly, outsourcing migration controls to citizens undermines *social trust* well beyond irregular migrants to all whose appearance, accent, or name raises doubts about their status.[101] Wary of immigration restrictions and regulations, some landlords and employers make discriminatory decisions that compound existing mistrust of migrants and foreigners. Obligations on lecturers and teachers to monitor student activities and report class attendance to immigration authorities undermines the trust of students, which is so essential to their education.[102] Similarly, co-opting charity workers to report homeless foreigners to immigration authorities radically erodes trust among society's most vulnerable communities, with serious adverse consequences for the welfare of rough sleepers and for public health—a fact made stark during the COVID-19 pandemic.[103] Generally, tasking citizens with duties to identify and report irregular migrants has the effect of exacerbating wider communal distrust of aliens and outsiders.[104]

Finally, a damaging consequence of mobilising 'categorical suspicion'[105] against migrants is their *marginalisation*, which in turn inhibits their democratic engagement, and undermines social harmony and civil peace. One study reported concerns that 'irregular migrants might avoid health services, which means that contagious diseases could remain untreated which also represents a threat for society'.[106] These prescient comments had serious implications during the COVID-19 pandemic. To make migrants, whatever their legal status, especially in already marginalised, vulnerable migrant and minority communities, wary of accessing public health services undermines state efforts to contain the virus.[107] The tangible harms inflicted on health, welfare, and

[99] Düvell, Cherti, and Lapshyna (n 26) 12.

[100] Pat O'Malley, 'Responsibilization' in Alison Wakefield and Jenny Fleming (eds), *The Sage Dictionary of Policing* (SAGE 2009) 276–78.

[101] Ana Aliverti, *Policing the Borders within* (n 19) 133 and *passim*.

[102] Karen Hodgson and others, 'Checks on Students Undermine Trust' *The Guardian* (2 March 2014) <https://www.theguardian.com/education/2014/mar/02/checks-on-students-undermine-trust> accessed 16 November 2021.

[103] Louise Casey and Niamh Mohan, 'It's Taken the Coronavirus Crisis for People to see Rough Sleeping for the Public Health Emergency it is' (*KCL News Centre*, 6 April 2020) <https://www.kcl.ac.uk/news/its-taken-the-coronavirus-crisis-for-people-to-see-rough-sleeping-for-the-public-health-emergency-it-is> accessed 16 November 2021.

[104] Barbara Hudson, 'Punishing Monsters, Judging Aliens: Justice at the Borders of Community' (2006) 39(2) Australian & New Zealand Journal of Criminology 232, 239; Andrew Ashworth and Lucia Zedner, *Preventive Justice* (OUP 2014) 226.

[105] Richard Ericson, *Crime in an Insecure World* (Polity 2007) 71.

[106] Düvell, Cherti, and Lapshyna (n 26) 20.

[107] ibid 21.

education provision exacerbate social divisions created by outsourcing 'everyday security'.[108] As Vaughan-Williams observes, mobilising citizens 'constitutes a new form of generalised borderwork whereby "good" subjects are constantly on the look-out for "suspicious" or "risky" subjects'.[109] Enlisting citizens as informers and gatekeepers creates a 'climate of suspicion'[110] that only increases the difficulties faced by non-citizens. Far from creating a more benign, compassionate milieu, the Compliant Environment raises the risk of non-compliance, and compounds the problem of 'making people illegal'.[111]

VII Conclusion

What are the implications of outsourcing border control for citizenship and state sovereignty? Does co-opting private individuals as border guards extend state power over its citizens and enhance state sovereignty?[112] Is 'governing at a distance' a more efficient tool of regulatory governance unfettered by democratic accountability?[113] Or is it better understood as delegating the state's sovereign right to police to private citizens, who act largely beyond state oversight and control? Outsourcing to private firms is subject to powerful, though scarcely infallible, legal regulation and contract terms that specify standards and enforce adherence. By contrast, outsourcing to private citizens lacks effective regulatory oversight, is enforceable only by sanction, and cedes control to a far greater extent. As Walsh observes of the Australian 'dob-in' scheme, the state, '[i]n summoning citizens to govern others ... authorizes dobbers to wield the state's sovereign powers to classify, decide, and exclude',[114] such that 'the sovereign state is no longer the sole executor of territoriality, but one, albeit critical, actor in a patchwork of practitioners'.[115]

The implications for state sovereignty are complicated by the fact that the question of whether citizen border guards are agents of the state or independent actors is contested, and the assumption that private citizens derive their authority from the state has been challenged in the courts. The Court of Appeal's finding that landlords are 'private individuals',[116] whose discriminatory application of statutory 'right to rent' checks cannot be imputed to the state, has led some to suggest that the case

[108] Adam Crawford and Steven Hutchinson, 'Mapping the Contours of "Everyday Security": Time, Space and Emotion' (2016) 56(6) The British Journal of Criminology 1184, 1190 ff.

[109] Nick Vaughan-Williams, 'Borderwork beyond inside/outside? Frontex, the Citizen–detective and the War on Terror' (2008) 12(1) Space and Polity 63, 64.

[110] ibid 68.

[111] Dauvergne (n 16).

[112] David Garland, 'The Limits of the Sovereign State: Strategies of Crime Control in Contemporary Society' (1996) 36(4) British Journal of Criminology 445; Georg Menz, 'Neo-liberalism, Privatization and the Outsourcing of Migration Management' (2011) 15(2) Competition and Change 116.

[113] David Osborne and Ted Gaebler, *Reinventing Government: How the Entrepreneurial Spirit is Transforming the Public Sector* (Penguin 1992).

[114] A 'dobber' is 'a person who secretly tells someone in authority that someone else has done something wrong' <https://dictionary.cambridge.org/dictionary/english/dobber> accessed 16 December 2021; Walsh (n 97) 285.

[115] Walsh (n 97) 278.

[116] *SSHD v Joint Council* (n 60) [148].

involved unwarranted 'political evaluation' by judges of immigration policy set by Parliament.[117] Allegations of judicial overreach seek to limit the scope of judicial power and purport to uphold parliamentary sovereignty. However, a more persuasive view is that the question of upon whose authority citizen border guards act is not a political matter beyond the jurisdiction of the courts, but a legal one that goes directly to state sovereignty. If citizen border guards do not derive their standing from the state, nor act as its agents, but act independently as private citizens, then the outsourcing of border control surely engages and diminishes state authority to police its sovereign territory.

How private citizens perceive their responsibilities, on what grounds they apply checks, and when and why they evade these duties remains little known, although it appears that fear of sanctions inclines some to be overly vigilant or outright discriminatory. In consequence, outsourcing to private citizens has had the effect of extending border checks well beyond their ostensible target of undocumented migrants to all who appear 'foreign'. By assigning responsibility to private agents who lack professional training and expertise, and who are largely unregulated, the state not only cedes power, but it also undermines its own legitimacy. Against claims that state power is enhanced or extended by enlisting private agents who can police immigration more flexibly, cheaply, and efficiently,[118] this chapter has suggested that in deploying private citizens as border guards, the state has significantly ceded dominion over its ultimate prerogative to determine who has access to citizenship. Outsourcing border control to private individuals undermines state sovereignty, delegitimises its authority, and far from enhancing efficiency has created a system lacking in the basic prerequisites of good governance, all of which is injurious to social trust, mutual tolerance, and civil peace.

References

Aliverti A, 'Enlisting the Public in the Policing of Immigration' (2015) 55(2) British Journal of Criminology 215

— —, *Policing the Borders within* (OUP 2021)

Andersson R, 'Profits and Predation in the Bioeconomy of Border Controls' (2018) 30(3) Public Culture 4139

Ashworth A, *Positive Obligations in the Criminal Law* (Hart 2013)

— — and Zedner L, *Preventive Justice* (OUP 2014)

Bosworth M, 'Border Control and the Limits of the Sovereign State' (2008) 17(2) Social and Legal Studies 199

— — and Guild M, 'Governing through Migration Control' (2008) 48 British Journal of Criminology 703

Chacón JM, 'Privatized Immigration Enforcement' (2017) 52 Harvard Civil Rights–Civil Liberties Law Review 1

Crawford A and Hutchinson S, 'Mapping the Contours of "Everyday Security": Time, Space and Emotion' (2016) 56(6) British Journal of Criminology 1184

[117] Ekins, 'The Court of Appeal's Powerful "Right to Rent" Judgment' (n 62).

[118] Oztig (n 5).

Dauvergne C, *Making People Illegal: What Globalization Means for Migration and Law* (CUP 2008)
Düvell F, Cherti M, and Lapshyna I, *Does Immigration Enforcement Matter? Irregular Immigrants and Control Policies in the UK* (COMPAS University of Oxford 2018)
Ericson R, *Crime in an Insecure World* (Polity 2007)
Garland D, 'The Limits of the Sovereign State: Strategies of Crime Control in Contemporary Society' (1996) 36(4) British Journal of Criminology 445
Guiraudon V and Lahav G, 'A Reappraisal of the State Sovereignty Debate: The Case of Migration Control' (2000) 33 Comparative Political Studies 163
Home Affairs Committee, *Immigration Policy: Basis for Building Consensus: Second Report of Session 2017–19* (HC 500, 2019)
Home Office, *Operation Vaken: Evaluation Report* (Home Office 2013)
Hudson B, 'Punishing Monsters, Judging Aliens: Justice at the Borders of Community' (2006) 39(2) Australian & New Zealand Journal of Criminology 232
Huysmans J, *The Politics of Insecurity: Fear, Migration and Asylum in the EU* (Routledge 2006)
Infantino F, *Outsourcing Border Control: Politics and Practice of Contracted Visa Policy in Morocco* (Palgrave Macmillan 2016)
James A, 'The Practice of Sovereign Statehood in Contemporary International Society' (1999) 47(3) Political Studies 457
Lahav G, 'Immigration and the State: The Devolution and Privatization of Immigration Control in the EU' (1998) 24 Journal of Ethnic and Migration Studies 675
Lazarus L, 'Positive Obligations and Criminal Justice: Duties to Protect or Coerce?' in Zedner L and Roberts JV (eds), *Principles and Values in Criminal Law and Criminal Justice: Essays in Honour of Andrew Ashworth* (OUP 2012)
Leerkes A, Bachmeier JD, and Leach MA, ' When the Border is "Everywhere": State-level Variation in Migration Control and Changing Settlement Patterns of the Unauthorized Immigrant Population in the United States' (2013) 47(4) Immigration Migration Review 910
Liberty, *A Guide to the Hostile Environment* (Liberty 2019)
Mantouvalou V, 'The UK Modern Slavery Act 2015 Three Years on' (2018) 81(6) The Modern Law Review 1017
Menz G, 'Neo-liberalism, Privatization and the Outsourcing of Migration Management' (2011) 15(2) Competition and Change 116
Mykkanen N and Simcock T, *The Right to Rent Scheme and the Impact on the Private Rented Sector* (Residential Landlords Association 2018)
O'Malley P, 'Responsibilization' in Wakefield A and Fleming J (eds), *The Sage Dictionary of Policing* (SAGE 2009)
Osborne D and Gaebler T, *Reinventing Government: How the Entrepreneurial Spirit is Transforming the Public Sector* (Penguin 1992)
Oztig LI, 'Rethinking Sovereignty: The Implications of the Role of Private Security Companies in the Prevention and the Regulation of Unauthorized Flows' (2020) 33(3) Cambridge Review of International Affairs 330
Parmar A, 'Arresting (Non)Citizenship: The Policing Migration Nexus of Nationality, Race and Criminalization' (2020) 24(1) Theoretical Criminology 28
Philpott D, 'Sovereignty' in *Stanford Encyclopedia of Philosophy* (Stanford Press 2003)
Rumford C, 'Citizens and Borderwork in Europe' (2008) 12(1) Space and Polity 1
Stageman DL, 'The Punishment Marketplace: Competing for Capitalized Power in Locally Controlled Immigration Enforcement' (2019) 3(3) Theoretical Criminology 394
Thorburn M, 'Reinventing the Nightwatchman State' (2010) 60 University of Toronto Law Journal 425

Torpey JC, *The Invention of the Passport: Surveillance, Citizenship and the State* (CUP 2018)
Vasanthakumar A, 'Privatising Border Control' (2018) 38(3) Oxford Journal of Legal Studies 411
Vaughan-Williams N, 'Borderwork beyond inside/outside? Frontex, the Citizen–detective and the War on Terror' (2008) 12 Space and Polity 63.
Walsh J, 'Report and Deport: Public Vigilance and Migration Policing in Australia' (2020) 24(2) Theoretical Criminology 276
Weber L, *Policing Non-citizens* (Routledge 2013)
— —, Wilson A, and Wise J, 'Cops and Dobbers: A Nodal Cartography of Onshore Migration Policing in New South Wales' (2013) 46(1) Australian & New Zealand Journal of Criminology 32.
Zedner L, 'Security, the State and the Citizen: The Changing Architecture of Crime Control' (2010) 13(2) New Criminal Law Review 379
— —, 'Is the Criminal Law only for Citizens? A Problem at the Borders of Punishment' in Franko Aas K and Bosworth M (eds), *The Borders of Punishment: Migration, Citizenship, and Social Exclusion* (OUP 2013)

Cases

SSHD v Joint Council for the Welfare of Immigrants [2020] EWCA Civ 542
Gureckis, R (On the Application of) v SSHD [2017] EWHC 3298 (Admin)
R (on the application of Joint Council for the Welfare of Immigrants) v SSHD [2019] EWHC 452 (Admin)

Legislation

Immigration Act 2014, s 23.
Immigration Act 2016, sch 7.

12
The Digitalisation of Border Controls and their Corporate Actors

Didier Bigo

I Introduction

This chapter focuses on the dematerialisation of physical border controls through the digitalisation of border entry processes. It aims to contribute to critical studies of borders and surveillance by demonstrating that remote policing and identity control are not new. To understand their beginnings, it is necessary to go back at least to the early days of the Schengen Information System (SIS 1) and analyse its transformation from a border control tool into a series of preventive policing tools for authentication, identification, automated detection of potential fraud and the production of watch lists on a transnational scale.[1] The chapter also highlights the role corporate actors specialising in data systems have played in designing and implementing the integration of data management into border security. I argue that these private actors are neither simply marginal players, nor pure technicians at the service of security professionals and national governments.

The vision of task delegation keeping sovereign decisions intact in public hands cannot hold in this field of digitalisation of security. On the contrary, corporate actors have been the driving force since the 1990s, in building the data 'highways' that have emerged across the Global North, and especially inside the European Union (EU), for information exchange between security professionals. Working with their partners—who were familiar with computer systems as well as being law-enforcement officers—computer (IT) systems corporate specialists planned some of the features that have changed the way border security is now conceptualised and delivered. These groups of individuals had different backgrounds and statuses, but their trajectories converged towards a specific ambition: to reframe local border management into integrated data management (labelled 'IDM'). From this aim has emerged a field that is transversal to both the US and the EU, and which has its own characteristics, but whose transnational links are very strong in terms of infrastructures and social use of digital technologies of surveillance and control. This field of practice has given birth to dominant positions by actors that I call a 'transnational guild of data managers and IT systems

[1] Evelien Brouwer, *Digital Borders and Real Rights: Effective Remedies for Third-country Nationals in the Schengen Information System* (Brill 2008).

Didier Bigo, *The Digitalisation of Border Controls and their Corporate Actors* In: *Privatising Border Control*.
Edited by: Mary Bosworth and Lucia Zedner, Oxford University Press. © Didier Bigo 2022.
DOI: 10.1093/oso/9780192857163.003.0013

engineers', which differs from traditional internal security bureaucracies and involves corporate knowledge of digital surveillance management.[2]

In the first part, the chapter will therefore show that remote policing and border surveillance is an old practice, but that its implementation differs from before as the digitalisation of controls delocalises the places of control, reinforces large-scale surveillance, and often privileges preventive logics over evidence-gathering or face-to-face border checks. In many scholarly articles which describe these evolutions of policing at a distance, the terminology of assemblage has gained ground to explain the complexity of the situation, the role of public–private partnerships in the process of de-assembling/re-assembling of the state,[3] and the crucial importance of multi-positioned actors (whether individuals or agencies) who destabilise, by their habitus and trajectories, the traditional dualist categories of public and private,[4] civil and military, and material and digital. In a more Marxist vein, some have also used the label of a border 'apparatus' to examine the role of a private industry that profits from the detention of foreigners, and from electronic walls and biometric identifiers.[5] Both science technologies and society (STS) and Marxist authors point to the importance of studying the specific trajectories of different social forces and the places they inhabit, as well as their previous practices regarding coercion, violence, state secrecy, and forms of effective freedom (thought, opinion, and movement) in order to understand the processes of transformation induced by digitalisation of security beyond borders. Nevertheless, these two approaches can also lead one to see only the alliances, similarities, and continuities between the dominant actors, and to merge them under one general category (neo-liberal managers, surveillance capitalism, and racial capitalism) with the effect of deflating the responsibilities of those specifically in charge instead of analysing their inner struggles around the different ways of organising security practices at borders.

Of course, from these different strands of research, important analyses concerning the impact of technologies on the daily routines of border guards exist for the North American, Australian, and EU cases,[6] but they rarely touch on the organisation of

[2] Didier Bigo, 'Sociology of Transnational Guilds' (2016) 10 International Political Sociology 398 <http://ips.oxfordjournals.org/content/10/4/398> accessed 16 January 2017; Didier Bigo, 'Adjusting a Bourdieusian Approach to the Study of Transnational Fields' in Christian Schmidt-Wellenburg and Stefan Bernhard (eds), *Charting Transnational Fields: Methodology for a Political Sociology of Knowledge* (Routledge 2020); Christian Schmidt-Wellenburg and Stefan Bernhard (eds), *Charting Transnational Fields: Methodology for a Political Sociology of Knowledge* (Routledge 2020).

[3] Rita Abrahamsen and Michael C Williams, 'Security beyond the State: Global Security Assemblages in International Politics' (2009) 3(1) International Political Sociology 1; EN Beck, 'The Invisible Digital Identity: Assemblages in Digital Networks' (2015) 35 Computers and Composition 125; Rita Abrahamsen and Anna Leander, *Routledge Handbook of Private Security Studies* (Routledge 2015).

[4] Bosworth and Singler, in this volume.

[5] Claire Rodier, *Xénophobie Business* (La Découverte 2012); Gregory Feldman, *The Migration Apparatus* (Stanford University Press 2020).

[6] Matthias Leese, 'Exploring the Security/Facilitation Nexus: Foucault at the "Smart" Border' (2016) 30(3) Global Society 412 <https://www.tandfonline.com/doi/full/10.1080/13600826.2016.1173016> accessed 19 January 2019; Karine Côté-Boucher, 'Smart Borders? Customs, Risk Targeting, and Internal Politics in a Border Agency' in Stacey Hannem, Carrie Sanders, and Christopher Schenider (eds), *Security and Risk Technologies in Criminal Justice: Critical Perspectives* (Canadian Scholars Press Inc 2019) 225–253; Julien Jeandesboz, 'Justifying Control: EU Border Security and the Shifting Boundaries of Political Arrangement' in Raphael Bossong and Helena Carrapico (eds), *EU Borders and Shifting Internal Security* (Springer 2016).

digital technologies as such (with the exception of Akkerman).[7] Thus, while the proliferation of so-called smart borders has been critically studied,[8] and while many evaluation reports have shown the limits of these technologies, the critique has focused more on the potential and actual social effects they imply concerning accountability, transparency, and human behaviour than on the process itself and the path dependency it may generate. Thus, while the consequences of these transformations are analysed in detail, the global transnational landscape of the 'system of systems' of these interoperable technologies and the number of participants in this electronic surveillance by dematerialised eyes are still a map of archipelagos within uncharted waters, where only a few institutional islands emerge, but where the knowledge is still rudimentary concerning the 'oceanic' flows of private companies, industries, and the myriad of practitioners who work closely together to produce these systems of systems; to collect data, store and organise them for different profiles, and resell them for different purposes. All these activities impact on the practices and conceptualisations of border controls. Building on Mathiesen's 2000 research,[9] which was one of the most detailed analyses of this early period of the process of 'globalisation of control', describing the Schengen Information System, I analyse here the delinkage between borders and controls, due to this digital globalisation, via a field approach, in the Bourdieusian sense. By doing so, this chapter hopes to repoliticise these developments concerning the emergence of a specific craft of security data management whose effects are less a way of achieving technical interoperability and enabling the detection of terrorist or illegal migrant suspects than a possibility for data analysts and systems engineers working for private firms to influence public decision-making power in respect of risk analysis and to challenge traditional visions of sovereignty at the borders. This impact of a stratum of specialists in charge of transnational police data highways, who have de facto subordinated the specific traditional stakes of border controls to their own overall strategy of developing preventive tools for data analytics via artificial intelligence, has led to (partially) unintended consequences. The potential replacement of personnel at the borders with remote data analysis tends to dehumanise border controls and to create a structural indifference on the fate of refugees, beyond current Frontex scandals of collusion with Libyan criminals wearing border guards' uniforms. Smart borders do not generate equal treatment and protection but even more suspicion, surveillance, and exclusionary practices than human controls.

[7] Mark Akkerman, *The Business of Building Walls* (Transnational Institute 2019) <https://www.tni.org/files/publication-downloads/business_of_building_walls_-_full_report.pdf> accessed 28 November 2021.

[8] Elspeth Guild and others, *An Analysis of the Schengen Area in the Wake of Recent Developments* (CEPS 2016) <https://www.ceps.eu/ceps-publications/analysis-schengen-area-wake-recent-developments/> accessed 28 November 2021; Médéric Martin-Mazé, 'Report: The Power Elite of Security Research in Europe: From Competitiveness and External Stability to Dataveillance and Societal Security' (2020) 6(1–2) International Journal of Migration and Border Studies 52; Médéric Martin-Mazé and Sarah Perret, 'Designs of Borders: Security, Critique, and the Machines' (2021) 6(3) European Journal of International Security 278 <https://www.cambridge.org/core/journals/european-journal-of-international-security/article/designs-of-borders-security-critique-and-the-machines/8DB8A6640CA79355650EE731EE4F5455> accessed 14 July 2021.

[9] Thomas Mathiesen, *Siste Ord Er Ikke Sagt. Schengen Og Globaliseringen Av Kontroll* (Pax Forlag 2000) 113.

Until now, this guild of data managers and systems engineers has rarely been studied in detail, except through the specific prism of a 'European war on migration', in which a defence-surveillance industrial complex is building physical, maritime, and virtual 'walls' (TNI reports, Fortress Europe blogs). My own research is based on the results of the FP7 and Horizon 2020 grant-funded projects in which I have participated, enhanced by archival research, detailed findings of the European Commission reports, and my own participation in reporting for the European Parliament.[10] From this background, I slightly disagree with the common framing in terms of a 'war machine', building 'electronic walls' blocking, stopping, and even killing people, as digitalisation of borders is based on the principle of 'letting people move', often presented as freedom of movement. But what have been called 'smart borders' are different from the principle of 'free movement'. They often involve a form of movement under permanent surveillance, as travellers forget that by delivering their data in advance they have allowed dataveillance by machines tracing their data doubles and checking them like objects at the point of 'delivery'.

The lack of physical checks during travel and the speed of this travel do not constitute a form of freedom, but a convenient way of accepting surveillance. So 'permitting mobility' works differently from stopping people and from the image of walls. Most people crossing borders accept the situation through the illusion that they are free because they are not stopped and checked as frequently as before. On the other hand, a small minority of travellers are under 'supplementary investigations' and blocked on the bases of poorly validated suspicions. This digitalisation of border security is therefore not identical to a military strategy of deterrence and combat; it is a 'ban-opticon' producing the othering of minorities and the normalisation of majorities that (in)security professionals implement.[11] It is a strategy of predictive

[10] Methodological note: after the FP7 research programme SOURCE, an informal group of researchers shared their different personal archives. Some were transcriptions of the early negotiations around Schengen, shedding light on some of the concerns raised at the time regarding 'compensatory measures', and the (un)desirable and technological solutions. They were completed with interviews and sessions of collective discussion after the colloquium '30 Years of Schengen' in 2015 organised by King's College London and CEPS-Brussels. A paper by Christina Oelgemöller, Leonie Ansems de Vries, and Kees Groenendijkhas has already been published: 'The Crafting of a Paradox: Schengen inside and out' (2020) 6(1–2) International Journal of Migration and Border Studies 7. Didier Bigo, Emma McCluskey, Elspeth Guild, and Federica Infantino have also contributed to the group, especially on the last-mentioned topic. Within this group, Didier Bigo, with the help of some professionals trainers of local trainers in police and border guard schools, carried out interviews with, and/or submitted questionnaires to, some of the first technicians of the companies involved at the beginning of Schengen. They asked for anonymity, including the names of their companies, as they were a very small group. In total, using the snowball effect strategy, we carried out more interviews (twenty-three in total) with their successors, and some who had entered into other groups such as the GoP (a group of personalities, composed of twenty-eight people set up in 2004 by DG Enterprise and DG Research for the EU Research & Development program in global security); ESRAB (European Security Research Advisory Board, which replaced the GoP in 2005, after it was extended to eighty-four people; and ESRIFF (the European Research and Immigration Forum, which followed ESRAB in 2007, consisting of sixty-five personalities and 600 experts of member states). This chapter is informed by these documents and interviews. See also the research of Martin Mazé and Sarah Perret, *The Power Elite of Security Research in Europe* (forthcoming 2023).

[11] Didier Bigo, 'Globalized-In-Security: The Field and the Ban-opticon' in Naoki Sakai and Jon Solomon (eds), *Translation, Biopolitics, Colonial Difference* (University of Hong Kong Press 2006) 109–156; Didier Bigo, 'Globalized (In)Security: The Field and the Banopticon' in Didier Bigo and Anastassia Tsoukala (eds), *Terror, Insecurity and Liberty: Illiberal Practices of Liberal Regimes after 9/11* (Routledge 2008)

policing based on detection of anomalies via algorithms, intelligence, and remote surveillance.[12]

This chapter focuses on the eu-LISA agency, which is officially small and was only created to provide a long-term solution for the operational management of large-scale IT systems, but which is also a de facto nexus of power for all agents straddling the public and private sectors, and who design the tools of the other agencies (Europol and Frontex), transforming by their action the way security is both framed and changed into a commodity.[13] It is this security commodity that the companies working for the eu-LISA agency are integrating, like many other 'objects', into the so-called data revolution of artificial intelligence.

II Sociogenesis of Policing at Distance: Sovereignty and Digitalisation

The interest in border controls and the control of foreigners by police officers, in addition to the forces in charge of passports and visas, is consubstantial with the beginning of national police forces in the nineteenth century,[14] while the development of bureaucracies issuing travel documents is even older.[15] The differentiation of the border guard profession from the military and police has, for some time, reinforced the idea of physical borders as symbols of entry into another state, often protected by a no man's land. The connection between sovereign narratives and border controls in a nationalist context has been crucial for politicians, despite the world's economic transformations, and the intensity and speed of the travel of goods, money, ideas, and people.

The terminology of sovereign borders, linked with right-wing narratives considering flows as a change to the identity of those living for a long time in a specific territory, is not the right depiction of reality; it is more a fantasy, or a mask allowing people to believe that, by erecting new walls and controls, the state can regain power alone, and afar from the international systems of states and the world economy.[16] Recent

10–48; Marie-Laure Basilien-Gainche, 'Leave and Let Die: The EU Banopticon Approach to Migrants at Sea' in Violeta Moreno-Lax and Efthymios Papastavridis (eds), *'Boat Refugees' and Migrants at Sea: A Comprehensive Approach* (Brill 2016) 327–350.

[12] Claudia Aradau and Tobias Blanke, 'Governing Others: Anomaly and the Algorithmic Subject of Security' (2018) 3(1) European Journal of International Security 1 <https://www.cambridge.org/core/product/identifier/S2057563717000141/type/journal_article> accessed 19 January 2019; Bonnie Sheehey, 'Algorithmic Paranoia: The Temporal Governmentality of Predictive Policing' (2019) 21 Ethics and Information Technology 49 <https://www.scopus.com/inward/record.uri?eid=2-s2.0-85056888956&doi=10.1007%2fs10676-018-9489-x&partnerID=40&md5=3388d8a852deb1e7b72fc60910f3af7f> accessed 28 November 2021; Didier Bigo, 'Sécurité Maximale et Prévention? La Matrice du Futur Antérieur et Ses Grilles' in Barbara Cassin (ed), *Derrière les grilles: sortir du tout évaluation* (Mille et Une Nuits 2013) 111–138.

[13] Lucia Zedner, *Security: Key Ideas in Criminology* (Routledge 2009).

[14] Gérard Noiriel, 'Chapitre 1—L'identification des Personnes' in Crettiez X and Piazza P (eds), *Du Papier à la Biométrie: Identifier les Individus* (Presses de Sciences Po 2006) 171–188.

[15] John C Torpey, *The Invention of the Passport: Surveillance, Citizenship and the State* (CUP 1999); Federica Infantino, 'The Politics of Management' in Federica Infantino (ed), *Schengen Visa Implementation and Transnational Policymaking: Bordering Europe* (Springer 2019) 125–154.

[16] Conor Gearty, *On Fantasy Island: Britain, Europe, and Human Rights* (OUP 2016).

outbreaks of ultra-patriotic (right-wing nationalist) narratives have reinforced this idea of a link between border and sovereignty, even if, as explained by Wendy Brown, the vision of protecting the country with electronic walls is more a sign of a 'waning' of sovereignty than a sign of reclaiming this sovereignty in the face of a global world.[17] This waning is the central element which leads to two crucial evolutions. First, the development of a border theatre where the different governments are happy to show that they brutalise unwelcome people at the borders in a false hope of deterring them. Second, the development of digital forms of surveillance—less coercive but more present than traditional security—by tracing the data doubles of people from their decision to travel to their arrival. This evolution towards digital surveillance creates a chasm between an apparent depoliticisation of security as a technical issue and a de facto political move in which bureaucrats and corporate actors decide about the effective travel measures and short-term migration rules: a sign of the ambiguous relationship between sovereignty, security, politics, and borders. Paradoxically, this technicisation of security gives state leaders and politicians more freedom to develop their own narratives on border policing, clearly disconnected from practice, by organising a political spectacle aimed at mobilising, within their political parties, the anxieties and uneasiness of an electorate in search of law and order, but without seeking to effectively regulate the long-term movement of foreigners. From the mid 1980s onwards, the strategy of transforming political choices concerning freedom and its limits in democracies into a technical debate on the best solutions for effective security has led, in many countries and at the institutional level of the EU, to the creation and multiplication of groups and subgroups of 'experts'. These European, and sometimes international groups have collaborated transnationally to develop more knowledge exchange, more information sharing, and thus more electronic data and the vision of a data 'container', accumulating as much electronic data as possible (including but not limited to personal data) allowing them to filter who travels.

Thus, politics has not disappeared. Rather, it has been displaced into bureaucratic networks and private corporate interests, the latest of which links border security to digital 'solutions'. The digital 'solutions' put in place have hardly ever been questioned and, on the contrary, they have been extended beyond the area, and have also been developed nationally by the opponents to this Schengen area of freedom of movement like the UK. The construction of a surveillance industry under the label of civil security has therefore developed silently with little criticism. How was this possible? How have countries like Sweden, for example, been able to develop such an industry while keeping the image of a peacebuilder? It is still difficult to answer these questions empirically. Nevertheless, some partial records of the discussions in the subgroup committees between 1985 and 1990 are now available after thirty years of silence, and they are illuminating about the discussions and objectives of that time.[18]

[17] Wendy Brown, *Walled States, Waning Sovereignty* (Zone Books/MIT Press 2010).

[18] A paper issued from the research described in n 10 has already been published: Oelgemöller, Ansems de Vries, and Groenendijk (n 10).

A The Schengen Agreements and the SIS-SIRENE Innovations

The Schengen Agreement (Schengen I) of 14 June 1985 regulated traffic between the Benelux countries, Germany, and France, while endorsing freedom of movement as a means of transforming the Common Market into an EU project. The principle of free movement of persons for all inhabitants of those countries that were ready to move in this direction was accepted. Nevertheless, negotiations continued after the signing of the 1985 text to resolve what the German minister of the interior saw as a risk of the free circulation of criminals. Specific subgroups were set up to draft the agreement of 1990. The linking of crime/terrorism with the international mobility of (certain) persons and the development of border control technologies were thus concomitant with the opening-up introduced by this rather confidential document.[19]

Within the various subgroups that aimed to create a convention—eventually signed as the Convention Implementing the Schengen Agreement (Schengen II) five years later in June 1990—a key subcommittee was called the 'Horizontal Group', as it crossed all areas of terrorism, crime, and migration, analysing ways of collaboration and introducing ideas of new technologies, beyond fax machines. At the beginning, it was only a small group of specialists from a few private companies linked to government authorities and even a few police officers with knowledge of computer systems who were involved in the development of a Schengen Information System or 'SIS' (competing at that time with another project called EIS—European Information System).[20] According to some of the practitioners, their different companies avoided centralising technology due to their concerns over a federalist view of the EU; in so doing they integrated politics into their technical designs. The German company Siemens teamed up with a Franco-Belgian-American company Honeywell Bull to form a consortium for the hardware of the SIS, while Steria (which would become later SopraSteria), a computer systems company of French origin, but widely distributed in Europe, developed specific software and data architecture. While the national defence industries were present in the competition to build the IT system, in the early 1990s they considered EU internal security to be too small a market. As a result, small start-ups challenged the traditional defence companies such as Thales or Finmeccanica (now Leonardo) and produced 'lighter' technologies adapted to police budgets; but this changed in the 2000s as we shall see.

The reason for emphasising these origins is that some of these early corporate players are still in the consulting business today and are influential beyond border management. This history is full of individual continuities masked by changes of companies and by mergers or the acquisition by large companies of smaller ones (for example, the creation of the DIS of Thales through the acquisition of a small company, or the financial merging of Sopra and Steria, and so on). Some of these 'pioneers', as they call themselves, explained during interviews that they regularly met among themselves and with their 'stakeholders' in specific subgroups, appreciating their diversity of nationalities but their technical homogeneity. They 'felt at home' and said

[19] Guild and others (n 8); Oelgemöller, Ansems de Vries, and Groenendijk (n 10).
[20] Didier Bigo and others (eds), *The Routledge Handbook of Critical European Studies* (Routledge 2020).

they were 'surprisingly free' to work, because the stakeholders could not give them a clear vision of what they wanted, except for basic arguments about the danger of centralisation if centralisation favoured the European Commission over the national ministries of interior. For thirty years, from the 1990s onwards, they have been in various colloquia and groups of 'personalities', a terminology later validated by the European Commission for setting up the first series of calls on internal security led by DG Research and DG Enterprise.[21]

As a result of these struggles over speed, capacity, price, and ease of use for end users, the first SIS consisted of a central technical node, C-SIS, based in Strasbourg, which did not contain any information but had the capacity to connect the various national databases where data were stored. The complete architecture included, in addition to the local SIS and C-SIS, the so-called SIRENE mechanisms, which allowed the national magistrates delegated to the 'additional information required at national entry' ('airne' or 'sirene') to assist law enforcement agents in querying other national authorities in order to identify suspects through requests for additional information. As Thomas Mathiesen and Statewatch revealed, the (then) confidential Sirene manual explained how to organise the operational links between the aliens databases and the police databases on criminals. Thus, even at its origins, the SIS-SIRENE was not only about border controls but was created with the aim of raising additional suspicions of criminality if persons were foreigners, migrants, or asylum seekers. While it was not an example of crimmigration as such, to the extent that the creation of criminal or administrative laws against foreigners was not involved, it was nevertheless a microprocess of (in)securitisation transferring logics applied to tackle serious criminality to petty illegalities.[22] This technological, digital system has helped to create a continuum of (in)security between anti-terrorist and anti-immigration practices,[23] generating discussions in critical security studies and immigration studies about its breadth and depth.[24]

In fact, the division into national markets did not work, and transnational companies played a key role in introducing innovations on the 'proactive' possibilities of digital applications. Corporate computer scientists, who were less mathematicians working on algorithms than systems engineers, became valuable, and many of them have, in the course of their careers, crossed the boundaries between the public and private sectors. Together, these IT system specialists with experience in security issues were mainly in control of the technical design and understood each other, but the traditional police and border organisations were nevertheless adamant about certain objectives, notably the speed of the system, which they saw as *the* symbol of efficiency. Very soon the question of the validity of the digital 'revolution' came to a halt and the interconnection of computers appeared to be the only solution to unify the geographical space of the growing number of Schengen countries. All the experts stated that,

21 J Peter Burgess, *Handbook of New Security Studies* (Routledge 2010).

22 Mathiesen (n 9).

23 Didier Bigo, 'Terrorisme, Drogue, Immigration: Les Nouvelles Figures de l'insecurite en Europe' (1995) 30(70) Revue Internationale d'Action Communautaire 43; Jef Huysmans, 'The European Union and the Securitisation of Migration' (2000) 38(5) Journal of Common Market Studies 751.

24 Mary Bosworth and Mhairi Guild, 'Governing through Migration Control: Security and Citizenship in Britain' (2008) 48(6) British Journal of Criminology 703.

without high-speed connections, the goal of control of people at the borders was not possible across such a large area. On arrival at external borders, checks on passengers had to be compatible with the imperative of not slowing down the flows beyond about twenty seconds per person. Freedom of movement and control of persons were thus linked and transformed into the speed at which controls occur.[25]

B Broadening of the Schengen Area, and Resistance to Reconfiguring the SIS Design into Predictive Policing Tools

Roughly finalised in 1988 at the Palma conference, the Schengen Convention of 1990 took two additional, crucial years of reflections on the nature of the Schengen Area in relation to free movement and security issues via the SIS. Events of 1989, including the end of the Cold War and the collapse of the Soviet bloc, which resulted in the reunification of East Germany with the West and the attachment of Central and Eastern European countries to NATO and the EU, further complicated matters in terms of freedom of movement in the Schengen Area. Borders in Europe were physically moving faster than EU politicians had envisaged.[26] The logics of control were changed materially in terms of infrastructure, beginning with Germany. Thinking of borders as more mobile and fluid, and less tied to their physical dimension, became an imperative that the digitisation of data made possible. What was still a marginal issue became an absolute priority in the various meetings of the Schengen subgroups.

Remote control by digital means was no longer a potentiality; it became a common practice. The control was to be carried out upstream and downstream of the border, with the border being only the place of expression of the data gathered previously by the security forces (police and intelligence), and the place where state coercion applied more easily to foreigners (the citizen of other states), in the name of a shared territorial sovereignty around a 'space' of free movement. Telecommunication companies and national technology leaders on computer systems have grouped themselves into associations lobbying for the police and vice versa. The struggles between the Schengen countries and the European Commission came to an end, first with the adoption of the Schengen system by almost all member states, and later when the Schengen agreements became part of the third pillar of the EU.

The enlargement of the EU with ten new member states from Central and Eastern Europe was less of a technical challenge for the SIS, as reported in the press, than a struggle of visions about the future role of digital technologies. Respondents recalled that the companies in charge of the Schengen infrastructure were in favour of developing search tools in the system to give a practical dimension to the discourse on preventive crime and proactive policing. They insisted on the creation of a SIS 2, in particular with the European Commission's DG, which wanted to have more direct contacts with the United States, Canada, and Australia. Nevertheless, this reframing of the tools was too costly, and the Portuguese Presidency succeeded in destabilising

[25] Vicki Squire, *The Contested Politics of Mobility: Borderzones and Irregularity* (Routledge 2010).

[26] Gerrit Huybreghts, 'The Schengen Convention and the Schengen Acquis: 25 Years of Evolution' (2015) 16 ERA Forum 379.

the technical oligopoly of these large firms from Germany and France, but also from Spain, Italy, and even Israel. With the help of a Portuguese start-up that offered all the new (Eastern) member states a technology called 'SIS 1 for all', they won most of the market. The Portuguese company was adjusted to the same logic of limiting digitalisation to border authentication but with fast connections. 'SIS 1 for all' was designed for border control, but not for police and suspect investigation. This reversal shows that the market was not completely in the hands of the initial actors and big companies. The major companies were upset by this 'unexpected' limit to their ambitions. But the situation changed after 2001, or more precisely for the EU after 2004.[27]

III The Changing Boundaries of the Digital Security Technology Domain and the Impact of Corporate Actors

As long as the number of internal security databases was limited and they were managed directly by the structures of the EU Commission, the empowerment of the field was a concern for border security actors, but the impact was still marginal for other security professionals. Nevertheless, the logic of preventive policing integrated with digitalisation tools explains why promoters of global counterterrorism after 2004 have facilitated the expansion of the field and its importance. The multiplication of the number of databases, the facilitation of access to them for various purposes, and the speed of connections, became key factors for the development of surveillance tools during the travel process. Corporate actors specialising in IT systems infrastructures met regularly with security professionals until a certain 'craft' shared by different people emerged and pushed them to try to institutionalise their relationships (see later). Specific grants, specific arenas, and specific agencies for IT systems have maintained this *'entre-soi'* around the idea of interoperability of IT systems designed for internal security, even if they are now challenged by the attractiveness of their own field, which attracts public and private defence actors, intelligence services, and/or cybersecurity specialists.

[27] Elif Kuskonmaz and Elspeth Guild, 'Rights-based Review of Border Surveillance' in Ramona Grimbergen, Aniel Pahladsingh, and Dean Spielmann (eds), *The Charter and the Court of Justice of the European Union: Notable Cases from 2016–2018* (Wolf Legal Publishers 2019) <https://researchportal.port.ac.uk/portal/en/publications/rightsbased-review-of-border-surveillance(f4c64e48-db64-4788-8b15-353123d3ec86)/export.html> accessed 14 July 2021; Niovi Vavoula, *European Travel Information and Authorisation System (ETIAS): A Flanking Measure of the EU's Visa Policy with Far Reaching Privacy Implications* (Queen Mary School of Law Legal Studies Research Paper) (2017); Niovi Vavoula, 'Interoperability of EU Information Systems: The Deathblow to the Rights to Privacy and Personal Data Protection of Third-country Nationals?' (2020) 26(1) European Public Law 131; Didier Bigo and others, 'Analytic Report: Visualisation on Societal Security Networks in Europe' <https://researchportal.port.ac.uk/portal/en/publications/analytic-report-visualisation-on-societal-security-networks-in-europe(a17e2c3a-1059-4225-9cbb-6a1570e2f721).html> accessed 7 February 2020; Didier Bigo, 'Interoperability: A Political Technology for the Datafication of the Field of EU Internal Security?' in Didier Bigo and others (eds), *The Routledge Handbook of Critical European Studies* (Routledge 2020).

A The Proliferation of Police Data Highways: An Anti-terrorist Solution or an Institutionalisation of the IT Systems inside the Security Field?

Since the declaration of the war on terrorism and the creation of a Department of Homeland Security, the US government has been pushing hard for transatlantic information sharing, especially on air travellers (API-PNR, visa programmes, entry/exit systems, travel authorisation, and no-fly lists). It is impossible to detail the transactions of this period, but many companies found that border security, which still had a small budget compared to defence, was nevertheless the most profitable of all time. Any bold idea was funded, and the development of the Internet, as well as the acceleration of broadband in submarine cables, gave data transfer the high speed needed for 'real time' action. The European Commission welcomed the 'pioneers' of the SIS and from then on EU money flowed in to develop this infrastructure linking the so-called external borders with internal controls. After the Madrid bombing in 2004, the EU pushed European Union Military Staff (EUMS) companies to create specific joint ventures in order to achieve economies of scale and compete with the US 'civil security' industry. In a few years, SIS became SIS2, transforming the use of SIS; SIS was complemented by a VIS (Visa Information System) and became interconnected with other databases (see below). The creation of multiple databases protected by the legal principle of purpose limitation, in terms of access, which was at the heart of the functioning of the area of freedom, security, and justice over the previous twenty years, has been reversed. Access to law enforcement authorities (police, border guards, criminal justice, and even administrative bodies (prefectures)) has been granted for almost all databases. This has radically changed practices and legal implications.[28]

In the mid 2000s, therefore, a series of 'internal' security databases in Europe proliferated and their interoperability was planned. But it nevertheless took ten years, until 2015, to give them some semblance of a legal basis, while their links, and interoperability tools, were similarly slow to implement. Connecting heterogeneous databases on consumer preferences, entry checks, and travel authorisations with specific categories of people wanting or needing to travel, in pursuit of the aim of turning this IT architecture into preventive policing tools, took time. The creation of these 'police data highways' by data analysts and systems engineers who simultaneously specialised over the years in border control and surveillance technologies, and in preventive and predictive tools based on the algorithmic claim to anticipate the future, has changed the dynamics of border control. The border controls are now increasingly relying on digital information arriving before people reach the border and they leave border guards with a narrow margin of autonomy. Thus, although most border guards still insist that they are based at the borders and have the ultimate and sovereign right to decide who enters and who is refused entry, the development of electronic visas, specific visitor programmes, and timely access to these data highways have de facto moved the modalities of authentication, verification of documents, and pre-travel authorisations

[28] Vavoula, 'Interoperability of EU Information Systems' (n 27).

'upstream'. 'Upstream' means that sending countries are obliged to collaborate with European police forces and to prevent part of their own populations from leaving; that consulates have an important role in filtering access to travel; and, most importantly, that temporal, predictive, or at least 'on-time', decision-making, aggregating digital data from different databases, is carried out. Digitalisation allows for pre-transit or in-transit surveillance of a specific identified person, and for some potential offences, the unidentified individuals are also tested against (semi-automatic) risk profiles based on categorical suspicion by association.

The interest in the avatar or 'data double' of suspicious persons and its *ex ante* identification even before the control of persons is becoming routine in airports, with Passenger Name Record (PNR), and new entry/exit systems. Of course, these territorial and digital logics have been combined, and this is why data management continues to use the territorial borders of the state as a place to extract (with a certain degree of discretion) data from people who want to travel; but their priority was and is to build algorithms on criteria of dangerousness, and to calculate scores on a scale of risk and suspicion, suggesting that individuals who have not yet done anything but resemble criminals are likely to be suspected a priori.

These changes were not made at random. They have been orchestrated by the 'new' eu-LISA agency, which has integrated into its staff the previous networks of corporate systems engineers, IT architecture designers, and public agents coming from proactive policing sectors.[29] This is why this European agency looks like the 'camera obscura' lens of the entire landscape of internal and border security. Certainly, information is still very fragmented and confidentiality—even secrecy—is very high. Nevertheless, more recently, some elements of its role have been studied by researchers.

B The Creation of eu-LISA, and the Role of Corporate Actors in the Making of a Specific Guild of Data Managers

Created in 2011 after a lapse of five or six years, and only operational on 1 December 2012, the eu-LISA agency presents its role as the implementation of EU justice and home affairs policies through the management of large-scale IT systems. Eu-LISA is responsible for all the interconnections between the databases and their future developments in terms of global interoperability, but it has no power over the day-to-day management given to the users, and is bound by the different legal agreements between the countries as well as the ongoing debate on the distinctions between internal or civil security and defence.

Always downplaying their role as mere 'digital plumbers', the staff of eu-LISA has shown restraint, with only 137 people in 2019 spread over three sites: the headquarters in Tallinn, Estonia; the operational site in Strasbourg, France; and a backup site in Sankt Johann im Pongau, Austria. Officially, they claim to support the technical infrastructure used by Europol and Frontex operations, but most of the few independent

[29] Georgios Glouftsios, 'Governing Border Security Infrastructures: Maintaining Large-scale Information Systems' (2021) 52(5) Security Dialogue 452.

studies show their key role and the agency's multi-positioning.[30] This 'modesty' contrasts sharply with the self-promotion of the other agencies, be it Europol, Frontex, or Eurojust. It also explains why the public and journalists and even 'experts' ignore them. On the other hand, according to the eu-LISA interviewees, they are not technicians at the service of the other agencies, but visionaries of a future in the making through the implementation of global smart cities in smart countries via smart borders. Eu-LISA's first major operation was to establish the full implementation of SIS 2 on 9 April 2013 after more than five years of delays and complaints between the company Sopra Steria and eu-LISA, but de facto pushed by the Commission and even more so by the European Parliament's LIBE Committee. Instead of highlighting the tremendous differences between SIS 1 and SIS 2, they present SIS 2 only as a more modern system, offering additional functionalities that have come into use and which concern objectives such as border control, national security, or law enforcement. Nevertheless, they stress that operational research and the ability to process images are essential for 'police work'.[31] SIS2 has also been complemented by the Visa Information System (VIS), and access to Eurodac has been extended to all national police forces and Europol, in order to compare fingerprints taken in criminal investigations with those of asylum seekers and migrants in Eurodac. In the near future (end of 2022–2023), three new databases will be operational into the EU IT architecture. They are the European Travel and Authorisation System (ETIAS), the European Electronic System (EES), and the European Criminal Records Information System for Third Country Nationals (ECRIS-TCN). Julien Jeandesboz has described these databases and their implications for travellers in detail.[32] The most important task was nevertheless to create the 'interchange' between these 'data highways'. This work, done in close association with the corporate companies they have worked with previously, and in particular the digital company Sopra Steria, has changed everyday practices at the borders and beyond. In November 2020, Krum Garkov, executive director of eu-LISA since the creation of the agency, declared:

> Digital transformation is one of the building blocks of Next Generation EU and eu-LISA is the Agency delivering the necessary digital platforms, to justice and home affairs communities, that provide tangible benefits for EU citizens, enabling the practical implementation of one of their fundamental rights –freedom of movement.

But can we agree with this statement? Are interoperable databases the implementation of freedom of movement or an instrument of surveillance? Contrary to many traditional analyses of European studies that read the interoperability programme as being a result of the 2015 terrorist attacks and the European Commission's desire to show that on these cross-border issues between France and Belgium they were useful

[30] Multi-positionality refers to actors who are in dominant positions in different fields, cf Didier Georgakakis, 'The Historical and Political Sociology of the European Union: A Uniquely French Methodological Approach?' (2009) 7(3) French Politics 437.

[31] Akkerman (n 7).

[32] Julien Jeandesboz, 'Smartening Border Security in the European Union: An Associational Inquiry' (2016) 47(4) Security Dialogue 292. See also migration, security, surveillance in Europe Ryerson workshop 2019–under publication.

and as 'tough' as national governments, we reject the idea that they were a result of this crisis of 2015 and that they are now the best tools of protection of our freedoms. As we have seen, the interoperability project existed long before, and if the attacks in Paris and Brussels were used as a political opportunity by a group of professionals to strengthen their positions, they were not a 'fresh response to the bombings'. In a discussion that started in 2005 in the transatlantic arenas and which crystallised in 2013, before being implemented in 2017 after four years of intense debate, the full discussion on interoperability and the construction of highway interchanges was, on the contrary, reduced to the IT tools already belonging to eu-LISA.

The five tools of the Commission proposal constituted a de facto induction course towards the goal of predictive analytics, and they were presented in a specific order, starting with a single search interface; then a uniform interface protocol; thirdly, a shared biometric system; fourthly, a common identity repository; and finally, a multiple-identity detector, wanted by the Commission despite the initial reluctance of the high- level expert group to validate this last 'tool'.[33] The argument for detecting fraudulent identification was envisaged to be applied against each passenger. This extension of targets was associated, beyond fraud, with the search for overstayers via the procedures of the European exit systems, and with the control of biometric identifiers, facial recognition, and internal EU PNR for the detection of suspected 'radicalised' EU citizens. Many non-governmental organisations therefore challenged the overall logic of connecting the dots at all costs on everyone. In this ongoing struggle, the weight of corporate actors who wanted to develop a digital industry in a context of 'global war' was crucial, but it should also be read also as a competition between the EU and the US for the control of the cybersecurity market. While some key players remain, it would be wrong to see only continuities. Seniority in the field has given powerful positions to the winners of the first battles, who have been influential in the way in which so-called technical solutions have framed the imaginary of the conceivable use of databases for security reasons. These winners, such as Sopra Steria or GMV, benefited from continuous subsidies, specific calls for tenders that they managed to 'inspire', in which they had niche markets, and social recognition abroad. Nevertheless, their previous autonomy changed when the big operators of the defence industry, such as Leonardo or Thales, after 2004, and more clearly after 2015, decided to recolonise the civil security market on border infrastructures, and also on digital technologies. Thales, for example, has proposed new packages with a wide range of military and security equipment, including biometric identification systems. Border infrastructure has been the logical entry point, through the connection with military logistics (see Thales, for example), but they have also acquired specific companies to complete their 'offer' for digital border technologies tenders.

In all these transactions, the current European Organisation for Security (EOS), which is now one of the most powerful lobbying organisations and has its origins in the SIS, organises the convergence of military and digital technologies under the name of cybersecurity. In conjunction with the Frontex and Law Enforcement Agency (LEA) networks, some colloquia have been de facto informal negotiations between

[33] For more details, see Emma Mc Cluskey, 'Freedom, technology and surveillance: everyday paradoxes on the EU-Morocco border' (2020) 6(1–2) International Journal of Migration and Border Studies 115.

the military and the civil security firms, and have been the vehicle for these mergers of interests. According to Akkerman, and to give just one example:

> In 2019, Thales acquired Gemalto, a large (biometric) identity security company, for €4.8 million, integrated as its Digital Identity and Security (DIS) division. In 2017, Gemalto had purchased 3M's identity management business, which included Cogent Systems (acquired by 3M in 2010) for $850 million. Between 2000 and 2017, Cogent and 3M were returning partners in a consortium led by Sopra Steria for several large European contracts for the development and maintenance of EURODAC, VIS and SIS II. Gemalto, formerly Cogent, also provides the fingerprint identification technology for the EURODAC database.[34]

Recently, most of the major EU contracts for digital security have been awarded to just two companies: Sopra Steria for data highways and GMV for Eurosur. It is far from an open competition and it seems that the logic follows more of a 'mercantilist approach' in a 'strategic area' than that of a free market. Nevertheless, the field of digital surveillance technologies, which was almost ignored, has become more visible due to the scandals involving its end users: Europol, but also and especially, Frontex. Their actions have created a backlash against the role of digital surveillance.[35]

IV Conclusion: Security Techno-solutionism—how to Fail Successfully

Intellectually, the distinctions between digital and physical, private and public, and data-embedded knowledge and privacy, which were the last boundaries, had to be dissolved in order to achieve a form of totalisation of security through its integration in a large-scale project linking military and civilian components, and national and European space. Security is no longer a goal to be achieved, but a condition of life in modernity. Technologies invented by private companies in the civil protection and security sector, designed to combat clandestine organised violence, are being tested for use to combat crime, incivilities, illegal aliens, or even deviant non-violent behaviour. The interoperability of data related to crowd detection and composite facial recognition, behavioural anxiety detectors, operate in certain locations (often airports) and work in a systematic way to do this kind of investigation while not spending too much time in human investigation. Or, at least, it is the dream of this programme that, if it is impossible to obtain intimate knowledge of all travellers protected by privacy regulations, they nevertheless have to detect weak signals of dangerousness remotely by associations based on suspicions only.

[34] Akkerman (n 7) 37.

[35] Claudia Aradau, 'Experimentality, Surplus Data and the Politics of Debilitation in Borderzones' (2020) 27(1) Geopolitics 26 <https://doi.org/10.1080/14650045.2020.1853103> accessed 14 July 2021; Martina Tazzioli, 'What Is Left of Migrants' Spaces? Transversal Alliances and the Temporality of Solidarity' (2020) 1(1) Political Anthropological Research on International Social Sciences (PARISS) 137.

The guild of data managers and IT systems engineers have, therefore, transformed what security does and what it means. As we have seen, they do not agree with traditional security professionals and in particular with border guards. They have different appreciations of the means of achieving security and they sometimes also prioritise the most important dangers differently. They are more pretenders than heirs in the general field of security professionals, but they have the advantage that their vision is attractive to politicians and the highest levels of management in public administrations. This gives them a strong influence today on all issues where digital technologies are involved in tackling terrorism, crime, migration, and fraud.

Nevertheless, it is important for scholars to ask what legitimacy the data managers have to decide in advance on these IT infrastructures of security and then to present them as necessities. Their narrative often recognises that these technologies can fail, but they consider that they just need to be improved, not discontinued. And to convince their opponents, they often insist that the cost of investment is so great that the only solution is to continue to develop and correct the technologies,[36] a narrative of techno-solutionism already used to justify smart cities initiatives. Their practices of digital security and building data highways have not created smart ways of travel with more protection and more freedom of movement; they have used border controls to their own aims, capturing more data for the global surveillance of travellers and the people who are receiving foreigners as guests too often (VIS, ETIAS, and PNR). They have accentuated the 'ban-opticon' logic described earlier. The digital technologies they use refine their targets through more complex profiling, but they also extend the observation of the social network via a suspicion of criminality by association, and they manage to do so without major protest, as long as they do not affect the majority of people and are presented to them as a benign protection of their way of life, or the means to achieve a bright utopian future of smart borders and cities regulated by future programmes integrating artificial intelligence.[37]

References

Abrahamsen R and Leander A, *Routledge Handbook of Private Security Studies* (Routledge 2015)

— — and Williams MC, 'Security beyond the State: Global Security Assemblages in International Politics' (2009) 3 International Political Sociology 1

Akkerman M, *The Business of Building Walls* (Transnational Institute 2019) <https://www.tni.org/files/publication-downloads/business_of_building_walls_-_full_report.pdf>

Aradau C, 'Experimentality, Surplus Data and the Politics of Debilitation in Borderzones' (2020) 27(1) Geopolitics 26 <https://doi.org/10.1080/14650045.2020.1853103>

Claudia Aradau and Tobias Blanke, 'Governing Others: Anomaly and the Algorithmic Subject of Security' (2018) 3(1) European Journal of International Security 1

[36] Paul Watzlawick, *Ultra-solutions: How to Fail Most Successfully* (WW Norton & Co 1988); Evgeny Morozov, *To Save Everything, Click Here: The Folly of Technological Solutionism* (US Public Affairs 2013).

[37] Marco Marsili and José Borges, 'The European Union Artificial Intelligence Strategy' (*Zenodo*, 28 June 2021) <https://zenodo.org/record/4972574#.YaPFDC2l10s> accessed 28 November 2021; see also the new Horizon Europe security research programme: <https://ec.europa.eu/programmes/horizon2020/en/area/security> accessed 16 December 2021.

Basilien-Gainche M-L, 'Leave and Let Die: The EU Banopticon Approach to Migrants at Sea' in Moreno-Lax V and Papastavridis E (eds), *'Boat Refugees' and Migrants at Sea: A Comprehensive Approach* (Brill 2016)

Beck, EN 'The Invisible Digital Identity: Assemblages in Digital Networks' (2015) 35 Computers and Composition 125

Bigo D, 'Terrorisme, Drogue, Immigration: Les Nouvelles Figures de l'insecurite en Europe (Terrorism, Drugs and Immigration: The New Faces of Insecurity in Europe)' (1995) 30 (70) Revue Internationale d'Action Communautaire 43

— —, 'Globalized-In-Security: The Field and the Ban-opticon' in Sakai N and Solomon J (eds), *Translation, Biopolitics, Colonial Difference* (University of Hong Kong Press 2006)

— —, 'Globalized (In)Security: The Field and the Banopticon' in Bigo D and Tsoukala A (eds), *Terror, Insecurity and Liberty: Illiberal Practices of Liberal Regimes after 9/11* (Routledge 2008)

— —, 'Sécurité Maximale et Prévention? La Matrice du Futur Antérieur et Ses Grilles' in Cassin B (ed), *Derrière les grilles: sortir du tout évaluation* (Mille et Une Nuits 2013)

— —, 'Sociology of Transnational Guilds' (2016) 10 International Political Sociology 398 <http://ips.oxfordjournals.org/content/10/4/398>

— —, 'Adjusting a Bourdieusian Approach to the Study of Transnational Fields' in Schmidt-Wellenburg C and Bernhard S (eds), *Charting Transnational Fields: Methodology for a Political Sociology of Knowledge* (Routledge 2020)

— —, 'Interoperability: A Political Technology for the Datafication of the Field of EU Internal Security?' in Bigo D, Diez T, Fanoulis E, Rosamond B, and Stivachtis YA (eds), *The Routledge Handbook of Critical European Studies* (Routledge 2020)

— —, Diez T, Fanoulis E, Rosamond B, and Stivachtis YA (eds), *The Routledge Handbook of Critical European Studies* (Routledge 2020)

Bosworth M and Guild M, 'Governing through Migration Control: Security and Citizenship in Britain' (2008) 48(6) British Journal of Criminology 703 <https://academic.oup.com/bjc/article-lookup/doi/10.1093/bjc/azn059>

Brouwer E, 'Digital Borders and Real Rights: Effective Remedies for Third-country Nationals in the Schengen Information System' (Brill 2008)

Brown W, *Walled States, Waning Sovereignty* (Zone Books/MIT Press 2010)

Burgess JP, *Handbook of New Security Studies* (Routledge 2010)

Côté-Boucher K, 'Smart Borders? Customs, Risk Targeting, and Internal Politics in a Border Agency' in Hannem S, Sanders C, and Schenider C (eds), *Security and Risk Technologies in Criminal Justice: Critical Perspectives* (Canadian Scholars Press Inc 2019)

Feldman G, *The Migration Apparatus* (Stanford University Press 2020)

Gearty C, *On Fantasy Island: Britain, Europe, and Human Rights* (OUP 2016)

Georgakakis D, 'The Historical and Political Sociology of the European Union: A Uniquely French Methodological Approach?' (2009) 7(3) French Politics 437

Glouftsios G, 'Governing Border Security Infrastructures: Maintaining Large-scale Information Systems' (2021) 52(5) Security Dialogue 452 <https://journals.sagepub.com/doi/10.1177/0967010620957230>

Guild E and others, *An Analysis of the Schengen Area in the Wake of Recent Developments* (CEPS 2016) <https://www.ceps.eu/ceps-publications/analysis-schengen-area-wake-recent-developments/>

Huybreghts G, 'The Schengen Convention and the Schengen Acquis: 25 Years of Evolution' (2015) 16 ERA Forum 379

Huysmans J, 'The European Union and the Securitisation of Migration' (2000) 38 Journal of Common Market Studies 751 <http://onlinelibrary.wiley.com/doi/10.1111/1468-5965.00263/abstract>

Infantino F, 'The Politics of Management' in Infantino F (ed), *Schengen Visa Implementation and Transnational Policymaking: Bordering Europe* (Springer 2019) <https://doi.org/10.1007/978-3-030-10647-8_5>

Jeandesboz, J, 'Justifying Control: EU Border Security and the Shifting Boundaries of Political Arrangement' in Bossong R and Carrapico H (eds), *EU Borders and Shifting Internal Security* (Springer 2016)

— —, 'Smartening Border Security in the European Union: An Associational Inquiry' (2016) 47 Security Dialogue 292

Kuskonmaz E and Guild E, 'Rights-based Review of Border Surveillance' in Grimbergen R, Pahladsingh A, and Spielmann D (eds), *The Charter and the Court of Justice of the European Union: Notable Cases from 2016–2018* (Wolf Legal Publishers 2019) <https://researchportal.port.ac.uk/portal/en/publications/rightsbased-review-of-border-surveillance(f4c64e48-db64-4788-8b15-353123d3ec86)/export.html>

Leese M, 'Exploring the Security/Facilitation Nexus: Foucault at the "Smart" Border' (2016) 30 Global Society 412 <https://www.tandfonline.com/doi/full/10.1080/13600826.2016.1173016>

Marsili M and Borges J, 'The European Union Artificial Intelligence Strategy' (*Zenodo*, 28 June 2021) <https://zenodo.org/record/4972574#.YaPFDC2l10s>

Martin-Mazé M, 'Report: The Power Elite of Security Research in Europe: From Competitiveness and External Stability to Dataveillance and Societal Security' (2020) 6 (1–2) International Journal of Migration and Border Studies 52

— — and Perret S, 'Designs of Borders: Security, Critique, and the Machines' (2021) 6 European Journal of International Security 278 <https://www.cambridge.org/core/journals/european-journal-of-international-security/article/designs-of-borders-security-critique-and-the-machines/8DB8A6640CA79355650EE731EE4F5455>

Mathiesen T, *Siste Ord Er Ikke Sagt. Schengen Og Globaliseringen Av Kontroll* (Pax Forlag 2000) (translated into English in Statewatch)

Mc Cluskey E, 'Freedom, Technology and Surveillance: Everyday Paradoxes on the EU-Morocco Border' (2020) 6(1–2) International Journal of Migration and Border Studies 115

Morozov E, *To Save Everything, Click Here: The Folly of Technological Solutionism* (US Public Affairs 2013)

Noiriel G, 'Chapitre 1—L'identification des Personnes' in Crettiez X and Piazza P (eds), *Du Papier à la Biométrie: Identifier les Individus* (Presses de Sciences Po 2006) <https://www.cairn.info/du-papier-a-la-biometrie-identifier-les-individus--9782724609891-page-29.htm>

Oelgemöller C, Ansems de Vries L, and Groenendijk K, 'The Crafting of a Paradox: Schengen inside and out' (2020) 6 International Journal of Migration and Border Studies 7

Rodier C, *Xénophobie Business* (La Découverte 2012)

Schmidt-Wellenburg C and Bernhard S (eds), *Charting Transnational Fields: Methodology for a Political Sociology of Knowledge* (Routledge 2020)

Sheehey B, 'Algorithmic Paranoia: The Temporal Governmentality of Predictive Policing' (2019) 21 Ethics and Information Technology 49 <https://www.scopus.com/inward/record.uri?eid=2-s2.0-85056888956&doi=10.1007%2fs10676-018-9489-x&partnerID=40&md5=3388d8a852deb1e7b72fc60910f3af7f>

Squire V, *The Contested Politics of Mobility: Borderzones and Irregularity* (Routledge 2010)

Tazzioli M, 'What is Left of Migrants' Spaces? Transversal Alliances and the Temporality of Solidarity' (2020) 1(1) Political Anthropological Research on International Social Sciences (PARISS) 137 <https://brill.com/view/journals/pari/1/1/article-p137_137.xml>

Torpey JC, *The Invention of the Passport: Surveillance, Citizenship and the State* (CUP 1999)

Vavoula N, *European Travel Information and Authorisation System (ETIAS): A Flanking Measure of the EU's Visa Policy with Far Reaching Privacy Implications* (Queen Mary School of Law Legal Studies Research Paper) (2017)

— —, 'Interoperability of EU Information Systems: The Deathblow to the Rights to Privacy and Personal Data Protection of Third-country Nationals?' (2020) 26 European Public Law 131 <https://www.kluwerlawonline.com/abstract.php?area=Journals&id=EURO2020008>

Watzlawick P, *Ultra-solutions: How to Fail Most Successfully* (WW Norton & Co 1988)

Zedner L, *Security: Key Ideas in Criminology* (Routledge 2009) <http://lib.myilibrary.com/?id=208467>

The Privatisation of Border Controls and the Limits of State Sovereignty

An Afterword

Ana Aliverti

I Introduction

The answer to the question of whether and how the privatisation of border controls affects state sovereignty is deceptively simple in appearance. As some scholars have argued, privatisation cedes to the private sector the monopoly of violence bestowed by the state as the core element of sovereignty and, in so doing, weakens it. Others argue that by privatising border control, the state does not surrender its powers over the exercise of legitimate violence, but rather expands its reach through the diversification and dispersion of actors and practices,[1] in what Stanley Cohen referred to as 'net-widening'.[2] In either case, the legal and normative implications of such trends are critical for both sovereignty and citizenship. The privatisation of coercive powers diminishes accountability and transparency; it subjects coercive powers to the rules of the market and creates spurious incentives for criminalisation; it augments the risks of abusive and discriminatory practices since many of those tasked with enforcement functions lack the appropriate training and expertise to carry them out; and it can heighten social fragmentation and entrench social inequalities. In examining the impact of privatisation on border controls, many scholars have rightly drawn on the literature of privatisation in the context of criminal justice given the parallels between the two institutional and legal fields.[3]

[1] See, eg Gallya Lahav, 'Immigration and the State: The Devolution and Privatization of Immigration Control in the EU' (1998) 24(4) Journal of Ethnic & Migration Studies 675; Huyen Pham, 'Private Enforcement of Immigration Laws' (2008) 96 Georgetown Law Journal 777; James P Walsh, 'Watchful Citizens: Immigration Control, Surveillance and Societal Participation' (2014) 23(2) Social & Legal Studies 237; Jennifer M Chacón, 'Privatized Immigration Enforcement' (2017) 52 Harvard Civil Rights–Liberties Law Review 1; Denise Gilman and Luis A Romero, 'Immigration Detention, Inc' (2018) 6(2) Journal on Migration and Human Security 145; Ingrid Eagly and Joanna Schwartz, 'Lexipol: The Privatization of Police Policymaking' (2018) 96 Texas Law Review 891; Daria Davitti, 'Beyond the Governance Gap: Accountability in Privatized Migration Control' (2020) 21 German Law Journal 487.

[2] Stanley Cohen, *Visions of Social Control: Crime, Punishment and Classification* (Polity Press 1985).

[3] See, eg Clifford D Shearing, 'The Relation between Public and Private Policing' (1992) 15 Crime and Justice 399; Trevor Jones and Tim Newburn, *Private Security and Public Policing* (OUP 1998); Daniel P Mears and Andrea N Montes, 'Introduction to the Special Issue on Privatized Corrections' (2019) 18(2) Criminology & Public Policy 213; John Rappaport, 'Criminal Justice, Inc' (2018) 118 Columbia Law Review 2551; Alessandro Corda and Sarah E Lageson, 'Disordered Punishment: Workaround Technologies of Criminal Records Disclosure and the Rise of a New Penal Entrepreneurialism' (2019) 60(2) The British

Ana Aliverti, *The Privatisation of Border Controls and the Limits of State Sovereignty* In: *Privatising Border Control.*
Edited by: Mary Bosworth and Lucia Zedner, Oxford University Press.
DOI: 10.1093/oso/9780192857163.003.0014

And yet, upon dissecting its many parts and subjecting them to scrupulous examination from a range of disciplinary standpoints, methodological approaches, and jurisdictions, the question and its answer get increasingly complicated, their certainties unsettled. This exercise is the hallmark of a robust intellectual enquiry. It is precisely what this volume does. This book deals with fundamental questions about the nature and legitimacy of state power in the context of globalised capitalism, and assesses its implications for entrenching social and global inequalities. I will use this afterword to outline these complexities, as richly developed throughout this book, and reflect on how studying privatisation might shed new light on our understanding of the nature of contemporary state sovereignty and governance. I will also reflect on the importance of ethnographic research to uncover these complexities. My afterword is structured into three parts in which I explore each of the critical concepts structuring the book: privatisation, border controls, and state sovereignty.

II Privatisation

I start with the notion of 'privatisation' to explore what it entails. According to the Oxford English Dictionary, it refers to 'the transfer of a business, industry, or service from public to private ownership and control'. Privatisation is often used interchangeably with 'outsourcing'—that is, the 'practice of handling over the control of public services to private companies'—although the latter is broader, admitting a wider range of practices, even within the private sector. This brief semantic analysis of a key term in this collection denotes very specific practice, which presupposes a strict differentiation between the private and the public, and some level of formal accord by the parties (including through contractual arrangements). While some of the practices covered in the volume (particularly the outsourcing of immigration detention to for-profit actors) fit squarely within this definition of privatisation, others—such as the imposition of reporting duties on citizens and the assumption of life-saving responsibilities by humanitarian organisations and private citizens—overstretch the term and demonstrate that new conceptualisations are needed to collectively understand this range of practices.

Indeed, some of these practices and relationships might be better framed as instances of pluralisation of controls, whereby the state is but one in the network of actors involved in the delivery of specific functions. Pluralisation, as the policing literature suggests, downplays the role of state as a central provider of (security) functions and hence departs normatively from a Weberian model of state sovereignty.[4] As opposed to privatisation, which demotes the normativity of state sovereignty and its monopoly on coercion, pluralisation embraces alternative forms of political and

Journal of Criminology 245; Tessa Diphoorn, *Twilight Policing: Private Security and Violence in Urban South Africa* (University of California Press 2016).

[4] Adam Crawford, 'Networked Governance and the Post-regulatory State? Steering, Rowing and Anchoring the Provision of Policing and Security' (2006) 10(4) Theoretical Criminology 449; Megan O'Neill and Nicholas R Fyfe, 'Plural Policing in Europe: Relationships and Governance in Contemporary Security Systems' (2017) 27(1) Policing and Society 1.

institutional organisation in the provision of security—more of which below. In so doing, it is more attuned to and better reflects contemporary transformations in governance, which cut across the national/global and public/private divides.

The 'privatisation' practices under analysis in this volume are varied, and have different legal, political, and institutional implications. Surely the contractual arrangements with private companies to enforce deportation orders raise distinct legal and political challenges to those arising from, for example, the outsourcing of food provision in detention centres. In a sense, public institutions and actors have relied on corporations for some time to deliver a range of services. Privatisation, outsourcing, and delegation of a range of services is far from novel. However, as the contributors rightly argue, some of the functions subject to subcontractual arrangements, particularly those involving coercive practices, deserve further scrutiny because they have potential social and legal implications.

In the specific case of the prisons and detention centres, as many scholars have shown, privatisation creates incentives to expand punitive powers, and entrenches social inequalities,[5] in what Jennifer Chacón in her chapter calls 'a mechanism of racialised capitalist extraction'. It is particularly telling that, even in countries with largely state-dominated prison estates, the imprisonment of migrants has been privatised. The case of the US, where for-profit corporations have a longstanding presence within the penal sector, provides important clues for the reasons behind this trend. Hallam Tuck in his chapter suggests that the proliferation of private prisons for foreign nationals is linked to various factors that relate to the civic and social status of those behind bars, and the political economy of punishment. Foreign-only prisons are cheaper to run because they do not offer provisions aimed at the reintegration of inmates. Crucially, the lack of citizenship works in more insidious ways with other social inequalities (including race, class, linguistic proficiency, and educational attainment) to make the detention of foreign nationals highly profitable. These structural and social factors enable corporations to operate prisons on a shoestring to 'keep people alive', which is evident in the downgraded infrastructure and caring facilities available. As sociologists of punishment have demonstrated, punishment has important material and symbolic functions for reinforcing social boundaries.[6] Prison privatisation, Tuck concludes, adds new layers to such functions by introducing an internal hierarchy within the prison based on citizenship status.

And yet, even in relation to the privatisation of immigration detention and deportation, contributors show that, far from abdicating power, in most of these contractual arrangements, the state retains a level of control over decision-making processes typical of neo-liberal governance whereby, rather than directly providing security, the state regulates the myriad of non-state actors delivering various border control 'services'.[7] Despite the extent of privatisation of immigration detention and deportation in

[5] Gilman and Romero (n 1).

[6] David Garland, *Punishment and Modern Society: A Study in Social Theory* (OUP 1990); Bruce Western and Becky Pettit, 'Incarceration & Social Inequality' (2010) 139(3) Daedalus 8.

[7] Nikolas Rose and Peter Miller, 'Political Power beyond the State: Problematics of Government' (1992) 43(2) The British Journal of Sociology 173; Nikolas Rose, 'Government and Control' (2000) 40(2) British Journal of Criminology 321; David Levi-Faur, 'The Global Diffusion of Regulatory Capitalism' (2005) 598 Annals of the American Academy of Political and Social Science 12; Crawford (n 4).

the UK, Mary Bosworth and Samuel Singler explain in their chapter that the state remains very much present during these processes and holds significant power over the oversight of private contractors' actions and decisions. In line with the 'net-widening' thesis, they argue, these practices show a dispersal of state power rather than its retreat.

Other contributions also highlight diverse relations between parties, ranging from formal or informal agreement (in the case of corporate actors and vigilante groups respectively), forced consent (by some private citizens), and outright usurpation and civil disobedience (in the case of the humanitarian interventions). This delegation or outsourcing of responsibilities creates legal challenges at times, which often dilute accountability. As Lucia Zedner explains in her chapter, even though private landlords are duty-bound to undertake immigration status checks on potential tenants, when doing so they are regarded as private citizens for the purpose of the pursuance of such duty and hence solely liable for any breaches committed during it. Without the training for exercising these checks and a clear contractual and regulatory framework to apportion civil or criminal liabilities, these new forms of delegation raise complex legal issues (and legal fictions) and, as she argues, undermine state legitimacy.

Critiques by linguists and contract lawyers notwithstanding, the collective analysis of these myriad forms of involvement by non-state actors in border control functions offers a unique opportunity to reassess the outer borders of the state and the nature of its power. Such reconceptualisation is needed, particularly given the distinctive questions and dilemmas that the exercise of border controls and its privatisation pose.

III Border Controls

The second key concept of the volume, 'border controls', presents similar complex questions. According to classical (Westphalian) conceptions of the state, territorial sovereignty is one of the core prerogatives of the state, and border control is one of the manifestations of this prerogative. Amid a rapidly globalised world, however, such power to defend the integrity of state's territory against foreign invasion has acquired a nationalistic dimension. Border controls are increasingly presented as the last bastion of state sovereignty and, particularly in relation to Northern states, as part of the state's prerogative to preserve the economic, social, and cultural survival of the nation state, which is arguably threatened by globalisation and mass migration.[8] The growing impetus to control 'the border' is thus a sign of a struggling and, as Peter Ramsay argues, in his contribution, decaying state.

Further, as many contributions in this collection point out, the contemporary configurations of the exercise of border controls have little or no relationship with the materiality of the territorial border. Such connection between state power and territory,

[8] Catherine Dauvergne, *Making People Illegal: What Globalization Means for Migration and Law* (CUP 2008); Wendy Brown, *Walled States, Waning Sovereignty* (Zone Books 2010); Katja Franko Aas, 'The Ordered and the Bordered Society: Migration Control, Citizenship and the Northern Penal State' in Katja Franko Aas and Mary Bosworth (eds), *The Borders of Punishment: Criminal Justice, Citizenship and Social Exclusion* (OUP 2013) 20–39; Vanessa Barker, *Nordic Nationalism and Penal Order: Walling the Welfare State* (Routledge 2017); Robert Koulish and Martje van der Woude (eds), *Crimmigrant Nations: Resurgent Nationalism and the Closing of Borders* (Fordham University Press 2020).

if it ever existed (we might think of European colonial expansion as a prime example of its negation), has been significantly eroded and diluted by the range of technologies that police at a distance,[9] the extraterritorial enforcement of border controls (through pre-entry controls in host countries and post-deportation arrangements),[10] and the growing networks of informants and controls within state territory.[11] Didier Bigo in his chapter made this point pristinely clear. Both the materiality of borders (walls and fences) and their 'stateness' (the bureaucratic architecture built around them) have been crucial in the production of the fantasy or myth of modern states. The proliferation of digital technologies, forming global 'data highways' and amassing huge amounts of data to scrutinise movements and filter out risky foreigners from 'bona fide travellers',[12] as both Bigo and Chacón demonstrate, have been developed, and are managed by, corporate actors with little scope for public accountability. In this context, it is worth interrogating the fantasy of hard borders policed by state guards altogether. Given the dislocation of the sites of control away from the territorial border, it might be more accurate to speak of migration controls instead of border controls. Equally, we might think of the relationship between borders and sovereignty in terms of a process. Borders, Madeleine Reeves reminds us, 'are less a simple reflection or manifestation of territorial sovereignty that is already fully formed than a site "to reflect on the *project* of territorial sovereignty"'.[13] Thus, through bordering practices, state sovereignty is continuously built, reproduced, and transformed.

Despite the parallels made with criminal justice and punishment, the exercise of power in this sphere is distinctive. As a form of sovereign power that licenses some of the most severe forms of coercion (that is, the deprivation of freedom, restrictions on the access to vital goods and services, and territorial exclusion) on individuals based on their citizenship status, the privatisation of this power presents distinctive moral and social challenges. Not only is the exercise of this power controversial, particularly given its disproportionate impact on poor and racialised groups,[14] but the power itself

[9] Didier Bigo and Elsepth Guild, 'Policing at a Distance: Schengen Visa Policies' in Didier Bigo and Elspeth Guild (eds), *Controlling Frontiers: Free Movement into and within Europe* (Ashgate 2005) 233–263; Elspeth Guild and Didier Bigo, 'The Transformation of European Border Controls' in Bernard Ryan and Valsamis Mitsilegas (eds), *Extraterritorial Immigration Control: Legal Challenges* (Brill 2010) 257–279.

[10] Bernard Ryan and Valsamis Mitsilegas (eds), *Extraterritorial Immigration Control: Legal Challenges* (Brill 2010); Leanne Weber, 'Policing the Virtual Border: Punitive Preemption in Australian Offshore Migration Control' (2007) 34(2) Social Justice 77; Mary Bosworth, 'Penal Humanitarianism? Sovereign Power in an Era of Mass Migration' (2017) 20(1) New Criminal Law Review 39.

[11] Ana Aliverti, 'Enlisting the Public in the Policing of Immigration' (2015) 55(2) British Journal of Criminology 215; Ben Bowling and Sophie Westenra, '"A Really Hostile Environment": Adiaphorization, Global Policing and the Crimmigration Control System' (2018) 24(2) Theoretical Criminology 163 ; Huyen Pham, 'When Immigration Borders Move' (2009) 61 Florida Law Review 1115.

[12] See also Katja Franko Aas, '"Crimmigrant" Bodies and Bona Fide Travelers: Surveillance, Citizenship and Global Governance' (2011) 15(3) Theoretical Criminology 331.

[13] Madeleine Reeves, *Border Work: Spatial Lives of the State in Rural Central Asia* (Cornell University Press 2014) 8.

[14] Jennifer M Chacón and Susan B Coutin, 'Racialization through Enforcement' in Mary Bosworth, Alpa Parmar, and Yolanda Vazquez (eds), *Race, Criminal Justice and Migration Control* (OUP 2018) 159–175; Alpa Parmar, 'Arresting (Non)citizenship: The Policing Migration Nexus of Nationality, Race and Criminalization' (2020) 24(1) Theoretical Criminology 28; Amanda Armenta, 'Racializing Crimmigration: Structural Racism, Colorblindness, and the Institutional Production of Immigrant Criminality' (2017) 3(1) Sociology of Race and Ethnicity 82.

is subject to heated contestation and faces a serious legitimacy deficit.[15] This deficit is felt by those tasked with border controls. As British immigration officers told me repeatedly, their everyday work exposes them to the fractured and contested politics of immigration where they are either accused of racism and xenophobia or charged with being too lenient towards migrants.[16] They are tasked with enforcing a global privilege arising from an accident of birth. As one of the very few non-privatised branches of the UK's border control apparatus, frontline immigration enforcement officers are one of the most tangible representations of the state on the streets.[17] By dint of their employment, they are subject to constant abuse and accusations of brutality and discrimination. Their profession is tainted, as they are tasked with a mandate that many sectors of society regard as unjust and illegitimate. Such mandate, far from capturing a 'public good' which is said to be best left to the state to bestow,[18] is beset with controversy and 'dirtiness'. This crucial aspect of border control might be one of the reasons why, in the British policing landscape, the police have been progressively spared the task of policing the borders within, while corporate actors have been hired to perform a wide range of distasteful and unpopular functions: from sending threatening phone messages to 'irregular migrants' to managing the immigration detention estate.

Controversy, public exposure, and stigma are not diffused or dissipated by outsourcing, though. As described by Federica Infantino in her chapter, the private guards inside British immigration detention centres reported a similar moral and political discomfort in working in those sites. Judged by the informal strategies that these guards learnt in their jobs to maintain order and placate resistance, as described by Infantino, and Bosworth and Singler (from which food to provide during deportation flights to how to speak to detainees), the task of forcing people out is emotionally and morally draining, and painful not only for detainees, but also for those executing it. Privatisation and illegalisation are said to be governmental strategies to obfuscate individual responsibility and create moral indifference. It is telling that, despite much investment by the state in these strategies, empirical research on border control workers continues to show instances of emotional distress and pain, which is evidence of the profound individual and societal ethical dilemmas involved in border controls. Understanding and galvanising such moral sentiments—and the legitimacy deficit that they expose—among officers and the wider population can be, as Emily Ryo and Ian Peacock suggest in their chapter, a critical avenue for resistance to privatisation and border controls more generally.

In her chapter, Ashwini Vasanthakumar considers another distinctive dimension of the legitimacy of state power in this context. She questions the extent to which, and

[15] Mary Bosworth, 'Can Immigration Detention Centres be Legitimate? Understanding Confinement in a Global World' in Katja Franko Aas and Mary Bosworth (eds), *The Borders of Punishment: Migration, Citizenship, and Social Exclusion* (OUP 2013) 149–165; Mary Bosworth, 'Affect and Authority in Immigration Detention' (2019) 21(5) Punishment & Society 542.

[16] Ana Aliverti, *Policing the Borders within* (OUP 2021); Ana Aliverti, 'Manufacturing Obedience: Coercion and Authority in Border Controls' (2021) Punishment & Society 146 <https://doi.org/10.1177/14624745211051320> accessed 21 December 2021.

[17] Behan Loftus, *Police Culture in a Changing World* (OUP 2009) 4.

[18] Ian Loader and Neil Walker, 'Policing as a Public Good: Reconstituting the Connections between Policing and the State' (2001) 5(1) Theoretical Criminology 9; Ian Loader and Neil Walker, *Civilizing Security* (CUP 2007).

under what conditions, the state is legitimised to exercise border control functions. Given that border controls transcend the domestic, and are directed towards non-citizens, she argues that we need a conceptualisation of legitimacy beyond the state–citizen relationship. This normative question connects to the more empirical one on the legitimacy and contested nature of border controls. Ultimately, both of these questions point to the urgency of reassessing key principles and concepts of state coercive powers in political theory, philosophy, and criminology.[19]

However, as many of the contributors have rightly argued, coercion does not exhaust the remit of border controls. Particularly under contemporary conditions, where vast regions of the world have become unliveable due to poverty, disease, climate emergencies, and wars, and border crossings are ever more precarious—to a large extent due to illegalisation and criminalisation—efforts to prevent arrivals and to enforce returns increasingly involve humanitarian interventions to save lives and provide care for vulnerable people.[20] While, as Anthea Vogl explains in her chapter, the humanitarian rationales and practices are often meant to legitimise and reinforce disciplinary and exclusionary ones, the injection of care and compassion in this sphere has important implications for our understanding of state sovereignty and the outsourcing of state functions.

It is curious that the welfare facet of state power has featured less regularly in criminological and philosophical accounts of the state, which have instead privileged, qua Hobbes and Weber, its coercive dimensions as its defining features. Historical analysis of 'the state' in countries around the world, however, suggest that such accounts are partial. In the first half of the twentieth century, the (welfare) state assumed key economic functions to limit the socially damaging nature of liberal capitalism and to empower the working classes.[21] In the UK, the welfare state sought to rebalance economic power relationships through expanding labour right protections and the liability of capital owners. As Peter Ramsay demonstrated, the growth of regulatory criminal law and its privileging of strict (or faultless) forms of criminal liability introduced during the interwar and post-war periods were very much shaped by changing ideas about (social) citizenship and the role of the state in guaranteeing minimum social rights:

> Strict liability regulatory law is therefore a means of ensuring that the burden of avoiding these risks will be borne by those most able both to bear them and to minimize them. By placing the burden where it does, the criminal law tends to make

[19] See also Arash Abizadeh, 'Democratic Theory and Border Coercion: No Right to Unilaterally Control your own Borders' (2008) 36(1) Political Theory 37; Lucia Zedner, 'Is the Criminal Law only for Citizens? A Problem at the Borders of Punishment' in Katja Franko Aas and Mary Bosworth (eds), *The Borders of Punishment: Criminal Justice, Citizenship and Social Exclusion* (OUP 2013) 40–57.

[20] Katja Franko Aas and Helene Gundhus, 'Policing Humanitarian Borderlands: Frontex, Human Rights and the Precariousness of Life' (2015) 55(1) British Journal of Criminology 1; Ana Aliverti, 'Benevolent Policing? Vulnerability and the Moral Pains of Border Controls' (2020) 60(5) British Journal of Criminology 117.

[21] In Argentina, for example, the 1950s were characterised by the strong involvement of the state in the economic market, with the substitution of imports, and the buttress of industrialisation. It also reshaped the social and economic status of the working classes, which, in turn, boosted consumption and expanded the internal market: Natalia Milanesio, *Workers Go Shopping in Argentina: The Rise of Popular Consumer Culture* (University of New Mexico Press 2013).

avoidance of these risks a business cost, and thereby tends to socialise the burden of risk. It has thereby contributed to the equalisation of the basic conditions in which people live.[22]

Although welfarism has receded in the last three decades across the world (albeit not uniformly), the repressive and protective nature of the criminal law, and the concomitant functions of the state endure.[23] Under contemporary conditions, characterised by a retraction by the state from its welfare role and the changing function of citizenship, as well as growing social hyperdiversity where the citizenship of those subject to state power cannot be presumed,[24] we need to ask whether and how this dual function of the state manifests itself and what the implications of privatisation of core state functions are. If, as Didier Fassin has argued, humanitarianism has become a form of governance of precarious lives which language 'serves both to define and to justify discourses and practices of the government of human beings',[25] it is pertinent to explore its centrality in the exercise, outsourcing, and legitimation of state power. Admittedly, as Vogl shows in her chapter, the work of non-government organisations (NGOs) in the care and control of asylum seekers in Australia—and elsewhere—differs from the core characteristics of the welfare state. Yet, she also shows that the assumption of such roles by 'humanitarian' NGOs distorts their remit and, as with the welfare state, breeds functional ambivalence resulting from the dual task of care and control of migrants.[26]

So too, humanitarian work—and its abdication by the state—can lead to very different results. In his analysis of the assumption of rescue duties by NGOs and private citizens, Valsamis Mitsilegas points out that such actions address the inaction, withdrawal, and even active obstruction of life-saving duties by the state. Private actors come to fill a void, often in blatant disobedience of state laws and practices, many of which have been ruled to be in violation of international human rights obligations. In so doing, not only do NGOs forge a more humane and universal sphere of rights and responsibilities that does not hinge on citizenship, they also cast serious doubt on the moral authority of the state and its political legitimacy. These actions, he suggests, raise issues of legitimacy which are distinct from those traditionally levelled at privatisation. The question is not that 'privatisation' is illegitimate due to the 'public' nature of the tasks being 'delegated', but because the very assumption of such tasks by private actors exposes a morally bankrupt state.

[22] Peter Ramsay, 'The Responsible Subject as Citizen: Criminal Law, Democracy and the Welfare State' (2006) 69 Modern Law Review 29, 49.

[23] Alan Bogg and Mark Freedland, 'Criminality at Work' in Alan Bogg and others (eds), *Criminality at Work* (OUP 2020) 592.

[24] Zedner (n 19).

[25] Didier Fassin, *Humanitarian Reason. A Moral History of the Present* (University of California Press 2012) 2.

[26] For a critique of penal welfarism, see Anthony Platt, *The Child Savers: The Invention of Delinquency* (Chicago University Press 1969); David Garland, *Punishment and Welfare: A History of Penal Strategies* (Quid Pro Books 2018).

IV State Sovereignty

Finally, the volume engages with the concept of state sovereignty—and more broadly with that of 'the state'. Much of the political theory and criminology scholarship discussions about the state build on specific ideas and images of it: the mighty Leviathan formed by a collection of little human beings comes immediately to mind. Such an artificial entity, either humanised in the figure of a paternal sovereign or epitomised in the 'bundle of widespread and globalized registers of governance and authority'—what Blom, Hansen, and Steputtat call 'languages of stateness'—commands authority and legitimacy.[27] Its construction as a separate domain, dissected from society, and endowed with superior capacities (omnipresence, rationality, boundedness, and impartiality) contributes to perpetuate state mythology.[28] However, as anthropologists of the state demonstrated, this idea of state sovereignty as absolute and all-encompassing is an illusion, particularly in post-colonial societies.[29] Ethnographic work on state bureaucrats has also shown that their everyday decisions are shaped not only by formal rules, but also by their moral dispositions, emotions, and subjectivities, thus constantly criss-crossing the boundaries between the official and unofficial, the personal and the impersonal.[30] By studying the state from the bottom up, ethnographers have uncovered how those at the frontlines of the state (its low-level personnel) do not just enforce state decisions, but are central in the material and symbolic construction of the 'state'. These officers are critical in making the state through their everyday work and interactions with other social actors. 'It is through such mundane activities', Gupta and Sharma explain, 'that the primacy of the state is reproduced, and its superiority over other social institutions established'.[31] The state is then conceptualised as a field where everyday practices and representations form part of its construction. Collectively, this work casts doubts on the image and idea of the state as a bounded, coherent, impersonal, disembodied, and complete entity.

[27] Thomas Blom Hansen and Finn Stepputat, 'Introduction' in Thomas Blom Hansen and Finn Stepputat (eds), *States of Imagination: Ethnographic Explorations of the Postcolonial State* (Duke University Press 2001) 5.

[28] Akhil Gupta, *Red Tape: Bureaucracy, Structural Violence, and Poverty in India* (Duke University Press 2012); Reeves (n 13); James Ferguson and Akhil Gupta, 'Spatializing States: Toward an Ethnography of Neoliberal Governmentality' (2002) 29(4) American Ethnologist 981.

[29] Thomas Blom Hansen and Finn Stepputat, 'Sovereignty Revisited' (2006) 35 Annual Review of Anthropology 295; Veena Das and Deborah Poole, 'State and its Margins. Comparative Ethnographies' in Veena Das and Deborah Poole (eds), *Anthropology at the Margins of the State* (School of American Research Press 2004) 3–33.

[30] Michael Lipsky, *Street-level Bureaucracy: Dilemmas of the Individual in Public Services* (Russell Sage Foundation 2010); Bernardo Zacka, *When the State Meets the Street: Public Service and Moral Agency* (Harvard University Press 2017); Didier Fassin (ed), *At the Heart of the State: The Moral World of Institutions* (Pluto Press 2015); Veena Das and Deborah Poole, 'State and its Margins. Comparative Ethnographies' in Mateusz Laszczkowski and Madeleine Reeves (eds), *Affective States: Entanglements, Suspensions, Suspicions* (Berghahn 2018) 3–34.

[31] Aradhana Sharma and Akhil Gupta, 'Introduction: Rethinking Theories of the State in an Age of Globalization' in Aradhana Sharma and Akhil Gupta (eds), *The Anthropology of the State: A Reader* (John Wiley & Sons 2006) 13.

The ethnographic, or 'practice', turn in the study of the state[32] is relevant for the analysis of privatisation, because it dispels myths about what the state is, and disrupts the seemingly clear boundaries between state and society, and between public and private on which much theorisation of the state in philosophy and political sciences has been built. As Malcolm Thorburn argues, the state is a distinct entity from the human beings that form it. It is endowed with specific qualities, such as non-partisanship and impartiality, that give an aura of legitimacy to its actions. On this account, the privatisation of border control functions, such as the exercise of coercion, to private actors and institutions is illegitimate, not because they are individually unfit to pursue them, but by dint of their private status. Such an argument has significant bite in light of evidence suggesting that the privatisation of prisons and detention centres has created economic incentives for their expansion. In the US, as Ryo and Peacock show, the steady increase in the immigration detention population since the early 2000s coincided with the takeover of detention centres by corporations. They suggest that both are casually linked, at least partly. A similar trend has been observed in other countries, such as the UK, where the rise in detention population since the late 1990s went hand in hand with the involvement of the security industry in various facets of immigration enforcement work.[33]

Yet, what empirical research shows is that private/individual motivations and subjectivities play a significant role in decision-making, and that such separation between the bureaucratic and institutional dimensions of the state, on the one hand, and personal, individual dimensions of those who act and speak in its name, on the other, is continually defied in practice. There is evidence that the legal and institutional lines separating private and public domains are in practice muddled: for example, private sector workers interviewed by Infantino referred to being attracted to the position of detention guards because '*you work for the government*'. The blurriness of such lines is also evident in the institutional language of the UK Home Office, which refers to the migration agency as a 'business',[34] and adopts practices and logics of the profit sector to fund its activities.[35]

The state-as-fantasy, its ideal type, also serves to measure up different versions of 'the state', as strong or weak. The monopolies on violence and territorial sovereignty are two hallmarks of strong states, and the absence of them its shadow image: the fragile state.[36] From this standpoint, the multiplicity of security providers with equal or

[32] Karine Côté-Boucher, Federica Infantino, and Mark B Salter, 'Border Security as Practice: An Agenda for Research' (2014) 45(3) Security Dialogue 195.

[33] Michael Welch and Liza Schuster, 'Detention of Asylum Seekers in the UK and USA' (2005) 7(4) Punishment & Society 397; Alice Bloch and Liza Schuster, 'At the Extremes of Exclusion: Deportation, Detention and Dispersal' (2005) 28 Ethnic & Racial Studies 491.

[34] Home Office, *UK Border Agency Business Plan April 2008–March 2011* (Home Office 2009); Home Office, *UK Border Agency Business Plan April 2009–March 2012* (Home Office 2010); Home Office, *UK Border Agency Business Plan 2011–15. Delivering our Commitments with a Smaller, More Efficient Agency* (Home Office 2011).

[35] Jon Burnett and Fidelis Chebe, 'Towards a Political Economy of Charging Regimes: Fines, Fees and Force in UK Immigration Control' (2019) 60(3) British Journal of Criminology 579.

[36] Achille Mbembe, *On the Postcolony* (University of California Press 2001) 17; James Ferguson, *Global Shadows: Africa in the Neoliberal World Order* (Duke University Press 2006) 16; Raza Saeed, 'The Ubiquity of State Fragility: Fault Lines in the Categorisation and Conceptualisation of Failed and Fragile States' (2020) 29(6) Social & Legal Studies 767 <https://doi.org/10.1177%2F0964663920906453> accessed 21 December 2021; Eva Magdalena Stambøl, 'Neo-colonial Penality? Travelling Penal Power and Contingent Sovereignty'

even superior power to that of state police in the Global South has been interpreted as a symbol of that fragility.[37] It is curious, then, that such a line of argument has not been made in relation to the contemporary proliferation of securitisation and privatisation in the Global North, a trend that has been framed through different theoretical lenses. And yet, as a number of scholars have argued, the idealisation of 'the state' and the universal image of the strong state are outdated and imperialistic. Through such constructs, as de Waal has argued, '[p]olitical science has played a role here in limiting our imagination of the possible'.[38] If such a strong state ever existed, it has been challenged by a range of contemporary developments arising from globalisation and transnationalism (including the growth of supranational governmental institutions and multinational corporations). These have given rise to new forms of governance and rule, displacing the state as supreme holder of political and economic power. Such portrayal of the modern Northern state as strong and sovereign is also inaccurate given historical evidence suggesting the importance of corporations and chartered companies in the formation and expansion of European states.[39] As Chacón explains in her chapter, if historically capitalist accumulation, racial violence and political authority are intrinsically connected in the US (through colonial expansion and slavery), we cannot understand contemporary border controls without attending to their functions for reproducing this same system of capitalist racialised extraction.

In offering alternative, non-binary, non-imperialist analytical frames to capture conceptually the empirically rich and complex nature of governance in this context, scholars have resorted to the notion of 'hybridity' and 'assemblages'. Following Homi Bhabha, the notion of 'hybridity' has been used by social scientists to designate the negotiated nature of political power and the entanglement or constellation of multiple (state and non-state) actors in the wielding of power over territory, thus avoiding the Eurocentric distinction between 'weak' or 'failed' and 'strong' states. Through the concept of 'hybrid sovereignties',[40] these scholars have questioned accepted binaries between state/non-state, legitimate/illegitimate, security/insecurity, and domestic/foreign, and demystified some states—from Lebanon to Jamaica—as failed. In dislocating the Northern state as normative, the notion of hybridity expands our

(2021) 23(4) Punishment & Society 536 <https://doi.org/10.1177%2F14624745211025745> accessed 21 December 2021.

[37] Jana Hönke, *Transnational Companies and Security Governance* (Routledge 2013). Specifically in relation to development programmes, which increasingly involve elements of border control imposed on recipients, such programmes are administered and delivered by corporations or non-profit organisations. As Hönke explains in her study on transnational security in Africa, Northern states providing development aid to African countries regard these non-state actors as more trustworthy than states, in relation to provision of security and 'good governance', in areas of 'limited statehood'.

[38] Alex de Waal, 'Power' in Veena Das and Didier Fassin (eds), *Words and Worlds: A Lexicon for Dark Times* (Duke University Press 2021) 137.

[39] Philip Stern, *The Company-state: Corporate Sovereignty and the Early Modern Foundations of the British Empire in India* (OUP 2011).

[40] Sara Fregonese, 'Beyond the "Weak State": Hybrid Sovereignties in Beirut' (2012) 30(4) Environment and Planning D: Society and Space 655; Rivke Jaffe, 'The Hybrid State: Crime and Citizenship in Urban Jamaica' (2013) 40(4) American Ethnologist 734; Simone Tholens, 'Border Management in an Era of "Statebuilding Lite": Security Assistance and Lebanon's Hybrid Sovereignty' (2017) 93(4) International Affairs 865.

imagination to other possible forms of political order, many of them fostered by colonial powers,[41] which may even be more mobile, adaptable, and resilient to the current global climate. Hybrid stateness is also more empirically accurate and analytically useful in that it acknowledges the power of neo-liberal capitalism to shape and penetrate power. The idea of the state as a political marketplace where business fuses with politics, as de Waal observes, is becoming a dominant phenomenon not only at the global margins but also at the centres of political and economic power: 'States are becoming political marketplaces, integrated across borders, dollarized, and disordered in many different ways.'[42]

This dynamic whereby political power is increasingly subject to economic bargaining blurs the lines between public and private. In the context of the security sector, as Bigo details in his contribution, the professional and institutional cultures of private and public sectors are hardly distinct, and these distinctions perish as actors constantly switch sectors and form part of the same 'global security assemblages'. This term captures the complex constellations of actors and networks, or 'geographies of power that are simultaneously global and national as well as public and private',[43] involved in the provision of security. Rita Abrahamsen and Michael Williams explained that such constellations reflect contemporary transformations in transnational governance.[44] Through such a lens, the involvement of non-state actors (from corporations to NGOs and citizens) in border control functions is not an anomaly or deviation from a supposedly universal rule—that is, the sovereign state—but is the norm. Such empirical fact may in turn lead us to rethink governance and demystify the state as supreme, bounded, impartial, and rational.

V Conclusion

To conclude, it may seem paradoxical that a volume on the privatisation of border controls tells us so much about the state and its place in broader structures of contemporary governance. In charting and subjecting to critical scrutiny the many practices through which state power is outsourced, shared, and abdicated, this volume sheds as much light on the plurality of actors involved in the exercise of state power as on the state itself. Challenging one-sided arguments on the relationship between state and capital, the authors have showed that this relationship is multifaceted (sometimes aimed at 'outsourcing failure' and depoliticising the exercise of coercion; at other times, at reducing costs and placating resistance), context specific, and far less straightforward than grand theories portray it to be. It is made much more complex when the question of border controls is added to the mix, because this exposes the

[41] See, eg the continuities drawn by Jaffe between the Maroons and the dons in colonial and contemporary Jamaica, respectively: Rivke Jaffe, 'From Maroons to Dons: Sovereignty, Violence and Law in Jamaica' (2015) 35(1) Critique of Anthropology 47.

[42] De Waal (n 38) 141.

[43] Rita Abrahamsen and Michael Williams, 'Security Privatization and Global Security Assemblage' (2011) 18(1) Brown Journal of World Affairs 171, 173. See also Paul Higate and Mats Utas (eds), *Private Security in Africa: From the Global Assemblage to the Everyday* (Bloomsbury Academic 2017).

[44] Abrahamsen and Williams (n 43).

distinct moral, political, and legal dilemmas of state power in a transnational world order. These dilemmas reveal, at once, a failed and decadent state, whose moral and political legitimacy is on the line.

We need to place these practices and developments within a wider global frame. While most chapters focused on the Global North, other scholars[45] have studied these processes in the South, where the privatisation of violence has long been prescribed and imposed by northern donors and international organisations in return for development funds and as an antidote to tackle problems of governance from state corruption to crime and migration. In both contexts, privatisation has been interpreted as an irregularity and a deviation from a normative idea of the state as the main provider of security. Such analytical frames have stymied theories and concepts that better reflect contemporary dynamics and flows of power, and they often served imperialist projects. Examining these practices, in all their complexities and diversity, and laying them open to empirical and normative scrutiny is essential for rethinking the place and function of the state in society.

References

Abizadeh A, 'Democratic Theory and Border Coercion: No Right to Unilaterally Control your own Borders' (2008) 36 Political Theory 37

Abrahamsen R, *Security Beyond the State: Private Security in International Politics* (CUP 2011)

— — and Williams M, 'Security Privatization and Global Security Assemblage' (2011) 18(1) Brown Journal of World Affairs 171

Aliverti A, 'Enlisting the Public in the Policing of Immigration' (2015) 55 British Journal of Criminology 215

— —, 'Benevolent Policing? Vulnerability and the Moral Pains of Border Controls' (2020) 60(5) British Journal of Criminology 117

— —, 'Manufacturing Obedience: Coercion and Authority in Border Controls' (2021) Punishment & Society 146

— —, *Policing the Borders Within* (OUP 2021)

Armenta A, 'Racializing Crimmigration: Structural Racism, Colorblindness, and the Institutional Production of Immigrant Criminality' (2017) 3(1) Sociology of Race and Ethnicity 82

Barker V, *Nordic Nationalism and Penal Order: Walling the Welfare State* (Routledge 2017)

Bigo D and Guild E, 'Policing at a Distance: Schengen Visa Policies' in Bigo D and Guild E (eds), *Controlling Frontiers: Free Movement into and within Europe* (Ashgate 2005)

Bloch A and Schuster L, 'At the Extremes of Exclusion: Deportation, Detention and Dispersal' (2005) 28 Ethnic & Racial Studies 491

Bogg A and Freedland M, 'Criminality at Work' in Bogg A, Collins J, Freedland M, and Herring J (eds), *Criminality at Work* (OUP 2020)

[45] See, eg Rita Abrahamsen, *Security Beyond the State: Private Security in International Politics* (CUP 2011); Hönke (n 37); Phillippe Frowd, *Security at the Borders: Transnational Practices and Technologies in West Africa* (CUP 2018); Eva Magdalena Stambøl, 'Borders as Penal Transplants: Control of Territory, Mobility and Illegality in West Africa' (2021) 25(3) Theoretical Criminology 474; Mark Duffield, 'Governing the Borderlands: Decoding the Power of Aid' (2001) 25(4) Disasters 308; Tholens (n 40).

Bosworth M, 'Can Immigration Detention Centres be Legitimate? Understanding Confinement in a Global World' in Franko Aas K and Bosworth M (eds), *The Borders of Punishment: Migration, Citizenship, and Social Exclusion* (OUP 2013)

— —, 'Penal Humanitarianism? Sovereign Power in an Era of Mass Migration' (2017) 20 New Criminal Law Review 39

— —, 'Affect and Authority in Immigration Detention' (2019) 21 Punishment & Society 542

Bowling B and Westenra S, '"A Really Hostile Environment": Adiaphorization, Global Policing and the Crimmigration Control System' (2020) 24(2) Theoretical Criminology 163

Brown W, *Walled States, Waning Sovereignty* (Zone Books 2010)

Burnett J and Chebe F, 'Towards a Political Economy of Charging Regimes: Fines, Fees and Force in UK Immigration Control' (2019) 60(3) British Journal of Criminology 579

Chacón JM, 'Privatized Immigration Enforcement' (2017) 52 Harvard Civil Rights–Liberties Law Review

— — and Coutin SB, 'Racialization through Enforcement' in Bosworth M, Parmar A, and Vazquez Y (eds), *Race, Criminal Justice and Migration Control* (OUP 2018)

Cohen S, *Visions of Social Control: Crime, Punishment and Classification* (Polity Press 1985)

Corda A and Lageson SE, 'Disordered Punishment: Workaround Technologies of Criminal Records Disclosure and the Rise of a New Penal Entrepreneurialism' (2019) 60(2) British Journal of Criminology 245

Côté-Boucher K, Infantino F, and Salter MB, 'Border Security as Practice: An Agenda for Research' (2014) 45(3) Security Dialogue 195

Crawford A, 'Networked Governance and the Post-regulatory State? Steering, Rowing and Anchoring the Provision of Policing and Security' (2006) 10(4) Theoretical Criminology 449

Das V and Poole D, 'State and its Margins. Comparative Ethnographies' in Das V and Poole D (eds), *Anthropology at the Margins of the State* (School of American Research Press 2004)

— — and — —, 'State and its Margins. Comparative Ethnographies' in Laszczkowski M and Reeves M (eds), *Affective States: Entanglements, Suspensions, Suspicions* (Berghahn 2018)

Dauvergne C, *Making People Illegal: What Globalization Means for Migration and Law* (CUP 2008)

Davitti D, 'Beyond the Governance Gap: Accountability in Privatized Migration Control' (2020) 21 German Law Journal 487

de Waal A, 'Power' in Das V and Fassin D (eds), *Words and Worlds: A Lexicon for Dark Times* (Duke University Press 2021)

Diphoorn T, *Twilight Policing: Private Security and Violence in Urban South Africa* (University of California Press 2016)

Duffield M, 'Governing the Borderlands: Decoding the Power of Aid' (2001) 25(4) Disasters 308

Eagly I and Schwartz J, 'Lexipol: The Privatization of Police Policymaking' (2018) 96 Texas Law Review 891

Fassin D, *Humanitarian Reason: A Moral History of the Present* (University of California Press 2012)

— — (ed), *At the Heart of the State: The Moral World of Institutions* (Pluto Press 2015)

Ferguson J, *Global Shadows: Africa in the Neoliberal World Order* (Duke University Press 2006)

— —

and Gupta A, 'Spatializing States: Toward an Ethnography of Neoliberal Governmentality' (2002) 29 American Ethnologist 981

Franko Aas K, '"Crimmigrant" Bodies and Bona Fide Travelers: Surveillance, Citizenship and Global Governance' (2011) 15 Theoretical Criminology 331

— —, 'The Ordered and the Bordered Society: Migration Control, Citizenship and the Northern Penal State' in Franko Aas K and Bosworth M (eds), *The Borders of Punishment: Criminal Justice, Citizenship and Social Exclusion* (OUP 2013)

— — and Helene Gundhus, 'Policing Humanitarian Borderlands: Frontex, Human Rights and the Precariousness of Life' (2015) 55(1) British Journal of Criminology 1

Fregonese S, 'Beyond the "Weak State": Hybrid Sovereignties in Beirut' (2012) 30 Environment and Planning D: Society and Space 655

Frowd P, *Security at the Borders: Transnational Practices and Technologies in West Africa* (CUP 2018)

Garland D, *Punishment and Modern Society: A Study in Social Theory* (OUP 1990)

— —, *Punishment and Welfare: A History of Penal Strategies* (Quid Pro Books 2018)

Gilman D and Romero LA, 'Immigration Detention, Inc' (2018) 6(2) Journal on Migration and Human Security 145

Guild E and Bigo D, 'The Transformation of European Border Controls' in Ryan B and Mitsilegas V (eds), *Extraterritorial Immigration Control Legal Challenges* (Brill 2010)

Gupta A, *Red Tape: Bureaucracy, Structural Violence, and Poverty in India* (Duke University Press 2012)

Hansen TB and Stepputat F, 'Introduction' in Hansen TB and Stepputat F (eds), *States of Imagination: Ethnographic Explorations of the Postcolonial State* (Duke University Press 2001)

— — and — —, 'Sovereignty Revisited' (2006) 35 Annual Review of Anthropology 295

Higate P and Utas M (eds), *Private Security in Africa: From the Global Assemblage to the Everyday* (Bloomsbury Academic 2017)

Home Office, *UK Border Agency Business Plan (April 2008—March 2011)* (Home Office 2009)

— —, *UK Border Agency Business Plan (April 2009—March 2012)* (Home Office 2010)

— —, *UK Border Agency Business Plan 2011–15. Delivering our Commitments with a Smaller, More Efficient Agency* (Home Office 2011)

Hönke J, *Transnational Companies and Security Governance* (Routledge 2013)

Jaffe R, 'The Hybrid State: Crime and Citizenship in Urban Jamaica' (2013) 40(4) American Ethnologist 734

— —, 'From Maroons to Dons: Sovereignty, Violence and Law in Jamaica' (2015) 35 Critique of Anthropology 47

Jones T and Newburn T, *Private Security and Public Policing* (Clarendon Press 1998)

Koulish R and van der Woude M (eds), *Crimmigrant Nations: Resurgent Nationalism and the Closing of Borders* (Fordham 2020)

Lahav G, 'Immigration and the State: The Devolution and Privatization of Immigration Control in the EU' (1998) 24 Journal of Ethnic & Migration Studies 675

Levi-Faur D, 'The Global Diffusion of Regulatory Capitalism' (2005) 598 Annals of the American Academy of Political and Social Science 12

Lipsky M, *Street-level Bureaucracy: Dilemmas of the Individual in Public Services* (Russell Sage Foundation 2010)

Loader I and Walker N, 'Policing as a Public Good: Reconstituting the Connections between Policing and the State' (2001) 5(1) Theoretical Criminology 9

— — and — —, *Civilizing Security* (CUP 2007)

Loftus B, *Police Culture in a Changing World* (OUP 2009)

Mbembe A, *On the Postcolony* (University of California Press 2001)

Mears DP and Montes AN, 'Introduction to the Special Issue on Privatized Corrections' (2019) 18 Criminology & Public Policy 213

Milanesio N, *Workers Go Shopping in Argentina: The Rise of Popular Consumer Culture* (University of New Mexico Press 2013)

O'Neill M and Fyfe NR, 'Plural Policing in Europe: Relationships and Governance in Contemporary Security Systems' (2017) 27 Policing and Society 1
Parmar A, 'Arresting (Non)citizenship: The Policing Migration Nexus of Nationality, Race and Criminalization' (2020) 24 Theoretical Criminology 28
Pham H, 'Private Enforcement of Immigration Laws' (2008) 96 Georgetown Law Journal 777
— —, 'When Immigration Borders Move' (2009) 61 Florida Law Review 1115
Platt A, *The Child Savers: The Invention of Delinquency* (Chicago University Press 1969)
Ramsay P, 'The Responsible Subject as Citizen: Criminal Law, Democracy and the Welfare State' (2006) 69 Modern Law Review 29
Rappaport J, 'Criminal Justice, Inc' (2018) 118 Columbia Law Review 2551
Reeves M, *Border Work: Spatial Lives of the State in Rural Central Asia* (Cornell University Press 2014) 8
Rose N, 'Government and Control' (2000) 40(2) British Journal of Criminology 321
— — and Miller P, 'Political Power beyond the State: Problematics of Government' (1992) 43(2) The British Journal of Sociology 173
Ryan B and Mitsilegas V (eds), *Extraterritorial Immigration Control: Legal Challenges* (Brill 2010)
Saeed R, 'The Ubiquity of State Fragility: Fault Lines in the Categorisation and Conceptualisation of Failed and Fragile States' (2020) 29(6) Social & Legal Studies 767 <https://doi.org/10.1177%2F0964663920906453>
Sharma A and Gupta A, 'Introduction: Rethinking Theories of the State in an Age of Globalization' in Sharma A and Gupta A (eds), *The Anthropology of the State: A Reader* (John Wiley & Sons 2006)
Shearing CD, 'The Relation between Public and Private Policing' (1992) 15 Crime and Justice 399
Stambøl EM, 'Borders as Penal Transplants: Control of Territory, Mobility and Illegality in West Africa' (2021) 25(3) Theoretical Criminology 474
— —, 'Neo-colonial Penality? Travelling Penal Power and Contingent Sovereignty' (2021) 23(4) Punishment & Society 536 <https://doi.org/10.1177%2F14624745211025745>
Stern P, *The Company-State: Corporate Sovereignty and the Early Modern Foundations of the British Empire in India* (OUP 2011)
Tholens S, 'Border Management in an Era of "Statebuilding Lite": Security Assistance and Lebanon's Hybrid Sovereignty' (2017) 93(4) International Affairs 865
Walsh JP, 'Watchful Citizens: Immigration Control, Surveillance and Societal Participation' (2014) 23(2) Social & Legal Studies 237
Weber L, 'Policing the Virtual Border: Punitive Preemption in Australian Offshore Migration Control' (2007) 34(2) Social Justice 77
Welch M and Schuster L, 'Detention of Asylum Seekers in the UK and USA' (2005) 7(4) Punishment & Society 397
Western B and Pettit B, 'Incarceration & Social Inequality' (2010) 139(3) Daedalus 8
Zacka B, *When the State Meets the Street: Public Service and Moral Agency* (Harvard University Press 2017)
Zedner L, 'Is the Criminal Law only for Citizens? A Problem at the Borders of Punishment' in Franko Aas K and Bosworth M (eds), *The Borders of Punishment: Criminal Justice, Citizenship and Social Exclusion* (OUP 2013)

Index

For the benefit of digital users, indexed terms that span two pages (e.g., 52–53) may, on occasion, appear on only one of those pages.